Jim Crow, Literature, and the Legacy of Sutton E. Griggs

EST. 75 1938
YEARS
THE UNIVERSITY OF GEORGIA PRESS 2013

Jim Crow, Literature, and the Legacy of Sutton E. Griggs

Edited by TESS CHAKKALAKAL
and KENNETH W. WARREN

The University of Georgia Press   *Athens and London*

Caroline Levander's "Sutton Griggs and the Borderlands of Empire" originally appeared, in somewhat different form, in *American Literary History* 22, no. 1 (2010): 57–84, and is reprinted here by permission of Oxford University Press.

© 2013 by the University of Georgia Press
Athens, Georgia 30602
www.ugapress.org
Set in Minion Pro by Graphic Composition, Inc.
Manufactured by Thomson-Shore
The paper in this book meets the guidelines for permanence and durability of the Committee on Production Guidelines for Book Longevity of the Council on Library Resources.

Printed in the United States of America
17   16   15   14   13   P   5   4   3   2   1

Library of Congress Cataloging-in-Publication Data

Jim Crow, Literature, and the legacy of Sutton E. Griggs / edited by Tess Chakkalakal and Kenneth W. Warren.
        pages cm. — (The New Southern Studies)
Includes bibliographical references and index.
ISBN 978-0-8203-4032-6 (hardcover : alk. paper) —
ISBN 0-8203-4032-4 (hardcover : alk. paper) —
ISBN 978-0-8203-4598-7 (pbk. : alk. paper) —
ISBN 0-8203-4598-9 (pbk. : alk. paper)
1. Griggs, Sutton E. (Sutton Elbert), 1872–1933—Criticism and interpretation. 2. Race relations in literature. I. Chakkalakal, Tess. II. Warren, Kenneth W. (Kenneth Wayne)
PS3513.R7154Z73 2013
813'.52—dc23   2012049539

British Library Cataloging-in-Publication Data available

Contents

Acknowledgments

This volume has been a collaborative effort, and we would like to thank Bowdoin College; the Chicago Humanities Visiting Committee; the Franke Institute for the Humanities; the Karla Scherer Center for the Study of American Culture; the Center for the Study of Race, Politics, and Culture; 3CT; and the University of Chicago Department of English for making it possible to bring together many of our contributors for scholarly exchange and fellowship.

Jim Crow, Literature,
and the Legacy of
Sutton E. Griggs

TESS CHAKKALAKAL AND KENNETH W. WARREN

Introduction

Who Was Sutton E. Griggs?

At the turn of the twentieth century, when state legislatures across the U.S. South had determined that the solution to the nation's so-called Negro Problem was to exile black Americans from the region's political life, the Baptist minister Sutton Elbert Griggs (1872–1933) embarked on a novel-writing career that was at once typical of and singular among early African American writers. Already a successful Baptist minister, Griggs turned to fiction writing with alacrity and in the brief span of less than a decade produced five novels that chronicled the challenges facing black Americans in the South and protested the region's assault on black political and civic rights. What made Griggs's career typical was that he was hardly alone among African American authors in believing that writing fiction and poetry was central to challenging the dismal political and social realities of the moment. As Dickson D. Bruce Jr. has observed in assessing the period between 1877 and 1915, the "virulence of white racism was a powerful spur to literary activity, as black writers sought to use their pens to fight against racist practices and ideas."[1] What set Griggs apart from many of his literary peers, however, was his long-term residence in the South. Most early African American writers were either from or pursued their professional careers in the northern states: Paul Laurence Dunbar was born in Dayton, Ohio; Pauline Hopkins in Portland, Maine; Charles W. Chesnutt in Cleveland, Ohio; and W. E. B. Du Bois in Great Barrington, Massachusetts.

To be sure, Griggs was not the only black writer at that time to count a southern state as his place of birth, but even here he differed in significant ways from his peers. Anna Julia Cooper was from North Carolina but attended Oberlin College before spending the bulk of her professional career in Washington, D.C. Also a southerner by birth, James Weldon Johnson was born in Florida, but his movements from Florida to New York, Venezuela, and Nicaragua, and his experience in New York's Tin Pan Alley may have helped persuade him that to participate in the region's politics he did not need to be located in the South, where most of the nation's black population resided.

By contrast, Griggs, who was born in Chatfield, Texas, in 1872, spent much of his professional career in southern states. The son of Allen R. Griggs, a former slave, Baptist minister, and educator, Sutton Griggs attended public schools in Dallas, Texas, before enrolling in Bishop College, established by the Baptist Home Mission Society in Marshall, Texas, and from which he graduated in 1890. Following in his father's footsteps, Griggs continued his religious education at the Richmond Theological Seminary in Virginia from 1891 to 1894, earning a bachelor of divinity degree before becoming an ordained Baptist minister. He received his first pastorate in Berkley, Virginia, where he served for two years, during which time he also married Emma J. Williams. From there Griggs and his wife moved to Nashville, Tennessee, where he became pastor of the East Nashville First Baptist Church. It was in Nashville that Griggs wrote his first novel, *Imperium in Imperio*, which was published by the Editor Publishing Company, a vanity press based in Cincinnati, Ohio. Although the writing of *Imperium* seemed to establish Griggs's ambition to become a novelist, he did not head to the nation's literary centers in New York and Boston. Instead, he stayed in Tennessee to establish his own publishing company, the Orion Publishing Company, in Nashville. Believed to be one of the first black-owned secular publishing companies in the United States, Orion would provide the imprimatur for Griggs's literary oeuvre until he moved to Memphis to become pastor of the Tabernacle Baptist Church in 1913. In Memphis, he became a member of the Inter-Racial League and created a second publishing company, the National Public Welfare League. In 1930, after the Tabernacle Baptist Church of Memphis was sold for failing to pay off its debts, Griggs returned to his native state, Texas, to serve as pastor of the Hopewell Baptist Church in Denison. Sutton E. Griggs died in Houston on January 2, 1933, and was buried in Dallas.

Although Griggs's novels amply display the range of political, social, and moral issues that preoccupied him throughout his career, his early years as a Baptist preacher just after his graduation from the seminary in Virginia reveal a young man already embroiled in the complex political and publishing world of the Baptist Church. Like his father, Griggs was an active member of the National Baptist Convention (NBC), which was viewed at the time as the largest constituency of African Americans in the United States. As much as the NBC was a religious organization based on the Baptist mission, it was also a political organization that purported to represent the specific needs and concerns of African Americans in the South, who were systematically excluded from the democratic process of electing representatives to state and federal governments. It is no wonder then that as a Baptist minister Griggs understood his religious mission to be inseparable from politics. Before taking on the job of pastor of the First Baptist Church in Berkley, Virginia, Griggs had already distinguished himself as a speaker much in demand by black audiences.

The *Richmond Planet*, Virginia's leading black newspaper, regularly reported on Griggs's public performances. In describing Griggs's first public lecture on May 5, 1894, the *Planet* characterized Griggs as having "an easy delivery and a fine voice, and [found that] his vivid portrayal of the achievement of the [American Home Mission] Society was attentively listened to."[2] Unlike the great black orators of the mid-nineteenth century whose voices can no longer be heard, Griggs's voice has been captured on sound recordings that we can still listen to today. Rediscovered and transcribed by Steven C. Tracy in the mid-1980s, these sound recordings "provide insight into Griggs' technique as a speaker and into the way he mixed the oral and written traditions in his sermons."[3] But Griggs did not limit his oratorical powers to the pulpit. He was the featured speaker at a debate that took place on March 12, 1894. Though the debate was held at the First Baptist Church and its proceeds were intended to assist the widow and seven children of a recently deceased minister, the topic of the debate had little to do with religion or charity. It concerned instead "the colored vote": "Resolved, that it is expedient for the colored people of the U.S. to cease voting with the Republicans and vote with the Prohibitionists." Arguing in favor of the resolution was, of course, "Sutton E. Griggs."[4]

The debate was the centerpiece of a larger program that included music, prayers, and a recitation delivered by Miss E. J. Williams, whom Griggs would marry three years later. Tickets for the event had to be bought in advance, for fifteen cents each, and they quickly sold out. Though the winner of the debate was not announced in the *Planet*, subsequent issues suggest that Griggs came out on top. Griggs was again the featured speaker at the "great denominational debate" on September 21, 1895, in which he defended the doctrines of the Baptist Church against those of the Methodist Church. "It will be," the *Planet* reported, "the hottest intellectual battle ever fought in the city of Richmond."[5]

The spirit of intellectual debate that soared among African Americans in the black churches of Richmond despite their exclusion from public life found an interesting corollary in print culture. The sentiments expressed by Elias Camp Morris, founder and president of the NBC, delineated the importance of publishing to the representation of African American views and opinions at the time. In a speech titled "The Demand for a Negro Publishing House," Morris argued that a black Baptist publishing house was necessary because it would provide "race employment," "race development," "a bequest to posterity," and business experience.[6] As an active member of the NBC, Griggs was one of several men who turned to the world of print culture to be heard by an audience beyond the church. Unlike those of many of his fellows Baptists, however, his publications were decidedly more secular than spiritual.

Griggs's oratorical performances took a different form when he became editor of the *Virginia Baptist* from 1894 to 1898. As editor, Griggs decided to take on the well-known and much-admired "Fighting Editor"—John Mitchell Jr.— of the *Richmond Planet*.[7] This move led to a series of exchanges between the two editors that ended in October 1898, when Griggs (along with several others from the *Virginia Baptist*) was charged with extortion and arrested.[8] Although the *Planet* praised Griggs's oral performances, the publication was quick and particularly ruthless in its criticism of his writings. The *Planet* openly denounced Griggs, calling him "a laughing-stock" and chastising him for using church funds to support his newspaper.

The catalyst for the war between Griggs and Mitchell was the *Planet*'s declaration that "the A.M.E. Church is the grandest Negro religious organization in the world" in terms of membership, financial resources, and independence from white influence. The last declaration in particular was a backhanded critique of the black Baptist Church that continued to work with white Baptist organizations. In the opinion of the editor of the *Richmond Planet*, the black Baptist Church risks "becom[ing] the doormat of every other organization that chooses to use us as such. We are tired of being used all the time and we should use others sometimes." Griggs had objected to these charges in the *Virginia Baptist*, and on Saturday March 5, 1898, the *Planet* printed a lengthy response to Griggs that comprised three full columns of its front page, taking apart Griggs's defense of his newspaper and the Baptist Church that he represented.

In his response Griggs waves aside Mitchell's challenge to prove the financial worth of the NBC, saying that unlike the AME Church, praised by the *Planet*, "with its magnificent organization," "its officers and its members," and valuable property, the Baptist Church refuses, in Griggs's words, "to reckon the worth of the church and its influence in the world from the dollars and cents that it collects."[9] Then in response to Mitchell's accusation that the "Colored Baptist" denomination was not sufficiently building itself up along material lines of racial advancement, Griggs is quoted as saying: "The lowest possible condition of Christian activity and life is the amassing of large property possession upon the part of the church to the neglect of the salvation of men."[10] Mitchell, however, was not impressed with Griggs's defense of his church and charged him with logical inconsistency. Indeed Mitchell found Griggs inconsistent on a variety of points. Elsewhere in this exchange, Mitchell, after claiming to have caught Griggs in a contradiction regarding the appropriateness of church organizations and publications accepting revenue derived from the sale of alcohol, crows in derision: "Brother Griggs is a curiosity. His writings would well-nigh make a 'horse laugh,' and his reasoning is so bow-legged that it reels and rocks like a drunken man. 'Go to, Brother Griggs!'"

But this issue of the *Planet* may be of significance for something more than the debate between Mitchell and Griggs. The paper notes in a brief commentary that at a recent meeting of President William McKinley's cabinet "the cowardly and brutal murder of Postmaster BAKER and babe and the maiming of his wife, son and daughter" was discussed. Although the president was said to be "shocked" by the accounts of the lynching, the *Planet*'s editor, far from convinced that justice would be done, concludes his commentary on a plaintive note: "Can the government protect its officials? Can it hunt down their murderers? If it cannot, it is a confession of weakness which is a disgrace to any nation afflicted therewith." It appears that Griggs may have used both his exchange with Mitchell and the outcry against Postmaster Frazier Baker's lynching in South Carolina as fodder for his first novel, *Imperium in Imperio* (1899). *Imperium* is a curious cross between utopian and historical fiction. Its narrative traces the life of Belton Piedmont as he rises from his one-room, ramshackle house in Virginia to become "the spirit of conservatism in the Negro race." Belton is killed in the end by his friend and nemesis, Bernard Belgrave, who embodies a form of political radicalism predicated on violent revolution that Griggs, for much of his life, opposed.

Debates such as that between Belton and Bernard would reappear with regularity in Griggs's subsequent four novels, each of which explores the theme of political opposition in different yet related ways. Each novel introduces characters from across the spectrum of possibilities for black activism: Bernard and Belton in *Imperium in Imperio*; Erma and her brother, John Wysong, in *Overshadowed*; Ensal Ellwood and Earl Bluefield in *The Hindered Hand*; Harry Dalton and Dorlan Warthell in *Unfettered*; and Letitia Gilbreath and Baug Peppers in *Pointing the Way*. Paralleling this juxtaposition of politically opposed black characters are similar political divisions among the novel's white characters.

We can only speculate about why Griggs turned to the novel form amid his very public dispute with John Mitchell, his arrest, and his eventual move to Tennessee. Based on the charges against him and Mitchell's vocal opposition to Griggs's position, the novel may have offered the young Griggs a forum in which to present his views in a more reasoned, less combative, dispassionate tone. Griggs could not convince individuals like Mitchell of his refusal to divide the Baptist Church between white and black or his desire to use the church—both its buildings and its publications—as a forum for lively political debate. Instead, Griggs would take his message to the people; it was a message, he believed, that must appear in print.

Though several critics have argued that a shift or "metamorphosis" from "Black Radical to Conservative," to borrow from the title of Randolph Meade Walker's 1990 study of Griggs's ideological and spiritual principles, occurred in Griggs's career around 1913, Griggs's early confrontation with Mitchell suggests the opposite. Griggs was remarkably consistent in his political opinions. Against the rising tide of antiblack sentiment during the period, Griggs believed that cooperation between the races remained the best and most effective policy. To secure such cooperation, however, he was often willing to speak up even when other prominent black spokespersons held their tongues. Griggs's response to the Brownsville affair in 1906 is a case in point. In August of that year, black infantrymen stationed in Brownsville, Texas, were accused of firing shots that had killed a white bartender and wounded a white policeman. Despite no evidence linking the soldiers to the incident, local authorities blamed them for the shootings. The War Department believed that the black troops knew who the responsible parties were but refused to identify them. President Theodore Roosevelt then stepped in and ordered that 167 of the infantrymen be dishonorably discharged. Although the wrongness of Roosevelt's actions was clearly visible to many observers, several prominent blacks, including Elias Camp Morris, president of the National Baptist Convention, and Booker T. Washington declined to speak out publicly against Roosevelt (Washington did, however, press Roosevelt privately to reverse his decision).[11]

Perhaps in part because the incident occurred in his home state of Texas, which Griggs loved despite, in his words, "whatever others may say," Griggs felt compelled to say something.[12] In doing so, he knew he was crossing some of those with whom he would have preferred to agree. But against what he termed the "Baptist silence" counseled by Morris, Griggs felt that Baptists needed to acknowledge publicly "a difference with [their] own President and a difference with the President of the United States."[13] Also, characteristically, Griggs did not criticize Roosevelt without at the same time extending the olive branch, assuring Roosevelt that blacks would be grateful were he to reconsider his decision. "In this time of exclusion from public life," Griggs wrote, "when sole reliance must be placed in the generous impulses of those of another race, we cannot afford to be stinted in praise of those who plead our cause."[14]

Griggs's insistence on working with whites to attain civil and political rights for African American citizens made him persona non grata among many who, like Mitchell, held all whites responsible for the injustices and daily humiliations blacks were forced to confront. Called everything from a "race traitor" to a "white folks nigger," Griggs continued to express his highly unpopular views in books and pamphlets and distributed them himself.[15] As he explains in his brief autobiography, *The Story of My Struggles* (1914), the cost of expressing his opinions was much higher than he could afford.

After abandoning fiction and having been forced to shut down Orion Publishing Company due to financial problems that year, Griggs turned to a new publishing venture, the National Public Welfare League, and devoted all his literary energy to nonfiction political pamphlets. Of these, *The Science of Collective Efficiency* (1923) encapsulates his political program most fully. Though Griggs remained a committed Baptist minister until his death in 1933, his prodigious literary and political activities often conflicted with his religious ministry.

As a minister whose primary mode of address was the sermon, Griggs was equally devoted to the printed word. In her study of the black Baptist Church, Evelyn Brooks Higginbotham points to Griggs as a representative of "the Talented Tenth"—in Du Bois's famous formulation—"who sought to subvert the power of illiterate leaders by privileging the written word."[16] Though Higginbotham is correct in noting Griggs's privileging of the written word, Griggs's membership in the Talented Tenth was complicated by his desire to disseminate "the word" among all African Americans, regardless of birth or talents. Griggs's privileging of the written word over the oral was consistent with his desire to increase the numbers of "talented" African Americans. Ultimately,

Griggs's investment in print culture was determined by a need to be "heard" by the masses, rather than just the talented few. "A speech," he explains, "would have been heard and would have vanished, leaving only memories behind, whereas the reader, if he feels so inclined, may now read, re-read and ponder every word that is here said."[17] Despite having made a reputation for himself as a speaker, devoted to the tenets of the NBC, Griggs still urged his fellow African Americans to "move up out of the age of the voice" as the only way to gain a political voice.[18] Indeed, it is for his turn to the written word, in its multiple forms, that Griggs is remembered today.

Aside from the numerous works of fiction and nonfiction that Griggs left behind, little information concerning his personal life remains. Finnie Coleman's recent book *Sutton E. Griggs and the Struggle against White Supremacy* provides the most detailed account of Griggs's childhood in Texas, compiling important information concerning the life and work of his father, Allen R. Griggs, who was particularly influential in his son's early career. Following the threads of information supplied by earlier critics, Randolph Meade Walker, Arlene Elder, Wilson Moses, and Betty Taylor Thompson, Coleman has done much to piece together the story of Griggs's life. But as Coleman admits, the pieces do not always fit. We still have much to learn about who Griggs was and how his books helped to shape African American literary culture at the turn of the twentieth century.

Griggs was, just as Mitchell complained, more interested in politics than preaching, yet his religious commitments seem to have obscured or "overshadowed" our understanding of his political interventions. The more we learn about the complexity of Sutton Elbert Griggs's personal and professional lives and his literary talents, the less we understand why his fiction and nonfiction have not received more scholarly attention. In spite of his many accomplishments, Griggs has remained at the margins of critical discourse regarding pre–Harlem Renaissance writers in particular and post-Reconstruction African American leaders more generally. The objective of this volume is to move Griggs from the margins to the center of African American literary history.

Literary Legacy

Following his departure from Virginia, Griggs continued to write fiction and in the brief span of less than a decade produced five novels—*Imperium in Imperio* (1899), *Overshadowed* (1901), *Unfettered* (1902), *The Hindered Hand; or,*

The Reign of the Repressionist (1905), and *Pointing the Way* (1908)—in which he chronicled the challenges facing black Americans in the South and protested the region's assault on black political and civic rights. Griggs's productivity mirrored that of his peers. The "last decade of the nineteenth century and the opening of the twentieth century," which according to Rayford W. Logan "marked the nadir of the Negro's status in American society," were remarkably productive for African American imaginative literature.[19] At the beginning of the 1890s, Frances E. W. Harper published her most distinguished novel, *Iola Leroy; or, Shadows Uplifted* (1892), while Anna Julia Cooper's *A Voice from the South* (1892) set out a program for black literary and artistic production that sought to align cultural production by black elites, most of whom resided in the northern states, with an effort to improve the political and social status of black Americans as a race. Paul Laurence Dunbar and Pauline Hopkins each published four novels during this period. Dunbar authored *The Uncalled* (1898), *The Love of Landry* (1900), *The Fanatics* (1901), and *Sport of the Gods* (1902), while Hopkins, in addition to editing *The Colored American Magazine*, wrote *Contending Forces: A Romance Illustrative of Negro Life North and South* (1900), *Hagar's Daughter: A Story of Southern Case Prejudice* (1902), *Winona: A Tale of Negro Life in the South and Southwest* (1902), and *Of One Blood; or, The Hidden Self* (1903). Not far behind these authors were Amelia E. Johnson and Charles W. Chesnutt with three novels apiece. Johnson published *Clarence and Corinne; or, God's Way* (1890), *The Hazeley Family* (1894), and *Martina Meriden; or, What Is My Motive?* (1901). Chesnutt's novels, in addition to his short-story collections, included, *The House behind the Cedars* (1900), *The Marrow of Tradition* (1901), and *The Colonel's Dream* (1905). It was also at this moment that W. E. B. Du Bois published both *The Souls of Black Folk* (1903), which has been a touchstone for formulating much literary criticism of the African American novel, and his first novel, *The Quest of the Silver Fleece* (1911), while James Weldon Johnson brought out his *Autobiography of an Ex-colored Man* (1912), often regarded as the first novel of the next major phase of black writing, namely, the Harlem Renaissance.[20]

Taken together, these novels constitute a collective response to the "Negro Problem" and to the system of Jim Crow segregation and political exclusion that was being devised by southern legislatures as its solution. The "Negro Problem" was the term that politicians and legislatures devised in the aftermath of the Civil War to rationalize and justify their commitment to ensuring that political power across the states of the former Confederacy would remain largely in the hands of the Democratic Party, a goal that required making black Americans a political nullity. As John David Smith has written, in purporting to solve a problem that they themselves had invented, "whites flooded popular magazines, newspapers, scholarly journals, polemical tracts, monographs, and 'scientific' treatises with writings on racial themes. Conferences, symposia, and public lectures underscored the sense of immediacy whites felt about the 'race problem.'"[21] The "solution," of course, was to make sure that any answer to blacks' second-class status would stop well short of full admission to the nation's polity, a solution that would commonly be referred to as Jim Crow.

This new social order would be recognized most immediately by its commitment to segregating blacks from whites in public spaces across the South, but its most visible manifestation was not its most profound. Of this period, historian Jane Dailey observes:

> Jim Crow did not draw its strength from segregation and should not be viewed as synonymous with it. Jim Crow's power over African Americans came from exclusion: exclusion from voting booths; from juries; from neighborhoods; from unions and management positions; from higher education; from professions; from hospitals and theaters and hotels. The "southern way of life" of racial hierarchy and segregation was backed up by white economic and political control and secured through the police power of the state.[22]

It was against the systematic exclusions of Jim Crow that writers turned to literature, almost as if they were heeding the words of Belton Piedmont, the co-protagonist of Griggs's first and most famous novel, *Imperium in Imperio*, who intones to his coconspirators, "If denied the use of the ballot let us devote our attention to that mightier weapon, the pen."[23]

Through Piedmont, Griggs was remarking a relation between the severe blow dealt to the political fortunes of blacks at the turn of the century and the early flowering of imaginative writing by black writers. Especially in the early 1890s, when a politics of disenfranchisement was gathering strength in the South, black authors and editors across the nation expressed the need for an African American literature. For example, in 1891 the *New York Age* published an article by Henry Clay Gray titled "Office of Distinctly Afro-American Literature." In this piece, Gray laments that notwithstanding abundant calls for "'race pride,' 'race unity' and the like,'" black people were as yet connected only "by a mere rope of sand—aimless talk." The remedy for this lack of cohesion, Gray asserts, is the development of a "distinctively Negro literature" that can provide "the cable of infinitely superior quality and tension which can bind the race into one coherent, materially helpful and heroic people." Although Gray is quick to note the "many obstacles in the way of [African Americans] having the advantage of such a unifying principle as that of a distinctively Negro literature," he nonetheless believes that these obstacles are "by no means insurmountable."[24] Likewise, J. McHenry Jones in his novel, *Hearts of Gold*—published in 1896, the same year of the U.S. Supreme Court's notorious ruling in *Plessy v. Ferguson* upholding racial segregation as constitutional—felt compelled to make a case for the importance of having a black literature. In that novel, one of Jones's characters, a newspaperman named Clement St. John, upbraids an unresponsive black readership by asking, "Is not a race literature just as necessary as a race church, club, or school?"[25] By publishing his novel, Jones sought to give an affirmative action to the question posed by St. John.

Recent scholarship on the turn of the twentieth century has affirmed that something new and unprecedented was happening among black writers and readers during this period. In many ways concurring with Griggs's Belton Piedmont, Rafia Zafar has remarked that the "situation at the end of the nineteenth century in fact promoted necessary changes in the literary tactics of African Americans [that] heralded the arrival of African American literature as we know it in the late twentieth century." In Zafar's view, black "writers of the nadir and immediately after, increasingly turning to attitudes and forms unique to their group, strove to create a more culturally specific literature within a structurally rigid society."[26] Even more recently, James Smethurst has tracked the roots of American literary modernism to this moment, arguing that "the establishment of Jim Crow as a national system" led some black writers "to feel a need for the creation (or recognition) of a distinct African American literature representing, channeling, and serving some notion of a black 'people' or 'nation.'"[27] Griggs, then, was participating in the emergence of a literary movement that would indelibly mark cultural production during the coming century.

For Griggs the solution of the "race problem" would remain central to his fictional work. Each of his novels seeks to provide direct solutions to the political plight of black Americans, proffering and experimenting with practical proposals for political action and affiliation in the South. Even in the face of disenfranchisement and racial violence, Griggs's novels portray direct challenges to southern state constitutions and social injustice via speeches crafted so that they could be lifted almost verbatim from the pages of his fiction and placed in the hands of white southern politicians. In his 1907 pamphlet, *The One Great Question: A Study Of Southern Conditions at Close Range*, which delineates the social and political damage wrought by what he terms "repressionist" regimes, Griggs quotes not only from the testimony of witnesses, victims, and perpetrators of southern white repression but also from his own novel *The Hindered Hand*, which he had written as a riposte to Thomas Dixon's *The Leopard's Spots*. In such portrayals, Griggs departs from those "post-bellum, pre-Harlem" novels that were committed to re-creating "group traditions obscured by the experiences of slavery."[28] Griggs's novels focus on a pressing issue, but one that he hoped would prove ephemeral: "the question as to whether the great American nation was to make good her grant of equality of citizenship to the race of darker hue."[29]

On July 1, 1912, the same year that James Weldon Johnson published his now-classic novel, *The Autobiography of an Ex-colored Man*, Griggs delivered a speech to the Young Peoples' Union Congress at Providence Baptist Church in Chicago. Though the gathering was primarily a religious one, Griggs spoke only of the contemporary political situation. "If the young Negroes of this country should believe in anything," Griggs began, "it should be in the square deal in the political affairs of this country." He went on to mark the difference between how African Americans had been oppressed in the past and how they were oppressed in his present: "The battle that was before the country in Civil War times is before the people of this country now in a new guise. The Negroes were held in bondage then by masters, but the great mass of the American people, white and black, are now under the bondage of political masters and seekers after special privilege."[30]

Griggs's commitment to his political present is, we believe, one of the main reasons he has presented difficulties to readers of African American literature today. In introducing Griggs's work here, from multiple vantage points, we hope to offer readers ways of understanding the formal and political objectives of this important but underappreciated writer.

By highlighting the political concerns that guided Griggs's fiction, we do not mean to convey the impression that he was indifferent to the art of the novel. However fundamental Jim Crow was to framing turn-of-the-century black writing, the influences on black writing were not confined to the constricted world that white southerners sought to construct for black Americans. As Ralph Ellison famously asserts about black writers during the segregation era, "If we are in a jug it is transparent, not opaque, and one is allowed not only to see outside but to read what is going on out there and to make identifications as to value and human quality."[31] Although Ellison would have counted Griggs among the writers he deemed "relatives" rather than "ancestors," Griggs believed that black writers needed to range far and wide in their reading if they were to realize their potential. He wrote fiction because he believed literature to be a high calling and that black writers could produce works that would rival the masterpieces of "Shakespeare, Bacon, Milton, Bunyan, together with the favorite sons of other nations adopted into the English language, such as Dante, Hugo, Goethe, Dumas, and hosts of others."[32] The challenge that Griggs's work presents to us is to devise ways to avoid dismissing his artistic ambitions even as we track how his ever-present political commitments structure and complicate his strategies for storytelling and characterization. The following ten essays on Griggs's five novels confront this challenge in new and innovative ways.

Sutton E. Griggs in the Twenty-First Century

In presenting these new essays on Sutton E. Griggs and Jim Crow America, we are responding to and participating in renewed scholarly interest in the literature and culture of the Jim Crow era. Recent efforts to rename and reassess the literary and cultural productions of the Jim Crow era have enabled scholars to take a closer look at the work of long-neglected African American writers. As a result of this recent scholarship, we have gained greater insights into the life and work of several black Americans who wrote during "one of the darkest periods in [the] history" of African American culture.[33] This collection of essays on the life and work of Sutton E. Griggs supplements recent edited volumes by Barbara McCaskill and Caroline Gebhard, *Post-Bellum, Pre-Harlem: African American Literature and Culture, 1877–1919*, and Brian Norman and Piper Williams, *Representing Segregation: Towards an Aesthetics of Living Jim Crow, and Other Forms of Racial Division*, which have helped to renew critical debate about the neglected writers and literature of the Jim Crow era. Like these editors, it is our hope that the essays collected here will invigorate the study of African American literature by grounding it in a deeper understanding of the literary works and the history that informed them. The collection proceeds chronologically, beginning with essays on *Imperium in Imperio*, first published in 1899, and concludes with essays on Griggs's last novel, *Pointing the Way,* published in 1908. While Griggs's nonfictional works, mostly produced after 1908, are considered by several of the authors, it is the novels that complicate generic representations of the Jim Crow era and thus form the cornerstone of the critical discussion of this collection.

The first section comprises essays by Caroline Levander, John Gruesser, and Robert Levine on Griggs's first and best-known novel, *Imperium in Imperio*. As all three authors note, part of the ongoing fascination with *Imperium* lies in its complex engagement with the politics and literature beyond the domain of the U.S. South. Although *Imperium* has been the subject of several critical assessments, these readings have been somewhat limited by their narrow focus on U.S. race relations. First published in *American Literary History* in 2010, Levander's essay has been reprinted here and opens this collection of *new* essays on Sutton E. Griggs. Taking the question of race beyond the United States, Levander's essay, "Sutton Griggs and the Borderlands of Empire," participates most directly in a new movement in studies of Griggs's writings specifically and American literature more generally. Levander invites us to read *Imperium* not just as another "race novel" but also as a novel of "the borderland." Resituating *Imperium in Imperio* in this way reveals that the border between Mexico and the United States "has long been subject to geopolitical disputes and struggles not only among Mexican, Mexican American, and Anglo-American groups but among multiple, at times overlapping nations, races, and ethnicities." Levander's hemispheric approach to the novel deconstructs, as it were, the binaristic terms that have confined *Imperium* to a black versus white conception of U.S. history.

Highlighting the vital and complex role that Texas plays in Griggs's fiction and in American history more generally, Gruesser contends in his essay, "Empires at Home and Abroad in Sutton E. Griggs's *Imperium in Imperio*" that "*Imperium* ends on neither a positive nor a negative note." Instead, Gruesser highlights the political tensions and textual ambivalences at the heart of this novel to help readers understand its broader implications. Examining in particular the apparent opposition between *Imperium*'s protagonists—Bernard Belgrave and Belton Piedmont—Gruesser shows the significance of Texas to Griggs's political strategy. He writes, "The plan to take control of Texas legally proposed by one of the novel's protagonists and then radicalized by the other can be read as a warning—work with the Piedmonts or create and later face the Belgraves." It is an ominous warning, one revealing the complexity of Griggs's engagement with the contemporary American political scene and the role black people played within it. Continuing the conversation on Griggs's engagement with political debates on race, patriotism, and imperialism, Robert Levine takes up intertextual connections between *Imperium*, *Overshadowed*, and Edward Everett Hale's enormously popular short story, "The Man without a Country" (1863). Foregrounding Griggs's reading practice—like Tess Chakkalakal and M. Giulia Fabi in subsequent sections—Levine provides a much-needed historical account of Griggs as an exemplary black reader of contemporary literature. Given Griggs's perspective on American politics, Levine shows how Griggs's reading of Hale's story discerns "in it something that was generally lost on readers of the nineteenth and early twentieth century." That "something" offers new insights not only into literary history but also into the political history of the United States following the Civil War. By reading Griggs with Hale, Levine reveals the importance, indeed the urgency, of crossing the color line in our readings of black and white authors.

Moving from Griggs's most talked-about novel to his least-discussed second novel, Andreá Williams's "Moving Up a Dead-End Ladder: Black Class Mobility, Death, and Narrative Closure in Sutton Griggs's *Overshadowed*" shifts our attention to the economic dimensions of Griggs's fiction. Focusing on Griggs's departures from literary convention and looking closely at "the serial endings" with which *Overshadowed* concludes, Williams weighs the political payoff of reading a novel that is so clearly preoccupied with loss and death. Williams presents a reading of *Overshadowed*—perhaps the first sustained interpretation of the novel—that builds on recent theoretical formulations of narrative closure to examine the manner in which Griggs deploys death as a potent metaphor for black Americans' second-class citizenship in the United States. By doing so, Williams seeks to overturn negative assessments of Griggs's literary talents.

Extending Williams's reading of Griggs's unorthodox literary methods, Finnie Coleman, in "Social Darwinism, American Imperialism, and the Origins of the Science of Collective Efficiency in Sutton E. Griggs's *Unfettered*," reads Griggs's fiction through his later nonfiction. Expanding on research conducted for his book-length study of Griggs, Coleman insists on connecting Griggs's later work with the scientific theories of Darwin and Benjamin Kidd so popular during Griggs's lifetime. To read Griggs's fiction *properly*, by which Coleman means historically, we must first understand the complex historical milieu that Griggs wrote from and about. By doing so, Coleman attributes Griggs's unpopularity as a writer to his sometimes harsh critique of the southern black community of which he was a particularly vocal and active member.

The question of Griggs's literary profile among African American writers has been a persistent one. As one of the most prolific late nineteenth- and early twentieth-century African American novelists, Griggs is impossible to ignore. But as Tess Chakkalakal argues in her essay, "Reading in Sutton E. Griggs," readers, at least during Griggs's lifetime, did ignore his novels. Of course, as Chakkalakal goes on to explain, this was not surprising, given the status of fiction among African Americans and the status of "the Negro" among general readers. Attracting an audience for fiction was a problem for even the now-canonical Charles Chesnutt and Paul Laurence Dunbar. What is surprising, Chakkalakal notes, is Griggs's tenacious commitment to the novel form despite lacking a readership for his novels. By surveying Griggs's publishing ventures and the role of the reader as articulated by Griggs through his fiction and nonfiction, Chakkalakal uncovers the importance of a private black reading practice that developed during the Jim Crow era and can be documented through a reading of Griggs's most successful novels: *Imperium in Imperio* and *Unfettered*.

Published in 1905, Griggs's fourth novel, *The Hindered Hand; or, The Reign of the Repressionist* is in many respects his most ambitious novel. The novel, as Hanna Wallinger explains in her essay, "Sutton E. Griggs against Thomas Dixon's 'Vile Misrepresentations': *The Hindered Hand* and *The Leopard's Spots*," the novel was originally commissioned by the National Baptist Convention to respond to Dixon's deeply damaging fictional portrayal of African Americans. But Griggs, as Wallinger contends, does a good deal more than merely respond to Dixon. Griggs weaves *The Hindered Hand* around a series of misunderstandings between various couples that harkens back to the sentimental conventions of the mid-nineteenth century. By embedding his critique of Dixon in a series of mysteries, mistaken identities, and misunderstandings, Griggs unravels "a history of slavery that highlights the legacy of bitter feelings and vengeance between the poor white class of the South and the 'Negro.'"

Continuing the story of the novel's historical narrative, John Ernest in "Harnessing the Niagara" reads *The Hindered Hand* as one in a long line of African American "appeals to reason" that falls, ultimately, on deaf ears. But rather than read Griggs's appeal as a failure, Ernest shows us how it actually worked. By embedding his appeal in fiction, Ernest reads Griggs's novels as exemplary of the African American intervention into official history. As Ernest points out, it is virtually impossible to read this novel without returning to the absurd and offensive white supremacist fictions that were pervasive during Jim Crow. Do we owe the existence of Griggs's plentiful literary productions—and African

American literature more generally—to the "vile misrepresentations" of Thomas Dixon and his ilk?

Indeed, both Ernest and Wallinger offer particularly nuanced accounts of Dixon's novels in their readings of Griggs. Calling Dixon's *The Clansman* (1905) "the most influential racist work the United States has yet produced" Ernest reveals the novel's complexity. However, it is a complexity, Ernest contends, that is contingent upon Griggs's novel. In other words, without understanding Griggs, readers in the twenty-first century cannot understand the social dynamics of Jim Crow that Dixon worked to manipulate with such great effect in his fiction. Extending Wallinger's contrast between Dixon and Griggs, Ernest paradoxically reveals the deep and troubling connection between black and white authors during the highpoint of racial segregation in the United States.

The final section of the collection comprises essays by M. Giulia Fabi and Kenneth W. Warren on Griggs's last novel, *Pointing the Way* (1908). Both of these essays present sustained discussions of Griggs's critically neglected novel and illustrate the interpretive conundrums contained within much of Griggs's fiction. In her essay, "Jim Crow and the House of Fiction: Charles W. Chesnutt's and Sutton E. Griggs's Last Novels," Fabi reads *Pointing the Way* as an intertextual revision of Charles Chesnutt's novel *The Colonel's Dream* (1905). Through a close comparative analysis of their narrative strategies and representational choices, she demonstrates that Griggs's novel, though typically seen as less accomplished and less innovative than that of his more critically esteemed contemporary, addresses key political and aesthetic concerns, certain key problems to which Chesnutt only alluded. Fabi argues that Griggs is able to complete what Chesnutt began with his portrayal of vernacular characters, namely, the full emergence of these characters into narrative heroes and avatars of black self-determination. Continuing the discussion of Griggs's final novel, Warren situates *Pointing the Way* centrally within the context of the U.S. Supreme Court case of *Giles v. Harris*, in which black plaintiffs sought unsuccessfully to overturn provisions of the Alabama State Constitution that virtually disenfranchised the entirety of the state's black population. By attending closely to Griggs's appropriation of that case to produce the plot and the resolution of his novel, Warren suggests that in this last novel, as well as in much of his fiction, Griggs attempts to elaborate the terms on which the franchise could be returned to black American men. Although Griggs would not publish another novel after *Pointing the Way*, he devoted the rest of his life to putting his controversial political opinions in print.

His subsequent books took a different form, however. Griggs set the narrative conventions and dramatic episodes of fiction aside to pursue a more direct mode of address in his writing. In book after book he argued against the repeal of the Fifteenth Amendment, outlining the importance of the franchise to improving the social and economic conditions of the South. Having abandoned fiction, Griggs homed in on the one issue that drove both his secular and his spiritual pursuits: "Strengthening the Negro's position in the body politic is a far better policy for the final good of the South than is the proposed policy of having him a permanent point of weakness. Let all political parties North and South throw open their doors to qualified Negro voters as to all other citizens. Let the Negroes enter the several parties, each according to his conviction on questions presented."[34] Although Griggs was chasing a will-o'-the-wisp in believing that the turn-of-the-twentieth-century Democratic Party could be made hospitable to the interests and needs of black Americans, he was on target in his conviction that black political participation and access to the franchise were requisite if the nation were to roll back the tide of racial inequality that had swamped the South during his years as a novelist. It would take slightly more than three decades after his death in 1933, with the passage of the Voting Rights Act in 1965, for the vision of his novels to begin to be realized. The essays collected here tell the story of Griggs's literary and political struggles, a story that reveals the importance of literature to the survival of democracy.

Notes

1. Dickson D. Bruce, *The Origins of African American Literature, 1680–1865* (Charlottesville: University of Virginia Press, 2001), 1–2.

2. "Richmond Theological Seminary," *Richmond Planet*, May 5, 1894, 4.

3. Steven C. Tracy, "Saving the Day: The Recordings of the Reverend Sutton E. Griggs," *Phylon* 47, no. 2 (1986): 160.

4. The topic of the debate would become the subject of his third and, as considered by critics, most political novel, *Unfettered* (1902). The novel introduces readers to Dorlan Warthell, a man who risks his life to persuade his fellow African Americans to leave the Republican Party.

5. "A Terrible Wreck!" *Richmond Planet*, September 21, 1895, 1.

6. E. C. Morris, "The Demand for a Negro Baptist Publishing House [Address Delivered before the National Baptist Convention at Washington, D.C., in 1893]," in *Sermons, Addresses and Reminiscences* (Nashville: National Baptist Publishing Board, 1901), 56.

7. See Ann Field Alexander, *Race Man: The Rise and Fall of the "Fighting Editor"* (Charlottesville: University of Virginia Press, 2002).

8. "Rev. Brown's Loan," *Richmond Planet*, October 29, 1898, 1.

9. Editorial, *Richmond Planet*, March 5, 1898, 2

10. Qtd. in *Richmond Planet*, March 5, 1898, 2.

11. See Louis R. Harlan, *Booker T. Washington: The Wizard of Tuskegee, 1901–1915* (New York: Oxford University Press, 1983), 311–14.

12. Sutton E. Griggs, *Wisdom's Call* (Nashville: Orion, 1911), frontispiece.

13. Sutton E. Griggs, *Pulled from Shelter* (Nashville: Orion, 1907), 6.

14. Ibid.

15. See "W. Allison Sweeney Breaks a Memphis 'WHITE FOLKS' NIGGER' on the Wheel!," *Chicago Defender* (big weekend ed.). The article appeared December 8, 1917. Like John Mitchell Jr., Sweeney was a powerful newspaper editor and used his position at the *Chicago Herald* to attack Griggs's positions repeatedly.

16. Evelyn Brooks Higginbotham, *Righteous Discontent: The Women's Movement in the Black Baptist Church, 1880–1920* (Cambridge, Mass.: Harvard University Press, 1993), 42.

17. Griggs, *Pulled from Shelter*, 3.

18. Sutton E. Griggs, *Life's Demand; or, According to Law* (Memphis: National Public Welfare League, 1916), 51.

19. Rayford W. Logan, *The Negro in American Life and Thought: The Nadir, 1877–1901* (New York: Dial Press, 1954), 52.

20. Of course, the novels produced by these writers are merely the tip of the iceberg. Dunbar was a prolific poet, short-story writer, and dramatist. Hopkins was a dramatist, and Chesnutt launched his career as a writer of short fiction.

21. John David Smith, general introduction, *Anti-Black Thought, 1863–1925* (New York: Garland, 1993), xiv.

22. Jane Dailey, *The Age of Jim Crow: A Norton Casebook in History* (New York: Norton, 2009), xiv.

23. Sutton E. Griggs, *Imperium in Imperio* (Miami: Mnemosyne, 1969), 246.

24. Henry Clay Gray, "Office of a Distinctively Afro-American Literature," *New York Age* October 23, 1891, n.p.

25. J. McHenry Jones, *Hearts of Gold* (Morgantown: West Virginia University Press, 2010), 141.

26. Rafia Zafar, *We Wear the Mask: African Americans Write American Literature, 1760–1870* (New York: Columbia University Press, 1997), 190.

27. James Smethurst, *The African American Roots of Modernism: From Reconstruction to the Harlem Renaissance* (Chapel Hill: University of North Carolina Press, 2011), 2.

28. Carla L. Peterson, "Commemorative Ceremonies and Invented Traditions: History, Memory and Modernity in the 'New Negro' Novel of the Nadir," in *Post-bellum, Pre-Harlem: African American Literature and Culture, 1877–1919*, ed. Caroline Gebhard and Barbara McCaskill (New York: New York University Press, 2006), 38.

29. Sutton E. Griggs, *Pointing the Way* (Kila, Montana: Kessinger, 2007), 220–21.

30. Sutton E. Griggs, "Black Educator Lauds Ted," *Evening Independent*, June 25, 1912, 1.

31. Ralph Ellison, "The World and the Jug," in *The Collected Essays of Ralph Ellison*, ed. John F. Callahan (New York: Modern Library, 1995), 163–64.

32. Griggs, *Imperium in Imperio*, 232.

33. Caroline Gebhard and Barbara McCaskill, introduction, *Post-bellum, Pre-Harlem: African American Literature and Culture, 1877–1919*, 1.

34. Griggs, *Wisdom's Call*, 34–35.

CAROLINE LEVANDER

Sutton Griggs and the Borderlands of Empire

"Equality and Independence" and "Equality or Death"

The first of these slogans graces a banner described in the "Plan de San Diego"—the fifteen-step revolutionary plan written in 1915 by an anonymous group of Mexican American and Mexican revolutionaries in South Texas who purportedly had the backing of Germany and Japan in their plan to reclaim the lands taken by the United States in 1846, establish an independent Negro and Native American republic, and put to death every "North American over 16 years of age" except women, children, and aged men. The banner was the emblem of the "Liberating Army for Races and Peoples," an army that planned to "proclaim liberty of all individuals of the black race and its independence of Yankee tyranny" and to declare the independence of the states bordering on the Mexican nation, which Mexico was robbed of "in a most perfidious manner by North American imperialism."[1] Regardless of whether or not they finally decided to annex their new nation to Mexico, the revolutionaries state in Article 11 that they will ensure that the newly independent "negroes" will have plentiful land upon which to "form a republic and . . . be independent."[2]

The second slogan is also plastered on the banner of a fictional black revolutionary independence movement along the Texas border—a banner that each of the student members of a secret society that the black Texas-born writer and minister Sutton E. Griggs depicts in his 1899 novel *Imperium in Imperio* simultaneously holds up to protest for racial equality. Staged by the secret society that the novel's protagonist Belton Piedmont forms at the fictional Stowe University, this open rebellion is meant to teach "the future leaders of their race"

21

the power of what Griggs would subsequently term "collective efficiency" or combining forces for the common good. In this case the common good ensures that the one black teacher at the university eats at the same table as the white teachers. But this is not an isolated win. When they see the white teachers "beat a hasty retreat and h[o]ld up a white flag," the students join the leadership ranks of the parent secret society called the Imperium that is building an independent black empire in Texas.[3] Indeed the slogan "equality or death" accurately encapsulates the Imperium's commitment to seize control of "that great state" of Texas or for "every man (to) die in his shoes" trying—"to die in honor rather than live in disgrace" defending their right to liberty in a region "broad in domain, rich in soil and salubrious in climate" (163).

So how is it that Griggs's 1899 novel could anticipate by a little over a decade so many aspects of the seditious "Plan de San Diego"? Uncanny resonances bind the two texts over the few years and few hundred miles that separate their writing. In addition to the two movements' overlapping slogans, their multistep plans of revolutionary aggression against the United States converge and echo one another in a myriad of ways, from their "secret negotiations with all of the foreign enemies of the United States" (167) to their commitment to "the independence of the negroes," to their choice of Texas as the site of revolution.[4] The answer is, in short, that the "Plan de San Diego" was not an isolated document but a textual instance or trace of a longer, protracted set of political frictions over nation, race, and empire that played out over a few hundred miles of territory and that erupted in both fictional and nonfictional textual form episodically over the second half of the nineteenth and early twentieth centuries. Indeed, two years after the "Plan de San Diego" was uncovered, the "Zimmerman Telegram" revealed another possible plot, proposed by Germany to Mexico as part of an alliance, to reclaim from the United States the territory lost during the Mexican-American War, should the United States declare war on Germany. As such documents as the "Zimmerman Telegram," the "Plan de San Diego," and Griggs's novel remind us, the border has long been subject to geopolitical disputes and struggles not only among Mexican, Mexican American, and Anglo-American groups but among multiple, at times overlapping nations, races, and ethnicities. Such narratives of racial and territorial aggression collectively remind us of the importance and prevalence of diverse racial constituencies to this long, knotty story and therefore suggest how the "Plan de San Diego" makes explicit provision for "the negroes," regardless of the final outcome of the plot. In so doing the "Plan" acknowledges the long-standing presence and importance of African Americans as a cultural, political, and military force along the border.

Literary studies of the U.S./Mexico borderlands have tended to emphasize a brown/white story with occasional reference to Native Americans, while studies of the U.S. South have tended to emphasize a black/white story. However, attention to the particular southern border territory that Griggs takes as the site for his black empire shows us that when we assume the Mason-Dixon Line as the geographical boundary between North/South and the Rio Grande as a brown/white dividing line between Mexico and the United States, we oversimplify the racial contours of the nation and overemphasize the ease of its imperial reach. Both endpoint and access point, the territory comprising what is now the state of Texas functioned as a fluid, multidirectional, multiracial grid—a dynamic field through which Mexican, Anglo-, and African American groups crossed, recrossed, and blended with each other. It is a space that challenges us to rethink geo-racial migration from antebellum times to the present—to revisit our tendency, on the one hand, to assume that blacks only migrated, before and after the Civil War, to the northern border of the United States and, on the other hand, to think of the Rio Grande as a significant border crossing for Mexicans only. At different times forming the outer rim of the former slaveholding galaxy, the threshold between the United States and Mexico, and its own independent nation, the area that Waldo Frank would term "the frontier of the Rio Grande" is a region comprised of overlapping and often conflicting geopolitical affiliations.[5] Documents like the "Plan" and Griggs's novel therefore emphasize these vanishing points and overlaps between the U.S. South and U.S./Mexico borderlands—the messy mélange where regions overlap and boundaries don't hold.

Scholars interested in reorienting the geospatial frames of American literature have recently turned critical attention to Griggs's writing precisely because of the hemispheric context in which novels like *Imperium in Imperio* operate—because the novel's critique of race relations in the U.S. South refers to hemispheric history of U.S. empire and the Spanish American War.[6] Once a relatively remote figure, Sutton Griggs and his work have recently been analyzed in prominent studies of race, empire, and American literature, such as Amy Kaplan's *The Anarchy of Empire in the Making of U.S. Culture* (2002) and Susan Gillman's *Blood Talk: American Race Melodrama and the Culture of the Occult* (2003), and his first novel has been recently republished by Modern Library with an introduction by Cornel West. Griggs's life and writing have also recently become the subject of a separate book-length study—Finnie Coleman's *Sutton E. Griggs and the Struggle against White Supremacy* (2007)—and articles on Griggs regularly appearing in important venues suggest that he is now widely recognized as an important writer and thinker in American and African American literary culture.[7] Whereas in 1987 historian William Loren Katz bemoaned being unable to find a review of *Imperium*—possibly because the novel was "too treasonous to evaluate"—twenty years later *Imperium* has become a significant object of study, especially for its commentary on race relations in an imperializing late nineteenth-century United States.[8]

Yet in this recent critical attention to the novel's strategic pairing of the contemporary extranational, imperial conflict epitomized by the "war between the United States and Spain" (137) with the intranational racial conflict epitomized by the brutal lynching of a postmaster in South Carolina (the actual mob murder of Postmaster Frazier Baker in 1898), scholars have consistently missed the nuances of Griggs's South—the variability and specificity of the particular region that the Imperium calls home. Griggs's observation that "in proportion as the Cubans drew near to their freedom, the fever of hope correspondingly rose in the veins of the Imperium" (137) makes clear the direct, dynamic relation between the Cubans' and the Imperium's political projects in racial self-determinacy. Given such lines, Kaplan's argument that Griggs projects U.S. racial anxieties onto the battlefield of Cuba or Gillman's suggestion that the Spanish-American War figures as a crisis point for U.S. domestic racial conflict make sense. Yet exclusive focus on the links between a uniform United States and Cuba can tend to obscure the rich, overlapping contexts, regions, and locales from which Griggs's text also derives its shape and meaning. Critical efforts to "world" American literature or to contextualize the United States within a transnational geopolitical frame, as José Limón reminds us, can run the risk of flattening the shape and texture of the distinct regions within which this literature is produced and can lead to totalizing readings of texts' complex regional engagements with global phenomena. In overlooking the importance of the Imperium's particular location to the novel's meaning, many recent analyses have rendered Griggs's novel placeless all over again.

So what happens if we locate Griggs's novel within the context of the specific region that the Imperium calls home, rather than within the context of a generic U.S. South or U.S. nation? In other words, what happens if we take Texas not as metonym or metaphor for the U.S. South but rather as a distinct, interconnected critical region, a sort of world apart as well as in relation, replete with specific local cultures whose critical interactions with global as well as national forces form the starting point for the novel's answer to a long U.S. history of racial injustice? Historians such as Gerald Horne, William Loren Katz, Barry Couch, James Leiker, Quintard Taylor, Neil Foley, Kevin Mulroy, Lawrence Rice, Philip Durham, Everett Jones, and Sara Massey have recently begun to tell the story of the African American slaves, freemen, fugitives, cowboys, and soldiers who occupied the U.S./Mexico borderlands during the late nineteenth century. By locating Griggs's fictional black empire within this regionally specific cultural context and, more particularly, within the dynamic and distinctive print culture that emerges in response to this multiracial populace, we can begin to see how Griggs's novel draws upon the area's rich racial legacy in order to imagine a new answer to a key question occupying both black and white citizens of the United States—where to place the nation's newly freed black citizens. As Trish Loughran has observed, local rather than "cross-regional" print culture helped to found the nation. However, this very same "proliferating variety of local and regional reading publics," as the following pages suggest, also posed key challenges to the nation as homologous entity.[9] By locating Griggs's writing within such a regional print climate, we can begin to see how Griggs's writing engages with the borderland's print culture and how this engagement helps Griggs to reformulate the terms in which an urgent national question is posed—the question of where free blacks should call home.

A Borderlands South: Beneath the South a Mine Has Been Dug

Locating Griggs's writing as part of the borderland region's ongoing textual dialogue about race, rights, and region allows us to make sense of key questions about black citizenship that his novel poses and attempts to resolve. As early as the 1850s Martin Delany and Frederick Douglass had recognized that blacks in the United States constituted "a nation within a nation," and both had advocated emigration outside the nation's southernmost borders to other countries in the Western Hemisphere as an answer to U.S. racism.[10] While Delany was a long-time proponent of emigration to Central and South America, Douglass's assertion that blacks might have to emigrate to points within the hemisphere where "we may still keep within hearing of the wails of our enslaved people in the United States" was an anomaly in his career-long opposition to emigration and African colonization.[11] Its title places Griggs's novel squarely in this protracted debate on the relative merits of emigration or assimilation that had absorbed both the African American press and political leaders throughout the century. But the novel suggests that the question of whether blacks should place themselves inside or outside the nation's borders to ensure equal political representation and protection—in short, whether they should amalgamate or emigrate—assumes the stability and permanence, rather than contestedness, of U.S. borders and, in so doing, overlooks another important option available to African Americans seeking equality.

Rather than advocating for the placement of this "nation within a nation" either inside or outside firmly fixed U.S. borders, Griggs's text suggests that there are strategic locations on the nation's edges from which to productively rethink some of the founding assumptions governing the geopolitics of African American rights. Wilson Jeremiah Moses has placed Griggs's novels in a black nationalist tradition that was, "like the nationalism of most colonial peoples, profoundly influenced by the culture of the dominant civilization."[12] It is true that Griggs's vision of a black empire at nation's edge largely ignores the black empire's potential impact on indigenous nonblack peoples.[13] Yet even as Griggs's novel may reproduce the strategic erasures of the "dominant civilization" it critiques, it also seeks alternatives to that civilization's either/or logics of racial integration by drawing on a borderlands history of racially hybrid peoples. By undertaking to "unite all Negroes in a body to do that which the whimpering government" will not do (183), the Imperium seeks to combat the U.S. federal government's failure to protect its black populace against racist violence—to leave "the Negro" an "unprotected foreigner in his own home" (125). But, once formed, the Imperium quickly dismisses the options of either amalgamation or emigration to the African Congo Free State with "hisses and jeers" (151) in favor of extended consideration of two plans to secure the entire territory of Texas for the black empire.

Indeed, when it convenes in its Waco, Texas, headquarters, the first subject that the assembly debates highlights the unilateral importance of the territory it occupies to the Imperium's project. Two competing plans for occupation of Texas are put forth by the novel's two protagonists, both of whom have suffered the ills of amalgamation—one's fiancée has killed herself rather than bear offspring that would further dilute the race, and one's wife has birthed a baby that appears to be white—and both of whom agree that the answer to the problem of U.S. racism is not to be found within the confines of the United States but rather in the region the Imperium has designated for its headquarters. Conflict between the two male protagonists about how to establish the Imperium—Belton Piedmont advocates initial nonviolence, while Bernard Belgrave is a proponent of armed resistance—on the one hand, threatens to split the Imperium but, on the other hand, reinforces a bipartisan agreement about where to establish it. Belton envisions blacks emigrating en masse to Texas, where they will secure lawful possession of the state majority vote and where they will work out their "destiny as a separate and distinct race in the Unites States of America" (164). Bernard, on the other hand, envisions an eight-step covert "Plan of Action" for taking over all "Texas land contiguous to states and territories of the Union" (167) that includes secret negotiations with foreign enemies of the United States and violent seizure of Texas land. At issue is the Imperium's capacity to accommodate dissent within its ranks, and in responding to Belton's disagreement, the Imperium both enacts its most important sovereign right— the right to put a citizen to death—and oversteps its bounds. Complete consent, however, does occur over the location, if not the implementation, of the empire. If they disagree over the how, in short, they do not disagree over the where, and the where is Texas.

As this uniform agreement over the empire's site suggests, territory will be key to the Imperium's project—not simply because the region's location on nations' periphery makes it a focal point for various efforts to reclaim lost rights, like that propounded by the "Plan de San Diego," but because such efforts raise important questions about black governance and civic representation that cannot be fully worked through within other parts of the United States. From the beginning, Piedmont attempts, with limited degrees of success, to create space within various parts of the U.S. South from which to "secure rights denied because of color" (47). As a young student in Winchester, Virginia, Belton prepares to undermine racist favoritism by digging a large underground room beneath "the platform of the school-room" upon which he will compete against the light-skinned Bernard in an oratory contest. Despite the fact that the judges recognize that Belton's speech on "The Contribution of the Anglo-Saxon to the Cause of Human Liberty" is better than Bernard's, they "don't like to see nigger blood triumph over any Anglo-Saxon blood" (29) and so find a loophole that lets them award the prize to Bernard. Belton interrupts this reaffirmation of white supremacy, however, by literally pulling the ground out from under the master of ceremony and dropping the hated headmaster into the dunking pool hidden under the platform's trapdoor. Temporarily short-circuiting racial hierarchies, Belton's orchestration of the racist schoolmaster's fall "from the sublime to the ridiculous" (30) prepares him for his future leadership role in "adjusting positions between the negro and Anglo-Saxon races of the South" (49)—more particularly, in bringing about the evacuation of "the Anglo-Saxon race from some of its outposts" and in forwarding "the march of the negro to occupation of these areas" (49–50).

His own geographic relocations within the U.S. national borders from Virginia to Tennessee to Louisiana enable Belton to test the likelihood that these southern regions within the United States could support the "forward march of the Negro" into "the beautiful land of the future" (50). In Richmond, Virginia, Belton starts a weekly journal, which is successful until it publishes an article that vigorously "attack[s] Southern Institutions" by critiquing voting fraud (88). Belton has fallen "into the well" of love for a Miss Nermal, and while the kissing game "in the well" allows the two to declare their love for each other, Belton cannot secure opportunities as an educated black man that would enable the two to pull themselves out of the well and thrive, despite his undercover explorations, impersonating a female nurse, of the labor opportunities available to blacks.

Frustrated blacks in Richmond think of rebelling against the United States and become willing to aid the foreign power that would invade it, but it is in Belton's next stop within U.S. borders, Louisiana, where "the colored people of the region far outnumber the white people" (101), that Belton sees firsthand what he needs to do in order to "command" his people to move forward to claim their "glorious destiny" (50). Belton is told that long ago blacks in the region had "absolute control of everything," because they organized their greater numbers into armed patrols and civic units. However, they did not have the "authority nor disposition to kill a traitor" when he appeared in their midst, and their inability to generate an "effective remedy against a betrayal" enables whites to strip them of their civil liberties. This political history of the region makes explicable to an initially confused Belton "what kind of a country he had entered" when he is arrested in Louisiana for being a "high-toned nigger" (99), but it also makes clear to him that a successful black society has to "exercise the sovereign right of life and death over its subjects" (129) in order to protect its members from white resistance.

It is from the outermost periphery rather than the center of the U.S. South—in a borderlands South—that the creation of an independent black society powerful and complex enough to defend African Americans against the racism that frustrates similar efforts in other parts of the South becomes imaginable. The physical structure of its Waco headquarters highlights the Imperium's ability to reorganize racial hierarchies and the space that blacks occupy relative to whites. Its main building has been constructed much as the platform that Belton initially built in Virginia—the top story is one large room that contains "an elevated platform" upon which stands what passes for "a gallows" (123). In this room, Belton initiates Bernard into the secrets of the Imperium, but he does so with a test that highlights the Imperium's power to do exactly what black social movements in places like Louisiana could not—the power to take life. After writing Bernard to "come to Waco at once," Belton tells Bernard of a "foul conspiracy" perpetrated by blacks that attempts to "unite all Negroes in a body to do that which the U.S. government says it cannot do—to secure protection for their lives and the full enjoyment of all rights and privileges due American citizens," and he asks Bernard to help him "expose the conspiracy before it is too late" (125). This test to see if Bernard is loyal to his race includes a pretend execution, and the blinded Bernard is led to the gallows platform, which he is told has "a trap door" that extends four floors and that, when sprung, will tear his arms from his body. Once the trapdoor opens, Bernard falls with terrific speed, but he drops safely into the Imperium Assembly, a large room with 145 occupied desks arranged in a semicircle around him, where he is hailed as the chief and president of the Imperium for his courage and loyalty to his race. The headmaster's precipitous fall through the platform trapdoor only temporarily challenges whites' prerogative to "keep blacks down," but Bernard's drop into the Imperium initiates an important next step in the Imperium's development, its ultimate goal of transforming "the Anglo Saxon who regards himself as a petty king and some community of negroes as his subjects" (218) from sovereign into subject—and of transforming black subjects of petty kings who "have chosen our race as an empire" into citizens of "an empire of their own" (218).

As is now apparent, the particular location of the Imperium on nation's periphery optimizes the success of this project to reorganize racial hierarchies within the nation. As the narrator observes, it is within this particular region "beneath the South [that] a mine has been dug and filled with dynamite," and this mine that is the Imperium has the capacity to generate a "terrific explosion" and to send "house, fences, trees, pavement stones, and all things on earth" (176) hurling into the air. Lying within the nation—in it but not entirely of it—this particular, outlying region provides an important leverage point for Griggs to rethink the geospatial assumptions of racial equality and blacks' placement inside or outside the United States. Its geographic location is not incidental but is rather essential to the Imperium's project. What is unsustainable in other parts of the South becomes imaginable in the Texas borderlands, both because of the region's particular geopolitical and racial history and because of the rich and varied regional print culture that springs up to adjudicate this history.

"Dreams of Freedom, Equality, and Empire"

Popular newspapers and magazines were important print forms for many late nineteenth-century American novelists, as Susan Mizruchi has observed, because they allowed authors interested in "shaping attitudes toward cultural others" to identify and engage the key concerns of public audiences and to market their novels to those audiences.[14] Griggs was "a significant pioneer" among African American novelists, in part, because he sought to harness the publishing industry's powerful role in transforming how reading audiences understood race.[15] He undertook to control all aspects of publication and marketing by operating his own publishing company and promoting the sale of his novels among black communities during his travels as minister and orator. In *The Story of My Struggles* (1914), Griggs describes going "from door to door . . . where plain workmen toiled" and "to schools where poor Negro boys and girls were struggling for an education" in order to sell his books. "These humble people of the race," he recalls, "came to me with their dimes" in order to buy the books that Griggs envisioned would help to further the race.[16] And he was partially successful. Rayford Logan estimates that Griggs "probably had more Negro readers than did Chesnutt and Dunbar."[17] Griggs believed that literature was fundamental to the successful "progress of the African American people"; Moses contends that Griggs was the "only black novelist of his period, with the possible exception of W. E. B. Du Bois, who deliberately undertook the writing of novels as part of a definite plan to create a national Negro literature."[18]

Yet this "national Negro literature" foregrounds the importance of region to the "progress" of the black audience for whom Griggs wrote. For example, Griggs dedicated writing like *Wisdom's Call* that addresses African Americans as a distinctive group "to Texas soil which fed me, to Texas air which fanned my cheeks, to Texas skies which smiled upon me."[19] In so doing, he suggests the region's larger importance to the literary project of forming an equal people. As has been the case with writing like Martin Delany's *Blake*, scholars have historically viewed the literary value of Griggs's writing as compromised by its awkward style, heavy didacticism, excessive polemics, and improbable plot twists.[20] One of the most widely read black novelists in the black communities of his day, Griggs has subsequently tended to be pushed to the sidelines of literary history.[21] However, what can appear nonsensical from a deterritorialized vantage point locks into focus once we recognize that *Imperium*'s narrative logic is embedded within the region's rich print culture and commentary on black equality—on race and place.

Griggs wrote, published, marketed, and sold *Imperium in Imperio* as the region's popular press was generating pro- and antiblack rights publications—as local periodicals were conducting an extended thought experiment on the place of blacks in the nation. These commentaries about blacks' rights moved easily from page to borderlands public sphere and shaped politics, practice, and possibilities for African American equality in the region. Highly politicized pro- and antiblack periodicals had long been a defining feature of the region, and by 1900 over two dozen black papers and periodicals were being published in Texas. One of the earliest to advocate for equal rights for black men had been the *Waco Spectator*, published in 1868 by Confederate veteran and philosophical anarchist Albert Parsons. The journal's goal of securing "the political rights of the colored people" generated "the hate and contumely" of many of its editor's "former army comrades, neighbors, and the Ku Klux Klan," and finally Parsons and the *Spectator* were run out of town.[22]

On the other side of the debate was the editor of the *Iconoclast*, a Waco-published journal of opinion that had a circulation of more than ninety thousand nationwide during its three-year life from 1895 to 1898. Self-dubbed the "Apostle," William Brann propelled his journal to national fame with his vitriolic commentary on social, political, and racial issues of the day. Brann was well known for his outlandish attacks on a number of groups including blacks, Baptists, Episcopalians, the British, and northeastern elites, and fashioned himself the Mark Twain of Texas. He was an entrepreneurial publisher, as well as author, who sold the *Iconoclast* to and repurchased it from his literary friend and colleague O. Henry. "Located in Texas," according to Brann, because the region has more "narrow-brained bigots and intolerant fanatics" than "any other section of these United States," the *Iconoclast* nonetheless foregrounded the importance of the region to answering the question confronting the nation—what to do with free blacks.[23]

According to Brann, the "best possible national policy" is one that reinforced cohesive national boundaries—that refused to let "the common people of this country" be divided into "two hostile camps" but that rather allowed "estrangement to be forgotten" and "a reunited people" to emerge out of North and

South.[24] Yet he is critical of "our northern neighbors who do not understand the negro" and of "the northern press," which had "reared up" and labeled his plan to forcibly expel blacks from the South "a damnable crime conceived in the brain of a Texas brute."[25] Because "no conceivable amount of training can transform the negro into a tolerable citizen," blacks, according to Brann, are the "black cloud hanging over every Southern home" and therefore should be "mercifully banished to a foreign shore" or "instantly executed."[26] Contending that the region "will quickly become the most populous, prosperous and progressive portion of the American Union" once "the negro is removed from the South," Brann challenged Massachusetts to take the black "away from the wicked Texans and carry him in triumph to the land of racial equality" or to let them be "roasted" in Texas.[27]

Despite Brann's commitment to a unified nation devoid of racial conflict, the year before Griggs wrote *Imperium*, local newspapers announced a "street duel to the death in Waco streets" between outraged citizens and Brann over his vitriolic editorials on local leaders' racial politics.[28] The region, according to the *Iconoclast*, was being compromised by its southern as well as its northern neighbors and by local leaders' ongoing illicit involvements with residents to their south. Tired of the dependence and disregard of "Spanish cavaleros and the half-civilized Aborigines to the south of us," Brann contended that the only way to stop their "flagrant insults to the American flag" was to sever ties with all countries "between our southern boundary and the Antarctic Circle" and to expel all South Americans from the region in order to protect its racial superiority.[29] But it was his coverage of a particular episode in the flow of people between this region and Texas that got Brann kidnapped, assaulted, and finally gunned down on the streets of Waco. Claiming that local residents of Waco had transported Latin American minors "to Texas to breed illegitimate Baptists," Brann antagonized area religious leaders with his justified allegation that Baptist administrators of Waco's Baylor University were sex-trafficking Brazilian minors, under the auspices of providing training for their missionary work in Latin America.[30] When a pregnant Brazilian exchange student accused a family member of Baylor's president of rape, Brann produced incendiary commentary declaring that her "ill-begotten babe" was "her diploma from Baylor" and that her "illegitimate childbirth constituted Baylor's graduation exercises."[31] His declaration that he had "nothing against the Baptists," he "just believed they weren't held under long enough" did nothing to appease outraged locals, many of whom tried to kill him before he was finally assassinated in April 1898.[32] The enduring animosity that the articulate savagery of his writing provoked is suggested by his tombstone, or more particularly the bullet hole shot through the profile of his head, next to the word "TRUTH." As Parsons's *Spectator* or Brann's *Iconoclast* suggest, the region's popular publications propounded radically differing positions on the place of nonwhites in the nation and generated heated, at times violent, reactions in their readers.

Griggs's novel took part in this protracted dialogue about race and region, place and politics, in large part by featuring print as key to these race debates. If the region's publication culture was a fiery, combustible blend of racial free-thinking and reactionism throughout the second half of the nineteenth century, Griggs generated text that featured the politically transformative power of print within its pages. Within such a milieu, it is therefore no surprise that the Imperium's new president would start a "fiery" "illustrated journal" that featured "pictures of horrors, commented upon in burning words" and that "spread fire-brands everywhere in the ranks of the Imperium" (137). The novel foregrounds the importance of print texts—from the multipage "PRESIDENT'S MESSAGE," a call to arms delivered to the assembly to the multistep "Plan of Action" and the "secret newspaper" that Bernard starts that chronicles "every fresh discrimination, every new act of oppression, every additional unlawful assault upon property, the liberty or the lives of any of the members of the Imperium" (137). Within the novel, this proliferation of textual production summons community into being—in short, to constitute—the community the assembly plans for and envisions. Belton's commencement address, for example, is printed in the *Richmond Daily Temps* and creates such "a great sensation in political and literary circles in every section of the country," that the oration is reprinted in "every newspaper of any consequence" and "commented upon by leading journals of England" (61) even inspiring the president of the United States to write a letter of congratulation to Belton. It moves one reader—the editor of the *Temps*—to pay for Belton's education because he recognizes the potential that the words on the page have to transform race relations and the potential of their author as a representative of his race's future. The printed word is later powerful enough to create "a great stir in political circles" (88) and to transform public opinion on questions of racial injustice.

Griggs not only features print as key to race debates in Imperium, but he also draws on popular print depicting the region as a separate nation, related to but distinct from the U.S. national project. Popular narratives had long shown the region's diverse independence experiments as both reenacting and refuting

U.S. nation formation. In its accounts of the founding of the independent Republic of Texas, for example, the *Telegraph and Texas Register* (1838), like many other publications, consistently figured the Texas Revolution of 1835–36 and the independent slaveholding republic that followed as upholding and extending U.S. narratives of nation formation and imperial ambition in order to legitimize the revolutionary effort. According to the *Telegraph and Texas Register*, those who fought for Texas independence understood "the present situation of Texas" to be "analogous to that in which American colonists were placed."[33] Writers modeled the Texas Declaration of Independence on the 1776 declaration, the republic's initial capital was named Washington on the Brazos, and men fighting at the Alamo mouthed the words of John Adams. Seeing their revolutionary struggle against Mexico as furthering the goals of the U.S. colonies' struggle against Great Britain, founders of the Republic of Texas identified the independent nation as fully realizing the incipient ideals of the nation to its north. William Allen summed up the situation thus in *Texas in 1840; or, The Emigrant's Guide to the New Republic*: its geopolitical genealogy enabled the new Republic of Texas to "establish a form of government upon the most perfect model the world has ever seen"—a superior "government of law, system of human rights, and security against the exercise of lawless power."[34] This new, independent republic upheld, extended, and finally threatened U.S. empire as well as nation, and many agreed with John Calhoun that the new slaveholding republic was uniting "the ambition of Rome and the avarice of Carthage," with the goal of becoming "the real Empire . . . of the country."[35] Enjoying "an empire and a history of her own," Texas, warns Edward Everett Hale, the anonymous author of *How to Conquer Texas, before Texas Conquers Us* (1845), has the capacity to "become the real Empire" of the continent.[36]

Like these popular print accounts of the region as a separate nation—even as a separate empire—Griggs uses U.S. patriotic narratives in order to conceptualize an independent empire in the region. Like the Texas Republic, the Imperium's "compact government" models its constitution after that of the United States, makes extensive use of Jefferson's writings, seeks in Bernard their own "George Washington," and debates the exact same laws and policy issues being considered by the Congress of the United States. By paying "especial attention to the history of the United States during the revolutionary period" (131), Imperium leaders seek to improve on what its founders managed to produce— they seek to correct "what the General Government could not do, because of a defect in the Constitution" (132). These painstaking reenactments of U.S. nation-formation at nation's edge both affirm the nation and underscore the nation's failure to implement its liberal democratic principles of liberty and justice for all.

This doubled relation to the nation to its north is nowhere more apparent than in the Imperium's capitol building, the facade of which is decorated with American flags and red, white, and blue bunting. Masquerading on the outside as Thomas Jefferson College to the uninitiated, the Imperium's capitol building contains inside all the apparatus of a second national government that has been "organized and maintained within the United States for many years," and that is comprised of a population of 7,250,000 (129). Underneath the patriotic cloak that attests to its national affiliation and protects it from the public eye, this building is covered in a second layer of black cloth that simultaneously represents the Imperium's critique of the United States, its mourning for the racial violence the United States continues to condone within its borders, and its aspirations to create an independent empire that threatens U.S. hegemony. As the multiple layers of fabric shrouding its capitol building suggest, the Imperium, just like the Republic of Texas, fashions itself on a U.S. constitutional model in order finally to pose a serious, covert challenge to this national government.

Fighting B(l)ack

As we have seen thus far, Griggs's text circulates in a vibrant array of local print debates about race, region, and national belonging that collectively highlight how the region's location at nation's edge complicates the concept of a firmly delineated national boundary upon which the ideas of emigration or assimilation depend. Griggs's novel engages with local print culture even as it addresses the alternative and experimental African American communities that had long typified the region. These communities, as we will see, refute the idea that assimilation or emigration were the only two answers available to those who wanted to challenge U.S. racial injustice.

At the same time that Anglo-Americans were constituting a new nation based upon racial hierarchies, African Americans were contesting the white privilege of the United States and of the Texas Republic. The region had long been home to experimental social efforts to refute and reimagine U.S. racial hierarchies. Even before Texas became an independent republic in 1836, blacks were living and working, in significant numbers, on the Texas plains. While a 1792 Spanish census indicated that 496 of Texas's 1,600 residents were black (Katz 63), it was the signing of Mexico's Plan de Iguala (1821), which guaranteed social equality, abolition of slavery, and the right of all races to hold office, that caused black settlement of Texas to skyrocket. Texas, the Mexican province most accessible to African Americans from the United States, became a principal area of settlement for blacks like Virginian John Bird, who believed that he and his son Henry would be received as citizens under Mexico's colonization laws and entitled as such to land. Their new rights inspired African Americans like Greenbury Logan to fight for Texas independence in 1836 because he felt himself "more a freeman [in Texas] than in the States."[37] By the time it was annexed in the 1840s, Texas was imagined by many northerners as the dumping ground for blacks—both free and slave—and as the natural portal through which blacks would emigrate to Mexico and the equator. Numerous postbellum experimental black colonies, such as William Ellis's and Jack Johnson's, continued to funnel blacks through Texas to northern Mexico. Johnson, for example, invited "colored people" who are "lynched, tortured, mobbed, persecuted and discriminated against in the boasted 'Land of Liberty'" to emigrate to the land of no "race prejudice."[38] For William H. Ellis the laws of Mexico as late as 1895 continued to be more fair and impartial than in the United States: "As long as the negro is suppressed as he is in the U.S., the better class will seek new fields, and Mexico, standing at the very doors of the U.S., offering inducements to all, will prove a welcome home to the negro."[39]

Using South Texas as their point of ingress and egress, Ellis's colonists became the subject of heated print debate—on both sides of the border—on questions of racial and national progress. Mexican presses like *El Tiempo* praised Ellis's effort as a "way of stopping the lynchings and helping the U.S. get rid of a race which the Yankee detest," and *El Heraldo* predicted "good results for the colony . . . but not for the country because the negro element is not an acceptable colonization," but some papers on the U.S. side of the border like the *San Antonio Express* were more critical of the experiment and complained that migrating blacks were destroying local communities.[40]

In his novel Griggs represents the complex civic position of blacks along the U.S./Mexico borderlands with a key question that organizes and seems to confuse the narrative from the start—whether key figures like the narrator and Belton are patriots or traitors. Although contemporaries like Brann may have argued for blacks' expulsion from the nation's borders, Griggs's novel points out that, from the vantage point of the region's fluid, multilayered racial makeup, the question of a citizen's unilateral, unequivocal national affiliation becomes impossible to determine. The text registers this impossibility in the founding tension that it creates between the opposing concepts of patriotism and treason—endpoints on a continuum of national affiliation. Griggs describes the writing of *Imperium* as a direct response to his dawning recognition that "men have a right to a voice in the government that exercises authority over them," but that the founding U.S. principle that "governments derive their powers from the consent of the governed" was being "violated with reference to the American Negro."[41] He therefore "wrote the book entitled Imperium in Imperio" because he believed "that a statement of our case in book form would accomplish good for our cause."[42]

The Imperium reflects the vexed relation of African Americans to their national government. The Imperium's reliance on and rejection of U.S. foundational narratives shape the narrative as well as the plot. It begins and ends with executions that reinforce the Imperium's legitimacy and its right to put a traitor to death, yet the narrative insists that Belton Piedmont and Imperium secretary of state Berl Trout are patriots as well as traitors, subject to competing, conflicting territorial affiliations that refuse nation logics of resolution. The novel formulates the choice between patriotism and treason as an overarching narrative problem in its preface—the Dying Declaration from Trout—beginning with the words "I am a traitor" (5). Trout has been identified as a traitor because he gives the story that we are about to read to Sutton E. Griggs to publish, and thereby destroys the secrecy upon which the Imperium depends for success. For this the Imperium assassinates him and buries his body face-downward, coffin-less, in an "old forsaken well," in accordance with Imperium law.

But if the narrative—or more particularly Griggs's publishing and our reading of it—is an act of traitorous betrayal of the Imperium, it is also the act of "a patriot" who defends the interests of the "whole human family" (6) against "a serious menace to the peace of the world" (176). Trout's decision to "prove traitor" to the Imperium rather than condone "internecine war" generates the text we read, and is reproduced within the text when Belton decides to break with the Imperium rather than support Bernard's violent and in Belton's estimation "treasonous" plan to take over Texas. Reminding Bernard that the Imperium was organized to secure their rights "within the United States" (168), Belton declares that he is "no traitor" to the United States and that he will "never fight to restrict [its] territory" (169) because he loves not only the Imperium and the

Union but, more particularly, "the South," on whose "soil" he "was born" and on whose "bosom [he] was reared" (154). The final, and fatal, conflict between Belton and Bernard is not about the geographic location of the Imperium—as we have seen, everyone agrees that it should be in the southern borderlands—but is rather endemic to this particular region. An inevitable outcome of the Imperium's location, the question of whether Belton is "patriot" or "traitor" or both represents the competing, overlaying affiliations that the region's racially diverse populace has to the various constituencies competing for control of the region.

Griggs's novel registers this enduring tension between affiliation with and resistance to the national corpus (between patriotism and treason), thus engaging the region's popular print commentaries on race and nation, but it also engages African American communities' lived experience in the region. The U.S./Mexico borderlands region did not immunize African Americans against the domestic racism of which Griggs is so critical in *Imperium*, but it did offer some strategic opportunities for African Americans to reconfigure the political, social, economic, and legal contours of postwar racism in America—to, as Griggs's narrator puts it, generate a "race that dreams of freedom, equality, and empire, far more than is imagined" (44). These regionally specific opportunities, as we will see, provide an explanatory logic for the seemingly fantastic elements of Griggs's text—from the armed march on the Texas capitol, to the establishment of a government replete with physical plant, to the start-up funds for the venture, to the accelerated purchase of all Texas land. African Americans' experiences in the region are integral to Griggs's vision of how to solve the national question of racial justice. But more fundamentally they collectively point out how "either/or" logics meant to resolve racial inequality either inside or outside the nation's borders fail to acknowledge the full range and complexity of citizens' "dreams of freedom, equality, and empire"—foreshorten far more ambitious, complex imaginings of racial equality.

The complex web of competing and, at times, conflicting loyalties and split affinities at the core of the region's African American civic participation is evident from African Americans' military service along the nation's blurry edge. From the time that Griggs was born in 1872 in the north central Texas town of Chatfield to the time that he wrote his first novel imagining a black empire in 1898, the region that he lived in and wrote about was transformed from a frontier into a national border. African Americans' territorial occupation played an essential role in this process. Black soldiers were key to the establishment of a

U.S. national border, and in 1873 more than 1,600 African American soldiers were stationed along the border, helping to solidify the United States' southernmost national boundary.[43] Buffalo soldiers had long fought for all sides during the multifront conflicts characterizing the region in the first half of the century, but the need of the United States after 1848 to rely on black troopers was heightened by the fact that U.S. authorities were not confident that they could count on Latino residents to confront Mexico, should open conflict between the two nations arise.[44] Depicted by the U.S. government as genuine Americans who could be trusted to defend national interests in contradistinction to these groups, black soldiers saw a unique opportunity to align their interests with the interests of the U.S. military in order to advance their own rights—to affiliate with the national corpus. Yet at the same time, conflicts with residents, as Horne and others have documented, placed black soldiers at odds with the citizens they protected; motivated them to mobilize when their civil rights were violated; and finally equipped blacks with the skills and experience necessary to reimagine their place within the nation.

In 1878, for example, the African American soldiers of Company D, Tenth Cavalry, rode into San Angelo, Texas, and opened fire in a white saloon after locals attacked a black sergeant. Immortalized by Frederic Remington's May 4, 1901, illustrated short story for *Collier's*, "How the Worm Turned," this conflict between Fort Concho troopers and local whites was, in Remington's words, "one of the wild notes that must sound when the great epic of the West is written."[45] Remington's story creates a clear line of influence between the 1878 "Texas fight" and the Spanish-American War. His first-person narrator was a bystander and most likely a participant in the saloon shoot out and tells the story to his comrade to pass the time while his company waits to fight the "Span-yards." The narrator disingenuously predicts that the Fort Concho fight will be forgotten, but "that Texas fight" at Fort Concho had a long-lived, as well as literary, legacy.[46] Individuals like Waco-born John B. Hayes, or "The Texas Kid," confronted "For Whites Only" saloon signs by asking for a drink and, upon being refused, backing his horse through the swinging doors and shooting out the lights. As late as 1917, 150 members of the Twenty-Fourth Infantry's Third Battalion marched on whites in Houston in retaliation for racial injustices, killing sixteen whites and suffering four casualties themselves. Organized in 1869, the Twenty-Fourth had served in the West before being deployed to Cuba in 1898 and then to Mexico through El Paso to fight Pancho Villa's forces in 1916. Seasoned on the U.S. imperial stage, these black soldiers had little patience for domestic racism. They put their military skills to work within the nation's border, in a two-hour march on the city, which came to be known as the Houston Riot of 1917 and precipitated the court-martial of sixty-four soldiers.[47] As these narratives suggest, African Americans actively and violently reclaimed their right to occupy space in the border region that they helped to stabilize for the United States. Through these aggressive self-defensive actions along the border, as Remington's story and the history of the Twenty-Fourth Infantry reminds us, African Americans were able to aggressively seek their own rights as they became more visible members of an imperial army—to dream and, increasingly, to act on their dreams of freedom, equality, and empire.

African American military service along the border reflected African American inhabitants' overlapping and at times competing drives to be assimilated within and autonomous from the United States—it made them at once "patriots" and "traitors," much like Griggs's characters. Their acquisition of real property, as well as military service, in the region also reflects the essentially fissured nature of black citizenship along the borderlands. On the one hand, African American land ownership rose more precipitously in Texas than in any other southern state, partly because Texas combined large tracts of abandoned land with liberal squatting laws. Many black Texas landowners resided in freedmen's settlements, informal communities of black farmers and stockmen that sprang up across the eastern half of Texas.[48] Some became landowners through land speculation and ranching opportunities. For example, William Goyens, a North Carolinian, settled near Nacogdoches in 1820, became a land speculator, and amassed nearly thirteen thousand acres in four East Texas counties by his death in 1856. The Ashworth brothers migrated to southeast Texas between 1831 and 1835 and soon became the largest and arguably wealthiest free black family in antebellum Texas, acquiring two thousand acres in southeast Texas, and 2,500 cattle, the largest herd in Jefferson County. Two of the Ashworths were wealthy enough to avoid military service in the Texas revolution, sending substitutes instead.[49] As Thad Sitton and James Conrad point out, historians as well as American studies and border studies scholars have commonly overlooked this phenomenon—partly because of difficulty in finding information on the settlements and their consequent erasure from official historical narratives but partly because we tend to think about this region in terms of land struggles between Anglo and Mexican residents, punctuated by such events as the Garza and Cortina rebellions and the Mexican Revolution. Yet the percentage of black Texas landowners increased fourteen times between 1870 and 1890, going from 1.8 to

26 percent and peaking at 31 percent in 1900.[50] By 1924 Clifton Richardson's article describing the region to readers of the *Messenger*, the national magazine of the Harlem Renaissance, observed that the state had a disproportionately large number of black property and landowners, and these residents, according to Richardson, were, like the leaders of Griggs's Imperium, determined to stay and "fight it out" "in the Lone Star State," regardless of trouble.[51]

And yet blacks, more often than not, still worked land they didn't or couldn't own. From the 1870s to the 1890s, over five thousand black cowboys (about 25 percent of all cowboys) worked the Texas cattle drives. The largest number of African Americans herding cattle worked in Texas—one-third of all black cowboys in 1890 and two-thirds by 1910—and black cowboys like Britton Johnson became legendary.[52] It was the locally developed skills of the black Seminoles in South Texas and ranch-working slaves, coupled with the challenging terrain, that made black cowboys so important to the development of late nineteenth-century Texas cattle empires like the King Ranch and the XIT Ranch. XIT (short for the number of initial investors, "Ten in Texas") was formed when the 1875 Texas legislature authorized the sale of over three million acres of land in the north central part of the state to underwrite the building of a new capitol house. A syndicate of private investors purchased the land, issued bonds to build the capitol (still in use in Austin), and then built a herd of over 110,000 cattle by 1886.[53] Covering an area of land larger than some eastern states, the XIT Ranch was an empire in which black cowboys had a significant part, but just as importantly, it offered a tangible example of the massive land purchases and acts of empire building ongoing within the state during Griggs's early life. Suddenly the plan of Griggs's Imperium to "quietly purchase all Texas land contiguous to states and territories of the Union" through "money raised by the issuance of bonds by the Imperium" (167) seems achievable rather than far-fetched, both because of massive land transfers ongoing in the area and because of the region's blacks' dual roles as laborers and landowners. Griggs could imagine the Imperium purchasing large tracts of Texas land not only because significant portions of the state were for sale but because by the 1890s African Americans had a track record of property acquisition in the state.

Griggs's novel represents the dual position of the region's black inhabitants' as both owners and occupants, both patriots and traitors, but in the Imperium itself, he also represents the powerful political societies that the region's African American communities formed to further their interests. As Griggs's narrator observes, "The negro has been a marvelous success since the war, as a builder of secret societies" (132). Once in the state, black residents quickly formed and joined organizations that gave them social, political, and economic leverage. As early as 1868 a freedmen's settlement eighty miles outside Houston formed an association, armed itself, and drilled daily, after Klansmen began threatening the settlers. Local whites filed a complaint with the local freedmen's bureau about the freedmen's "military organization" and requested that the local bureau agent forbid the community from bearing arms. The bureau issued a formal order that any "armed band, organization or secret society" was banned, but brokered a successful compromise by securing the Klan's agreement to stop harassing the freedman community if it ceased engaging in "any warlike preparations."[54] The same year ten blacks were elected delegates to Texas's Constitutional Convention. During the 1870s freedmen and Republicans joined forces, with political success for both groups. Twelve African Americans served as legislators during the 1880s, and four were elected to the Senate in the nineteenth century. Many had originally been brought to Texas as slaves. Black Texans also formed fraternities, lodges, and societies, and the wealth of black organizations in Texas was nothing less than "staggering," according to Richardson.[55] Associations such as the Colored Knights of Pythias and Court of Calanthe; the Masons, Knights and Daughters of Tabor; and United Brothers of Friendship and Sisters of the Mysterious Ten held accumulated wealth of multiple millions of dollars.[56] In addition, these groups bought or constructed enormous temples, meeting structures, and buildings—the $250,000 temple that the Odd Fellows built was not atypical.[57] Indeed, such a building serves as a model for the Imperium headquarters, but as importantly it indicates the extent to which African Americans in the region achieved social and economic self-determinacy.

Griggs harnesses this complex, regionally specific African American legacy to imagine, within the pages of popular print, a powerful all-black governing body at nation's edge. His novel operates in dynamic relation to a geopolitical landscape where black as well as white and brown residents had long engaged in ambitious and vital experiments in self-determination that make "patriot" and "traitor" overlapping rather than mutually exclusive terms. Even as the Imperium upholds and extends U.S. national genealogies, this "other government" has the political ambition to reconstitute U.S. government and the economic, political, and military means by which to do so. It has already used its influence secretly to have teachers appointed in southern schools who will teach black students to aspire for equality. It has "army drills" after "lodge sessions" adjourn; branch legislatures in multiple states; and a congress and constitution. It has purchased "good land" that was offered "after the war for twenty-five cents an acre" (133) and boasts a treasury of $500 million. Its leaders are compared to "Julius Caesar, on entering Rome in triumph," "Napoleon," or "General Grant, on his triumphal tour around the globe" (39), at the head of "an immense army of young men and women" who have been trained to determine "the future of the race" (40) and who are "ready to march" (50) for their rights. A natural expression and logical endpoint of African Americans' complex regional footprint, the Imperium utilizes the deep contexts of the local African American community to conceptualize a place not inside or outside but at the interstices of the nation's borders from which blacks can most effectively reconfigure the political, economic, legal, and social contours of their built environment.

Conclusion

From Brann to Parsons to Remington, writers of short stories and editors of periodicals sought to determine as well as document—to write as well as to report—the chapter that the region contributes to "the great epic" of the nation, a chapter that is, as Remington observed, too easily forgotten. Like his contemporaries, Griggs published to make as well as record history—to contribute to debate regarding the place of blacks within the nation's borders. Griggs used local print culture to begin to answer a national question regarding black citizenship, but the race and print communities in which he worked collectively generated a new frame of reference for these national debates on race.

As we have seen, Griggs's text illustrates how civic affiliation is comprised of a grid of multidirectional links and connections that mutually enforce even as they finally undo each other. In so doing, the novel offers a strategic geopolitical location from which to rethink the binary logics that tended to govern African American rights talk during Griggs's literary career. As Griggs suggests, framing the question of African American rights as a choice between assimilation within the nation or emigration from it overlooks the complex logics and opportunities inhering in the nation's blurry edges. Adjacent to and embedded within the United States, the region featured in *Imperium* offers Griggs a new territorial coordinate from which to rethink U.S. racism during the age of empire.

When scholars approach *Imperium in Imperio* with the geographic coordinates of Cuba and a generic U.S. South in mind, they miss the complexity and geographic specificity of Griggs's conceptual engagement with territoriality, race, and nation-building. From the vantage point of the borderlands South in which Griggs's text circulates, we can begin to see that 1898 was not only the culmination of protracted racial conflict between U.S. North and South—the last battle of the Civil War, as scholars have importantly observed—but that it was also a tipping point in the long history of black militarism and civil rights struggles typifying the geographic area stretching from the north central Texas area of Waco all the way to the nation's blurry edge. The novel asks us to draw new lines between U.S. sites of conquest outside the nation's borders to specific regions within its boundaries that remain liminal. Doing so complicates two-dimensional narratives of displacement, domination, and national building—be they directed across or framed within firmly fixed national borders—that can all too easily stand in for the myriad unfinished processes, multidirectional movements, and ongoing relocations giving local communities and the texts produced within them their distinctive shape and texture.[58] Such analysis of the fluid movement of blacks in the border region over long historical time brings to the fore a rich, multidimensional cultural field defined less as a single great migration and more as an ongoing oscillation of people

Griggs's imagined answer to U.S. racism is not to be found within frames of reference located inside the nation's bisected regional North/South frame nor outside the nation's borders on its imperial playing field, but rather within the unwieldy racial mixture, movement, and mélange defining the region apart but integrally connected to U.S. struggles for dominance. Griggs's novel asks us to read from the vantage point of the regional logics in which it is embedded—to read within a dynamic language of text and territory, race and region produced by African Americans along the U.S./Mexico borderlands. In so doing it asks us to rethink what we think we know about past, place, and prose.

Notes

1. "Plan de San Diego," in *Fragments of the Mexican Revolution: Personal Accounts from the Border*, ed. Oscar J. Martinez (Albuquerque: University of New Mexico Press, 1983), 145–48.

2. Ibid.

3. Sutton E. Griggs, *Imperium in Imperio* (New York: Modern Library, 2003), 46. Subsequent references to this work are cited parenthetically in the text.

4. "Plan de San Diego," Article 15.

5. Waldo Frank, *America Hispana: A Portrait and a Prospect* (New York: Charles Scribner's Sons, 1931), 233.

6. James Robert Payne's "Afro-American Literature of the Spanish-American War," *MELUS* 10, no. 3 (Fall 1983): 19–32, provides an important account of African American writing on the Spanish American War. Payne's analysis of Griggs's novel as part of this tradition constitutes an important context for subsequent Griggs scholarship.

7. Amy Kaplan, *The Anarchy of Empire in the Making of U.S. Culture* (Cambridge Mass.: Harvard University Press, 2002); Susan Gillman, *Blood Talk: American Race Melodrama and the Culture of the Occult* (Chicago: University of Chicago Press, 2003); Finnie Coleman, *Sutton E. Griggs and the Struggle against White Supremacy* (Knoxville: University of Tennessee Press, 2007). For additional recent Griggs scholarship, see Kali Tal's "That Just Kills Me: Black Militant Near-Future Fiction," *Social Text* 20, no. 1 (Summer 2002): 65–91; Maria Karafilis's "Oratory Embodiment, and U.S. Citizenship in Sutton E. Griggs's *Imperium in Imperio*," *African American Review* 40 (Spring 2006): 125–43; and Stephen Knadler's "Sensationalizing Patriotism: Sutton Griggs and the Sentimental Nationalism of Citizen Tom," *American Literature* 79, no. 4 (December 2007): 673–701.

8. William Loren Katz, *The Black West: A Documentary and Pictorial History of the African American Role in the Westward Expansion of the United States* (New York: Simon & Schuster, 1987), 322.

9. Trish Loughran, *The Republic in Print: Print Culture in the Age of U.S. Nation Building, 1770–1870* (New York: Columbia University Press, 2007), xix.

10. Martin Robison Delany, *The Condition, Elevation, Emigration, and Destiny of the Colored People of the United States, Politically Considered* (Philadelphia: printed by the author, 1852), 209.

11. Philip Foner, ed., *The Life and Writings of Frederick Douglass* (New York: International Publishers, 1950), 2:252.

12. Wilson Jeremiah Moses, *The Golden Age of Black Nationalism, 1850–1925* (New York: Oxford University Press, 1988), 189.

13. Griggs's novel is not unusual in this regard but rather reflects contemporary tensions between races. As Neil Foley observes, in Texas, unlike any other part of the South, white meant not only not black but also not Mexican. Therefore Mexicans and blacks found themselves unexpected partners as well as opponents in a myriad of power struggles along the border. See Neil Foley, *The White Scourge: Mexicans, Blacks, and Poor Whites in Texas Cotton Culture* (Berkeley: University of California Press, 1997).

14. Susan Mizruchi, *The Rise of Multicultural America: Economy and Print Culture 1865–1915* (Chapel Hill: University of North Carolina Press, 2008), 6.

15. Hugh Gloster, "Sutton Griggs, Novelist of the New Negro," *Phylon* 4, no. 4 (1943): 335–45, quote on 345.

16. Sutton E. Griggs, *The Story of My Struggles* (Nashville: Orion, 1916), 14.

17. Rayford Logan, *The Betrayal of the Negro: From Rutherford B. Hayes to Woodrow Wilson* (New York: Collier, 1965), 357.

18. Sutton E. Griggs, *Wisdom's Call* (Nashville: Orion, 1911), frontispiece; Moses, *Golden Age of Black Nationalism*, 171.

19. Griggs, *Wisdom's Call*, frontispiece.

20. See Gloster's "Sutton Griggs, Novelist of the New Negro," as an example of this trend in Griggs scholarship. For critical commentary on this trend, see Andy Doolen's "'Be Cautious of the Word 'Rebel'": Race, Revolution, and Transnational History in Martin Delany's *Blake; or, The Huts of America*," *American Literature* 81, no. 1 (March 2009): 153–79.

21. As Wilson Moses notes, "Griggs is conspicuous by his absence from standard anthologies of black literature published since the late 1960s," and "few readers treat Griggs with any serious appreciation." See Moses, *Golden Age of Black Nationalism*, 203–4.

22. Albert Parsons, *Life of Albert Parsons: With a Brief History of the Labor Movement in America* (Chicago: Mrs. Lucy E. Parsons, 1880), 14. Seeing parallels between the abuse that the capitalists heaped on Chicago's working poor and the "actions of the late southern slave holders in Texas toward the newly enfranchised slave" (16), Parsons continued to defend the weak and was finally executed in 1887 for his role as one of the Haymarket Riot ringleaders.

23. William Cowper Brann, "Texas and Intolerance," in *Brann the Iconoclast: A Collection of the Writings of W. C. Brann*, ed. J. D. Shaw (Waco: Herz Brothers, 1911), 1:164–70, quotes on 165.

24. William Cowper Brann, "Blue and Gray: An Address to the Old Veterans," in Shaw, *Brann the Iconoclast*, 1:50–55, quotes on 55.

25. William Cowper Brann, "The Rape Fiend Remedy," in Shaw, *Brann the Iconoclast*, 9:37–39, quotes on 38.

26. William Cowper Brann, "Beans and Blood: The South Again in the Soup," in Shaw, *Brann the Iconoclast*, 1:325–32, quotes on 329.

27. Ibid., 331.

28. T. E. Davis, "The Street Duel to the Death in Waco Streets. There Are Two More Widows and Eight More Orphans," *Waco Weekly Tribune*, April 2, 1898.

29. William Cowper Brann, "The Monroe Doctrine," in Shaw, *Brann the Iconoclast*, 1:116–19, quote on 119.

30. William Cowper Brann, "Antonia Teixeira," in Shaw, *Brann the Iconoclast*, 1:187–92, quote on 191.

31. William Cowper Brann, "The Teixeira-Morris Case," in Shaw, *Brann the Iconoclast*, 1:320–25, quote on 322.

32. William Cowper Brann, "Baptism by Immersion," in Shaw, *Brann the Iconoclast*, 10:31–33, quote on 32.

33. *Telegraph and Texas Register*, October 26, 1838, n.p.

34. William Allen, *Texas in 1840: or, The Emigrants Guide to the New Republic* (New York: William Allen, 1840), 260.

35. John C. Calhoun to Abel P. Upshur, letter, August 27, 1843, Calhoun Papers, South Carolina Historical Society, Charleston, 17:381.

36. Edward Everett Hale, *How to Conquer Texas, before Texas Conquers Us* (Boston: Redding, 1845), 4.

37. Katz, *Black West*, 64.

38. These words are featured in a 1919 advertisement from the *Messenger* that is reprinted in Theodore Vincent, *Voices of a Black Nation: Political Journalism in the Harlem Renaissance* (New York: Africa World Press, 1991), 260.

39. This July 1895 correspondence from Ellis is cited in Alfred W. Reynolds's "The Alabama Negro Colony in Mexico, 1894–1896, Part II," *Alabama Review* 6, no. 2 (April 1953): 31–58.

40. Reynolds, "Alabama Negro Colony in Mexico," 260.

41. Griggs, *Story of My Struggles*, 7.

42. Ibid.

43. For commentary on African American soldiers' presence along the border, see James Leiker's *Racial Borders: Black Soldiers along the Rio Grande* (College Station: Texas A&M University Press, 2002).

44. At various times projections of the number of U.S. residents of Mexican heritage who would raise arms against the United States ranged from 10,000 in Brownsville to 8,000 in San Antonio and 20,000 in El Paso. As Gerald Horne details in *Black and Brown: African Americans and the Mexican Revolution, 1910–1920* (New York: New York University Press, 2005), African American soldiers occupied a complicated position in relation to resident Mexican Americans—on the one hand, sharing a history of disenfranchisement and racial prejudice, on the other hand, finding themselves in a position to leverage their own race's relative position in U.S. public opinion by protecting the nation's border.

45. Frederic Remington, "How the Worm Turned," *Collier's*, May 4, 1901, in *Voices of the Buffalo Soldier: Records, Reports, and Recollections of Military Life and Service in the West*, ed. Frank Schubert (Albuquerque: University of New Mexico Press, 2003), 115.

46. Ibid., 117.

47. For commentary on the Texas Kid and on the 1917 Houston riot, see Katz's *Black West*.

48. For commentary on these trends, see Thad Sitton and James Conrad's *Freedom Colonies: Independent Black Texans in the Time of Jim Crow* (Austin: University of Texas Press, 2005); and Clifton Richardson's "Texas—the Lone Star State," in *These 'Colored' United States: African American Essays from the 1920s*, ed. Tom Lutz and Susana Ashton (New Brunswick, N.J.: Rutgers University Press, 1996), 255–61.

49. For commentary on African American land ownership, see Sarah Massey, ed., *Black Cowboys of Texas* (College Station: Texas A&M University Press, 2000).

50. Sitton and Conrad, *Freedom Colonies*, 2.

51. Richardson, "Texas—the Lone Star State," 261.

52. See Katz's *Black West* for commentary on Johnson and others.

53. For accounts of the XIT ranch and the role of black cowboys in the region, see Philip Durham and Everett Jones's *The Negro Cowboys* (Lincoln: University of Nebraska Press, 1965).

54. Barry Crouch, *The Dance of Freedom: Texas African Americans during Reconstruction* (Austin: University of Texas Press, 2007), 231.

55. Richardson, "Texas—the Lone Star State," 255.

56. Ibid., 258.

57. Ibid.

58. For relevant commentary on migration, see Tiffany Ruby Patterson and Robin D. G. Kelley's "Unfinished Migrations: Reflections on the African Diaspora and the Making of the Modern World," *African Studies Review* 43, no. 1 (April 2000): 11–45; and Rodrigo Lazo's "Migrant Archives: New Routes in and out of the Nation," in *States of Emergency: The Object of American Studies* (Chapel Hill: University of North Carolina Press, 2009), 36–55.

JOHN GRUESSER

Empires at Home and Abroad in
Sutton E. Griggs's *Imperium in Imperio*

The older idea was that the whites would eventually displace the native
races and inherit their lands, but this idea has been rudely shaken in the
increase of American Negroes, the experience of the English in Africa,
India and the West Indies, and the development of South America. The
policy of expansion, then, simply means world problems of the Color
Line. The color question enters into European politics and floods our
continent from Alaska to Patagonia.
—W. E. B. Du Bois, "The Color Line Belts the World"

What to that redoubted harpooner, John Bull, is poor Ireland, but a
Fast-Fish? What to that apostolic lancer, Brother Jonathan, is Texas but a
Fast-Fish? And concerning all these, is not Possession the whole of
the law?
—Herman Melville, *Moby-Dick*

One of the most notable developments in twenty-first-century scholarship, the
movement away from U.S.-centered approaches to America, enables scholars
to cross disciplinary boundaries, make connections among texts heretofore associated with discrete national literatures or regional area studies, and delin-
eate the global forces operating in literary texts. Such a critical methodology is
especially appropriate for U.S. black writing, particularly those texts published
at the end of the nineteenth century and the beginning of the twentieth century, when the country vigorously pursued an imperialist agenda and acquired
an overseas empire.[1] In the late 1800s and early 1900s, white imperialists and
white anti-imperialists subscribed to the scientific racism and social Darwinism of the day.[2] To be sure, U.S. blacks were influenced by the era's ideas about

49

race, yet in their responses to expansion they differed profoundly from their white counterparts because they rejected racist assumptions and insisted on the salience of the country's founding documents, which whites considered null and void in connection with U.S. blacks, Filipinos, Puerto Ricans, and Hawaiians.[3] During these difficult and rapidly changing times, African American literary artists rarely adopted and maintained a fixed position on imperialism—their position depended on several factors, including the overseas location in question (e.g., Cuba or the Philippines), the stage of the author's career, and the text's relationship to specific generic conventions and literary traditions. No matter what their disposition toward imperialism, the fact of U.S. expansion allowed and in many cases compelled these authors to grapple with empire; moreover, they often used texts about expansion to address directly or obliquely the situation facing blacks at home during a period in which their citizenship rights and very existence were increasingly in jeopardy.

Between 1899 and 1908, Sutton E. Griggs published five long works of fiction, making him the most prolific late nineteenth- and early twentieth-century African American novelist. For a variety of reasons, these texts about black and white southerners have frustrated attempts by critics to arrive at definitive interpretations. In contrast to his more famous contemporaries Paul Laurence Dunbar and Charles Chesnutt, whose books, brought out by mainstream northern publishers, were marketed to white readers, Griggs "spoke primarily to the Negro race," using his own Nashville-based Orion Publishing Company to print all but the first of his novels.[4] Not only do individual texts by Griggs alternate between gloom and hope, but his fiction, taken as a whole, follows a similar pattern with each book following *Imperium in Imperio* (1899)—his best-known novel and the only one currently in print—serving as a response or counterpoint to the previous one, as is suggested by their titles: *Overshadowed* (1901), *Unfettered: A Novel* (1902), *The Hindered Hand; or, The Reign of the Repressionist* (1905), and *Pointing the Way* (1908).[5] Complicating matters, his first and fourth novels not only have open-ended conclusions but also give nearly equal time to coprotagonists with contrasting worldviews and political agendas. As Arlene Elder observes, the rival main characters in these books "have names beginning with the same letters because Griggs conceives them not so much as individuals but as alter egos, symbols of the opposing impulses within the new generation of blacks."[6] The idiosyncrasies, ambivalences, and ambiguities of Griggs's texts, coupled with the tendency of critics to read them in binary terms, have resulted in widely diverse and in some cases starkly discrepant responses to the author.[7] These include characterizations of Griggs as a militant (Gloster, Tucker, Lamon), radical black Baptist (Frazier), accommodationist (Bone), black nationalist (Gayle, Moses, Gillman), black chauvinist (Logan), marginal (Fullinwider), transitional (Elder), melodramatic sentimentalist (Rampersad), near-futurist (Tal), black utopian (Fabi, Winter, Kellman), and sensationalist (Knadler) novelist, who, in the eyes of some scholars, admired Booker T. Washington and supported his political program and, according to others, criticized and satirized the era's most influential black leader.[8]

In his novels, Griggs portrays U.S. blacks driven to desperation as a result of widespread disenfranchisement, unchecked white-on-black violence, and discriminatory justice.[9] In response to these conditions, his African American characters seriously contemplate or actively pursue various options, most notably amalgamation, emigration, and armed resistance. Since the early 1800s, U.S. black leaders had debated the pros and cons of both assimilation into the white race and transportation to Africa or other locations beyond the borders of the United States. However, the possibility of organized violence was not, for obvious reasons, openly discussed during the antebellum period, nor was it explicitly raised in the decades immediately following emancipation. Thus, the proposals made and the actions taken in Griggs's novels to respond to the denial of black citizenship with armed revolt represent a notable departure from the writings of his African American precursors and contemporaries, and critics have, understandably, regarded them as one of the most striking features of his fiction. Yet because of the reluctance until quite recently to address the relationship between U.S. expansion and literary texts, particularly those by African Americans, scholars have for the most part failed to situate Griggs's texts within the larger political context of the era, typically reading them exclusively in the light of U.S. race relations.

Griggs raises the option of armed violence in fiction that was composed during and immediately following—and that explicitly grapples with—the imperialistic wars at the turn of the twentieth century, the first conflicts against foreign peoples since the Mexican-American War and the first major wars of any kind since the Civil War. In *Imperium*, *Unfettered*, and *The Hindered Hand*, Griggs addresses the Cuban revolution, African American military service in the conflict against Spain, the frustrations of black war veterans, the controversy over the annexation and subjugation of the Philippines, and the connections between U.S. imperial policy overseas and domestic race relations. Although it does not specifically address the Spanish-Cuban-American or the

Philippine-American War as three of the other novels do, *Overshadowed* links the situation of U.S. blacks to people of color throughout the world.[10] Whereas *Imperium* explicitly thematizes the prelude to the war with Spain, *Unfettered* and *The Hindered Hand* address different aspects of its aftermath. The former directly links national electoral politics with expansion and compares the status of newly annexed Filipinos to that of U.S. blacks during and after slavery, raising legitimate concerns about the consequences of imperialism, both abroad and at home. In doing so, it repeats assertions Griggs made in the November 3, 1900, issue of the *Indianapolis World*. In this article, he urged readers to support the Democrats because of the Republican administration's policy "responsible for enslaving 'the colored peoples of the Philippines and for worsening the plight of black citizens in the United States,'" adding, "If the Negro aids the Republican party in the political murder of the Filipino, . . . we will not have long to wait before there is a political hanging in America with the Negro as the victim."[11] Ultimately, however, and for reasons that are not adequately explained, Griggs chooses not to condemn expansion in the last third of *Unfettered*, in part because of its potential to provide welcome opportunities for African Americans and people in overseas locations that have recently come under U.S. control.[12] Written in response to a request from the 1903 National Negro Baptist Convention in Philadelphia for him to respond to Thomas Dixon's recently published, race-baiting novel *The Leopard's Spots: A Romance of the White Man's Burden—1865–1900*, *The Hindered Hand* depicts the often harrowing experiences of a trio of African American veterans of the Cuban conflict upon their return to the South.[13] Inspired by the Cuban revolution, one of the book's coprotagonists organizes a rebel force of five hundred armed men designed to compel the United States to address the oppression of its black population. Rejecting the options of organized violence and biological warfare against whites, the novel's other main character writes and widely disseminates a pamphlet calling for key changes in the United States' racial policies. Believing that the nation has betrayed the black men who fought for it, a third character, who likewise saw action at the Battle of San Juan Hill, dismisses the U.S. flag as a "dirty rag"; in doing so, he echoes African Methodist Episcopal bishop Henry McNeal Turner's notoriously incendiary statement made in the light of the violence directed at African American troops who were slated to serve in Cuba. In 1899, Turner, whom Abraham Lincoln appointed as the first black army chaplain in 1863, decried African American enlistment in the Philippine-American War and, citing the violence directed at black soldiers who served in the Caribbean, declared of the U.S. flag: "It is a symbol of liberty, of manhood, sovereignty and of national independence to the white man, we grant, . . . but to the colored man that has any sense, any honor . . . , it is a miserable dirty rag."[14]

This essay examines Griggs's perspicacious linking of empires abroad and at home in *Imperium in Imperio*, a novel about contrasting main characters, Bernard Belgrave and Belton Piedmont, who play key roles in a widespread, well-funded, and clandestine black organization called the Imperium that in the closing chapters initially advocates a mass African American migration to and the political takeover of Texas and later approves a plan to make war on the United States in conjunction with foreign powers to create a Texas-based black empire.[15] Although unquestionably a work of speculative fiction, Griggs's first novel looks less fantastic and bizarre than several critics have claimed when read in the context of, first, actual and proposed nineteenth-century black immigration to and emigration from Texas; second, the sometimes outlandish proposals at the turn of the twentieth century to ship large numbers of African Americans from the South to such places as the southwestern United States, northern Mexico, Hawaii, Cuba, and the Philippines put forward by southern politicians, northern publications, and some leading African American figures; and, third, U.S. imperialism—especially the Spanish-Cuban-American War—and its domestic and international ramifications.

Given Texas's liminal location and transnational history, Griggs's choice of the Lone Star State as the site for the Imperium has resonances that reach far beyond the "Negro Question" within the United States that he addresses in his fiction and nonfiction and that has often been the focus of critical readings of his novels. Caroline Levander remarks in a recent essay on *Imperium*, "Sutton Griggs and the Borderlands of Empire," included in this volume, that to think only in terms of a North/South divide within the United States or to regard the Rio Grande as a white/brown dividing line is to "oversimplify the racial contours of the nation and overemphasize the ease of its imperial reach. Both endpoint and access point, the territory comprising what is now the state of Texas functioned as a fluid, multidirectional, multiracial grid—a dynamic field through which Mexican, Anglo-, and African American groups crossed, recrossed, and blended with each other." She adds that to frame "the question of African American rights as a choice between assimilation within the nation or emigration from it overlooks the complex logics and opportunities inhering in the nation's blurry edges. Adjacent to and embedded within the United States, the region featured in *Imperium* offers Griggs a new territorial coordinate from which to rethink U.S. racism during the age of empire." Although Griggs received his doctor of divinity in Virginia and spent most of his career as a Baptist minister in Tennessee, he was born and raised in and had an intimate knowledge of Texas, where his father, the Reverend Allen Griggs, who had been a slave in Georgia, founded numerous churches, a religious academy, Dallas's first black high school, and four black colleges, including Bishop College, from which the younger Griggs graduated in 1890.[16] The widely read Sutton Griggs had a firm grasp of the history of his native state, which remained in his thoughts despite the years he spent away from it, as indicated by his act of "affectionately" dedicating his 1911 nonfiction tract *Wisdom's Call* to "the imperial state of Texas."[17]

The influx of African Americans into as well as their departure from Texas during the 1800s constitutes less "a single great migration," as Levander observes in her essay, than "an ongoing oscillation of people." In accordance with an agreement worked out with Spain in 1820, Stephen Austin eventually led three hundred white families and their slaves into what is now Texas. Mexico, which won its independence from Spain in 1821, rejected repeated offers by the United States to buy Texas, outlawed slavery in 1829 (which the so-called Old Three Hundred circumvented by nominally converting their slaves into indentured servants), and banned the immigration of U.S. citizens into Texas in 1830.[18] Five years later, Texans revolted against Mexico, and within six months the Republic of Texas was born. Although some Texans supported continued independence, Sam Houston lobbied for annexation by the United States, finding support among a coalition of northern expansionists and proslavery southerners. As Neil Foley explains, "Texas, it was supposed, would become a safety valve for attracting both slaves and freed blacks to the doorstep of Latin America, where they could cross the border and become mingled with Mexicans. Annexation, then, would facilitate the relocation of blacks from the South to the 'dumping ground' of the far-western frontier and hasten . . . the 'natural emigration' of blacks to Mexico and the equator," thereby solving the supposed problems posed by free African Americans.[19] Early in 1845, Congress passed and President John Tyler signed a bill, effective by the end of that year, authorizing the annexation of Texas, and in the interim, Texans voted in favor of a state constitution legalizing slavery.

In a January 2, 1846, speech delivered in Belfast, Ireland, titled "Texas, Slavery, and American Prosperity," Frederick Douglass, who like other antislavery advocates had vehemently opposed the annexation of Texas, expressed his disgust and disappointment over these developments: "Two years ago, I had hoped that there was morality enough, Christian-mindedness enough, love of liberty enough, burning in the bosoms of the American people to lead them to reject for ever the unholy alliance in which they have bound themselves to Texas." Seeing the prospect of the Civil War on the horizon, Douglass nevertheless adamantly asserted that he did not wish to behold the devastation this would entail visited on the United States: "I do not know but the spirit of rapine and plunder, so rampant in America will hurry her on to her own destruction. I hope it will not, for although America has done all a nation could do to crush me . . . yet, I trust in God, no ill may befall her. I hope she will yet see that it will be her duty to emancipate the slaves."[20] His efforts and those of other abolitionists in the North were not successful in preventing what he termed a "most deep and skillfully devised conspiracy—for the purpose of upholding and sustaining one of the darkest and foulest crimes ever committed by man." And indeed Douglass's worst fears did come to pass. The cotton industry brought so many immigrants and slaves to Texas that by 1860 there were over 182,566 bondmen and women, roughly one-third of the entire population, an exponential rise from the total of 5,000 slaves in 1836.[21]

Early in 1861, Texas seceded from the Union and joined the Confederacy, and during the Civil War it supplied a significant number of soldiers to the rebel cause. On Juneteenth, June 19, 1865, federal troops landed at Galveston to take control of the state and liberate the slaves. Although there were notable exceptions, as Levander notes, for the overwhelming majority of black Texans, the postwar era brought economic hardship and political disenfranchisement rather than opportunity and prosperity. Indications of their desperation can be seen in various emigration movements and schemes. Over twelve thousand blacks left Texas for Kansas in 1879 in response to reports that free land could be found there, others migrated to Oklahoma when this option became available, and beginning in the late 1870s, there was considerable interest in emigration to Liberia; moreover, in 1880 a Boston philanthropist secured the endorsement of an African American convention in Dallas for a black colony in northwest Texas, which never materialized.[22] Summing up his discussion of late nineteenth-century African American emigration, Alwyn Barr states, "Though the exodus never included more than a small percentage of black Texans at any time, only the costs of emigration or total despair held back thousands of others."[23] Griggs's use of Texas as the location of the Imperium's headquarters and the focal point of the plan for mass African American immigration should thus be seen, at least in part, in connection with the many actual and proposed movements of blacks to and from Texas from the 1820s through the 1890s.

Besides paying homage to U.S. black migration into and out of his home state, Griggs implicitly addresses proposals at the turn of the twentieth century to ship large numbers of African Americans abroad, which the federal government did not take steps to implement but was nevertheless forced to study and contemplate. Southern Democrats, editorial writers for mainstream publications, Republican legislators and policy makers, and U.S. black leaders proposed and debated schemes for the mass emigration of African Americans. Such suggestions were, of course, nothing new; back-to-Africa initiatives dated from the early part of the nineteenth century. What was new, however, was the nation's acquisition of an overseas empire—the annexation of Hawaii (as well as Guam, American Samoa, and Puerto Rico), the occupation of Cuba, and the takeover and bloody pacification of the Philippines. These new territories made it possible for influential Alabama U.S. senator John T. Morgan and others to propose transporting blacks from the South not to Africa but to the newly acquired lands in the Pacific and the Caribbean, where they would be removed from the continental United States but still subject to the nation's control.[24] Recalling earlier Confederate schemes, late 1890s and early 1900s expansionist ambitions even included plans to take over sovereign nations within the Western Hemisphere, reflected in *Harper's Weekly*'s proposal that the United States purchase sparsely populated northern Mexican states as the site for the resettlement of southern blacks.[25] Furthermore, prominent African American leaders, including Bishop Turner, educator William Saunders Scarborough, and newspaperman T. Thomas Fortune, as well as lesser-known figures, such as Bishop Lucius H. Holsey of the Colored Methodist Episcopal Church and the Baltimore Baptist minister Harvey Johnson, advocated the relocation of U.S. blacks. Holsey urged the federal government to establish a black state in the Indian Territory of New Mexico.[26] Meanwhile, Johnson proposed a scheme whereby the U.S. government would buy up the entire state of Texas by means of eminent domain and then sell parcels of land to African Americans so that they could establish a separate black state within the union.[27] In *Imperium* Griggs responds to the era's many emigration schemes, some of which were at least as far-fetched as his own Texas-takeover scenario. His fictional vision of a black-run Texas serves in part to highlight the impracticality if not the downright absurdity of actual proposals, endorsed by whites as well as blacks, to remove as many as five million blacks from the continental United States.

In addition to its implicit and explicit allusions to and commentary on nineteenth-century black migrations to and from Texas and turn-of-the-twentieth-century proposals to relocate African Americans abroad, references to imperialism generally and the run-up to the war against Spain specifically abound in *Imperium*. The narrative early on refers with apparent approbation to African American aspirations for "freedom, equality, and empire."[28] However, in the light of post-Reconstruction-era conditions, U.S. blacks constitute not only a nation within a nation but also an "empire," in the sense of a colonized people, within the larger American empire, as Belgrave explicitly states in a speech to the Imperium's legislative body: "They have apparently chosen our race as an empire, and each Anglo-Saxon regards himself as a petty king, and some gang or community of negroes as his subjects" (147). Griggs, moreover, titles chapter 17, in which the Imperium debates the possibility of war against the United States, "Crossing the Rubicon," a reference to Julius Caesar's irrevocable decision in 49 BCE to violate the law on *imperium* and take the battle to Rome, the seat of empire, itself.

The event that brings the Imperium to its moment of crisis in the final chapters of the novel is a white mob's murder of U.S. postmaster Felix Cook (based on the February 1898 lynching of Frazier Baker in Lake City, South Carolina), which happens in close proximity to the sinking of the *Maine* in Havana Harbor.[29] In a rousing speech, Belgrave, the privileged, light-skinned, Ivy League–educated, newly elected president of the Imperium, reviews the history of white atrocities against blacks in the United States and calls upon the organization's legislators to take some decisive course of action. Quickly rejecting amalgamation into the white race and immigration to Central Africa, the Imperium seems to have only one option: an official declaration of war on the United States roughly coinciding with the U.S. Congress's proclamation of war on Spain. At this key moment, however, the novel's other main character, a dark-skinned man of humble origins and the speaker of the Imperium's legislature, rises to speak. Espousing views on patriotism closely resembling those that Griggs expresses and directly connects to *Imperium* at the beginning of his autobiographical sketch, *The Story of My Struggles* (1914), Piedmont makes an impassioned plea for the organization to continue to try to work within the Union. He offers a spirited defense of American ideals, enumerates the benefits that U.S. blacks have gained from their association with white southerners, and proposes that the Imperium reveal its existence to the rest of the nation and give the United States four years to restore to African Americans their constitutional rights.[30] If the Imperium's demands are not met by the end of this period, then U.S. blacks shall all, says Piedmont, "abandon our several homes in the various other states and emigrate in a body to the State of Texas, broad in domain, rich in soil and salubrious in climate. Having an unquestioned majority of votes we shall secure possession of the State government" (163). Once lawfully in charge of the state, African Americans will defend to the death their newly acquired rights and, as Piedmont puts it, "sojourn in the State of Texas, working out our destiny as a separate and distinct race in the United States of America" (163–64). This bold plan thus attempts to straddle both loyalty to the race and fealty to the nation.

Piedmont's resolution passes; however, it gives Belgrave an idea for a more radical scheme, which, after lining up support from key members of the organization, he proposes to the Imperium the next day. It calls for the takeover of Texas by the Imperium, the mutiny of strategically placed black sailors in the U.S. Navy, and the declaration and prosecution of war—in conjunction with foreign powers—on the United States. These actions will secure the Imperium's sovereignty in Texas and result in the ceding of newly captured Louisiana to the Imperium's foreign allies, thereby providing a buffer state for the Imperium. Belgrave's ultimate goal, in contrast to that of Piedmont, who wants to reform the United States but not break from it, is to lead a Texas-based African American empire. Here I must take issue with Levander's contention in her essay in this volume that Piedmont's and Belgrave's proposals constitute "two plans to secure the entire territory of Texas for the black empire." Unlike Belgrave, Piedmont consistently makes clear that he wants the Imperium to remain a part of the United States—with blacks enjoying citizenship rights either throughout the country or at a minimum in Texas, where they will have vast numerical superiority and control the organs of political power. Belgrave's scheme links the Imperium to the Confederacy, which not only seceded from the Union and appealed to European powers to assist it in remaining separated but also envisioned the establishment of an empire based on slavery comprised of territories acquired beyond the borders of the United States.[31] It also looks ahead to Marcus Garvey's dream of founding a black empire expounded in such writings as "African Fundamentalism."[32] As Addison Gayle observes, "Marcus Garvey probably never read Sutton Griggs' *Imperium in Imperio*, but had he done so, he might have been accused of plagiarism. For the Imperium that Garvey desired to establish on African soil was established here in America in this novel by a virtually unknown nineteenth-century Black writer."[33]

Housed under the guise of Thomas Jefferson College in Waco, Texas, the organization's ruling body is modeled on that of the United States; however, it requires that all decisions be unanimous, with dissent being ruthlessly punished. Thus, when everyone else approves of the radical plan for war and Piedmont resigns from the Imperium in protest, his decision, according to the organization's laws, carries with it a sentence of death. In his important, multilayered, and provocative reading of *Imperium*, first published in 2007 and reprinted in revised form in *Remapping Citizenship and the Nation in African-American Literature* (2010), Stephen Knadler sees Griggs using Piedmont to satirize Washington's accommodationist policies. He asserts that in the wake of the war against Spain "many African American leaders such as Booker T. Washington drew on the long history of romantic racist imagery, from Harriet Beecher Stowe's *Uncle Tom's Cabin* to the more recent plantation fiction of Thomas Nelson Page, to portray African Americans as patriotic 'Citizens Toms.'" During the late 1890s and early 1900s, when flag-waving rituals reached a peak in part as a response to the influx of immigrants, the figure of the naturally loyal and dutifully obedient 'Citizen Tom' made it possible for U.S. blacks to participate in the "sentimental patriotism" of the era, which Knadler contends Griggs seeks to unsettle "traumatically" through a series of sensational scenes involving Piedmont.[34] Similar to Pauline Hopkins in *Contending Forces* (1900), Griggs does indeed create opposing characters who resemble Washington and W. E. B. Du Bois, in Piedmont and Belgrave—the former a man who rises from humble Southern origins to become a college president, regards slavery as a kind of fortunate fall for U.S. blacks, and in the end places his country ahead of his race; the latter a Harvard graduate who chooses race over country, at times advocates vengeance against U.S. whites, and dreams of a black empire.[35] Yet, despite the novel's description of Piedmont in the final chapter as "the last of that peculiar type of Negro heroes that could so fondly kiss the smiting hand" (175), Knadler too easily conflates Piedmont and Washington, overlooking the resistance that Griggs's character frequently offers to white oppression and minimizing both the duration and the depth of his commitment to the Imperium. At all-black Stowe University, Piedmont forms a "secret organization" with the password "Equality or Death" (44) that protests the segregation of the school's lone black professor from other faculty members during meals. When the astonished white teachers wave "the white flag," the student body celebrates its victory by holding up "a black flag" and, significantly, singing "John Brown's Body" (46). This act of resistance orchestrated by Piedmont not only indicates that the "cringing, fawning, sniffling, cowardly Negro which slavery left, had disappeared, and a new Negro, self-respecting, fearless, and determined in the assertion of his rights was at hand" (46) but also inspires similar "combinations" involving "one hundred thousand students" of African descent throughout the country (47). Piedmont's actions against white oppression, moreover, do not cease upon graduation, for he founds a popular newspaper that boldly exposes "frauds at the polls" before it is shut down (87). The protest at Stowe also portends the pivotal role that he will play in the Imperium: "Remember that this was Belton's first taste of rebellion against the whites for the securing of rights denied simply because of color. In after life he is the moving, controlling, guiding spirit in one on a grand scale" (47). It must also be noted that Piedmont, "a member for years" (133), invites Belgrave, who knows nothing about the Imperium, to join the organization and oversees the harrowing loyalty test that his friend must pass to gain admittance.

At the end of the novel, Belgrave's plan to make war on white America does not come to fruition because Berl Trout, the main narrator of Griggs's novel, the Imperium's secretary of state, and a member of the firing squad that kills Piedmont, betrays the Imperium to white authorities. Trout explains that he does so because, with the execution of Piedmont, "the spirit of conservatism in the Negro race died," and without anyone capable of tempering the president's militancy, Belgrave "was a man to be feared" (175). Trout's action must therefore be seen in connection with the dynamic relationship between Belgrave and Piedmont that structures the entire book (and links it in particular to *The Hindered Hand*, in which a mulatto likewise struggles with a more conservative man of darker hue for the hearts and minds of the race). Although Trout begins the book with the words "I am a traitor" (5), he declares he is also "a patriot" (6) and concludes the narrative with the assertion that he did what he did "in the name of humanity" (176). As Knadler notes, Griggs in the final chapter complicates the conflict between allegiance to race and allegiance to nation by introducing another alternative in the form of what might be called global or universal patriotism.[36] Trout also issues the plea that "all mankind will join hands and help [his] poor downtrodden people to secure those rights for which they organized the Imperium," adding, "I urge this because love of liberty is such an inventive genius, that if you destroy one device it at once constructs another more powerful" (177).

Some controversy surrounds when and how Trout betrays the Imperium. Levander suggests in her essay in this volume that the novel itself—which in the prefatory "To the Public," someone signing himself "Sutton E. Griggs" claims, after defending Trout's "strict veracity," to be merely "editing," and "giving . . . to the public" (3–4)—constitutes Trout's betrayal: "Trout has been identified as a traitor because he gives the story that we are about to read to Sutton E. Griggs to publish, and thereby destroys the secrecy upon which the Imperium depends on success." In other words, Levander contends that the United States first learns about the Imperium—and then presumably takes action against it—through the narrative. Trout states, "I decided to prove traitor and reveal the existence of the Imperium that it might be broken up or watched. My deed may appear that of a vile wretch, but it is done in the name of humanity" (176). The use of the present tense in the second sentence may seem to suggest that the betrayal has not yet occurred—and that the text is itself the act of betrayal. However, the next sentence—"Long ere you shall have come to this line, I shall have met the fate of a traitor" (176–77)—indicates that the betrayal has already taken place and Trout has already paid the price for it. Moreover, simply revealing the existence of the Imperium, which is exactly what Piedmont had proposed doing—and the Imperium's legislators initially unanimously had agreed to do—would not in and of itself amount to an all-out betrayal of the organization. It seems much more likely that Trout has (already) specifically exposed Belgrave's plan to make war on the United States.

   Imperium ends on neither a positive nor a negative note. On the one hand, Trout's betrayal means that a bloody race war has been averted, which Griggs clearly regards as a good thing. On the other hand, the future for U.S. blacks seems particularly bleak. Thus, I cannot concur with M. Giulia Fabi's upbeat reading of the novel's conclusion in *Passing and the African American Novel*: "Th[e] spirit of self-determination and self-reliance, which gave birth to the Imperium in the first place, survives and is even kindled by Belton's death and the dismantlement of the organization. The possibility and explicit threat of constructing an even 'more powerful' organization are reiterated at the very end of the novel and sustain the utopian vision of unstoppable black empowerment and liberation Griggs projects."[37] Trout, however, actually uses the word "device," which is much hazier than Fabi's "organization"; moreover, with the venerable, well-funded, and powerful Imperium dismembered and their most dynamic leaders presumably jailed or executed, disenfranchised U.S. blacks find themselves entirely at the mercy of an increasingly violent and intolerant white population and with little or no hope of protection from the nation's discriminatory justice system.

In a sense, Griggs's novel offers his black readers a chance to indulge momentarily their revenge fantasies and dreams of power—and even empire—but also shows them that they must be rejected. Piedmont's dissension from and especially Trout's betrayal of the Imperium can thus be seen as actions designed to deflect African Americans—and by extension the country as a whole—from such fantasies so that they will address soberly and constructively the situation here (and for Griggs this always meant the South) and now. His message to white southerners in *Imperium* functions in a somewhat different way—he vividly imagines the potentially nightmarish consequences of the continued oppression of blacks but then defuses the incendiary scenario he so powerfully envisions in order to persuade white southerners to abandon their own fantasies—either of continuing to rule over African Americans as an empire or of ridding the land of blacks through mass emigration—so that they, too, will realistically face the here and now. The plan to take control of Texas legally proposed by one of the novel's protagonists and then radicalized by the other can be read as a warning—work with the Piedmonts or create and later face the Belgraves.

In three novels published between 1899 and 1905, *Imperium in Imperio*, *Unfettered*, and *The Hindered Hand*, Sutton Griggs profoundly engages with the Spanish-Cuban-American and Philippine-American Wars and their domestic implications. Seen within the context of nineteenth-century black migration to and away from Texas and the turn of the twentieth century's chaotic and deadly serious combination of black disenfranchisement, mob violence, rigidly enforced segregation, mass African American emigration schemes, and overseas expansion, Griggs's vision of a black-run Texas in his first novel becomes far less fantastic than it may initially appear. Beyond engaging with the empire abroad through the parallels it draws to the war with Spain, *Imperium* expands the notion of an empire at home by comparing U.S. blacks to colonized people and by imagining a black empire existing within and upon the borders of the nation.

Notes

This essay would not have been written if I had not been a participant in Hemispheric American Literature, a 2007 National Endowment for the Humanities Summer Seminar held at Columbia University, codirected by Rachel Adams and Caroline Levander. For an overview of Hemispheric Studies, see Ralph Bauer, "Hemispheric Studies," *PMLA*

124, no. 1 (January 2009): 234–50. For an elaboration of and justification for an inter-American or hemispheric approach to American literature, see Earl E. Fitz, "In Quest of 'Nuestras Américas' or Inter-American Studies and the Dislocation of the Traditional 'American' Paradigm or (with Apologies to José Martí and Stanley Kubrick) How I Learned to Stop Worrying and Love Academic Change," *AmeriQuests* 14, no. 2 (2004). For a collection of essays that vividly illustrates such an approach, see Caroline F. Levander and Robert S. Levine, eds., *Hemispheric American Studies* (New Brunswick, N.J.: Rutgers University Press, 2008).

Epigraphs are from W. E. B. Du Bois, "The Color Line Belts the World," in *W. E. B. Du Bois on Asia: Crossing the World Color Line*, ed. Bill V. Mullen and Cathryn Wilson (Jackson: University Press of Mississippi, 2005), 33–34; Herman Melville, *Moby-Dick*, 2nd ed., ed. Hershel Parker and Harrison Hayford (New York: Norton, 2002), 310.

1. For examples of transnational readings of African American literary texts, see Ifeoma C. K. Nwankwo, "The Promises of U.S. African American Hemispherism: Latin America in Martin Delany's *Blake* and Gayl Jones's *Mosquito*," in Levander and Levine, *Hemispheric American Literature*, 187–205; Stephen Knadler, *Remapping Citizenship and the Nation in African-American Literature* (New York: Routledge, 2010); Gretchen Murphy, *Shadowing the White Man's Burden: U.S. Imperialism and the Problem of the Color Line* (New York: New York University Press, 2010).

2. See Christopher Lasch, "The Anti-Imperialists, the Philippines, and the Inequality of Man," *Journal of Southern History* 24, no. 3 (August 1958): 319–31. On social Darwinism and racist science, see Thomas F. Gossett, *Race: The History of an Idea in America* (Dallas: Southern Methodist University Press, 1975).

3. See Kwame Anthony Appiah, *In My Father's House: Africa in the Philosophy of Culture* (New York: Oxford University Press, 1992), 28–46.

4. W. E. B. Du Bois, "Negro Art and Literature," in *The Oxford W. E. B. Du Bois Reader*, ed. Eric J. Sundquist (New York: Oxford University Press, 1996), 318.

5. Unrelentingly pessimistic, *Overshadowed* (Nashville: Orion, 1901) tells the story of the Job-like trials and sad demise of the tragic mulatta Erma Wysong. In stark contrast, *Unfettered: A Novel* (Nashville: Orion, 1902) claims that when the protagonist's "Plan" for solving the race problem is implemented, it enjoys remarkable success, vastly improving conditions for not only U.S. blacks but also Africans and other peoples of the diaspora. Gloom, however, pervades the next book, *The Hindered Hand; or, The Reign of the Repressionist* (Nashville: Orion, 1905), which graphically depicts the torture, burning, and mutilation of an innocent black couple, includes a woman literally driven insane by the South's pursuit of racial purity, and concludes with one of the protagonists leaving for Liberia, where he will strive to provide a refuge for U.S. blacks denied their citizenship rights in the land of their birth, should this prove necessary. If the pessimism of the fourth novel recalls that of the second, the optimism of Griggs's final fiction resembles that of the third. Like *Unfettered*, *Pointing the Way* (Nashville: Orion, 1908) offers a solution to the race problem, this one engineered by a coalition of talented blacks and enlightened whites that begins in one southern city and spreads throughout the nation.

6. Arlene Elder, *The "Hindered Hand": Cultural Implications of Early African American Fiction* (Westport, Conn.: Greenwood, 1978), 101.

7. Perhaps Elder has come as close as anyone has to summing up the writer's fiction: "Sutton Griggs's novels are literary collages, part propagandist blueprint for political action, part gothic romance of the maze and morass of miscegenation, and part symbolic description of the conditions threatening the internal and external life of the 'New Negro' of the turn of the century" (ibid., 69).

8. For the various characterizations of Griggs, see Hugh M. Gloster, preface to Sutton E. Griggs's *Imperio in Imperio* (New York: Arno, 1969), iii–viii; David M. Tucker, "Black Pride and Negro Business in the 1920s: George Washington Lee of Memphis," *Business History Review* 40, no. 4 (Winter 1969): 435–51; Lester C. Lamon, *Black Tennesseans 1900–1930* (Knoxville: University of Tennessee Press, 1977); Robert Bone, *The Negro Novel in America* (New Haven, Conn.: Yale University Press, 1965); Larry Frazier, "Sutton E. Griggs's *Imperium in Imperio* as Evidence of Black Baptist Radicalism," *Baptist History and Heritage* 35 (Spring 2000): 72–91; Rayford W. Logan, *The Betrayal of the Negro: From Rutherford B. Hayes to Woodrow Wilson* (New York: Da Capo, 1997); Addison Gayle, "The Harlem Renaissance: Towards a Black Aesthetic," in *The Addison Gayle Jr. Reader*, ed. Nathaniel Norment Jr. (Urbana: University of Illinois Press, 2009), 71–80; Wilson Jeremiah Moses, *The Golden Age of Black Nationalism, 1850–1925* (New York: Oxford University Press, 1988); Susan Gillman, *Blood Talk: American Race Melodrama and the Culture of the Occult* (Chicago: University of Chicago Press, 2003); S. P. Fullinwider, *The Mind and Mood of Black America* (Homewood, Ill.: Dorsey, 1969); Arnold Rampersad, "Griggs, Sutton E[bert]," in *Dictionary of American Negro Biography*, ed. Rayford W. Logan and Michael R. Winston (New York: Norton, 1979), 271; Kali Tal, "'That Just Kills Me': Black Militant Near-Future Fiction," *Social Text* 20, no. 2 (Summer 2002): 65–91; M. Giulia Fabi, *Passing and the Rise of the African American Novel* (Urbana: University of Illinois Press, 2001); Molly Crumpton Winter, *American Narratives: Multiethnic Writing in the Age of Realism* (Baton Rouge: Louisiana State University Press, 2007); Steven G. Kellman, "Imagining Texas as a Black Utopia," rev. of *Imperium in Imperio* by Sutton E. Griggs, *Texas Observer*, February 27, 2004; Knadler, *Remapping Citizenship*. Whereas Fullinwider, Gloster, Winter, and Knadler regard Griggs as an anti-Bookerite, Bone and Elder see him supporting Washington's policies.

9. Griggs also addresses the political, physical, and judicial assaults on U.S. blacks in *The One Great Question: A Study of Southern Conditions at Close Range* (Philadelphia: Orion, 1907), a fifty-eight-page nonfiction tract that characterizes the South generally—and Nashville in particular—as "repressionist" and includes passages from his fiction that he claims are based on events he witnessed personally or were widely documented.

10. At the conclusion of *Overshadowed*, Astral Herndon buries his wife, Erma Wysong, at sea rather than on U.S. soil, proclaiming himself "A CITIZEN OF THE OCEAN" instead of the country of his birth and asserting, "This title shall be entailed upon my progeny unto all generations, until such time as the shadows which now envelop the darker races in all lands shall have passed away, away and away" (217). The epilogue does hold out

the faint hope that Erma and Astral's son shall inspire "the Negro" to "emerge from his centuries of gloom" (219).

11. See Willard B. Gatewood, *Black Americans and the White Man's Burden, 1898–1903* (Urbana: University of Illinois Press, 1975), 249.

12. Gillman quite appropriately terms *Unfettered* "Griggs's most political novel" (*Blood Talk*, 105).

13. Woolford Damon, "Twenty-Third Annual Session of the National Negro Baptist Convention at Philadelphia," *Colored American Magazine*, November 1903, 778–93.

14. See Henry McNeal Turner, "The Negro and the Army," in *Respect Black: The Writings and Speeches of Henry McNeal Turner*, ed. Edwin S. Redkey (New York: Arno, 1971), 184–85.

15. With the exception of James Robert Payne's early essay, "Afro-American Literature of the Spanish-American War" (*MELUS* 10, no. 3 [August 1983]: 19–32), only recently have critics such as Gillman; Knadler in "Sensationalizing Patriotism: Sutton Griggs and the Sentimental Nationalism of Citizen Tom" (*American Literature* 79, no. 4 [December 2007]: 673–99), which is reprinted in *Remapping Citizenship*; and Caroline Levander in her essay on *Imperium in Imperio* in this volume, "Sutton Griggs and the Borderlands of Empire," begun to address connections between Griggs's novels and the Spanish-Cuban-American War, the Philippine-American War, and U.S. expansion. In their extended readings of all five of Griggs's novels, Moses, Winter, and Elder do not address U.S. imperialism. The first two make no mention of the Spanish-Cuban-American and Philippine-American Wars, and the third only briefly addresses the latter in connection with *Unfettered*. Moreover, one recent critic, John David Smith, dubiously asserts that Griggs "advocated both American imperialism abroad and the establishment of a black empire at home." See Smith's "'My Books Are Hard Reading for a Negro': Thomas Dixon and His African American Critics, 1905–1939," in *Thomas Dixon Jr. and the Birth of Modern America*, ed. Michele K. Gillespie and Randal L. Hall (Baton Rouge: Louisiana State University Press, 2006), 54.

16. Finnie D. Coleman, *Sutton E. Griggs and the Struggle against White Supremacy* (Knoxville: University of Tennessee Press, 2007), vii, 13, 18. Biographical information on Griggs remains somewhat sketchy. Some of the published chronologies of his life, including that in the 2003 Modern Library edition of *Imperium*, contain inaccuracies. Randolph Meade Walker's "The Metamorphosis of Sutton E. Griggs: A Southern Black Baptist Minister's Transformation in Theological and Sociological Thought during the Early Twentieth Century" (PhD diss., Memphis State University, 1990) offers reliable information but focuses on the latter half of the writer's career. Coleman's *Sutton E. Griggs*, the only published monograph devoted exclusively to the author, provides many tantalizing tidbits about Griggs's life, but its documentation is not as thorough as it might be.

17. Griggs, *One Great Question*, v.

18. See Alwyn Barr, *Black Texans: A History of African Americans in Texas, 1528–1995* (Norman: University of Oklahoma Press, 1996), 15; Frederick Douglass, "Texas, Slavery, and American Prosperity: An Address Delivered in Belfast, Ireland, on January 2, 1846,"

in *The Frederick Douglass Papers: Series One, Speeches, Debates, and Interviews* (New Haven, Conn.: Yale University Press, 1979), 1:118.

19. Neil Foley, *The White Scourge: Mexicans, Blacks, and Poor Whites in Texas Cotton Culture* (Berkeley: University of California Press, 1999), 20.

20. Douglass, "Texas, Slavery, and American Prosperity," 118.

21. Ibid. and Barr, *Black Texans*, 17.

22. See Jackson Lears, *Rebirth of a Nation: The Making of Modern America, 1877–1920* (New York: HarperCollins, 2009), 123–24; Barr, *Black Texans*, 96, 97.

23. Barr, *Black Texans*, 98.

24. For information on Morgan, see Thomas Adams Upchurch, "Senator John Tyler Morgan and the Genesis of Jim Crow Ideology, 1889–1891," *Alabama Review* (April 2004): 110–31.

25. In February 1903, the mainstream northern publication *Harper's Weekly*, responding to—and greatly misrepresenting—a speech by Secretary of War Elihu Root to the Union League in New York, floated a relocation plan of its own. The magazine recommended that the U.S. government pay Mexico $200 million for Chihuahua and two or three other sparsely populated northern states to be used for the voluntary resettlement—"Compulsory deportation is, of course, impracticable" (not unconstitutional or immoral)—of African Americans: "If the northern section of the Mexican Republic could be bought and erected into a Territory for the exclusive benefit of our colored people, and if it were distinctly understood that they not only would receive grants of land and cattle, but would enjoy educational facilities and a monopoly of political privileges, it is by no means incredible that a large body of negroes might be inclined to migrate thither." *Harper's Weekly* cites as a precedent the relocation of Native Americans to lands acquired as a result of the Louisiana Purchase, an act that, the magazine asserts, "neither the Indians nor we have had cause to regret." This relocation scheme dovetailed perfectly with the expansionist furor of the era, because it would have, with the subjugation of the western frontier completed, extended U.S. territory further south. See "Elihu Root on the Negro Problem," *Harper's Weekly*, February 12, 1903, 307. For Root's speech, see Elihu Root, "The Union League Club," in *Miscellaneous Addresses*, ed. Robert Bacon and James Brown Scott (Cambridge, Mass.: Harvard University Press, 1917), 123–27.

26. Clarence A. Bacote, "Negro Proscriptions, Protest, and Proposed Solutions in Georgia, 1880–1908," *Journal of Southern History* 25, no. 4 (November 1959): 493–94.

27. It is not clear whether Johnson's plan may have inspired Griggs's *Imperium* or vice versa. In *The History of Black Baptists*, Leroy Fitts claims that Johnson first proposed the "Texas Movement" in the early 1890s. Others, including A. Briscoe Koger, who wrote a 1957 biographical sketch of Johnson, date the "National Texas Purchase Movement" after 1900. Although Koger describes Johnson's proposal as "unworkable," he goes on to state, "As fantastic as it may appear, however, several organizations endorsed the plan and sought information and advice about its workings." See Leroy Fitts, *A History of Black Baptists* (Nashville: Boardman, 1985), 247; A. Briscoe Koger, *Dr. Harvey Johnson—Pioneer Civic Leader* (Baltimore: n.p., 1957), 16.

28. Sutton Griggs, *Imperium in Imperio* (New York: Modern Library, 2003), 44. Subsequent quotations from the novel are cited parenthetically in the text.

29. As George P. Marks documents, the African American press frequently connected the sinking of the *Maine* and the lynching of Baker, as does "Negroes Who Protect American Rights Abroad Must Be Protected at Home," a letter addressed to the U.S. Senate that was drafted following "a mass meeting of colored citizens" at Boston's Faneuil Hall on February 28, 1898, "to protest against the murder of the colored postmaster of Lake City, S.C." See George P. Marks, *The Black Press Views American Imperialism (1898–1900)* (New York: Arno, 1971), 199–200.

30. The histories that Belgrave and Piedmont offer in their extended speeches to the members of the Imperium are strictly U.S.-centered—and Anglo-Saxon U.S.–centered at that. The focus is always Anglo-Saxons and (or versus) U.S. blacks—there is no sense of diasporic or hemispheric connections, with the exception of a brief mention of a racial link between African Americans and Cuban freedom fighters. For example, the black presence in America starts in 1619 in Virginia—not fifty years before this in Florida or over a century earlier in Santo Domingo and Puerto Rico.

31. See Caroline Levander, "Confederate Cuba," *American Literature* 78, no. 4 (December 2006): 821–45.

32. See Marcus Garvey, "African Fundamentalism," in *Marcus Garvey: Life and Lessons*, ed. Robert A. Hill and Barbara Bair (Berkeley: University of California Press, 1987), 3–6. Additionally, the proposed but swiftly rejected option of mass emigration of U.S. blacks to Africa discussed by the Imperium targets the Congo Free State with the intent either to take the colony away from the Belgians by force or to purchase it from King Leopold, a plan that foreshadows Harry Dean's early twentieth-century dream of buying Portuguese East Africa for the establishment of an African American–led Ethiopian empire. See Dean's autobiographical work *The Pedro Gorino* (Boston: Houghton, 1929).

33. Gayle, "Harlem Renaissance," 75. Logan in *The Betrayal of the Negro* echoes and Wilson J. Moses ("Literary Garveyism: The Novels of Reverend Sutton E. Griggs," *Phylon* 40, no. 3 [Fall 1979]: 203–16) expands on Gayle's statement.

34. See Knadler, *Remapping Citizenship*, 144, 145.

35. See Pauline E. Hopkins, *Contending Forces: A Romance Illustrative of Negro Life North and South* (New York: Oxford University Press, 1988). M. Giulia Fabi notes that Griggs consistently opposes the irresponsible actions of the privileged, fair-skinned Bernard with "the self-discipline that Belton has painfully had to acquire in his life as a lower-class, visibly black person" (*Passing*, 54).

36. Knadler, *Remapping*, 160. In some respects, the dilemma facing the members of the Imperium over whether to be loyal to their country or to their race foreshadows the one that confronted African American soldiers fighting in the Philippines, a very small number of whom deserted the U.S. Army to fight with the Filipinos. See Gatewood, *Black Americans*, 287–90; Jennifer C. James, *A Freedom Bought with Blood: African American War Literature from the Civil War to World War II* (Chapel Hill: University of North Carolina Press, 2007), 125–66; Scot Ngozi-Brown, "African-American

Soldiers and Filipinos: Racial Imperialism, Jim Crow and Social Relations," *Journal of Negro History* 82, no. 1 (Winter 1997): 42–53; Michael C. Robinson and Frank N. Schubert, "David Fagen: An Afro-American Rebel in the Philippines, 1899–1901," *Pacific Historical Review* 44, no. 1 (February 1975): 68–83; Rene G. Ontal, "Fagen and Other Ghosts: African-Americans and the Philippine-American War," in *Vestiges of War: The Philippine-American War and the Aftermath of an Imperial Dream 1899–1999*, ed. Angel Velasco Shaw and Luis H. Francia (New York: New York University Press, 2002), 118–33.

37. Fabi, *Passing*, 55.

ROBERT S. LEVINE

Edward Everett Hale's and Sutton E. Griggs's Men without a Country

Edward Everett Hale's "The Man without a Country" (1863) was arguably the most widely read short story in the United States from 1863 to 1945; Sutton Griggs's first two novels, *Imperium in Imperio* (1899) and *Overshadowed* (1901), the second of which was self-published, were barely noticed at the time of their publication. This chapter examines intertextual connections between Hale's popular short story and Griggs's first two novels, focusing on the authors' narrative figurations of nation (or country) in relation to debates on race, patriotism, and imperialism. In his first two novels, Griggs, I suggest, honors, revises, and recuperates Hale's phenomenally popular short story, discerning in it something that was generally lost on readers of the nineteenth and early twentieth century: its expression of anger at the U.S. nation, and its thematic emphasis on connections between dispossession and patriotism.

Hale published "The Man without a Country" anonymously in the December 1863 *Atlantic*, and over the next several decades the story was republished numerous times under Hale's name (and always with a preface by Hale).[1] By the 1890s, it had become a standard school text, and it would have been as a school text or widely anthologized and reprinted story that Griggs would have encountered it. In the versions published between 1863 and 1898, Hale linked the story to goals that Griggs would have applauded: support for the Union cause in the Civil War, which included emancipation, and thus an implied support for Reconstruction. In the post–Civil War context, the antislavery and antiracist motifs of the story, including a scene in which Africans are liberated from a slaver, would have been especially resonant for Griggs. I will be focusing on Griggs's narrative strategies in *Imperium*, which bear some resemblance to the narrative strategies of "The Man without a Country"; his use of flag imagery and other patriotic icons in *Imperium* (which draws on the flag imagery and other patriotic icons in "The Man without a Country"); his conception of Texas as a site of black conspiracy in *Imperium* (which has clear overlaps with Hale's depiction of the Burr conspiracy in "The Man without a Country"); and, with respect to *Overshadowed*, his bold revision of Hale's iconic image of the patriot at sea.

Edward Everett Hale (1822–1909), a white antislavery Unitarian minister from Massachusetts, published his most famous story in the midst of the Civil War, nine years before Griggs's birth. "The Man without a Country" tells the story of one Philip Nolan, an army officer who in 1805 joins with Aaron Burr in his alleged western conspiracy (which is implicitly analogized to southern secession) and is captured and tried at a court-martial. When Nolan is asked by the court to attest to his loyalty, he shockingly declares: "D——n the United States! I wish I may never hear of the United States again!"[2] Granting his wish, the court subsequently sentences Nolan to a life at sea, and from the moment of his sentencing in 1807 to his death in 1863, Nolan resides on various U.S. naval vessels in which the sailors work strenuously to make sure he learns nothing about the United States. They censor newspaper articles, deny him access to ever-changing maps, and guard their conversations in his presence. As Nolan becomes infirm and aged, however, some information about the United States is leaked to him, though it is agreed that no one will tell him about the Civil War. Aware that he's dying, Nolan reveals to an officer named Danforth that over the years he has built a shipboard shrine to the United States, which Danforth describes in a letter to the story's narrator:

> The stars and stripes were triced up above and around a picture of [George] Washington, and he had painted a majestic eagle, with lightnings blazing from his beak and his foot just clasping the whole globe, which his wings overshadowed. The dear old boy [Nolan] saw my glance, and said, with a sad smile, "Here, you see, I have a country!" And then he pointed to the foot of his bed, where I had not seen before a great map of the United States, as he had drawn it from memory, and which he had there to look upon as he lay. Quaint, queer old names were on it, in large letters: "Indiana Territory," "Mississippi Territory," and "Louisiana Territory," as I suppose our fathers learned such things: but the old fellow had patched in Texas, too; he had carried his western boundary all the way to the Pacific, but on that shore he had defined nothing. (235–36)

With the help of his shipboard shrine, Nolan displays U.S. continental expansion up to the time of the Civil War, making the acquisition of Texas and westward movement to the Pacific key to his passion for U.S. nationalism. There is a sense that Nolan, in the spirit of his shrine's majestic eagle, has himself taken Texas and the western territories as an imaginative act of patriotism, thereby redeeming his youthful actions. After describing the shrine, Danforth reports on the death of Nolan, who leaves among his papers the epitaph that he wants engraved on a stone somewhere in New Orleans:

"In Memory of
PHILIP NOLAN,
Lieutenant in the Army of the United States.
He loved his country as no other man has loved her; but no
man deserved less at her hands." (241)

Ironically, then, "The Man without a Country" presents the life history of a man who could have entered the annals of American history as one of its most notorious traitors and instead ends up as an iconic figure of U.S. patriotism. It is the paradoxical nature of this patriot-traitor that may well have caught Griggs's attention. In a provocative critical reassessment of the story, Carrie Hyde shows how nineteenth-century readers gained instruction in patriotic thinking not only from Revolutionary heroes such as Patrick Henry and George Washington but also from "negative figures of citizenship" who are denied full political autonomy: "traitors, expatriates, and slaves," such as Major John André, Frederick Douglass, and even Burr himself. As she remarks about Hale's tapping into this tradition: "By prioritizing negative examples of citizenship, 'The Man without a Country' makes the pathos of dispossession a precondition for the patriotism of the protagonist and reader alike. As a result, Hale's seemingly simple allegory of loyalty interrogates the categories of political belonging—expanding readerly sympathy to the nation's outcasts as well."[3] Nolan is entrapped for over fifty years on a naval vessel, and his identification at a key point in the story with equally homeless African slaves speaks to the pathos of his own homelessness and sense of dispossession. Hale himself made the connection between Hale and black Americans in his 1886 preface to "The Man without a Country," stating that when he heard from a friend in Virginia about "the death of PHILIP NOLAN, a negro from Louisiana, who died in the cause of his country in service in a colored regiment, I felt that he had done something to atone for the imagined guilt of the imagined namesake of his unfortunate god-father."[4] A black Philip Nolan atoned for a white Philip Nolan who, Hale suggests, had nothing much to atone for.

Though "The Man without a Country" had a pervasive presence in late nineteenth-century American culture, we lack definitive evidence that Griggs read it (because we lack most of Griggs's letters and journals). And yet both Griggs's *Imperium* and his *Overshadowed* portray black men and women who want to love their country and receive less at its hands, and there is considerable textual evidence suggesting that Griggs learned from Hale's famous story about what Hyde terms "outcast patriotism."[5] At various moments in Griggs's first two novels, the leading characters state, in effect, "D——n the United States," and make decisive moves to act on their anger. In *Overshadowed*, the main character chooses exile; and in *Imperium*, the two main characters, instead of building a shrine to Texas, develop plans (like Burr and Nolan at the opening of "The Man without a Country") to take Texas in order to create a new country. As I discuss later, Griggs's most direct "quotation" from "The Man without a Country" can be found at the end of *Overshadowed*, but the Texas plot in *Imperium* resonates with the account of Texas at the beginning and the end of "The Man without a Country." In Hale's story, the plot to take Texas is foiled by the U.S. government; in *Imperium*, it is foiled by the narrator of the novel, Berl Trout. But Berl does more than foil the plot: as a participant-narrator he complicates our understanding of the plot. The participant-narrator of "The Man without a Country" similarly complicates interpretation of Hale's story. Though there are significant differences between the narrators of "The Man without a Country" and *Imperium in Imperio* as characters (one is a white naval officer and the other a black ex-conspirator), there are enough similarities in the works' destabilizing narrative strategies to suggest that Griggs learned something about narrative from Hale as well.

Both "The Man without a Country" and *Imperium* set up complicated relationships between the author and the narrator that can frustrate (or inspire) interpretation. In the 1863 anonymous printing of "The Man without a Country," we have a narrative of Philip Nolan told by Frederic Ingham of the U.S. Navy, who first met Nolan around 1820 and had last seen him around the time of the war with Mexico. When Ingham notices Nolan's obituary in 1863, he decides to tell "this poor creature's story" (203). With the help of legal and naval documents, letters, and oral history, the narrator pieces together an account that runs from 1805 to 1863. Remarking on Burr and Nolan's activities in 1805, Ingham confesses: "What Burr meant to do I know no more than you, dear reader" (205), and it's clear that there are a number of other incidents he describes that ultimately elude him. "I imagine his life," he says about Nolan's history, "from

what I have seen and heard of it" (222). He first meets Nolan on a ship enforc-
ing "our Slave-Trade treaty" (224) and is moved by Nolan's efforts to return liberated slaves to their homeland in Africa. Eventually he loses touch with Nolan,
and the final report of Nolan's death comes to the narrator from the naval officer Danforth, who sends a letter that allows Ingham to complete the story. But
in ways that Hale may not have intended, the assembled story, with its conjec-
tures and lacunae, suggests that U.S. nationalism can be understood as a form
of national fantasy.[6]

Subsequent reprintings of "The Man without a Country" include an author's preface from Hale that insists on the fictionality of Philip Nolan (but
not of the equally made-up Ingham), perhaps because there was a historical
figure circa 1800 named Philip Nolan. He also discusses the story's Civil War
context, conceding that there are different ways of reading a story that he no
longer fully controls. In 1863, Hale's goal was to encourage a patriotic love for
the Union as the U.S. nation, disturbed as he was by the 1863 absentee run for
the Ohio governorship by Clement Vallandigham, a southern sympathizer, or
Copperhead. And yet by the time the story was published in the *Atlantic*, Vallandigham had lost the election and been exiled South by the Union army. To
some extent, then, the story had lost its original purpose. But perhaps this was
all for the good. Saying the story "passed out of my hands" (199), Hale implied
that it could do larger and more important cultural work in the service of U.S.
nationalism.

There is much in "The Man without a Country," however, that shows the
darker and more disturbing sides of national power and thus encourages reader
identification with the traitor-patriot Nolan. At the close of his 1868 preface,
Hale notes that a reader from Connecticut told him "the story must be apol-
ogized for, because it was doing great injury to the national cause by asserting such continued cruelty of the Federal Government through a half-century"
(203), a comment that perceptively links Nolan's "fit of frenzy" (206) in damn-
ing the United States with a comparable juridical fit of frenzy in the sentencing
and open-ended enforcement. Moreover, the narrator Ingham calls the decision to keep information about the United States from Nolan "a little cruel"
(212), and he says about his own post-1830s efforts to free Nolan, in light of
Nolan's heroic service during the War of 1812, "It was like getting a ghost out of
prison. They pretended there was no such man, and never was such a man. . . .
It will not be the first thing in the service of which the Department appears to
know nothing!" (230). Perhaps because he is aware of that darker reading of

an arbitrary and heartless national power, Hale begins the 1868 preface with a strong assertion of the story's patriotic dimension, stating that he wrote it during the summer of 1863 "as a contribution, however, humble, towards the formation of a just and true national sentiment, or sentiment of love to the nation" (199).

Griggs's *Imperium* begins with similar claims about the patriotic motives behind the storytelling, but those claims are made not by Griggs but by his narrator, Berl Trout. "I . . . pronounce myself a patriot," the narrator states in the prefatory "Berl Trout's Dying Declaration."[7] However, the opening words of his preface are as follows: "I am a traitor" (5). Like Hale, in other words, Griggs works with a complex thematic tension between the traitor and the patriot. What is vague at the outset is exactly what the condemned Berl means by terming himself a patriot or a traitor. Is he talking about being a traitor to the U.S. nation, or another social entity, or, as he says, "the whole human family" (6)? Adding to the uncertainty is Griggs's own prefatory "To the Public," which introduces the narrator's preface. In his post-1863 printings, Hale established himself in his prefaces as the author of "The Man without a Country"; in contrast, Griggs presents himself as an editor rather than an author, which is to say that the Griggs of the preface is more a fictional character than an actual historical author, even as he insists that he is telling a true story. He states that Berl "was a warm personal friend" of the two main characters, Belton Piedmont and Bernard Belgrave, and that Berl not only "learned from their own lips the stories of their eventful lives" (3) but also, in the tradition of Hale's Ingham, developed his narrative from "documents" (4) that are now in the possession of Griggs, who asserts that he fulfilled Berl's "dying request by editing his Ms." (3). Griggs's opening gambit of presenting two prefaces raises questions about how to read the narrative that follows.[8] As in "The Man without a Country," there is a participant-narrator (who nonetheless is not described in the novel until the very last chapter) and a nagging sense that we are forever at a distance from the novel's main characters.

Unlike "The Man without a Country," however, the narrative of *Imperium*, which is supposedly constructed from documents and personal testimony, seems to be a conventional third-person narrative. Still, there is a strong interpretive narrative voice that is best linked to the traitor-patriot Berl, who seeks to highlight the significance of the patriotic treason to come. Thus, we are told that Belton's mother's decision to send him to the school run by the learned racist Tiberius Gracchus Leonard in Winchester, Virginia, "vitally affected the destiny of the nation and saved the sun of the Nineteenth Century, proud and glorious, from passing through, near its setting, the blackest and thickest and ugliest clouds of all its journey" (7). When Belton's benefactor, the white newspaper editor V. M. King, advises Belton to appeal to the good side of whites, the narrator portentously tells us: "This is one of the keys to his [Belton's] future life. Remember it" (37). As someone who thinks well of whites, Belton attends the appropriately named Stowe University, and when he is caught spying on a black teacher at a faculty meeting, he pretends to be a chicken thief and makes his escape before he can be identified. The narrator remarks: "Thus again a patriot was mistaken for a chicken thief; and in the South to-day a race that dreams of freedom, equality, and empire, far more than is imagined, is put down as a race of chicken thieves" (44). Iconic images of flags, as in Hale's story, are crucial to the representation of the black patriot, who is described by his white benefactor King as "living . . . beneath the American flag, known as the flag of freedom" (33). Consistent with the presentation of Belton's desires for freedom and equality in an American mode, the white president of Stowe University charges him to "play a part in the adjusting of positions between the negro and the Anglo Saxon races of the South" (49) and in so doing become one of America's "true patriots" (50).

But as we follow Belton's history as a patriot, we see him increasingly disillusioned by the virulent racism of southern whites. He joins with the unemployed blacks of Virginia who "grew to hate a flag that would float in an undisturbed manner over such a condition of affairs" (91; Griggs regularly uses the nautical "float" in relation to the flag). In a striking image of the emasculation he experiences while unemployed, Belton disguises himself as a woman, as a way of spying on white culture, and is nearly raped, and when his wife gives birth to a light-complected baby, he connects his near-rape to the possible rape or adultery of his wife. His (mis)reading of his wife leads to further alienation from the country, which is again underscored (by Berl as portentous narrator) through the image of the flag: "But ah! what were his feelings in those days toward the flag which he had loved so dearly, which had floated proudly and undisturbed, while color prejudice, upheld by it, sent, as he thought, cruel want with drawn sword to stab his family honor to death" (95). Moving to Cadeville, Louisiana, to assume the presidency of a black university, Belton faces such intense racial hatred that he can only ask "what kind of a country he had entered" (99). In the most melodramatic (and unforgettable) scene of the novel, Belton is lynched after helping a young white woman locate a song in her hymnal, and a Dr. Zackland takes the body to his medical office, where the still-living Belton stabs Zackland in the throat and leaves him dead on the dissecting table. Although Belton is arrested for murder, he gains his freedom from the Supreme Court with the help of his long-lost lawyer friend Bernard. The narrator sums up where Belton is at this point in the novel: "Thus ends the tragic experience that burned all the remaining dross out of Belton's nature and prepared him for the even more terrible ordeal to follow in after years" (109). This is the moment when Belton could easily say, "God d——n the United States!" And indeed his subsequent actions suggest that he had uttered or thought a version of such sentiments.

I have focused on Belton because he is the character who most clearly embodies the Nolan role of traitor-patriot. It is important to underscore that it is Belton, and not Bernard (typically read as the novel's most radical figure), who initially embraces the Texas-based secretive black Imperium in Imperio (nation within the nation) and is initially presented as its leader. But *Imperium* presents two men without a country, Belton and Bernard, and in crucial ways shows how these eventual antagonists are not so very different after all. Griggs had depicted the dark-skinned Belton working in relation to black communities, while the light-skinned Bernard attends Harvard (with the help of his white senator father), wins a congressional election when the "masses of colored people rallied around his flag" (74), and falls in love with the dark-complected Viola Martin, who shockingly kills herself rather than marry a mixed-race man who, she fears, will "whiten" the black race and contribute to its extinction. Her suicide note charges Bernard to work against miscegenation, and Bernard vows to follow her edict. In short, when the Imperium in Imperio hinted at in Berl's preface is finally introduced, about two-thirds into the novel, both main characters are at a loss. And it is here, in its account of black patriots and traitors in Texas, that key themes and motifs of Hale's story come to the forefront of the novel.

"The Man without a Country" begins with Burr's apparent plot to take western territory (which includes lands that would become part of the state of Texas) in the immediate wake of the Louisiana Purchase, which itself could be read as Jefferson's successful "taking" of the same territory from the French. In this respect, Hale's story provides an important prehistory to the Civil War. By thwarting Burr's alleged conspiracy, the United States maintained its hold on southwestern lands, a crucial precondition for the eventual war with Mexico, the admission of Texas as a slave state, and the national crisis over slavery that the Compromise of 1850 failed to resolve. Griggs evokes that history through the name of the Louisiana doctor Zackland (an allusion to Zachary Taylor, who played a key role in the war with Texas) and through the name of the headquarters of the Imperium: Thomas Jefferson College (the man who embodied the nation's contradictory commitment to human equality and slavery, and who made the purchase that helped bring forth the slave state of Texas). Given Hale's strong antislavery position, Texas has an odd place in his story. The dying Nolan is "wild with delight" (237) at the hints he's received that Texas has become part of the Union, and accordingly he gives Texas a central place in his shrine to the United States. But the specter of Texas ultimately disrupts the story, for the simple reason that, ever since the 1830s, southerners who dreamed of extending U.S. slavery into the southern Americas had greatly desired the acquisition of Texas as a slave state. As described in "The Man without a Country," naval officials watching over Nolan at the time of Texas's annexation wonder "whether they should get hold of Nolan's handsome set of maps, and cut Texas out of it,—from the map of the world and the map of Mexico" (231). As the map imagery suggests, Texas has been "cut" from Mexico, but Hale doesn't follow up on this suggestion of imperialism in the name of the slave power, perhaps because he expected the Civil War to bring about the end of slavery and thus change the nature of American global expansionism. Nevertheless, by bringing Texas into the story, indeed into Nolan's shrine, Hale would seem to be doing contradictory and even incoherent cultural work, closing his eyes to the connections between the acquisition of southwestern lands for slaveholders, which he strongly opposed, and the expansionism that he seems to be celebrating through the image of Nolan's eagle "clasping the whole globe."

Because he wrote his novel at a different historical moment and from a very different perspective, Griggs had a clearer view of Texas's connections to histories of slavery and racism.[9] Should the black Imperium successfully take back Texas, Griggs suggests, it would to some extent rewrite, or unwrite, the U.S. nationalist history of slavery and empire limned in Hale's story. There are ambiguities in Griggs's presentation. Is the Imperium conceived as a reformist challenge to the U.S. nation or as a hostile, separatist alternative? In his initial account of the Imperium, Belton tells Bernard of its founding during the post-Revolutionary period by an unnamed influential black scientist. As celebrated by Belton, this organization, whose "Capitol at Waco was decorated in American flags" (138), is inspired by American Revolutionary ideology and is in large part devoted to revitalizing that ideology in the face of the dire developments of the post-Reconstruction moment: the Supreme Court's overturning of the Civil Rights Bill; and the ongoing attacks on and lynchings of blacks. The black members of the Imperium, Belton believes, are patriots who are worth dying for, and thus when he recruits Bernard to assume the presidency of the Imperium, he puts him through a bizarre loyalty test, urging Bernard to expose the Imperium or die (to the point where he stages a mock execution). But Bernard resists Belton's threats, defiantly asserting to his friend (who of course secretly agrees with him), "I think . . . those whom you call conspirators are a set of sublime patriots" (125).

At the moment when Bernard assumes the presidency, then, the two friends share a vision of the patriotic goals of the organization, even if there is something vague about whether their fundamental loyalty is to the Imperium or to the U.S. nation. In his presidential speech, Bernard reports on injustices against blacks with respect to labor, civil rights, education, and other areas, basically remarking on problems that have already been exposed through the account of Belton's experiences in the South.[10] The speech takes an even more aggressive turn, however, when Bernard urges blacks to resist volunteering to fight in the Spanish-American War, demanding to know why African Americans should defend a country that "treats [them] in a manner to make [them] execrate it" (145). When the Imperium's congress responds to Bernard's speech with the chant of "War! war! war!" (152), Belton takes it upon himself to respond with an affirmation of his larger loyalty to the U.S. nation. In an echo of a similar theme in Hale and in relation to a key patriotic image that is also central to Nolan's shrine, he insists that his experience of dispossession has only added to his love of country:

> The Anglo-Saxon has seen the eyes of the Negro following the American eagle in its glorious flight. The eagle has alighted on some mountain top and the poor Negro has been seen climbing up the rugged mountain-side, eager to caress the eagle. When he has attempted to do this the eagle has clawed at his eyes and dug his beak into his heart and has flown away in disdain; and yet, so majestic was its flight that the Negro, with tears in his eyes, and blood dripping from his heart has smiled and shouted "God save the eagle." (162)

Belton concludes his talk by calling on blacks to continue to immigrate to Texas in order to influence the popular vote and develop a black nationalism that remains a constituent part of the United States—a plan that is in the direct line of Hale's 1845 *How to Conquer Texas, before Texas Conquers Us*, which called on antislavery people to immigrate to Texas in order to build up voting majorities that would bring about "the conquest of Texas, by the peaceful weapons of truth, of freedom, of religion, and of right."[11]

The Imperium's congress unanimously approves Belton's speech, but a new crisis develops when the two leaders have a night meeting and Bernard, in the manner of Aaron Burr, proposes a more radical plan that would accomplish what Burr failed to accomplish (if this was indeed his intention): the taking of the Southwest. Clearly treasonous with respect to the United States, Bernard proposes "A PLAN OF ACTION FOR THE IMPERIUM IN IMPERIO" (167) in which blacks would infiltrate and ultimately subvert the U.S. Navy, build up a stockpile of weapons in Texas, secretly negotiate with foreign countries, and "hoist the flag of the Imperium" (168) at Texas's capital city of Austin, while giving Louisiana to the foreign power that chooses to aid the black rebels (thereby in effect undoing the history of the Louisiana Purchase). Belton responds to Bernard's image of the flag of the Imperium with the flag of the United States: "Our Imperium was organized to secure our rights within the United States. . . . Our efforts have been to wash the flag free of all blots, not to rend it; to burnish every star in the cluster, but to pluck none out" (168). Stars are indeed "plucked out" of the Hale story because of the mandate that Nolan not learn of any developments concerning the United States, such as the addition of new states. In Hale, to be plucked out or cut out is to be added; here Belton is concerned that Bernard's plan would result in states truly being plucked out.

In his 1868 preface, Hale insists that the large aim of "The Man without a Country" is to develop "love to the nation," and in his story that love is cast in relation to the flag and other national symbols. Belton's expression of his opposition to Bernard's radical vision brings together a number of Hale's themes about the love of country and its symbolic incarnations. Belton declares to Bernard: "I love the Union and I love the South. Soaked as the Old Glory is with my people's tears and stained as it is with their warm blood, I could die as my forefathers did, fighting for its honor and asking no greater boon than Old Glory for my shroud and native soil for my grave. This may appear strange, but love of country is one of the deepest passions in the human bosom. . . . I shall never give up my fight for freedom, but I shall never prove false to the flag" (168). Like the dying Nolan, Belton looks forward to his end, in effect providing Bernard with instructions for his burial that Bernard will indeed honor. Even when facing execution for his decision to resign from the Imperium, he refuses to back down, putting "duty to country above everything else" (172). Just before being shot on Bernard's order, he offers his last words, which, like Nolan's closing words in his death letter, are meant to provide his epitaph: "Tell posterity . . . that I loved the race to which I belonged and the flag that floated over me; and, being unable to see these objects of my love engage in mortal combat, I went to my God, and now look down upon both from my home in the skies to bless them with my spirit" (173–74). He is subsequently shot and killed, with the narrator stating in the concluding sentence of the chapter: "On the knoll where he fell he was buried, shrouded in an American flag" (174). Hale's naval officer Danforth remarks on the death of Nolan: "And now it seems the dear old fellow is dead. He has found a home at last, and a country" (233). The same could be said for Belton as well.

Had *Imperium* ended with this penultimate chapter, we would have a man without a country who, in death, nonetheless has more of a country (and home) than his countrymen. It is the pathos of Belton's patriotic martyrdom that has persuaded many critics that Belton at the end of the novel speaks for the historical Griggs. For example, Coleman writes, "In the denouement of the novel, Belton's conservative, perhaps even ultraconservative, remarks and resolutions are cast as the morally correct choice against Bernard's more militant program." But cast by whom? As Coleman goes on to remark, "This is all, of course, presented through an unreliable narrator, whose conservative aphorisms end up sounding like Griggs's personal opinion."[12] But do we know Griggs's personal opinion outside of the dynamic formalistic workings of the novel itself? We need to consider the novel's problematic ending, which brings us back to its problematic beginning, which points to Griggs's revisionary reworking of a key aspect of Hale's story.

As in "The Man without a Country," the account of the hero at his final moments comes mediated by a narrator. The mysterious Berl Trout of the novel's opening now reveals himself as one of the five executioners of Belton. Repentant about his actions, he takes the position of Belton that the Imperium should hold off on (but not renounce) the option to use violence. He thus chooses to do what Belton himself had told Bernard was worthy of death: expose the Imperium. Concerned about the weapons that Bernard and the Imperium are stockpiling, Berl states at the end of his narrative, as he announced at the start: "I decided to prove traitor" (176). But he's a traitor not to the U.S. nation but to the Imperium, even as he upholds the group's reformist aims, offering the hope

"that all mankind will join hands and help my poor downtrodden people to secure those rights for which they organized the Imperium, which my betrayal
has now destroyed" (177).

Berl appeals to humanity and pleads in "the spirit of conservatism" (175) for
the rights of blacks, but on the basis of the systemic racism that we've read
about in the novel, we should resist linking his naive optimism directly to
Griggs's own views. Might the specter of Bernard's rage also be seen as a moti-
vator for change? For example, consider the extraordinary public memorial that
the Imperium erects in a seat of its congress for former member Felix Cook,
who was attacked and murdered by white racists: "a golden casket containing
his heart, which had been raked from the burning embers on the morning following the night of the murderous assault" (139).[13] Those burning embers suggest a still-burning anger. In this respect, I would argue that Griggs sees Berl's
conservatism and Bernard's rage as a dualism rather than a binary. Again, it is
worth remembering that it is Belton who recruited Bernard and taught him
that betrayal of the Imperium was an act of treason worthy of death. In the
end, Belton doesn't categorically reject Bernard's radical plan; instead, he asks
for a four-year waiting period. Viewing the two men without a country as one,
we can regard Bernard's final remarks on Belton, which are also the novel's
final remarks on the U.S. flag, as an effort to talk back to "The Man without a
Country" by suggesting the limits of Hale's patriotic vision for black Americans: "Float on proud flag, while yet you may. Rejoice, oh! ye Anglo-Saxons,
yet a little while. . . . Exhume Belton's body if you like and tear your flag from
around him to keep him from polluting it!" (176). A similar rage against white
supremacist U.S. nationalists can be discerned in Griggs's next novel and his
other extant writings of the time, even as the image of the Imperium congress's
honoring of the burned heart in a casket speaks to the tortured nature of the
sentimental nationalism that will remain an important part of Griggs's work.

"The Man without a Country" moves from the patriot's renunciation of the
United States to an embrace of Texas, and in certain respects *Imperium in Imperio* follows that trajectory, however ironically or sociocritically. In his next
novel, the 1901 *Overshadowed*, Griggs ends where Hale begins: with the protagonist renouncing country and assuming a life at sea. In effect, Griggs's protagonist makes himself into an icon whose exile at sea parodically revises (but
also discerns a certain truth of) Hale's story in order to suggest the importance
of (self-)exile to patriotism. The title of Griggs's second novel, published two
years after *Imperium*, may have also drawn from Hale. Consider again the fa-

mous description of the eagle in Nolan's shrine: "The stars and stripes were triced up above and around a picture of Washington, and he had painted a majestic eagle, with lightning blazing from his beak and his foot just clasping the whole globe, which his wings overshadowed." *Overshadowed* was published at a time when Hale was celebrating turn-of-the-century U.S. military actions abroad, while Griggs was increasingly concerned about the damage being done by the eagle's beak, foot, and wings. It was also written during a time when Hale's "The Man without a Country" had come to be read, with Hale's help, as an unambiguously patriotic embrace of the war against Spain. In a new preface written expressly to celebrate the invasion of Cuba, Hale offered a reading of the story that robbed it of its ambiguities and complexities, stating in jingoistic terms

> the calm historical fact is that we are at war with Spain. In that war it is time again for young men and young women, and old men and old women, for all sorts of people, to understand that the Country is itself an entity. It is a Being. The Lord God of nations has called it into existence, and has placed it here with certain duties in defence of the civilization of the world. It was the intention of this parable ["The Man without a Country"], which describes the life of one man who tried to separate himself from his country, to show how terrible was his mistake.[14]

A short story that could be read as antislavery and as a profound meditation on outcast patriotism was now, with Hale's help, put to the service of imperialism.

In his 1902 novel, *Unfettered*, Griggs's main character, Dorlan Warthell, initially opposes the war with Spain and the subsequent invasion of the Philippines as military actions intended to further the agenda of white racist imperialists, only to be persuaded by the woman he loves that the northerners who are managing the invasion are doing the laudable "work of leading the Filipinos into all the blessings of higher civilization."[15] But in an earlier November 1900 letter to the *Indianapolis World*, Griggs offered a more jaundiced perspective on U.S. imperialism, blaming the Republicans for enslaving "the colored peoples of the Philippines and for worsening the plight of black citizens in the United States." Disillusioned by the continuing erosion of rights for blacks in the Jim Crow South, he invoked U.S. ideals going back to the revolutionary period in urging blacks to consider that the Democratic Party under the leadership of William Jennings Bryan, as opposed to the Republican Party under McKinley, could perhaps offer "that same political freedom for which Patrick Henry pleaded."[16] And yet by the time of Griggs's 1901 *Overshadowed*, he would appear to have little faith that the U.S. nation was capable of living up to its revolutionary ideals in the immediate future.

As with all of Griggs's novels, the plotting of *Overshadowed* is complicated and at times confusing. In order to tease out the Hale dimension, I focus here on the plot line involving Astral Herndon, the African American who by the end of the novel is a man without a country.

Set in Richmond, Virginia, the novel opens with Astral courting Erma Wysong, the daughter of a white father and a black mother (now dead). After Astral moves North to pursue his schooling, there are two large plot developments: the white James Lawson, son of a former governor, attempts to seduce Erma, making use of one Dolly Smith as his go-between. As it turns out, Dolly is the sister of Erma's dead mother, and she is now seeking revenge on Lawson because years earlier she had acted as a go-between in his father's seduction of her sister, which had destroyed her family. When she reveals the history that makes the Lawson family look so bad, and which reveals as well that Lawson and Wysong are half brother and sister, she is tarred and feathered by a white citizenry that simply doesn't want its secrets aired in public; shortly thereafter, she commits suicide. Right around the same time, Erma's younger half brother, John, is experiencing his own troubles. Fired from the Bilgal Iron Works because the labor union will not accept blacks as members, he decides to kill the union chief after he hears him declare, "If a foe stands in our way and nothing will dislodge him but death, then he must die." Initially John is not suspected as the killer, but when his conscience bothers him, he confesses to his sister. Inspired by the hopeful tenor of Booker T. Washington's speech on the "Race Problem," which he had recently delivered in Richmond, Erma urges her brother to confess, which he does, with the predictable result: he's sentenced to death.[17] Perhaps also inspired by Booker T. Washington's address, several members of Virginia's House of Delegates begin meeting with educated young black women in order to better understand black people, again with the predictable result: Horace Christian, a politician who had earlier overseen a black lynching, sexually violates Erma's friend Margaret. In a characteristically Griggsian textual moment of dark irony and violence, an honorable white, the speaker of the house Lanier, gets the intoxicated Christian masked in black face and manages to have him hanged instead of John. So the white lyncher is lynched, while John makes his way to Florida, where he deliberately commits a crime so he can ease his conscience by serving a prison term.

At this point Astral returns to the novel, still in love with Erma. Despite the opposition of aristocratic light-complected blacks, who are bothered by Astral's dark complexion, the two are married and have a child, Astral Herndon Jr. Seven years later, John appears in their home as an escaped convict, worn down by the Florida prison system, and dies before Erma's eyes. Shocked and grief-stricken, Erma dies as well, and policemen arrive on the scene and assault Astral. He's delirious at first, but he appears at the funeral for Erma and declares that he cannot allow her to be buried in the racist United States. The good Lanier urges Astral to change his mind, insisting that "with all its faults, this country is by far the greatest on earth." Still, he says he'll support whatever Astral decides to do, and Astral, given the antiblack violence that has been featured throughout the novel as the defining characteristic of the nation, is approaching Nolan's state of mind when he declares "God d——n the United States!" Unlike Nolan, however, who's sentenced to life at sea by a vindictive court, Astral self-sentences himself to an undetermined time at sea. He travels to New York harbor with his son and the bodies of Erma and her brother and embarks on a ship whose destination his friends and associates think is Africa. But that is not his choice; he chooses to live at sea. When "in mid-ocean," "the caskets containing the remains of the two departed were gently lowered into the depths of the ocean and committed to the keeping of the waves." Then, with his son by his side, Astral offers this closing speech:

> My son, . . . your mother had been buried in these domains, because here there abides no social group in which conditions operate toward the overshadowing of such elements as are not deemed assimilable. And now, I, Astral Herndon, hereby and forever renounce all citizenship in all lands whatsoever, and constitute myself A CITIZEN OF THE OCEAN, and ordain that this title shall be entailed upon my progeny unto all generations, until such time as the shadows which now envelope the darker races in all lands shall have passed away, away, and away!"[18]

This is a remarkable rewriting of "The Man without a Country," as the protagonist embraces his noncitizenship and disconnection from the country. For those critics invested in Griggs's notion of "The Science of Collective Efficiency," which he elaborated in his 1923 *Guide to Racial Greatness*, the seeming individualism of Astral's self-exile has been taken as a mark of his failure.[19] But read in relation to Hale's story and in relation to Griggs's anger about the social situation circa 1900, Astral's final speech and decision to remain at sea can be understood as a powerful testament of his patriotism *and* as a form of collective leadership that comes about through his strong individualism.[20] In effect, Astral has made himself into an icon, "A CITIZEN OF THE OCEAN," in the same way that Hale created an icon, "The Man without a Country," that is meant to inspire collectivities. The narrator of Hale's story, Ingham, insists on seeing Nolan as an icon, telling his readers that he offers Nolan's history "by way of showing young Americans of to-day what it is to be A MAN WITHOUT A COUNTRY" (204). It is worth underscoring, then, that by the end of Hale's story, when Nolan has emerged as an inspiring superpatriot, he embraces not the United States but the sea. In a passage that would seem to have resonated for Griggs, the dying Nolan requests of the naval officers who have him in custody: "Bury me in the sea; it has been my home, and I love it" (240–41). In the ocean burial that concludes *Overshadowed*, Griggs thus in effect takes back "The Man without a Country" from those who were using it to legitimate U.S. imperialism, showing that exile from one's country in the service of a deeper patriotism might not be such a "terrible . . . mistake." In an act of authorial revision and recuperation, Griggs finds wisdom in a work that Hale now more sanctimoniously linked to U.S. wars abroad. Hale's story came to serve as war fodder for patriotic Americans during World War I and World War II, becoming even more popular than it was in the nineteenth century, while Griggs's neglected novels retained their power—in the way of the patriotic outcast—by remaining overshadowed and without a country.

Notes

1. On the phenomenal popularity of "The Man without a Country," see Brook Thomas, *Civic Myths: A Law-and-Literature Approach to Citizenship* (Chapel Hill: University of North Carolina Press, 2007), 55–57; Hsuan L. Hsu, "Contexts for Reading 'The Man without a Country,'" in *Two Texts by Edward Everett Hale: "The Man without a Country" and Philip Nolan's Friends*, ed. Hsu and Susan Kalter (Lanham, Md.: Lexington Books, 2010), 1–16.

2. Edward Everett Hale, "The Man without a Country," in *If, Yes, and Perhaps* (Boston: Ticknor & Fields, 1868), 206. This is the first book publication of Hale's 1863 story, with the first printing of his introduction. (Hale titled subsequent editions of this volume *The Man without a Country and Other Tales*.) Subsequent quotations from the story are from this 1868 edition and are cited parenthetically in the text.

3. Carrie Hyde, "Outcast Patriotism: The Dilemma of Negative Instruction in 'The Man without a Country,'" *ELH* 7 (2010): 916, 915, 919.

4. Edward Everett Hale, *The Man without a Country and Other Tales* (Boston: Roberts Brothers, 1886), 8.

5. See Hyde, "Outcast Patriotism," 915–39. In a provocative essay on Griggs's depiction

of black patriotism in a racialist, Uncle Tom tradition, "Sensationalizing Patriotism: Sutton Griggs and the Sentimental Nationalism of Uncle Tom" (*American Literature* 79 [2007]: 673–99), Stephen Knadler notes similarities between Griggs's novel and "The Man without a Country" with respect to their depictions of Texas as a site for conspiracy.

6. On Hale and national fantasy, see Elizabeth Duquette, *Loyal Subjects: Bonds of Nation, Race, and Allegiance in Nineteenth-Century America* (New Brunswick, N.J.: Rutgers University Press, 2010), 49–51.

7. Sutton E. Griggs, *Imperium in Imperio* (1899; New York: Modern Library, 2003), 6. Subsequent quotations from *Imperium* are from this edition and are cited parenthetically in the text.

8. On pioneering aspects of Griggs's narrative strategies in *Imperium*, see Raymond Hedin, "Probable Readers, Possible Stories: The Limits of Nineteenth-Century Black Narrative," in *Readers in History: Nineteenth-Century American Literature and the Contexts of Response*, ed. James L. Machor (Baltimore: Johns Hopkins University Press, 1993), esp. 197–200. Critics are divided about whether Griggs's use of Berl as narrator is successful. Finnie D. Coleman states that "this experiment fails miserably at a number of levels" (*Sutton Griggs and the Struggle against White Supremacy* [Knoxville: University of Tennessee Press, 2007], 45). For an important defense of Griggs's narrative strategy, see Eric Curry, "'The Power of Combinations': Sutton Griggs' *Imperium in Imperio* and the Science of Collective Efficiency," *American Literary Realism* 43 (2010): 23–40.

9. For a richly textured account of the histories of blacks in the southern borderlands that Griggs both drew on and contributed to in his portrayal of the Imperium's home base in Waco, Texas, see Caroline F. Levander's essay in this volume.

10. On the importance of oratory in the novel, see Maria Karafilis's "Oratory, Embodiment, and U.S. Citizenship in Sutton E. Griggs's *Imperium in Imperio*," *African American Review* 40 (2006): 125–43.

11. [Edward Everett Hale], *How to Conquer Texas, before Texas Conquers Us* (Boston: Redding, 1845), 13.

12. Coleman, *Sutton Griggs*, 69.

13. As critics have pointed out, Felix Cook, a postmaster, is based on the black postmaster Frazier Baker, who was murdered in South Carolina in 1898.

14. Hale added these sentences in his introduction to a republication of the story in *New Outlook* 59 (1898): 116; this new introduction accompanied subsequent reprintings of *The Man without a Country and Other Tales*.

15. Sutton E. Griggs, *Unfettered: A Novel* (Nashville: Orion, 1902), 156.

16. Quoted in Willard B. Gatewood Jr., *Black Americans and the White Man's Burden, 1898–1903* (Urbana: University of Illinois Press, 1975), 249. On Griggs and the Spanish-American War, see Susan Gillman, *Blood Talk: American Race Melodramas and the Culture of the Occult* (Chicago: University of Chicago Press, 2003), 73–116.

17. Sutton E. Griggs, *Overshadowed: A Novel* (Nashville: Orion, 1901), 102, 127.

18. Griggs, *Overshadowed*, 214, 216, 217.

19. See, for example, Arlene A. Elder's critical remarks on Astral in *The "Hindered Hand": Cultural Implications of Early African-American Fiction* (Westport, Conn.: Greenwood, 1978), 82–84.

20. It is worth noting that Griggs writes at the end of the *Guide to Racial Greatness; or, The Science of Collective Efficiency* (Memphis: National Public Welfare League, 1923): "The greatest of all agencies capable of bringing about transformation is the individual" (218).

ANDREÁ N. WILLIAMS

Moving Up a Dead-End Ladder

Black Class Mobility, Death, and Narrative Closure in Sutton Griggs's Overshadowed

In Sutton Griggs's second novel, *Overshadowed* (1901), black Americans face tragic outcomes when they threaten existing class hierarchies. In fact, nearly every ambitious, upwardly mobile black American in the novel meets what might be called a "dead end": whether physical demise or the more figurative social death of silencing, exile, and marginalization that signals characters' expulsion from the novel's fictional world. In this way, though *Overshadowed* shares with Griggs's other four novels a focus on challenging Jim Crow racism, *Overshadowed* more specifically emphasizes how racism operates by limiting black Americans' economic opportunities. Still, despite the dismal fates that several black characters encounter, the narrative nevertheless self-consciously promises that "somehow good will be the final goal of ill."[1] By examining the resolution of individual plot lines, as well as the novel's final pages, I show how Griggs struggles to offer a realistic, yet optimistic, representation of the stifling economic conditions for postbellum southern blacks. The multiple endings depicted in *Overshadowed* reveal much about the author's broader social agenda to develop and inspire an African American readership, demand political representation, and protest Jim Crow educational and labor practices that, in effect, kept black Americans subjugated to whites. By showing how often black Americans' attempts at upward mobility end tragically, *Overshadowed* enacts a public politics of mourning to rally for black people's full inclusion in the American political economy.

Set in Richmond, Virginia, *Overshadowed* centers on the plight of Erma and John Wysong, African American siblings who encounter both institutional and social challenges to their self-sufficiency. Racially excluded from the semiprofessional work appropriate to her capabilities, Erma accepts work as a domestic servant, which jeopardizes both her personal safety and her reputation. As a servant, Erma is pursued by lecherous white men and ostracized by her elite black peers who denigrate physical labor. However, after proving her work ethic and virtue, she later secures a gainful marriage to physician Astral Herndon, a longtime friend who ignores the stigma projected onto black working women. In contrast to Erma's ascendance, her brother, John, unfairly loses his job at the ironworks, and in retaliation, he kills the white labor union leader whose discriminatory policies led to his termination. Though John manages to evade being hanged for his crime (thanks to an elaborate cross-racial disguise), he serves a harsh prison sentence, then escapes to seek out his sister. The siblings' reunion is spoiled when John dies shortly after arriving at Erma's home, causing her to die from shock. Although the novel's two central characters die, two additional developments destabilize a patently tragic reading of the text. First, after Erma dies, her husband, Astral, leaves the United States, embittered by the race and class inequality that had foreclosed his wife's lifelong desire for peace and prosperity. Second, in an epilogue, the narrator prophesies that Erma's son later will return to the States to pursue social reform. Stretching over multiple pages, the novel's resolutions evoke emotions ranging from joy and grief to indignation and a final bittersweet hopefulness. Each increasingly extravagant ending works against the previous one, complicating its effect.

Scholars often have read the unwieldy conclusions of Griggs's novels as evidence of the author's supposed aesthetic ineptitude. In an early review, critic Hugh Gloster set the tone by applauding the author as "outstanding for his productivity and influence," but "weak according to artistic standards."[2] Similar sentiments echo in a recent assessment that Griggs "lacks the artistry to convey the feeling of tragedy."[3] By contrast, in a more generous evaluation, Maria Karafilis suggests that in Griggs's best-known novel, *Imperium in Imperio* (1899), the "aporia, the lack of narrative closure" intends to "resist a symbolic resolution" to social problems that admittedly are "not immediately resolvable."[4] Extending Karafilis's brief attention to the lack of narrative closure in *Imperium in Imperio*, I focus on the serial endings of *Overshadowed* and gesture toward Griggs's other novels to elucidate how narrative endings are one of the most deliberate and provocative—rather than oversimplified or botched—means by which Griggs endorses racial uplift via nonviolent political activism.

If authors privilege particular elements of their texts to signal readers and guide their interpretations, as Frank Kermode, Peter Rabinowitz, and others have argued, then the endings of texts are especially significant points. As Rabinowitz proposes, authors lend careful attention to "titles, beginnings and endings (not only of whole texts, but of subsections as well—volumes, chapters, episodes), epigraphs, and descriptive subtitles."[5] In turn, readers can expect that the most revealing elements of a story will be placed in these positions. Authors and readers thus often share an understanding of literary conventions, anticipating how narratives should be structured and how they may be decoded or consumed in the reading process.[6] However, when an author departs from a literary convention by delaying, parodying, or evading it, the departure may critique the convention itself or comment on the extratextual social conditions that the convention describes.[7] For instance, in keeping with romantic conventions, Griggs inscribes Erma's marriage as a reward for her moral constancy. But Erma's subsequent death revokes the expected happy ending. Through this reversal, *Overshadowed* tellingly suggests that black families such as Erma's cannot presume to maintain the secure domesticity afforded to white protagonists.

The nuanced distinction between an "ending" and "closure" helps in further interpreting the narrative structure of *Overshadowed*. As Ibrahim Taha explains, an ending or conclusion is "the definite and actual part of the text," while closure refers to "the process by which the text achieves a benefitting, satisfying, and proper conclusion."[8] In *Overshadowed*, individual story lines constantly and sometimes abruptly end throughout the novel, as well as in its final pages. But the novel altogether culminates in untidy closure. The happy ending remains deferred, always only promised in the novel's final pages, which extend their temporality to a future undesignated time when Erma's son will redeem black Americans from "centuries of gloom."[9] The dissonance between ending and closure in the novel exemplifies how, in Russell Reising's terms, narratives about fraught social issues "can't close, precisely because their embeddedness within the sociohistorical worlds of their genesis is so complex and conflicted."[10] The real-world problems engaged by socially conscious narratives persist and disrupt the story's satisfactory closure. Indeed, narratives that work hardest to neatly tie up what Reising calls "loose ends" paradoxically expose how unsettled their resolutions remain.[11]

In the endings that punctuate the intervening story lines and chapters of *Overshadowed*, Griggs deploys death as a potent metaphor for black Americans' second-class citizenship in the United States. Though physical death often is considered the most extreme or undesirable state of the human condition, the novel indicates how the machinations of Jim Crow—ranging from its subtle indignities to the outright dehumanization of black Americans—constitute a veritable version of death. Drawing the connection between economic deprivation and social death, historian Orlando Patterson has noted that in systems of bondage predating American chattel slavery, a financially insolvent person could be relegated to the social death of enslavement, stripped of the right to property, self-possession, honor, and community.[12] Much the same could be said for the postbellum U.S. South that Griggs depicts, where Jim Crow laws and practices aimed to ensure that African Americans remained without property and status. In this regard, to recall Patterson's observation about the comparative experiences of social death from one location to another, "History did not repeat itself; it merely lingered."[13] In a pivotal chapter of *Overshadowed* titled "Worse than Death," Griggs traces John's descent from being an ambitious worker, to being unemployed and underemployed, to serving time in a convict lease camp, where inmates are treated like "a herd of cattle" exploited by white capitalism.[14] This chapter's telling title might be said to extend elsewhere within the novel, which exposes the economic underpinnings of the New South as uncannily reminiscent of the old one.

Griggs's meditations on social death resonate elsewhere in African American cultural representations. In *Raising the Dead: Readings of Death and (Black) Subjectivity*, Sharon Patricia Holland posits death as "a cultural and national phenomenon or discourse, as a figurative silencing or process of erasure, and as an embodied entity or subject capable of transgression."[15] Death is universal, but it is not entirely arbitrary; rather, the details of when, why, and how an individual dies may depend largely on the social and environmental conditions in which he or she lives. In the cultural study *Passed On: African American Mourning Stories*, Karla Holloway recognizes African Americans as much more likely than white Americans to be legally executed, violently murdered, sentenced without a fair trial, or victims of suicide. As Holloway insists, "Instead of death and dying being unusual, untoward events, or despite being inevitable end-of-lifespan events, the cycles of [African Americans'] daily lives were so persistently interrupted by specters of death that [they] worked this experience into the culture's iconography and included it as an aspect of black cultural sensibility."[16] In this regard, dead ends become a convention within the stories black Americans tell in writing, visual and performance art, music, and commodity culture; death emblematizes the state of black life.

Yet while Holloway and Holland draw their examples primarily from later twentieth-century African American culture, the saturation of death and loss in Griggs's work marks the postbellum South, in which he sets all his novels, as a particularly fraught site of death-inducing racial violence and subjection.[17] Griggs's fiction is exceptional even among African American narratives generally thought to fixate on death. Black Americans seldom die from old age or proverbial "natural causes" in Griggs's story lines; rather, nothing could be more unnatural than how his characters perish or experience loss. Arlene Elder provides an inventory of the startling body count that accumulates across the course of the author's five novels:

> His books contain more deaths and disasters than those of his [black literary] predecessors combined. Within the five plots appear two sudden insanities, three deathbed scenes, two deaths in a fire, five supposed deaths in a fire, two fatal heart attacks, two killings in self-defense, one attempted murder, two slayings with sexual overtones, four shootings, four suicides, one attempted suicide, one legal hanging, one tarring and feathering, four lynchings, one attempted lynching, and two political executions![18]

Elder interprets these tragic plot developments as less an aesthetic decision on Griggs's part than a sociohistorical one. For Elder, "Griggs generally abandons sentimental or melodramatic depictions as irrelevant" and instead relies on such plots to indict "the irresponsible and widespread destructiveness of a racist climate."[19]

Yet the documentary and artistic functions of dead ends in Griggs's fiction are not mutually exclusive. Death is a recurrent topic for the author not only because it was a concrete reality during the nadir, which his fiction could reflect, but also because death and suffering are compelling narrative devices to call readers to action. Instead of avoiding melodramatic representation, as Elder presumes, Griggs indeed shows how the narrative form of melodrama—characterized by emotional excess, multiclimactic structure, dualities, and sudden reversals of fortune—mimics the extremes of black life and death. As Linda Williams provocatively argues, melodrama potently reveals "why it is that in a democracy ruled by rights, we do not gain the moral upper hand by saying simply that rights have been infringed. We say, instead, much more powerfully: 'I have been victimized; I have suffered, therefore give me rights.'"[20] By building a cumulative account of the subtle and more appalling suffering that African Americans experienced under Jim Crow, *Overshadowed* enacts a politics of mourning, "that creative process mediating a hopeful or hopeless relationship between loss and history."[21] The politics of mourning not only allow for cathartic expressions of grief, but also may incite people to transform the conditions that precipitate loss. David L. Eng and David Kazanjian's sense that mourning can foster a "hope*ful* or hope*less*" response is crucial to understanding Griggs's reliance on dead ends.[22] For *Overshadowed* does not merely testify to southern African Americans' dire positions but also aims to inspire political and socio-economic transformation for an alternative future.

The period of the 1880s to the second decade of the twentieth century has been called the nadir of black experience—a period that ushered in the codi-fication of Jim Crow, a spike in racial violence, and the continued exploita-tion of African American agricultural and manual labor. But while the majority of African Americans remained poor after emancipation, by the last quarter of the nineteenth century, a small percentage of the black population consti-tuted a middle class distinguished by its relative wealth, education, (semi)pro-fessional occupations, and patterns of consumption.[23] The development of a black middle class heightened tensions for both black and white communities, however. For black Americans, the middle-class group that Du Bois would des-ignate as the Talented Tenth constituted the self-chosen leaders of the race but sometimes estranged themselves from the black masses for whom they claimed to speak. Never enjoying the political rights or accumulated wealth of the white middle class, middle-class black Americans remained vulnerable to downward mobility. As one historian explains, from the perspective of white southerners, "black [upward] mobility could be tolerated so long as claims to middle-class status in the form of political and civic equality were never made. Still, an un-dercurrent of hostility remained."[24]

As in Griggs's fiction, the focus on black class aspirations that lead to dead ends appears, to a lesser degree, in the fiction of turn-of-the-century black writ-ers W. E. B. Du Bois and Paul Laurence Dunbar. In the final lines of Du Bois's short story "Of the Coming of John" (1903), the college-educated eponymous character awaits his death at the hands of a lynch mob. Though the mob pur-sues John because he has killed a white man who threatens his sister, the mob is incited as much by what they consider John's "almighty air and uppish ways."[25] Likewise, in Dunbar's short stories about black professionals, including "One Man's Fortune" (1900) and "Mr. Cornelius Johnson, Office-Seeker" (1900), occupational hierarchies constrain upwardly mobile black men and relegate them to ill-paid jobs with little social esteem. Following an unfair termina-tion as a law clerk, Bertram Halliday in "One Man's Fortune" pens a good-bye letter in the tone of a suicide note. "I now see why so many promising young men, class orators, valedictorians and the like fall by the wayside and are never heard from after commencement day.... Southward Ho," Bertram exclaims.[26] Though the story does not conclude with Bertram's literal death—he resigns himself to accepting undesirable work—the letter signifies the death of his ideal career ambitions. The story's bitter closing lines observe, "A colored man has no business with ideals—not in *this* nineteenth century!"[27] Rather than providing a settled moral for the tale, the ironic one-liner emphasizes the term "this" to critique current conditions and differentiate them from *that* unattained nineteenth-century United States in which black Americans may more freely pursue both business and ideals.

Griggs's fictions address the dual force of a post-Reconstruction class structure that maintains racialized boundaries between blacks and whites, as well as fosters an intraracial social hierarchy among African Americans. By exposing the mutually constitutive relationship between racism and class disparities, Griggs joins other late nineteenth-century thinkers such as Ida B. Wells who understood white violence as being, in part, a disciplinary tactic for undermining black Americans' economic gain and maintaining white supremacy in every area of public and private life. Following the lynching of three black businessmen in Memphis in 1893, Wells would respond, "Until this past year I was one among those who believed ... that when wealth, education and character became more general among us, the cause being removed the effect would cease, and justice be accorded to all alike."[28] She found instead that "no matter what the attainments, character or standing of an Afro-American," his or her livelihood and life remained in jeopardy.[29] Indeed, upwardly mobile blacks were often the especial targets of violence and discrimination. In *Overshadowed*, when the all-white labor union bars black workers such as John Wysong, the national union leader explains, "We [white Americans] cannot afford to enter into competition with the Negro. For it would not be a question of dollars. It would be a question of home against home."[30] Like Wells's nonfiction polemic, *Overshadowed* would grapple with how to interpret the gradual advances that some black Americans make up the social ladder: whether as evidence of the race's progress or as inconsequential exceptions to the general rule of black economic disadvantage. The novel ultimately suggests that black middle-class status was unsustainable so long as racist U.S. laws and social customs denied blacks the means to pursue, defend, and maintain the accumulation of wealth.

By offering several seemingly discordant endings to *Overshadowed*, Griggs experiments with narrative closure as he does in each of his novels, in which appended documents or secondary characters expound upon and sometimes contradict the novel's apparent message. Griggs's first novel, *Imperium in Imperio*, generally has been read as promoting black nationalism, given the novel's representation of the Imperium as a separatist, black-run government that plans to sabotage U.S. armed forces. Yet the novel's conclusion troubles such an interpretation when Berl Trout, a first-person participant in the Imperium, confesses to U.S. authorities in order to have the Imperium dismantled. Trout anticipates that the Imperium's black leaders will have him killed as a traitor, but he justifies himself, explaining, "I die for mankind, for humanity, for civilization. . . . When will all races and classes of men learn that men made in the image of God will not be the slaves of another image?"[31] Allowing Trout to articulate the novel's final words, Griggs privileges a character and a conservative ideological position that plays only a minor role in the novel's building action. Critic Stephen Knadler further observes, "The universalism behind this eleventh-hour appeal is never defined but accepted as a given."[32] Trout's confession unravels the novel's black nationalist claims for liberty. Instead of containing or neutralizing the explosive topic of black separatism that *Imperium in Imperio* engages, the ending leaves loose ends as one notes that the black man (in Trout's case) must die to achieve freedom.

If the preponderance of death in Griggs's fiction appears melancholic, the author recognized the need to vary the conclusions of his novels for the benefit of readers. According to Finnie Coleman, Griggs partly attributed the disappointing sales of *Imperium in Imperio* to its nationalist themes, though the addition of Berl Trout's self-sacrificial confession aims to temper overt nationalism.[33] In the two novels that followed, *Overshadowed* and *Unfettered*, Griggs adjusts his approach by wedding the imperatives of political discourse with a romance plot. The leading story line of *Unfettered* (1902) concludes with the marriage of Morlene Dalton and Dorlan Warthell, lovers whose long-awaited union signifies a change in the South's political climate. Morlene initially had declined Dorlan's marriage proposal because, as she reasons, racial conditions in the South subvert the ideals of black domesticity and class advancement. Morlene believes that a wife should support her husband's ambitions, but "in the South the Negro wife is robbed of this holy task" since encouraging her mate's ascendancy or political activism would put his very life in danger.[34] Her hesitancy to marry Dorlan motivates his quest to dismantle the color line, and when he succeeds, the two marry as readers "bid this loving and laboring couple a fond adieu."[35]

Griggs's authorial commentary in *Unfettered* challenges the critical notion that he was naive about the mechanics of narrative endings. Rather, he shrewdly recognizes the limits of romance for conveying his politicized message and then hybridizes the form by supplementing the novel's ending. Although the story line of *Unfettered* formally ends with marriage, Griggs intercedes to guide the audience's attention from the story's well-rounded ending to lingering, extratextual social dilemmas. Although the race problem is resolved within the fictional world of *Unfettered*, Griggs appends a fifty-two-page treatise to outline the still-present racial disparities for his actual readership. In "Dorlan's Plan: A Dissertation on the Race Problem," the author conveys his own social theories, while attributing them to the fictional Dorlan. Anticipating that readers may object to the move from fiction to nonfiction, Griggs uses false self-deprecation to signal his bait-and-switch strategy for closure. As he mentions in an authorial note preceding "Dorlan's Plan," readers attracted by the fictional plot now have to "wearily plod their way through the Plan . . . proclaiming what dull reading the Plan makes."[36] Meanwhile, the author "shall chuckle gleefully and rub [his] hands joyfully" at having gained readers' attention to serious matters.[37]

As in the authorial note in *Unfettered*, *Overshadowed* reveals Griggs's self-consciousness about structuring his novels to offer a clear social agenda while appealing to audiences' possible desire for an emotionally gratifying reading experience. In the preface to *Overshadowed*, the author indicates his purpose to grant "reverence . . . to the memory of those slain."[38] Likewise, the opening poem proposes, "To be true to life, the story must indeed be a somber one," and the dead ends throughout the text accord with this sentiment.[39] But what, readers might ask, is the use of attempting racial uplift through mobility if one merely and inevitably ends up dead, often as a direct or indirect result of one's class ambition? To move the audience beyond somberly mourning the wrongs against black Americans to anticipating and working toward future rights and opportunities, Griggs offers an intermediate, redemptive ending by allowing Erma to secure a gainful, middle-class marriage, albeit before her untimely death. Yet by accruing so many conflicting endings, *Overshadowed* casts doubt that the problems of elitism and racism that it engages can ever be concluded, either in the novel or in the real world.

The fast-dwindling cast of characters in *Overshadowed* indicates the effect of social death and physical demise for ambitious black Americans. Reading closely, one notes how frequently people go missing from the novel: many characters appear in only a few scenes before they meet their end or disappear for chapters at a time before surprisingly reemerging in the plot. Rather than reading this as a sign of Griggs's poor character development, suggesting that the author uses each character as an ideological mouthpiece and then discards it, we instead might ask what these characters' disappearances from the world of the text suggest about the parallel disappearance or marginalization of African Americans in the post-Reconstruction South.[40] Fictional instances that initially appear sensational or exceptional—including the kind of strikingly violent deaths that Elder catalogs as appearing throughout Griggs's novels—arise from the ordinary, precarious circumstances of African American life. Even those characters in *Overshadowed* who have few direct encounters with white Americans feel the effects of white supremacy, hiring discrimination, and elitism that shape and inevitably foil African Americans' advancement.

Griggs marks each black American's dead-end exit from the novel as a moment of heightened emotion, framing occasions of social or physical death within a range of modes from mild disappointment and humor to shame and grief over the seemingly needless loss or degradation of black lives. Each character employs a specific, fruitless strategy for attaining upward mobility: the Reverend Nerve, a local minister, desires to pursue education but instead attempts insurance fraud to gain money. Erma Wysong's brother, John, depends on the work ethic, but after an unfair dismissal from work, he turns to retaliatory homicide. Meanwhile, Erma's former classmate Margaret Marston attempts to gain status through the performance of gentility but then turns to a sexual liaison with a powerful white man. Erma alone withstands the temptations of immoral or extralegal means to move up the social ladder. Yet because her ending also is forecast early in the text, Griggs reveals how absolutely southern society constrains even the most respectable black Americans' from gaining the social status that would make them equal to their white counterparts.

Erma encounters loss from the opening pages of the story. As an orphan whose parents have died before the story's beginning, she is a likely model for testing the American myth that one's work ethic can earn due rewards. But unlike either the orphaned white females of the mid-nineteenth-century "woman's fiction" that Nina Baym categorizes or the white homeless youngsters of Horatio Alger's postbellum tales, Erma finds that additional stigmas attend her attempted rise as an African American working woman.[41] As one white man warns, ironically while plotting his own sexual conquest of Erma, "While there are service girls of sterling worth, a bad odor attaches to the calling."[42] Like historical African American household servants who were vulnerable to the sexual predations of their employers, Erma has few protections while working in a white household.[43] Though she manages to protect her virtue, hardships and losses diminish her initial optimism about the character-building qualities of physical labor.

As black Americans in *Overshadowed* realize that their individual strategies for gaining additional wealth or social status fail, each contemplates his or her situation in revelatory conversations, letters, and monologues that constitute the novel's most striking analyses of class fixity. The Reverend Nerve, a local unlettered minister who hopes to bolster his educational credentials, makes an untimely departure when he is unable to pierce the class boundaries erected within black communities. Speculating on why he was dismissed from a previous preaching position in Richmond, the Reverend Nerve explains:

> All-of-the-mulattoes, whose-skins-are-such-that-their-blue-blood-shows, have-decided-to-form-an-aristocracy. If-you-are-yellow-and-don't-work-any-with-your-hands, you-are-all-right. That-is-condition-number-one. If-you-are-black-and-don't-work-any-with-your-hands-and-are-smarter-than-the-whole-lot-of-them-blue-veiners-put-together, you-will-be-accepted-until-they-get-something-on-you. That-is-condition-number-two. . . . I-did-not-work-with-my-hands, but-I-was-not-smart-enough. So, being-black, they-put-me-out.[44]

In representing the minister's speech, Griggs goes beyond the usual heavy use of apostrophes, misspellings, and malapropisms that many nineteenth-century black and white authors used to represent black vernacular. Instead Griggs features dashes between each word, emphasizing the difficulty with which the Reverend Nerve attempts to imitate sophisticated enunciation. Just as the Reverend Nerve's diction draws attention to itself as performative and artificial, so, too, do the social standards of the black elite that he both critiques and envies. As an unlettered preacher, the Reverend Nerve is excluded by African Americans who, anxious to challenge stereotypes of racial inferiority, demand an educated clergy while devaluing folk wisdom, manual labor, and cross-class racial solidarity. The Reverend Nerve further points to colorism, the preoccupation with skin complexion, as foiling darker-skinned African Americans' progress up the social ladder. The minister articulates what appears to be Griggs's own point: that black intraracial stratifications based on skin color and occupation reinforce the exclusionary practices that racism already imposes on black communities.

The Reverend Nerve's subsequent disappearance contributes to the cumulative number of characters who encounter dead ends, whether as a result of structural inequities or personal negligence that seems at least partly related to the inequalities they face. Though the pastor observes that intraracial class bias may have led to his earlier dismissal, his former parishioners have likely expelled him because of his shady ethics. Readers can interpret the Reverend Nerve's analysis with a bit of humor when, in the following chapter, he burns down his present church to get the insurance money. Then "Rev. Josiah Nerve, D.D.S., was not heard from in Richmond again."[45] Though the Reverend Nerve is presented comically, Griggs posits Erma as the moral compass whose response models for readers a more sobering interpretation of the Reverend Nerve's fraudulent practices that lead to his self-exile. As the narrator explains, "The tragic, not the humorous in the experiences of Rev. Josiah Nerve, appealed to Erma."[46] As the Reverend Nerve stealthily leaves town to avoid investigators or church members who may have discovered his arson plot, Griggs shifts the judgment from the Reverend Nerve's individual improper behavior to the social exclusions that foreclose his legitimate rise.

In tracing the eventual dead end of one of Erma's former classmates, Margaret Marston, Griggs relies on a similar transition from humor to seriousness, a move that attempts to balance the entertaining and polemical intents of the novel. As a gatekeeper of the black elite, Margaret draws strict lines of exclusion against physical laborers, such as Erma, insisting that the black elite class must be distinguished by its leisure. Margaret herself is the daughter of a laundress, whose hard work barely affords Margaret's lifestyle as a black society belle. As Margaret expresses her intense unwillingness to work, despite the benefits her earnings could provide her family, Griggs satirizes her as so self-centered and irrational as to be laughable. She insists, "White girls occupying the social station in their race that we do in our race would suffer themselves to be carried out of their homes dead before they would perform such menial tasks" (37). Margaret hyperbolically associates labor with death, though it is her acute desire for upper-class luxuries that actually leads to her dead end. She later tries to parlay her status within segregated black communities into a parallel status across the color line by secretly courting a white politician. When he seduces Margaret, her misguided efforts at upward mobility lead to her dead end as a fallen or "ruined girl" (148).

Though the novel initially critiques Margaret and reveals her folly, one may conclude that her outcome also partly reflects the limited means by which southern black women legitimately may gain both wealth and public respectability, as enjoyed by the white women with whom Margaret compares herself. In a letter disclosing her pregnancy, Margaret pleads that other black women avoid the untoward advances of white men who promise them leisure, status, or material gain. Recognizing her racial and gender disadvantage, Margaret soberly ends by writing, "I go on my downward journey, and Mr. Christian moves upward to the highest places. . . . Farewell" (149). Banished from Richmond, Margaret goes pregnant and alone to New York, a morally forbidden urban landscape in nineteenth-century black fiction.[47] Compounded with the Reverend Nerve's dramatic exit, Margaret Marston's fateful end conforms to Griggs's pattern of exiling from the black community those African Americans who pursue an elite status in order to distance themselves from their working-class roots.

However, this pattern is not limited to those who privilege leisure and gentility over physical labor, for even black Americans who follow pragmatic career paths come to disconcerting ends. Erma's younger brother, John, deliberately foregoes a liberal education to pursue a trade, which he considers a sure, if less prestigious, means to financial solvency. In describing John's work experiences at the Bilgal Iron Works, Griggs raises and then deflates the reader's possible expectations that John's hard work will be rewarded according to the nation's myths of unbounded opportunity. As John anticipates a special meeting with his boss, he is "whistling and singing and planning great things out of his four dollars per day," confident that he will be offered a promotion.[48] Instead he is barred from the all-white labor union and fired. As John's dreams of career advancement are shattered undeservedly, Griggs introduces only the first of a sequence of dead ends that John encounters. Excluded from the work for which he has been trained, John can find work only as a low-paid, unskilled carriage driver, who, coincidentally, has to escort the "Master Workman of the Labor Union of the United States," the national union leader whose racially exclusive policies lead to John's firing. While serving as coachman for the master workman, John overhears his vehement antiblack speech: "So we of the Labor Unions have decided that either our homes must be crushed out or the Negro. . . . The Anglo-Saxon has never gotten anything for which he did not fight. . . . If a foe stands in our way, and nothing will dislodge him but death, then he must die."[49] Though the master workman speaks specifically on behalf of white organized labor, his sentiments more broadly indicate how thoroughly white supremacy authorizes and engineers many black Americans' inevitable dead ends. By pushing the union leader over a ledge to kill him, John puts into practice the master workman's own policy that one's economic competitors must be killed. Though John surreptitiously escapes execution for his crime, his conscience later leads him to concede to imprisonment, a condition that, as previously asserted, Griggs interprets as yet another form of living death.

With an established pattern of "offing" ambitious characters, the author misleads readers into anticipating such an ending before actually delivering it in Erma's case. In the chapter "Erma and an Assassin," the title presupposes a possible murder plot against Erma. Recognizing how Erma's upward mobility from servant girl to society belle transgresses the trenchant intraracial class hierarchy, black elite rivals hire someone to kill her. Yet in the suspenseful moment before the expected homicide, Griggs asserts humor and irony to lighten the tone. Startled by Erma's striking beauty, the assassin aborts his mission because he has been directed "to kill a woman, and, dad gum it, this is an angel."[50] Rather than concluding with a death, the chapter culminates with Erma's marriage to her longtime suitor, Astral Herndon, a doctor whose status confirms Erma's place in the black middle class. The narrator announces Erma's marriage by explaining, "Erma Wysong had passed away, and . . . it was happy Erma *Herndon* now."[51] The play on the phrase "passed away" serves to frustrate the envious characters who ordered Erma's murder, as well as to tease readers who may anticipate death as the heroine's expected outcome. In this instance, the narrative postpones Erma's physical death, though only to reserve it for more elaborate symbolism later in the novel.

In the interim, marriage serves as another form of closure in *Overshadowed*. As several feminist scholars have argued, female protagonists in nineteenth-century novels conventionally attain two possible outcomes: death or marriage. In one regard, as the narrative shifts from the female quest of a woman coming into her own, it appears that the married heroine's "prospects are scaled down . . . by the fulfillment of an inexorable communal wish for her romantic union and silence."[52] But rather than reading marriage as analogous to death or silence, recent critics argue that turn-of-the-century black writers and readers often interpreted marriage as mobilizing personal and racial advancement. Claudia Tate, Ann duCille, Frances Smith Foster and Tess Chakkalakal contend that the narrative trajectory toward marriage in African American literature can show, in Foster's words, how "African Americans considered themselves competent to define and to discipline, to regularize and record for themselves the most intimate aspects of their lives."[53] By allowing Erma to avert death at the hands of an assassin and instead enjoy marriage, Griggs both adheres to romantic conventions and endorses family as the locus of civil society. In one scene during which Erma is enjoying the pleasures of family life, however, a visitor interrupts the happily ever after of the conventional marriage plot. The emaciated, fugitive prisoner who comes to the Herndons' doorstep proves to be John Wysong, who had been legally sentenced to execution many years earlier. Unknown to Erma, John had avoided being hanged, but he willingly had resigned himself to imprisonment in Florida. He lands at the Herndon home moments before dying. And when Erma sees her dead brother, whom she thought had been killed many years ago, she, too, dies. By allowing Erma to die after she has achieved a middle-class marriage and family life, the novel shows how black Americans' everyday experiences prove to be as dangerous as the more spectacular murder plot forecast in the earlier chapter "Erma and an Assassin."

Because John has been absent from the plot for multiple chapters, his return from long confinement may be a surprise to the reader, as well as to Erma and her family. Griggs resurrects John in the plot only to have him die a more melodramatic death in his sister's presence. Erma invites the fugitive into her home, responding with compassion and curiosity that gives way to shock, as though she has encountered a ghost: "The longer she looked, the more and more her feelings began to assume definite form, and a sensation of terror crept over her until she had to get up and move away."[54] In many respects, John is a veritable ghost, a haunting figure whose protracted death reifies the effects of inequality. Denied both the rights and the means to pursue the class attainment he desires, John is rendered as "living dead" long before his actual demise. In such cases, as Russ Castronovo has proposed, "for a moment, literal and figurative meanings of death blur so that . . . severe estrangement from the community tracks across both simile and statement of fact."[55] Griggs shows that there is little difference between being an actual corpse and being an economically stifled black worker, "grabbing here and there in a desultory manner at every little job of work," a would-be hanging victim, or a prisoner suffering inhumane conditions in the state-sanctioned labor camps where John serves time.[56]

By provocatively titling the chapter in which the double deaths occur "Name the Chapter After You Read It," Griggs invites his audience, if not into the actual production of the text by sharing his pen, then into the process of interpreting the dead ends. Erma's husband, Astral, also tellingly interprets how the ailing and dead black body symbolizes the society's failures. As Astral describes, "[Erma] suffered countless ills. Her heart, unable longer to bear the strain, gave up the struggle and ceased its pulsations."[57] Likewise, because John is the model of the working-class work ethic gone awry, his haunting reappearance intrudes to demythologize black middle-class security. Grief stricken, Astral notes that his own domestic happiness and movement up the social ladder have been voided by the parallel course of "fate [that] had so needlessly reared a ladder to the unspotted blue of his sky, and climbing there, had fanned out the sun of his firmament."[58] The double death plot undermines the Herndons' middle-class achievement by showing that they cannot escape the realities of class inequality or racism experienced by most other black Americans.

The characters within *Overshadowed*, as well as the readers, are called to witness the spectacle of death and respond to it through the exercise of mourning. In the chapter "The Funeral," Erma's death opens up a space for interracial exchange, bringing together black and white mourners across race and class boundaries. In this regard, mourning becomes a politicized act to reconcile divided factions. White Americans who had known Erma challenge segregation practices, at least temporarily, and "petitioned that an opportunity be given them to publicly manifest their esteem" by attending the funeral.[59] Yet rather than endorsing grief as a universalized, transcendent mode that can smooth over differences, Astral uses the funeral rites as a platform for his hardhitting analysis, lobbying for an end to the inequity that leads to black Americans' death: "You now desire that [Erma's] body shall go to enrich this soil. . . . Will this land which her dust would help to compose—will this land render to the son of another mother more than it will to the son that [Erma] leaves behind? . . . You are unable to assure me that her son shall not be confronted with the same unequal conditions she so often encountered."[60] Associating Erma's decomposing body with the soil of the South, Astral powerfully ascertains how, as Holland argues, "the dead and the black subject all serve a double sentence in the national economy and imagination."[61] Though hyperbolic, Astral's statement exposes how black bodies contribute their labor to the U.S. economy, which perpetuates their continued exclusion or exploitation. This use of the black subject continues even after death, as the deceased becomes a symbol around which a nation, region, or group defines itself. Rather than allowing mourners to celebrate Erma's virtue alone, Astral emphasizes her victimization to show how she has been denied full citizenship in life and will not serve the nation in death. As he claims his wife's remains and exhumes his brother-in-law's body, Astral displaces the two from possible recirculation in the South's economy. Instead, after boarding a ship accompanied by his son and his family members' remains, Astral buries his wife in the ocean "because here there abides no social group in which conditions operate toward the over-shadowing of such elements as are not deemed assimilable." He declares, "And now, I, Astral Herndon, hereby and forever renounce all citizenship in all lands whatsoever, and constitute myself A CITIZEN OF THE OCEAN."[62]

Had the novel concluded with Astral's final words, "away, away, and away," *Overshadowed* would appear to privilege advocates who, at the turn of the twentieth century, contemplated whether African Americans' most advantageous environment might lie outside the United States. Yet Griggs opposed both black northward migration and back-to-Africa movements, insisting instead that African Americans could best prosper in the southern United States, if only allowed to do so.[63] To align the narrative's conclusion with his own sociopolitical stance, Griggs inserts a two-page epilogue that tempers Astral's proclamation. Using the first-person collective "we," the narrator recruits the reader in devising an alternative to the story's initially bitter ending: "We who have followed [Erma and Astral's] fortunes, lo, these many days, are loth to leave them until our minds can fasten on some circumstance external to our being, to confirm the thought that perennially rises within and bids us believe that their lives have not been spent in vain; that 'somehow good will be the final goal of ill.'"[64] The narrative intrusion works to restore faith among Griggs's mostly black readership in the ideal of ultimate good. Through this move to fashion a possibly hopeful moral, the epilogue contrasts the bitterness evident in the ending of works such as Dunbar's "One Man's Fortune," in which Bertram complains, "We have been taught that merit wins. But I have learned that the adages, as well as the books and the formulas were made by and for others than us of the black race."[65] Written for "the black race" by a self-published black author, Griggs's novel ultimately propounds the racial uplift rhetoric that Dunbar's character critiques as irrelevant or ineffective.

The epilogue reframes the symbolic meanings assigned to dead ends, extending the story's frame beyond Erma's death to her legacy. Titled "A Lay to the Coming King," the epilogue projects toward the future when Astral Jr. will recant his father's denunciation and instead work toward devising circumstances under which "the Negro shall emerge from his centuries of gloom, with a hope-emblazoned brow."[66] Strikingly, in a 1971 reprint of *Overshadowed* that omits the two-page epilogue, this omission might mislead readers about Griggs's final polemical message in the novel.[67] Read without the epilogue, the text seems to privilege Astral Sr.'s expatriate militancy, while the epilogue instead posits young Astral as a messianic figure for black Americans' socioeconomic and political advancement stateside. Noting how the black messiah figure functions in Griggs's fiction, as well as other American cultural representations, Wilson Moses explains, "The myth of black messianism reconciles the sense of separateness that black people feel and their fundamental belief that they are truly American. It is the point at which their black nationalism and their American nationalism overlap."[68] Griggs balances Erma's achievement of the ultimate upward mobility—presumably to heaven, in keeping with Griggs's own Protestant beliefs—with a prophecy of black Americans' rise into "the hall of fame."[69]

Despite beginning with a fairly large number of characters, *Overshadowed* concludes with two—Erma and Astral Jr., one dead, one alive—wholly responsible for redeeming hope from a history of death and loss. The novel's final exclamatory lines foretell a new beginning for African Americans and the South: "In that day, pleasing thought, Erma shall live again in the wondrous workings of the child whom she has brought to earth. All hail to Erma."[70] These final lines offer a reverent but celebratory tone that invests Erma with sacred and secular significance. As a holy mother valued for her reproductive capacities, Erma literally generates the change that society needs, Astral Jr. As a working woman who manages to move up the social ladder to the middle class (at least temporarily before her death), Erma provides the model of a work ethic that Griggs often exposes as limited, even while he perpetuates it.

Examining narrative closure in *Overshadowed* not only reveals Griggs's authorial strategies but also demands that we consider why mediating the relationship between the fictional ending and its real-life implications is significant enough for Griggs to belabor in ways I have proposed here. The provocative last sentence, "All hail to Erma," is, in fact, an invitation—or rather invocation—for the book to end and for readers to begin the process of interpretation by taking Erma as an exemplar. As Rabinowitz reminds us, "Last sentences, of course, cannot serve to focus a reading experience (at least, not an initial reading experience). But they do often serve to scaffold our retrospective interpretation of the book."[71] For its original readers, *Overshadowed* may have warranted such a retrospective, repeated analysis of its final lines. In a 1909 advertisement for the novel, one synopsis describes *Overshadowed* as a "charming story of which colored women especially never grow weary. Some have read it through as many as ten times."[72] Likely written by Griggs himself or a staff member of his firm, Orion Publishing, this promotional description strikingly mentions the audience's rereading, a process that is, as Taha explains, a "post-ending activity."[73] Rereading both relishes and nullifies the work of arriving at the novel's end by starting all over again. In rereading *Overshadowed*, the audience repeatedly memorializes Erma Wysong, just as elicited by the concluding line, "All hail to Erma."[74] Like Griggs's act of writing the novel, the audience's re-creative act of reading, rereading, and interpreting the text becomes part of the politics of mourning to foster better conditions for ambitious African Americans.

By highlighting the dead ends that upwardly mobile black Americans encounter in the segregated South, *Overshadowed* offers an account of loss that eventually is mitigated by the promise of hope. As southern blacks such as John Wysong, the Reverend Nerve, and Margaret Marston lose their livelihoods or lives, the narrative exposes the difficulty and near futility of black upward mobility. Yet the serial turns in Erma's outcome—first her marriage, then her tragic but glorified death, followed by her family's radical expatriatism, and finally her son's imminent repatriation—display the intense authorial labor Griggs exerts to make black Americans' endings presentable, and even inspiring, for his readers. Griggs transforms death, loss, and mourning not only to shape a positive response to his novel but, more importantly, to promote the epilogue's injunction to "calmly abide" while nonviolently working toward socioeconomic and political change.[75] *Overshadowed* evades finite closure because, as Griggs offers in the novel's preface, the "attempt of the Negro to journey by the side of the white man . . . [is] still in process of unfoldment."[76] Just as the loose ends of Griggs's fiction invited his first, turn-of-the-century readers to return to the text, modern readers can reassess Griggs's strategies for narrative closure to trace his shrewd understandings of race, class, and novelistic form.

Notes

1. Sutton Griggs, *Overshadowed* (Nashville: Orion, 1901), 218.

2. Hugh M. Gloster, "Sutton E. Griggs, Novelist of the New Negro," *Phylon* 4, no. 4 (1943): 337, 345.

3. Jerry Bryant, *Victims and Heroes: Racial Violence in the African American Novel* (Amherst: University of Massachusetts Press, 1997), 91.

4. Maria Karafilis, "Oratory, Embodiment, and U.S. Citizenship in Sutton E. Griggs's *Imperium in Imperio,*" *African American Review* 40, no. 1 (2006): 141.

5. Peter Rabinowitz, "Reading Beginnings and Endings," in *Narrative Dynamics: Essays on Time, Plot, Closure and Frames*, ed. Brian Richardson (Columbus: Ohio State University Press, 2002), 300.

6. Ibid., 303.

7. Ibid., 306.

8. Ibrahim Taha, "Semiotics of *Ending* and *Closure*: Post-ending Activity of the Reader," *Semiotica* 138, no. 1–4 (2002): 260.

9. Griggs, *Overshadowed*, 219.

10. Russell Reising, *Loose Ends: Closure and Crisis in the American Social Text* (Durham, N.C.: Duke University Press, 1996), 11.

11. Ibid., 3.

12. Orlando Patterson, *Slavery and Social Death: A Comparative Study* (Cambridge, Mass.: Harvard University Press, 1982), 41.

13. Ibid., 76.

14. Griggs, *Overshadowed*, 175.

15. Sharon Patricia Holland, *Raising the Dead: Readings of Death and (Black) Subjectivity* (Durham, N.C.: Duke University Press, 2000), 5.

16. Karla F. C. Holloway, *Passed On: African American Mourning Stories* (Durham, N.C.: Duke University Press, 2002), 6.

17. Referring specifically to the deaths of an African American couple in Griggs's novel *The Hindered Hand* (1905), Holloway surmises, "Griggs's scene foreshadowed the role lynching would play in both black literature and black life." Holloway's focus on violent death in this passage leads her to highlight one of the most often cited, gruesome deaths in Griggs's fiction, but a broader survey of his oeuvre reveals the author's sustained attention to mortality and more-figurative dead ends. Holloway, *Passed On*, 61.

18. Arlene A. Elder, *The "Hindered Hand": Cultural Implications of Early African-American Fiction* (Westport, Conn.: Greenwood, 1978), 72.

19. Ibid., 72.

20. Linda Williams, *Playing the Race Card: Melodramas of Black and White from Uncle Tom to O. J. Simpson* (Princeton, N.J.: Princeton University Press, 2001), 9.

21. David L. Eng and David Kazanjian, *Loss: The Politics of Mourning* (Berkeley: University of California Press, 2003), 2.

22. Ibid., emphasis added.

23. W. E. B. Du Bois's *The Philadelphia Negro* offers one account of the existence of a class he alternately terms "well-to-do" and "the 'middle classes' and those above." Du Bois, *The Philadelphia Negro: A Social Study*, ed. Elijah Anderson (1899; repr., Philadelphia: University of Pennsylvania Press, 1996), 311, 60. Likewise, more recent "community-based studies" of the black middle class focus on its late nineteenth-century formation in particular locations, such as Birmingham, Charlotte, Atlanta, Boston, and Washington, D.C. See Joseph O. Jewell, *Race, Social Reform, and the Making of a Middle Class: The American Missionary Association and Black Atlanta, 1870–1900* (Lanham, Md.: Rowman & Littlefield, 2007), 185.

24. Jewell, *Race, Social Reform*, 72.

25. W. E. B. Du Bois, *The Souls of Black Folk*, in *Oxford W. E. B. Du Bois Reader*, ed. Eric J. Sundquist (1903; repr., New York: Oxford University Press, 1996), 228.

26. Paul Laurence Dunbar, "One Man's Fortunes," in *The Complete Stories of Paul*

Laurence Dunbar, ed. Gene Andrew Jarrett and Thomas Lewis Morgan (Athens: Ohio University Press, 2005), 138.

27. Ibid., 139, original emphasis.

28. Ida B. Wells, "Lynch Law in All Its Phases," in *With Pen and Voice: A Critical Anthology of Nineteenth-Century African-American Women*, ed. Shirley Wilson Logan (Carbondale: Southern Illinois University Press, 1995), 81.

29. Ibid., 86.

30. Griggs, *Overshadowed*, 100.

31. Sutton Griggs, *Imperium in Imperio* (1899; repr., New York: Modern Library, 2003), 177.

32. Stephen Knadler, "Sensationalizing Patriotism: Sutton Griggs and the Sentimental Nationalism of Citizen Tom," *American Literature* 79, no. 4 (2007): 694.

33. Finnie D. Coleman, *Sutton E. Griggs and the Struggle against White Supremacy* (Knoxville: University of Tennessee Press, 2007), 21.

34. Sutton Griggs, *Unfettered* (1902; repr., New York: AMS, 1971), 174.

35. Ibid., 215.

36. Ibid., 220, 221.

37. Ibid., 221.

38. Griggs, *Overshadowed*, 6.

39. Ibid., 7.

40. I find useful here a similar observation that M. Giulia Fabi makes about the plotting and characterization in William Wells Brown's *Clotel; or, The President's Daughter* (1853). As Fabi suggests, "having characters appear and disappear without previous notice from the text . . . gives [the] audience a readerly experience of the familial disruption caused by slavery." Fabi, introduction to *Clotel: or, The President's Daughter*, by William Wells Brown (New York: Penguin, 2004), xvii. This pattern of disappearing characters has a comparable effect in Griggs's novel, as he indicates how black lives are disrupted and treated as expendable at the turn of the century. In only one instance is such a disappearance favorably depicted in *Overshadowed*. When, in the novel's early pages, Astral Sr. leaves Richmond to attend medical school, his later return and betrothal affirm his middle-class status.

41. See Nina Baym, *Woman's Fiction: A Guide to Novels by and about Women in America, 1820–1870* (Urbana: University of Illinois Press, 1993).

42. Griggs, *Overshadowed*, 48.

43. For historical accounts of turn-of-the-century black working women's sexual exploitation at the hands of white men, as well as black women's strategies for resisting such predations, see Tera Hunter, *To 'Joy My Freedom: Southern Black Women's Lives and Labors after the Civil War* (Cambridge, Mass.: Harvard University Press, 1997); Jacqueline Jones, *Labor of Love, Labor of Sorrow: Black Women, Work and the Family, from Slavery to the Present* (New York: Vintage, 1985); Darlene Clark Hine, "Rape and the Inner Lives of Black Women in the Middle West: Preliminary Thoughts on the Culture of Dissemblance," in *Words of Fire: An Anthology of African-American Feminist Thought*, ed. Beverly Guy-Sheftall (New York: New Press, 1995), 380–87.

44. Griggs, *Overshadowed*, 63–64.

45. Ibid., 81.

46. Ibid.

47. Critics disagree whether Margaret Marston's pregnancy signifies an irrevocable dead end to her class ascendancy. John Vassilowitch Jr.—one of the few critics to focus specifically on *Overshadowed*, rather than examining it as part of a survey of all Griggs's fiction—suggests that Marston's outcome after leaving Richmond is "left an open question" ("The Example of 'Horace Christian': A Central Irony in *Overshadowed*," *American Literary Realism* 14, no. 1 [1981]: 68). My reading of Margaret's exile is more in concert with Arlene Elder's observation that the chance that Marston "will succeed in salvaging her life seems unlikely." Elder, "*Hindered Hand*", 81. I interpret Marston's banishment within the novel's sequence of black Americans' increasingly severe downward class mobility or immobility.

48. Griggs, *Overshadowed*, 92.

49. Ibid., 100, 101.

50. Ibid., 196.

51. Ibid., original emphasis.

52. Alison Booth, ed., *Famous Last Words: Changes in Gender and Narrative Closure* (Charlottesville: University Press of Virginia, 1993), 2. For studies of contemporary women writers who complicate or subvert marriage and death as devices of narrative closure, see also Rachel Blau DuPlessis, *Writing beyond the Ending: Narrative Strategies of Twentieth-Century Women Writers* (Bloomington: Indiana University Press, 1985); Laura Doan, ed., *Old Maids to Radical Spinsters: Unmarried Women in the Twentieth-Century Novel* (Urbana: University of Illinois Press, 1991).

53. Frances Smith Foster, *Love and Marriage in Early African America* (Boston: Northeastern University Press, 2008), xxii. See also Claudia Tate, *Domestic Allegories of Political Desire: The Black Heroine's Text at the Turn of the Century* (New York: Oxford, 1992); Ann duCille, *The Coupling Convention: Sex, Text, and Tradition in Black Women's Fiction* (New York: Oxford University Press, 1993); Tess Chakkalakal, *Novel Bondage: Slavery, Marriage, and Freedom in Nineteenth-Century America* (Urbana: University of Illinois Press, 2011).

54. Griggs, *Overshadowed*, 203.

55. Russ Castronovo, *Necro Citizenship: Death, Eroticism, and the Public Sphere in the Nineteenth-Century United States* (Durham, N.C.: Duke University Press, 2001), xi.

56. Griggs, *Overshadowed*, 98.

57. Ibid., 211.

58. Ibid., 206.

59. Ibid., 209.

60. Ibid., 211–12.

61. Holland, *Raising the Dead*, 25.

62. Griggs, *Overshadowed*, 217.

63. Coleman, *Sutton E. Griggs*, 74.

64. Griggs, *Overshadowed*, 218.

65. Dunbar, "One Man's Fortunes," 160.

66. Griggs, *Overshadowed*, 219.

67. Throughout this essay, I refer to the first edition of the novel. It is unclear whether the omission in the 1971 reprint by Books for Libraries (Freeport, N.Y.) occurs as a technical error or as a deliberate, politicized omission by the modern-day editor in favor of Astral Sr.'s expatriatism.

68. Wilson Moses, *Black Messiahs and Uncle Toms: Social and Literary Manipulations of a Religious Myth* (University Park: Pennsylvania State University Press, 1982), xiii.

69. Griggs, *Overshadowed*, 219.

70. Ibid., 218.

71. Rabinowitz, "Reading Beginnings and Endings," 303.

72. This advertisement is featured as the back matter of one of Griggs's later nonfiction volumes, *The Race Question in a New Light* (Nashville: Orion, 1909).

73. Taha, "*Ending* and *Closure*," 263.

74. Griggs, *Overshadowed*, 218.

75. Ibid., 219.

76. Ibid., 6.

FINNIE COLEMAN

Social Darwinism, American Imperialism, and the Origins of the Science of Collective Efficiency in Sutton E. Griggs's *Unfettered*

Of the five academic disciplines Griggs references in his definition of the Science of Collective Efficiency, I am most interested in theories and ideas he selects from sociology and history and how he uses them to illuminate the contemporary events and issues that dominate his fiction.[1] It is noteworthy that Griggs does not mention religion or religious studies as one of the disciplines that inform his "science." Understanding that Griggs was a seminary-trained Baptist minister from a prominent religious family, we are left to speculate about why he does not include his religious training as an important influence in his most important theory. Not until *Kingdom Builders' Manual*, late in his career, do we see Griggs turn his hand to explicitly nonsecular writing. In this chapter I focus on two texts, Griggs's *Science of Collective Efficiency* (1921) and his third novel, *Unfettered; or, Dorlan's Plan* (1902).

My work here shares some resonances with Eric Curry's exceptional article "The Power of Combinations: Sutton Griggs' *Imperium in Imperio* and the Science of Collective Efficiency," where Curry uses Griggs's *Guide to Racial Greatness* (1925) to contextualize his reading of *Imperium in Imperio*. This work does much to eliminate our ignorance of the *Guide* and offers another engaging reading of *Imperium*. Curry treats these two texts as bookends to Griggs's career, "first and final efforts," even though Griggs continued to publish until at least 1930. *Missing Links, or Unfolding the World's Greatest Mystery* (1923), *Kingdom Builders' Manual: Companion Book to Guide to Racial Greatness* (1924), *Negroes Steadily Recording Progress* (1924), *Triumph of the Simple Virtues, or, The Life Story of John L. Webb* (1926), and *Co-operative Natures and Social Education: A Philosophy of Civic Life* (1929) are the primary works in the final period of Griggs's career, when he offers his first nonsecular text, completes his first and only biography, and begins reformulating the Science of Collective Efficiency with an eye toward building autonomous civic institutions dedicated to social and economic uplift. These institutions would complement the black church and black academic institutions that provided black America with spiritual and intellectual uplift. *The Guide to Racial Greatness* punctuates this final period of scholarly activity, but it does not mark the end of a career. While the *Guide* is the fullest articulation of the Science of Collective Efficiency, the more concise *The Science of Collective Efficiency* summarizes more than twenty years of thinking about the causes and cures for the so-called Negro Problem and marks the first mature version of Griggs's most important contribution to racial uplift doctrine. Given the fact that the specific teachings of social Darwinism circulate more prominently in *Unfettered* than in any of Griggs's other works of fiction, this least-studied novel helps us to trace the intellectual roots of the "Science of Collective Efficiency" more succinctly than any of his other works of fiction, including *Imperium in Imperio*.[2]

Like Curry, I see the value in revisiting the key tenets of the Science of Collective Efficiency, but not to formulate a lens for reading Griggs's fiction. For me, the Science of Collective Efficiency reflects the maturation of a body of thought that was still evolving when Griggs penned his early novels. In these novels we see Griggs struggling with the various contradictions that attend racial uplift doctrine at the end of the nineteenth century. Whereas Curry is interested in using the Science of Collective Efficiency to inform his reading of Griggs's fiction, I revisit Griggs's fiction to more closely observe the incubation of the Science of Collective Efficiency. Historical context and the array of archetypal structures that Griggs deploys are important to my reading of his fiction. For that reason, I devote time here to reviewing the key tenets of the Science of Collective Efficiency, discussing the historical milieu that Griggs wrote from and about, teasing out a fundamental architecture for his fiction, and discussing how that architecture worked to advance the tenets of social Darwinism that shape both his fiction and his subsequent political writings. In the process, I hope to shed additional light on Griggs the person. As we look deeper into Griggs's life and work, we find that while he was a prolific writer, he was by no means universally popular in the black community.

Griggs begins the *Science* by drawing distinctions between two categories of beings that may be found in groups of animals or humans, individualistic and cooperative. Griggs goes on to argue that human communities are successful or unsuccessful depending on how well they meet their "Joint Tasks." Griggs believed that a group "possesses collective efficiency when it has the capacity for, and the habit of concentrating all of its potential and necessary forces behind the joint tasks of mankind." Using terms like "social paralysis," "social deformity," and "social epilepsy," Griggs constructs an analogy between the social interactions and the healthy functioning of the human body. Communities that fail to manifest collective efficiency in their daily interactions (internal and external) risk more than maladies and illnesses; those communities risk death. For Griggs, the "Negro Problem" seems to have been two-tiered. The first tier involved resolving the disjuncture between the national reality for blacks and what Gunnar Myrdal would eventually describe as the "American Creed," which called for fair treatment and equal opportunity for all American citizens, unfettered access to the American dream. The first tier of the problem required resolving the dysfunctional relationship between blacks and whites, a process that lay largely in the hands of whites. The second tier concerned resolving what Griggs felt were internal failings of the black community, failings that could only be rectified by blacks. In Griggs's estimation, this second tier of the "Negro Problem" had to be resolved before blacks could expect broader results in the first tier. The Science of Collective Efficiency systematically addresses the second-tier concerns, paying close attention to characteristics of the black community that Griggs felt were self-defeating or destructive.

Griggs especially despised black-on-black violence and felt that the "common" element in the black community should submit to the leadership of the Talented Tenth, who could help to extirpate embarrassing, antisocial behaviors. For Griggs, any submission to leadership was complicated by what he saw as unconscionable divisiveness even among black leaders themselves. If the community intended to survive, it would have to learn how to choose strong leaders and then champion those leaders as they assumed the business of leadership. Good choices were important but just as important were processes by which mistakes could be rectified without damaging the progress that the group had made. If the black community could accomplish these things, it could then begin moving toward earning the esteem and admiration of other races. It would be important for all members of the black community to cultivate the goodwill of other racial groups. Griggs believed that this would require a transformation of the very nature of the black community, a nature that Griggs believed was steeped in individualism. For Griggs, the absence of cooperation among blacks was the most debilitating of all the community's faults.

Collective Efficiency would be something that the black community would have to work hard to develop, but it was possible. All the community had to do was embrace a stronger moral foundation, strengthen its mental traits, and develop a temperament different from the one that other races had come to attribute to the group. The ten "Joint Tasks of Mankind" and the "Essential Traits" central to the Science of Collective Efficiency directly address the very specific issues Griggs sees in the black community that he and others attributed to the "nature" of black folk and flaws in that community's social inheritance. These ideas did not, of course, come to Griggs as he was writing *The Science of Collective Efficiency*, though it is clear from the text that he was drawing his ideas almost verbatim from Benjamin Kidd's recently published *Science of Power* (1918). Appreciating how Griggs arrives at his "New Science" requires a bit of historical contextualization. We quickly find that Griggs's reliance on Benjamin Kidd was anything but new in 1921.

Rapid advancement in technologies, paradigmatic shifts in communication technologies, the potential for dramatic extension of human life expectancy, pressure to move from one energy family to another, unprecedented upheaval in financial markets, the omnipresence of war, and fundamental shifts in social relations are but some of the issues, problems, advances, and opportunities that colored life in the United States of America in the late 1900s. One might argue cogently that success or failure in managing watershed moments in national histories may rest in how well or how poorly intellectual and political leaders understand concomitant shifts in human psychology and behavior. In our readings of Griggs's Science of Collective Efficiency, we see that Griggs understood these shifts as black communities, North and South, began to prepare for life in post–World War I America. Griggs rightly imagined that the rapid advancement in technologies, new methods of communicating, advances in biology and medicine, dramatic economic growth, and the birth and surprisingly solid growth of the black middle class would fundamentally change the world for blacks at home and abroad.

The rapidly deteriorating political and social conditions for blacks in the 1890s were inextricably bound to broader shifts in American society wrought by the Second Industrial Revolution (1870–1914). This revolution brought with it unprecedented change in the material realities of people around the world. Many of the inventions, micro-inventions, and technological advancements that we associate with this revolution were brought to market before Griggs was born in 1872. Crude oil products had replaced whale oil as a common source of energy, and the Bessemer process, the telegraph, the cable car, the electric light bulb, and even the vacuum cleaner had already significantly impacted the world before Griggs was born. However, it was during his youth that the most impactful advances were made: the telephone eclipsed the telegraph, germ theory led to the development of preventative and life-saving vaccinations, electricity became a medium for conducting kinetic energy for common use inside the home, and the automobile had begun replacing the horse and buggy. Although paradigm shifts in communication, medical advances, and unprecedented social upheaval dominate our memory of the past, the combination of mechanization and applied technology produced the greatest impact on American society. These innovations were all geared toward improving "efficiency," the hallmark of Progressive Era thinking. These efficiencies would generate surpluses that would support the rapid expansion of the middle classes in the United States, Britain, and Europe more generally.

Depending on one's race, ethnicity, or place of origin, the technological advancements made during the Second Industrial Revolution proved to be a mixed blessing, for the fruits of these advancements were jealously guarded and systematically disseminated. While the inequitable distribution of wealth and other benefits of the revolution changed the world, that change did not cause late nineteenth- and early twentieth-century thinkers to move beyond cursory reevaluations of and challenges to existing systems of privilege based on race. In fact, just the opposite is true of the era's greatest thinkers; instead of challenging the status quo where race, class, and gender biases were concerned, the majority of intellectuals actually strengthened existing hegemonic structures. Instead of improving the world for all humanity, scientists, pseudoscientists, and sociologists of all stripes joined with politicians, liberal and conservative, to effectually tighten economic, social, and political strictures on people of color not just in the United States but around the world. The result was devastating for non-Europeans because any benefits that accrued to them would be largely tangential, ancillary, "trickle-down" benefits. This was especially true where access to and exploitation of economic markets was concerned. Policing the discontent produced by these inequities required the development of tiered social-justice systems derived from caste-based systems of privilege concocted during slavery.

The Second Industrial Revolution saw European and American societies redouble their commitment to mercantilism, the same economic philosophy that dominated economic thought and practice during the first Industrial Revolution (1760–1830). Ironically, the insistence on having national exports exceed imports resulted from the notion that national wealth consisted of the resources within a nation's borders. The expansion and redefinition of national borders promulgated by advances in maritime travel and mobility of military technologies produced the world's most aggressive strain of imperialism. This unswerving commitment to mercantilism came with another fateful twist; greater productivity and efficiency fostered by advances in industrial processes, the expansion of existing markets, and the creation of new markets led to revisions of colonialism as a viable economic model. This new brand of imperialism forced the conversion of the colonial subject from "reluctant producer" of low- or zero-cost raw materials for use by the mother country to "eager consumer" of finished products shipped to the colonies from homeland factories. This conversion entailed additional inequities, instances of wanton abuse, and otherwise unconscionable exploitation of non-Europeans that were rarely questioned at the time, never extirpated, and continue to fester in today's global marketplace.

The philosophical contradictions of empire were glaring and simply could not go unjustified. As during the Enlightenment period, late nineteenth-century European governments and principalities turned to the intelligentsia to provide a philosophical rationale for the dominance and subjugation that accompanied their racially inflected imperialist expansion. Though the term is anachronistic for that period, "social Darwinism" was ready-made for just this purpose.[3] If we are not careful, we might accept at face value claims that social Darwinists like William Graham Sumner, Herbert Spencer, Francis Galton, and Benjamin Kidd overextended Charles Darwin's work with animal species, applying what they learned about rules governing the animal kingdom to the governance of human society, a ready intellectual rationale for imperialist expansionism. To accept this claim is to fail to differentiate between the various species of political, social, economic, and biological determinism synonymous with the term "social Darwinism." In truth, it is the biological determinism associated with the term that modern-day scholars find most repugnant, especially where earlier thinkers conflated race, culture, and ethnicity. Scientific racism was but part of a much more convoluted complex of ideas that supported imperialism. In fairness to Spencer and Sumner in particular, neither economist actually supported the notion of natural selection being used to explain societal or cultural efficiencies and inefficiencies.[4] What these scholars did do, however, was to revise intellectually dishonest ideas inherited from Enlightenment thinkers to fit the racial dynamics and exigencies of their moment.

The intellectual inheritance from the Enlightenment came with significant flaws that fin de siècle thinkers did not challenge before accepting. Sutton E. Griggs believed that the worst of these flaws involved assumptions about the negative aspects of human nature, which were used to justify ideas and behavior ranging from supporting the idea that whole groups of men and women were "naturally inferior" to other groups to excusing the remarkable aggression associated with imperialism, as if that aggression were a "natural" rather than a preternatural reality. Griggs's ideas and preoccupations about human psychology and sociology can be traced back to the works of Sigmund Freud, Benjamin Kidd, Herbert Spencer, and Karl Marx. Griggs relied heavily on these thinkers as he attempted to resolve the conflict between his positivist conceptualizations of humanity and the negativity that colored "accepted theory."

While shaping the general contours of *The Science of Collective Efficiency*, Griggs took prominent cues about "social efficiency" from Benjamin Kidd, who in 1911 wrote the *Encyclopedia Britannica* entry defining sociology. It is useful to quote that entire entry:

> In trine of the evolutionary view, the development of human society is regarded as the product of a process of stress, in which progress results from natural selection along the line not of least effort in realizing human desire, but of the highest social efficiency in the struggle for existence of the materials of which society is composed. In the intensity of this process society, evolving towards higher efficiency, tends to become increasingly organic, the distinctive feature being the growing subordination of the individual to the organic social process. All the tendencies of development—political, economic, ethical and psychological—and the contents of the human mind itself, have therefore to be regarded as having ultimate relations to the governing principles of the process as a whole. The science of social evolution has, in short, to be considered, according to this view, as the science of the causes and principles subordinating the individual to a process developing by inherent necessity towards social efficiency, and therefore as ultimately over-ruling all desires and interests in the individual towards the highest social potentiality of the materials of which society is composed.[5]

This biblically sanctioned point about self-sacrifice was one with which Griggs was familiar. Citing John 18:14, Griggs makes this specific point in "Dorlan's

Plan" regarding the expediency of an individual perishing for the benefit of the group. Throughout his career, Griggs demonstrated that he was personally committed to this pillar of the Science of Collective Efficiency and wrote it into virtually every chapter of *Unfettered*.

Even though *Unfettered* has not garnered much critical attention, the novel demonstrates that Griggs was as deeply engaged in the intellectual debates of his day as any other "American" writer of the period and cognizant of the day-to-day injustices endured by the black community. And while some scholars have dismissed Griggs as an "old-fashioned southerner," there is much to be said for him as a thinker and lay sociologist trying to develop a systematic approach to the issues of his day. The aforementioned "Dorlan's Plan" is a sixty-page "dissertation on the Race Problem" that Griggs appends to *Unfettered*.

In *Unfettered*, the stakes are the highest in any of Griggs's novels, in that Dorlan Warthell must literally "solve the race problem" if he is to win the hand of Morlene Dalton, who unsurprisingly is herself a paragon of intelligence, morality, and beauty. These variations on common themes and characterization do not in themselves create significant distance between *Unfettered* and Griggs's other novels. What does set this novel apart from his other fiction is the manner in which Griggs imagines real-life occurrences in *Unfettered*. While Beulah's lynching sounds familiar, Griggs does not write any identifiable specific event or personage into the novel. Instead, in support of the novel's philosophical contentions, Griggs has his characters reference specific texts from his intellectual benefactors. Most of Griggs's readers would not have known a great deal about the works of evangelist and professor Henry Drummond, Columbia University sociologist Franklin Henry Giddings, biologist Thomas Henry Huxley, sociologist Benjamin Kidd, historian William E. Lecky, and, most important, the eminent biologist, philosopher, and sociologist Herbert Spencer, all of whom are written into the novel. It is also noteworthy that with the exception of Giddings, all these scholars hailed from the British Isles. The Spanish-American War (1898–1902) and the potentially dangerous generational shifts in white supremacy in the United States during the Progressive Era (1890–1920) figure more prominently in *Unfettered* than in any of his other novels. Griggs understood that white supremacy as an overarching national ideology was inherently dangerous and that this ideology would become even more dangerous in a country that embraced the naturalistic tenets of expansionism and the logic of imperialism. In his first three novels, Griggs foretells the horrific consequences that would result from yoking superabundant resources to Nietzsche's notion of "the will to power," driven by a nationalistic political philosophy akin to the United States' Manifest Destiny. In *Unfettered*, Griggs leverages the research of the aforementioned scholars to illuminate the contours of the "Negro Problem" and then actively revises their work to craft specific strategies for the advancement of the black community and thus produces the rudiments of his *Science of Collective Efficiency*.

Questioning traditional black loyalty to the Republican Party forms one of the central tensions of *Unfettered*. Griggs first touched on that tension in *Imperium in Imperio* and again in *Overshadowed*. In both of these earlier novels, he arrives at fantastic alternatives for casting off ties to the Republican Party that constituted an underexamined barrier to full political expression by members of the black community. In route to these alternatives, Griggs developed six postulates that would find their fullest expression in *Unfettered*. (1) The greatest challenge the nation faced was the race or "Negro Problem"; (2) white America was unable or unwilling to solve the "Negro Problem"; and (3) neither the Democratic Party nor the Republican Party could be depended on to address the problem. (4) Consequently, blacks were essentially a nation within a nation; (5) Africans—and by extension blacks in America—were in fact late arriving at the table of civilization and were by dint of time socially inferior to the more advanced civilizations of the earth. (6) The "New Negro" armed with social Darwinist theories about the true nature of the black community was actually capable of solving the race problem.

When Griggs published *Friction between the Races: Causes and Cure* in 1930, the "Negro Problem" remained alive and well. The truth that Griggs faced at the end of his life was that progress toward "solving" the problem had been incremental, and although white Americans in greater numbers spoke out passionately against racial injustices, very little progress had been made toward having large numbers of whites in various walks of American life take the lead in addressing one of the nation's greatest shames. Segregation persisted in the United States, and Jim Crow laws governed social and political relations in the South and much of the North. Griggs also continued to believe that black America lagged behind white America in most respects. He also had not abandoned the idea that adherence to his Science of Collective Efficiency would lead the black community toward resolution of the "Negro Problem." Although the world had changed forever, these things remained stubbornly in place. In 1902, however, Griggs wrote with a sense of possibility.

Of course, Griggs was not alone in his beliefs regarding most of these postulates, especially the first: *the greatest challenge the nation faced was the race or "Negro Problem."* In the oft-quoted proclamation that opens the second chapter of *The Souls of Black Folk* (1903), W. E. B. Du Bois offers the most recognizable rendering of this postulate:

> THE PROBLEM of the twentieth century is the problem of the color-line,—the relation of the darker to the lighter races of men in Asia and Africa, in America and the islands of the sea. It was a phase of this problem that caused the Civil War; and however much they who marched South and North in 1861 may have fixed on the technical points of union and local autonomy as a shibboleth, all nevertheless knew, as we know, that the question of Negro slavery was the real cause of the conflict. Curious it was, too, how this deeper question ever forced itself to the surface despite effort and disclaimer. No sooner had Northern armies touched Southern soil than this old question, newly guised, sprang from the earth,—What shall be done with Negroes?[6]

Griggs did not question the key tenets of social Darwinism but was suspicious of the imperialist impulse influencing American foreign policy and directly threatening the window of opportunity offered by the Science of Collective Efficiency. His critique of imperialism was essential to his attempt to successfully address the "Negro Problem" before that window closed. It must be noted, however, that Griggs's work was complicated by the fact that there was no clear consensus on the nature of the problem and no clearly defined plan for how to best proceed; merely criticizing white America for not doing more would not be enough to solve the problem. A look at Griggs's intellectual debt to Frederick Douglass helps us to recognize the multiple perspectives (complicating factors) surrounding the very essence of the "problem." It also reveals one of Griggs's more questionable rhetorical strategies.

Griggs begins "Dorlan's Plan" with words from Frederick Douglass's memorable speech "The Lessons of the Hour," delivered in 1894 to the Metropolitan African Methodist Episcopalian Church in Washington, D.C., a speech that was especially useful to Griggs as he wrote *Unfettered*: "The solution of the Negro Problem involves the honor or dishonor, the glory or shame, the happiness or misery of the entire American people."[7] Capturing his contention that the "Negro Problem" was at core an "American" problem, Douglass's speech touches on each of the novel's major themes: lynching, mob violence, disenfranchisement, and the embrace of expansionism in American political life. Reversals or accommodations of Douglass's ruminations alleging indolence on the part of white southerners, the exploitation of black labor, notions of a separate political party for blacks, the baseness of the new generation of whites, and the supposed nobility of former slaveholders all factor prominently in the plot of *Unfettered*. Although Griggs uses this speech to suggest that the preceding generation was exhorting the coming generation to take up the mantle and responsibility for solving the "Negro Problem," a signal difference emerges between Douglass's and Griggs's perspectives on the matter. Douglass asserted,

> There is one thing, however, in which I think we shall all agree at the start. It is that the so-called, but miscalled, negro problem is one of the most important and urgent subjects that can now engage public attention. It is worthy of the most earnest consideration of every patriotic American citizen. Its solution involves the honor or dishonor, glory or shame, happiness or misery of the whole American people. It involves more. It touches deeply not only the good name and fame of the Republic, but its highest moral welfare and its permanent safety. Plainly enough the peril it involves is great, obvious and increasing, and should be removed without delay.[8]

In sharp contrast to Griggs, Douglass argued that blacks were not the cause of the problem nor could they be expected to solve the problem. Douglass proudly defied the notion that blacks were somehow morally or physically less than whites. Douglass pilloried those who would claim that black men had developed a new penchant for raping white women when nary an instance could be substantiated during the Civil War when black men had unprecedented access to white women in the South or during Reconstruction, when they had greater access to power. Douglass believed that lynching and "Mobocracy" were but the latest tools of white supremacists who used "slave revolt" conspiracies to justify their violent treatment of blacks during slavery and "negro domination" to justify similar treatment during Reconstruction. For him, the rape of white women was an absolutely pathetic shibboleth for the disenfranchisement of an entire people.[9] Douglass argued that the "Negro Problem" would end only when whites changed *their* behavior and not before then. Blacks were largely hard-working, law-abiding citizens who did not lynch, did not mob, did not strip away the rights of others, who did not believe that they as a group should rule over any other group in an ostensibly "free" nation. Moreover, Douglass made clear that if whites were taken at their word, then it was obvious that *white America was unable or unwilling to solve the "Negro Problem,"* Griggs's second postulate.

Douglass was especially critical of colonization schemes that would remove blacks from the land of their birth and, then, only because their presence caused offense to a class of whites who had traditionally used and abused them, a group that included some members of the so-called better classes of whites that endorsed lynching and mob rule. Ironically, Griggs supplements Douglass's epigraph with a line from the final speech of white supremacist Henry W. Grady, perhaps the most ardent southern supporter of black colonization to Louisiana and Texas, a theme that dominates Griggs's first novel, *Imperium in Imperio*. On December 12, 1889, Grady delivered a speech in Boston at Faneuil Hall titled "The Race Problem in the South." In what would become his final speech, Grady claimed, "I had rather see my people render back this question rightly solved than to see them gather all the spoils over which faction has contended since Cataline conspired and Caesar fought."[10]

Douglass and Grady, for very different reasons, agreed that the solution to the "Negro Problem" rested in the hands of whites—Douglass on the grounds that blacks were not culpable and Grady on the grounds that blacks were not capable; neither man would have endorsed Griggs's thesis to the contrary—that blacks should take full responsibility for solving the race or "Negro Problem." More than that, the current social hierarchy, as during slavery and Reconstruction, rested on the endurance of twin myths, white supremacy and black inferiority. The maintenance or destruction of these myths was very much in play for Griggs and his peers. Indeed, if whites like Grady were in fact given absolute control of and responsibility for solving the "Negro Problem," it appeared that these myths would likely remain intact. More was at stake than merely solving the problem; the very real question of social equality would need to be addressed as well. Griggs knew that blacks must be intimately involved in the process and that a more nuanced approach would have to be taken. Appropriating the master's tools for that purpose would prove to be a complicated effort and would generate its own set of problems and unintended repercussions. The best that Griggs could muster was a pragmatic approach to the race problem and the complex of ideas that attended it.

Griggs was one of many scholars who believed that the remarkable technological, political, economic, and scientific progress that marked the fin de siècle could also provide a long-awaited window of opportunity to substantively address the underlying causes of the "Negro Problem" as a new generation of blacks and whites came into control of the country's political, social, and economic apparatuses. The battle was against Jim Crow and the incredible range of violence, from physical to psychological, that supported it. Jim Crow, more than anything else, served as the chief barrier to even second-class citizenship, much less access to the elusive American dream. When we begin here to discuss agency and action, the terms "generation" or "community" are clearly too broad. What Griggs and, more famously, Du Bois imagined was that a talented percentage of that generation would rise to lead the rest. Just one generation removed from slavery, Griggs was one of the elite members of the Talented Tenth, someone whose family had managed to shake off the chains of poverty and ignorance and who saw clearly the value of attaining full, unfettered citizenship in the United States. The franchise was the chief instrument against Jim Crow, both literally and metaphorically. This new generation included Charles Chesnutt, Maggie Lena Walker, James Weldon Johnson, Mary McLeod Bethune, William Stanley Braithwaite, Madame C. J. Walker, with William Monroe Trotter, Solomon Carter Fuller, Paul Laurence Dunbar, and Sutton Griggs, the latter four all born in 1872. Of this new generation of thinkers, the "New Negroes," Griggs took important cues from his idol, Kelly Miller, who understood as well as anyone else of his generation the importance of challenging the intellectual roots of white supremacy.

Much of the political and social science content we find in *Unfettered* is repeated in "Dorlan's Plan," revised in *Wisdom's Call*, and formalized in *The Guide to Racial Greatness*, ideas that were deeply influenced by Miller's brand of pragmatic utilitarianism. Griggs begins *Unfettered* by strategically misquoting Miller: "The chains that bound the body ** were as tender cords of mercy compared with the shackles that gyved his mind**." This quote was taken from Miller's article "The Negro and Education," published the February before *Unfettered* appeared.[11] In this article Miller makes a number of points that Griggs takes up whole cloth in the plot of *Unfettered* and in the key tenets of "Dorlan's Plan." The article begins with the "Lincolnesque" observation that the dogmas of the past were rapidly becoming inadequate for the turbulent present. In homage to the recently deceased Douglass, Miller writes the following: "When it is demonstrated that the negro has capacity for knowledge and virtue, he thereby establishes his title clear to the opportunity for their development and exercise. The chains that bound the body of Frederick Douglass to a cruel servitude were as tender cords of mercy compared with the shackles that gyved his mind to a degrading ignorance."[12] Using asterisks to elide Douglass's name in his epigraph and the phrase "gyved his mind to a degrading ignorance," Griggs invokes the idea that the transformation of the "Negro" was at hand, not some subset of the black community or a particular individual as in the past. There was some pride taken in the supposition that the newly emerging black middle class represented the coming of an exemplary generation of individuals as opposed to a generation marked by exemplary individuals. Griggs knew that this also meant shifting away from thinkers of previous generations to the work of the new generation. The coming generation would have to contrive new solutions to the "Negro Problem." This shift would entail significantly more than changes in methodology or particular tactics. The new generation would have to see the problem in a much different light. For example, it was important to scholars like Miller and Griggs that individual shortcomings be dismissed as "individual" shortcomings and not as a reflection on the race as a whole. The problem, then, did not concern individual aberrations but rather the broader behavioral patterns of the community. That "critical stage" was bound up in the generational shift away from older modes of thinking among the black intelligentsia. For Griggs, blacks were very much a part of "the entire American people" and bore some responsibility for solving this problem. As mentioned earlier, *Unfettered* and "Dorlan's Plan" demonstrate that Griggs would have blacks assume the entirety of this responsibility. The Science of Collective Efficiency that flows from those documents is but a blueprint for how the black community might assume more responsibility for its welfare, for its honor and glory.

As indicated in the author's preface of *Unfettered* and the epigraph that precedes it, both Griggs and Miller realized that the generational change they saw swaying and shaping the black community was also at work in white communities. The trick was to figure out how to take advantage of those shifts rather than being significantly harmed or even destroyed by them. Even as the material excesses of the Gilded Age were grudgingly giving way to a new austerity and desire for accountability in the Progressive Era, Griggs and his peers knew that blacks would have to illuminate the physical danger for whites that the "Negro Problem" had produced in the past (namely, the Civil War), highlight acts of brutality on the part of whites in the near past that threatened to plunge the nation into another violent internal conflict, and exploit the new generation's desire to create some distance between themselves and their less enlightened parents. Essentially, Griggs, Miller, and other intellectuals advocated shaming the rising generation of white Americans to nobly embrace black America before the arrival of the "day of final adjustment," when the nation would be "summoned" to deal with the "Negro's strength, to kindly accept or reject all that he can do." For that to happen with any success, the debate would have to be shifted away from achievements of particular black individuals to a broader conversation about the capacity of the black community. Standing in the way of this effort was the uncertainty about the true nature and character of the coming generation of white Americans, a preoccupation that dominates the early chapters of *Unfettered*.

The first two chapters of *Unfettered* are titled "An Anglo Saxon's Death" and "A New King ... Which Knew Not Joseph." The first chapter captures the essence of black leaders' concerns regarding the transition from the old guard that they knew and understood to a new set of leaders who ostensibly championed social justice while remaining silent or even defending segregation and lynching. The second captures the idea that this new generation perceives blacks as a threat, and that if blacks are not careful, they could find themselves in a much worse situation than in the past. In these two chapters, it is not the new generation but the old that understands honor and nobility and that the new generation could quite easily morph into a group that is far worse than its forefathers. In its hands would rest unearned resources bequeathed to it without any agreement to maintain the noblesse oblige of white southern heritage.

Griggs crafts Lemuel Dalton as the embodiment of this new generation of white men in the South who are bent on creating a segregated society and Congressman Bloodworth as a representative of the utilitarian, egocentric, opportunistic generation of whites coming to power in the North. Dalton is especially mean spirited and vindictive in ways that are an embarrassment to his elders. His first act upon the death of his uncle is to expel every black on the plantation including the loyal mammy, Aunt Catherine, and the gorgeous, brilliant, would-be tragic mulatta Morlene. In keeping with the tenets of the trope, she remains unaware of her "true" parentage, the secret dying with Maurice Dalton, the family patriarch. Instigating a fight to avenge a childhood insult, Lemuel Dalton shoots an unarmed Harry Dalton, who is a member of a respected family of former slaves living near the plantation that Lemuel has recently inherited. Morlene cares for Harry, who falls in love with her and, predictably, will die unless she agrees to marry him. The incident provokes a mass exodus of blacks who would rather leave the community than continue to suffer abuse at the hands of brash young whites like Lemuel. Angered by the realization that they will now be required to perform the manual labor that blacks had always performed, a mob of young white men led by Alfred Mullen, the son of a prominent squire, burns Harry Dalton's home and then murders his defenseless younger sister, Beulah Dalton, as she attempts to escape.

Through these two incidents, Griggs effectively captures what he imagines are the most dangerous generational shifts in white supremacy: the inexplicable mean-spiritedness, abject cowardice, and precipitous decline of personal honor that for generations served as the touchstone of the "Anglo-Saxon Race." More than that, this new cowardice was *in the blood* of the new southern gentleman. Beulah's father, after failing to incite a confrontation with the men who have killed his daughter, remarks: "Ah! Gentlemens, you kill er pore gal when her daddy wuz erway, but you won't fight him, I see. Gentlemens, dare uster be bettah blood dan dat. I was in de war wid my marster, an' he showd good blood to de Yankees. Is it all gone, dat three uv you won't fight ur nigger,' ez you call him?" (*Unfettered*, 60).

Beyond a ritual banishment ceremony presided over by the elderly Squire Mullen and his peers, Griggs does not immediately deploy a youthful example of the "better element" of southern white men to counter the negative image that Lemuel and the younger Mullen provide of the "new southerner." In the shooting incident, the gathered Anglo-Saxons observe that white men fighting black men on equal footing smacks too much of equality and that Lemuel should have simply struck Harry Dalton with his whip while remaining in his saddle. Pulling from Herodotus's *Histories*, Griggs touches on the maintenance of black inferiority as an active enterprise in white America:

> "Permit me to add a word," requested a feeble-voiced young man, rising in a most timid manner, rubbing his hands together nervously.
>
> 'Squire Mullen gave him a reassuring look and he proceeded.
>
> "I simply wish to reinforce what 'Squire Mullen has said by a historical incident.—On a certain occasion when the Scythians were returning from a war in which they had been engaged, they received news that the servants whom they had left behind had mutinied and taken possession of the city and the households of their former masters. The Scythians were preparing to attack the slaves with a full accoutrement of arms when one of their number protested. He told his fellows that the best way to conquer the slaves was to discard arms and go with whips simply. He held that arms would suggest equality, while whips would be a reminder to the slaves as to what they were. The experiment succeeded and the Scythians effected a re-enslavement without any bloodshed. So, I agree with 'Squire Mullen that it is a great help to superiors to keep alive in inferiors a well developed sense of their inferiority. It certainly helps to keep them in subjection. The Scythian whips, which had as an aid the feeling of inferiority, were more successful than arms would have been, carrying along with them the idea of equality." (*Unfettered*, 32)[13]

Lemuel explains that by not fighting Harry, he would have left in Harry's mind the memory of a previous victory over a white man, something that the latter might have continued to refer to as proof positive that whites were not in fact intellectually *and* physically superior to blacks. After some deliberation, the Anglo-Saxon elders agree with Lemuel, and the shooting is forgiven. The second offense, the unprovoked murder of a defenseless woman, cannot be forgiven, and the perpetrator is expected (by his family) to commit suicide. The young man does not possess the courage or honor requisite for taking his own life, an act that Griggs romantically or perhaps facetiously imagines that members of the previous generation would not have hesitated to commit. In either case, Griggs wants to sort out how whites collectively come to imagine that they are "superior" in the face of cowardly acts like lynching.

Pulling from an 1881 article by Herbert Spencer in *Popular Science Monthly* regarding the development of political institutions, Griggs has one of his characters offer the following:

> A profound thinker of our day sets forth this idea in these words:
> "'There are the respective mental traits produced by daily exercise of power and by daily submission to power. The ideas, and sentiments, and modes of behavior, perpetually repeated, generate on the one side an inherited fitness for command, and on the other side an inherited fitness for obedience; with the result that, in course of time, there arises on both sides the belief that the established relations of classes are the natural ones.'" (*Unfettered*, 33)[14]

Citing community dietary practices and restrictions, Spencer explains how seemingly far-removed circumstances and practices can lead to false notions about inherent traits. The distribution of food along class lines where the higher classes are allowed to partake of better-quality foods than their "inferiors" leads to disparities in physical stature that in turn serve as markers of natural superiority. The physical differences in such communities has more to do with forced malnutrition than with natural superiority. Recognizing how myth passed from one generation to the next was only part of Griggs's broader concern. In "Dorlan's Plan," he returns to Spencer to help explain those characteristics that he believed truly did pass from one generation to the next, especially the transgenerational transfer of character:

> The traits of character acquired in one generation were transmitted to succeeding generations, so that notions of inherent superiority and the belief in the right of repression became ingrained in Southern character.

In confirmation of this conclusion, we again quote from Mr. Herbert Spencer, who says: "The emotional nature prompting the general mode of conduct is derived from ancestors is a product of all ancestral activities. * * * The governing sentiment is, in short, mainly the accumulated and organized sentiment of the past." (*Unfettered*, 227)[15]

Of course, this supposition cuts both ways. If this were true for whites in terms of perceived supremacy, it would be true of blacks as well in terms of accepting notions of innate inferiority, and that acceptance of inferior status in and of itself represented a tangible species of inferiority. It was not a major step then for Griggs to move beyond applying such notions to individuals and communities to applying them to notions of race and nation just as other social Darwinists were apt to do. Griggs did not give himself the luxury of picking and choosing in this regard. Consistent to the end, he accepted all of the theory, not just those parts that suited his purpose. If social Darwinism could explain why whites imagined that they were superior, then he would have to explain the inferiority of blacks in terms suggesting that it was artificially created and could be overcome under the proper conditions. In some ways mirroring the 1880s and 1890s phase of the Great Migration, the mass exodus of blacks in *Unfettered* is a rather heavy-handed symbolic rendering of Griggs's point that new whites in the South were indefatigable contributors to the race problem and certainly were not inclined to solve that problem to the liking of the black community. This exodus allows Griggs to temporarily remove the South from the race-problem equation. With the community removed to R——, Griggs turns his attention to party politics and the unswerving loyalty of African Americans to the Republican Party.

The Republican betrayal of 1876 was arguably the most important of several acts of political mischief against blacks in the last quarter of the nineteenth century. The 1890s, often referred to as the nadir in the history of blacks in America, were particularly rife with examples of the deteriorating conditions between black and white Americans. The sharp increase in lynching in the early 1890s, the enigmatically racist Columbian Exhibition, the coup d'état that punctuated the Wilmington riots in 1898, the wholesale disenfranchisement of blacks in the South via "grandfather clauses," and even the enduring and overwhelming popularity of the minstrel show all foreshadowed a grim future for blacks as the nation approached the twentieth century. The absence of a strong black voice in American politics was made more prescient by the fact that the novel appears as southern states were redoubling their legal and ex-tralegal efforts to disenfranchise black voters. In fact, between 1890 and 1908, every state in the South revised and adopted new state constitutions that specifically disenfranchised black voters. These matters, coupled with the virtual absence of support or meaningful concern for the welfare of blacks from the Cleveland and McKinley administrations, the majority and dissenting opinions in *Plessy v. Ferguson*, and Congress's long-standing disinterest in passing antilynching legislation, sustained Griggs's distrust of the United States government more generally and led to his third assertion that *neither the Democratic Party nor the Republican Party could be depended upon to address the Negro problem.*

Even so, blacks continued to look to the Republican Party for assistance in issues ranging from redressing the proliferation of Jim Crow legislation to abating the public shame that was lynching. It bears mentioning that the novel's core narrative and internal arguments rest precariously on the assumption that blacks actually possessed an unfettered voice in national politics. In *Unfettered*, Griggs directly questions the wisdom of unswerving loyalty to the Republican Party that demanded that blacks remain uncritical of anything in the party's platform, including imperialism and expansionism.

Though couched in fiction, Griggs's premise was indeed a risky if not dangerous one for a black writer at the turn of the century. It was one thing to challenge or even demonize racist whites in the South; it was something altogether different to challenge in print one's benefactors, Republicans in the North. In Dorlan Warthell, described as an ebony Apollo, Griggs constructs the exemplary "New Negro." Dorlan, self-educated political genius, enters the novel just as he prepares to depart the Republican Party. After serving several years as a ghostwriter and the brains behind Republican congressman Bloodworth, Dorlan decides to leave the Republican Party because it champions military action in the Philippines. When a newspaper editor questions Dorlan's party loyalty, he replies:

A noble man does a cripple a kindness. The man dies and a thrifty neighbor comes into possession of the shoes, clothes and hat that he wore at the time of helping the cripple. The neighbor puts on the leavings of the dead man, appears before the cripple and demands his allegiance because of the clothes worn. The cripple yields the devotion asked for, giving evidence that he was ready to consider the dead man and the clothes as one and inseparable. We are charged with acting like unto this cripple, in the matter of rendering devotion to the party name and machinery, the clothes left behind by the men who did the actual work of liberating us. (*Unfettered*, 95)

This is certainly one of the more succinct and successful analogies to be found in Griggs's fiction. Of even more interest here is Dorlan's intention to found an independent political party in which blacks would be allowed to choose between Republicans, Democrats, or an independent candidate based on how well a candidate's positions aligned with the needs and desires of the black community. This was an attractive alternative to voting along any particular party line out of sheer loyalty. Griggs takes care to tease out the contours of both sides of the debate regarding expansion, painting Morlene Dalton as an ardent expansionist and her husband, Harry, as a fanatical supporter of the Grand Old Party.

Morlene, brilliant in her own right, believes that expansionism will result in world peace. She reasons that the destruction of "pseudo-national boundaries" will hasten the day when all governments will be combined into one entity (*Unfettered*, 87). She goes on to reiterate the pro-expansionist arguments of the day: excess production and creating external markets for excess goods, military exigency in capturing outlying possessions of strategic value, raw desire for political power on the part of politicians, and the humanitarian argument for elevating "weaker people" (*Unfettered*, 88). Dorlan counters these arguments in turn with one glaring elision. As James Robert Payne points out in his essay "Afro-American Literature of the Spanish-American War," Griggs has Dorlan advocate not for immediate freedom for the Filipino people but rather for full rights under the American flag.[16]

The manuscript for *Unfettered* seems to have gone to print just before the United States "officially" ended hostilities in the Philippines in 1902. Hostilities with Spain actually ceased in a matter of weeks, but violence in the Philippines persisted for more than a decade after Spain sold the islands to the United States under the favorable provisions of the Treaty of Paris (1898), and dissidents in Cuba would resist U.S. intervention as late as 1934. This resistance was due to the fact that the United States entered the war under a transparent but nonetheless startling political ploy. Conveniently ignoring clauses regarding noninterference with existing colonies, the United States used the anticolonialist expansion provisions of the Monroe Doctrine to hedge its claims against Spain. In a matter of weeks, the United States had simply replaced Spain as colonial master in both Cuba and the Philippines. On the home front, this act of political hypocrisy fostered two popular debates that Griggs hoped to influence. The first debate revolved around whether expansionism should be allowed to function as a legitimate component of U.S. foreign policy. Assuming that expansionism would be accepted as policy, the nation was left to wrestle with the second question, what should be done with newly annexed peoples? The second debate was uncomfortably similar to the then centuries-old debate regarding "what should be done with the Negro," a question that remained unresolved in 1898.

Would new populations be granted the rights and privileges that accrued to U.S. citizenship and the protections of the Constitution? Would yet another group be added to the United States' list of underclass citizens? African Americans were especially divided in opinion about the Spanish-American War, tenuously balancing patriotism and unyielding support of the Republican Party against the solidarity that some members of the community felt with other oppressed people around the globe. Griggs recognized that support for the war was inflected by sectional differences—homing in on the fact that with the election of William McKinley, the U.S. government was securely in the hands of the Republican Party: white men in the North. Noting the violent oppression of blacks at the hands of southern whites, Griggs viewed the United States' entry into the war as proof of the moral compromise of the last major group of whites in the world who were not actively oppressing and exploiting some non-European group at home or abroad. Republican support for expansionism signified the arrival of a powerful and potentially unbreakable compact.

Rudyard Kipling's "The White Man's Burden" was published in *McClure's Magazine* in 1899. The poem is largely remembered for its unapologetic embrace of European imperialism and expansionism. However, the poem's full title: "The White Man's Burden: The United States and the Philippine Islands" attests to the fact that Kipling was speaking not to the general idea of expansion or about Europe's role but rather directly to the people of the United States about becoming more actively involved in a broader race-based enterprise that went beyond merely looting and plundering distant lands. Kipling saw U.S. domination of the Philippines as the "fulfillment of an obligation." White Americans, as members of the white race, were expected not just to join in domination of the "uncivilized" parts of the world but also to take the lead in the enterprise. In *The Americanization of the World; or, The Trend of the Twentieth Century*, British proto-tabloid journalist William T. Stead took Kipling's exhortation to the United States a step further. Stead believed that given its vast natural resources, Yankee ingenuity, willingness to wage war, and credibility as an "Anglo-Saxon" nation, the United States was destined to "Americanize" the world. He went so far as to advocate for the establishment of the "United States of Europe" in which European nations would actually become part of the United States.[17] Stead's argument was not convincing, at least not in the United States. However, his and Kipling's messages were not lost on ardent U.S. expansionists like Theodore Roosevelt, Henry Cabot Lodge, and the segment of the population that also believed that the United States was and should remain a white man's country. Kipling's poem, Stead's journalistic pieces, and other pro-expansionist writings also showed Griggs and his peers that literature could serve as a powerful vehicle for influencing general debate, supplementing, supporting, clarifying, simplifying, and otherwise making accessible to the untutored masses more complicated arguments proffered by politicians and "scientists."

As mentioned earlier, the Science of Collective Efficiency was Griggs's attempt at constructing a doctrine specially tailored for the elevation of blacks in the United States of America. Unfortunately, at least in its initial iterations, Griggs's attempt to replicate Darwinist theories merely reproduced essentialist notions about the nature of the black community and inadvertently reinforced a number of existing stereotypes about individual life habits of people of African descent more broadly. It is disappointing, to say the least, that Griggs, a remarkably well-educated intellectual, well versed in the psychological dynamics of white supremacy, accepted the biological determinism embedded in social Darwinism so readily. He believed and argued that Africans—and by extension blacks in America—were in fact late arriving at the table of civilization and were by dint of time socially inferior to the more advanced civilizations of the earth, the most important being the Anglo-Saxon. This, of course, is precisely what social Darwinists had been arguing for decades and what ethnologists and eugenicists had posited for more than a century. Again, it is significant that Griggs was not alone in his thinking among the black intelligentsia of his day, with Booker T. Washington and Kelly Miller standing as the most obvious examples. In our efforts to better understand Griggs, it is instructive to return again to Miller's thoughts on solving the "Negro Problem."

Miller and Griggs understood that the manifold solutions for the "Negro Problem" were even more numerous than the myriad political perspectives that produced them. Both men searched for constants that might anchor their theories. Miller settled on two profoundly problematic constants in the opening paragraphs of "The Negro and Education," constants that Griggs accepted without complaint or revision:

> Two facts stand out bold and pronounced, which must be the determining factors in any scheme for the betterment of the negro's status.
>
> 1. The *negro belongs to an undeveloped race*, and is, therefore, many centuries behind his Aryan competitor in the cultivation of those qualities which make for progress. *He possesses only such promiscuous experiences as he has picked up during the past two or three hundred years while confined to the backyard of civilization.*
> 2. *For all time with which we may wisely concern ourselves, his religious, social, and cultural life will be relegated to a separate sphere.* The African and the Anglo-Saxon will come together for purposes of business and philanthropy; but for pleasurable intercourse and social satisfaction each will return to his own company. The *social isolation of the negro* makes imperative an educational scheme which provides for a wise and competent self-direction. The negro has now reached a critical stage in his career.[18]

Had these lines come from Grady, Kipling, or Stead, we could easily dismiss them. The echoes of Washington are obvious, and the clumsy anticipation of Aryanism in the coming decades is palpable. We must recognize even if we fail to respect the not-so-subtle rhetorical shift away from arguments of "innate inferiority" to openly embracing the lesser evil that blacks were an "underdeveloped" people. The latter of these offered at least the possibility for progress; the former suggested that very little could be done to elevate the race. If blacks were descended from a backward people, it was possible that members of both groups, Africans and blacks in America, could be redeemed. Although "Dorlan's Plan" takes the elevation of blacks in the United States as its primary focus, the most important of the final chapters in *Unfettered* concern the "backwardness" of Africa and its inhabitants. Recruiting the work of Huxley, Spencer, Kidd, and Stanley Livingstone, Griggs uses these final chapters to engage several of the more specious social Darwinist arguments about the nature of Africans and, by extension, their not-so-distant cousins in the United States.

Just before closing *Unfettered*, Griggs melodramatically reveals that the novel's hero, Dorlan Warthell, is a long-lost African prince. Kumi, one of the many emissaries who have fanned out across the globe in search of the lost monarch, finds Dorlan and informs him that he is now king and one of the richest men in the world. Predictably, Dorlan is torn between pursuing the recently widowed Morlene and lifting his country and Africa above its degraded position. More for the sake of the plot than fidelity to logic, Kumi explains that Dorlan does not need to return to his people immediately or at all:

> "How so?" asked Dorlan, arising and drawing near to Kumi.
>
> The latter began: "We Africans are engaged in a sociological investigation of many questions. We are seeking to know definitely what part the climate; the surface, the flora and the fauna have played in keeping us in civilization's back yard. Huxley thinks that our woolly hair and black skins came to us only after our race took up its abode in Africa. He holds that it was nature's contribution to render us immune from the yellow fever germs so abundant in swampy regions.
>
> "He thinks that those of our race who did not take on a dark hue and woolly texture of hair were the less adapted to life in the tropics and eventually died out, leaving those that were better adjusted to survive.
>
> "He thinks that these beneficial modifications were preserved and transmitted with increasing strength from generation to generation until our hue and our hair or the physical attributes for which they stand rendered us immune from yellow fever. I may add that Livingstone says of us, 'Heat alone does not produce blackness of skin, but heat with moisture seems to insure the deepest hue.'" (*Unfettered*, 165–66)[19]

Livingstone made his observations in his *Missionary Travels* (1857), but appears in Griggs's work courtesy of Herbert Spencer's "Climate and Social Development" published in *Popular Science* in July 1874. In this essay Spencer uses Livingstone's observations in southern Africa to support his contention that there were "recognizable, corresponding differences in energy and social advance." It would appear that Huxley, Spencer, and Livingstone, like Jefferson and so many others before him, felt compelled to explain away the physiological differences between sub-Saharan Africans and Europeans, imagining that these physical differences were actually viable and indispensable markers of real differences in physical and intellectual endowments, a preoccupation and intellectual investment that yielded the true source of the "Negro Problem." It would appear that the same article also led Griggs to Huxley's work. When Griggs wrote *Unfettered*, biblical explanations of differences in color were discounted in some quarters as a misreading of scripture and accepted in others as the gospel. Griggs accepted Huxley's thoughts about racial differences but drew the line when the Bible was recruited for an explanation:

"Now, nature, in thus protecting us against yellow fever, by changing our color from the original, whatever it was, has painted upon us a sign that causes some races to think that there is a greater difference between us and them than there really is. So much for our color and the ills that it has entailed."

Dorlan interrupted Kumi to remark very feelingly:

"I am truly glad that you are not inoculated with that utterly nonsensical view to be met with in this country, which represents that the Negro's color is the result of a curse pronounced by Noah upon his recovery from a drunken stupor. Please proceed." (*Unfettered*, 166)

Griggs and his peers preferred naturalist explanations of racial differences to explanations that these differences were indelible. More than that, the Bible itself was used to support any negative traits associated with those differences. Dispensing with biblical explanations, Griggs returns to Spencer for assistance:

Kumi resumed his remarks. "Mr. Herbert Spencer holds that our comparative lack of energy is due to heat and moisture. He states that 'the earliest recorded civilization grew up in a hot and dry region Egypt; and in hot and dry regions also arose the Babylonian, Assyrian and Phoenician civilizations.' He points out that all 'the conquering races of the world have hailed from within or from the borders of the hot and dry region marked on the rain map rainless districts,' and extending across North Africa, Arabia, Persia and on through Thibet into Mongolia." (*Unfettered*, 167)

Spencer revises this idea in *Principles of Sociology* (1881), adding that "original superiority of type was not the common trait, of these races: the Tartar type is inferior, as well as the Egyptian. But the common trait, as proved by the subjugation of other races, was energy."[20] Kumi concludes:

He [Spencer], therefore, would ascribe our backwardness principally to a woeful lack of energy, a condition brought on by our hot and moist climate.

"When our investigation of these questions is complete," continued Kumi, "we will know just what has brought us where we are and can determine whether artificial appliances sufficient to counteract existing influences can be discovered and instituted." (*Unfettered*, 167)

Understanding what we know today about human biology, it is difficult not to be judgmental about Spencer's conclusions and Griggs's dependence on them. In much the same way that it must have been difficult for Griggs to look back on Jefferson's *Notes on the State of Virginia* with anything other than shock and dismay, it is difficult for us to believe that Griggs actually accepted Spencer's work without some conditions. His acceptance of Benjamin Kidd's work, as expressed in Kumi's declamation, is just as problematic, if not more so:

> Mr. Benjamin Kidd seems to think that the tropics can never develop the highest type of civilization. In the event that the government of the tropics is to be conducted from the temperate zones, we tropical people will desire Negroes to remain in the temperate zones, to advocate such policies and form such alliances as shall be for our highest good.
>
> So, it may turn out to be the best for you, our king, to remain here, for our welfare, owing to our peculiar environments, depends, just now, as much upon what others think of us as upon what we ourselves may do. The question of your going to Africa is not, therefore, a pressing one, yet. (*Unfettered*, 167–68)

The notion that the abundance of fauna and flora produced an indelible indolence in the people from these regions seems to have been an especially compelling one for Griggs. The logic that flowed from this was simple enough: people from more austere climates were naturally fit to rule people who had grown up unchallenged in civilization's backyard. Although Kidd's profoundly condescending original text *Control of the Tropics* (1898) came just in time to justify the latest wave of imperialist behavior, especially the United States' engagement in the Philippines and Cuba, the question of how Africans in particular would be regarded by European powers had been decisively settled before the Berlin Conference of 1884–85.[21] Griggs must have known that Kidd's rationale for European dominance of the tropics held implications for descendants of those people who resided in other parts of the world. Highly civilized Dorlan, only recently removed from Africa, comes to stand as an enigmatic exception to Griggs's premise regarding the civilizing effect of contact with the Anglo-Saxon, a premise derived directly from Kidd's work. Dorlan also brings into relief another long-standing tension within the black community in the United States with regard to recently arrived Africans and African Americans whose families left Africa a finite, but most often indeterminate, number of generations beforehand.

This tension has retained its significance over the centuries and has been brought back to popular attention most recently with the election of Barack Obama as president of the United States. For Griggs, the question was simple enough: what were the traits and characteristics that set the "Negro" apart from his or her cousins in Africa? If social Darwinists were correct, then there should be significant innate differences between the two. In "Dorlan's Plan" and elsewhere in his fiction and nonfiction, Griggs appears to agree with this analysis, yet he gives us in chapter after chapter a character who functions as an exemplar of the "Negro" in America only to reveal in the final passages of the novel that this is not the case. Even though Griggs writes in "Dorlan's Plan" that "the Negro has but lately entered civilization's parlor. He possesses an oriental nature called to service in an occidental civilization" (*Unfettered*, 229), it is clear that he imagines that all "Negroes" were not the same: that blacks in America were further along in terms of civilization than their African counterparts. It is more than "slippage," then, that an "American Negro" does not craft "Dorlan's Plan," Griggs's plan for solving the "Race Problem." Moreover, the plan that Dorlan develops is not just for the uplift of blacks in America but for the eventual uplift of Africa as well:

> It so happens that Africa has but recently bestowed upon me, Dorlan Warthell, untold millions. I have no qualms of conscience in thus applying to the Negroes of America funds derived from Africa, for I firmly believe with Mr. Wm. T. Stead in the Americanization of the globe, and believe that in due time the Negroes of America are to be the immediate agents of the Americanization of Africa. Money spent in the uplift of the American Negro is, therefore, an investment in the interests of Africa that will pay a glorious dividend. (*Unfettered*, 257)

Even if Dorlan's personal identity has become ambiguous at this point in the narrative, it is clear that Griggs believed that blacks in America, by dint of traits acquired through contact with whites in America, would eventually reach the point where they would be able to dramatically change Africa. In 1897 Miller published *A Review of Hoffman's Race Traits and Tendencies of the American Negro* for the American Negro Academy, a pamphlet written in response to Frederick L. Hoffman's article "Race Traits and Tendencies of the American Negro" published in 1896. We know from passages in *Unfettered* that Griggs knew this text, if only through his reading of Miller's work. Hoffman, a statistician for the Prudential Insurance Company of America, had written what Miller described as "by far the most thorough and comprehensive treatment of the Negro problem, from a statistical standpoint, which has yet appeared. In fact, it may be regarded as the most important utterance on the subject since the publication of 'Uncle Tom's Cabin'; for the interest which the famous novel aroused in the domain of sentiment and generous feelings, the present work seems destined to awaken in the field of science and exact inquiry." Miller's critique of Hoffman's article is simply astonishing:

> The superintendent of the tenth census writes on this subject: "I entertain a strong conviction that the further course of our [Negro] population will exhibit that tendency in a continually growing force; that this element will be more and more drained off from the higher and colder lands into the low, hot regions bordering on the Gulf of Mexico." Commenting on this subject Mr. Hoffman says: "This tendency if persisted in will probably in the end prove disastrous to the advancement of the colored race, since there is but the slightest prospect that the race will be lifted to a higher plane of civilization except by constant contact with the white race." It is undoubtedly true that the Negro has not the initiative power of civilization. What race has? Civilization is not an original process with any race or nation known to history. The torch has been passed from race to race and from age to age. Where else can the Negro go? The white race at present has the light. This concession is no reproach to the Negro race, nor is it due to any peculiar race trait or tendency.[22]

Miller exhibits here a species of logic that Griggs shared without revision, the tendency to counter the substance of arguments by citing exceptions to the rule while explicitly ignoring underlying logical fallacies that impugned the entire black community. The "concession," while not a "reproach" to blacks, complicates the notion that there was such a thing as the "American Negro" and that there is any signal difference between this type and the African.

The corpus of Griggs's writing, both fiction and nonfiction, contains passages about the nature of black Americans that are just as shocking as anything we find in Miller's work. One of the most prescient of these passages is found in "Dorlan's Plan," where a thinly veiled Sutton Griggs outlines the primary tasks for the "racial organization" that will become the instrument for solving the race problem as defined in Miller's analysis:

> Recognizing the fact that, in the interests of a composite American civilization, it is desirable that the Negro be imbued with many of the qualities of the white man, care should be taken that the Negro population be so diffused throughout the country, that no section of the white race shall have more work of this character than it can well perform. Our racial organization shall therefore establish an emigration bureau, that shall drain off unduly congested regions and locate Negroes in more desirable localities. (*Unfettered*, 268)[23]

Passages like this one explain why Griggs's work incensed many in the black community both during his lifetime and afterward. These passages also offer us something perhaps more valuable: an unobstructed glimpse into the inner workings and complexity of thought, the inherent contradictions, and apparent intellectual confusion and cognitive dissonance that colored the work of so many black public intellectuals of that era. Moreover, Griggs and his peers understood very well what their audiences were expecting and what they would accept. Griggs was writing specifically to members of the newly established, educated middle class that was still establishing the values and pretentions that would form the core of its identity. Throughout his career, Griggs kept this audience first and foremost in his writings. The Science of Collective Efficiency was crafted with the greatest of intentions but yielded its own problems and contradictions. Even so, the proliferation of uplift organizations that came into being just years after the publication of *Unfettered* and "Dorlan's Plan" is not wholly coincidental. We know with certainty that Griggs's work influenced Du Bois and that Griggs was an active member of the Niagara Movement. Although we might find the literal roots of the Science of Collective Efficiency in the pages of "Dorlan's Plan," it is in the narrative that precedes that pamphlet that we find the most important clues to the ideological origins of that science. In the end, Sutton E. Griggs's work provides a useful set of cautions about the remarkable complexities of being black in the United States at the beginning of the twentieth century and more generally the inevitable difficulties inherent in solving real-world problems with the latest social or political theory. That lesson alone is worth remembering.

Notes

1. Griggs defines this "science" in a 1921 pamphlet titled *The Science of Collective Efficiency* (Memphis: National Public Welfare League): "The new science of collective efficiency is subsidiary to sociology as the latter in turn is subsidiary to anthropology. Sociology concerns itself 'with the origin and development of arts and sciences, opinions, beliefs, customs, laws and institutions generally within historic time.' The science of collective efficiency selects from sociology, history, ethics, psychology, nature studies and all other available sources, just the things necessary to enable groups of men to function successfully and enduringly as groups, meeting in adequate fashion their civic needs" (3).

2. Although it is necessary to delve into "Dorlan's Plan (Sequel to 'Unfettered': A Dissertation on the Race Problem)" appended to the novel, in the pages that follow, I consciously restrict my reading of Griggs's fiction to the novel as much as possible.

3. T. C. Leonard points out that the term "social Darwinism" did not come into popular usage until after World War I. Moreover, in his study of Richard Hofstadter's

influential *Social Darwinism in American Thought, 1860–1915*, Leonard affirms that the term has not always been a pejorative one. More important, the concept itself was not discredited during the Progressive Era. Thomas C. Leonard, "Origins of the Myth of Social Darwinism: The Ambiguous Legacy of Richard Hofstadter's *Social Darwinism in American Thought*," *Journal of Economic Behavior and Organization* 71 (2009): 37–51.

4. Even though Spencer coined the term "survival of the fittest," he did not apply that term to human society. Citing Howard L. Kaye, *The Social Meaning of Modern Biology: From Social Darwinism to Sociobiology*, T. C. Leonard clarifies this point with respect to Spencer and Sumner: "Howard Kaye, a careful scholar of social Darwinism, summarizes the historiography that revises Hofstadter: 'a close reading of the theories of Sumner and Spencer exonerates them from the century-old charge of Social Darwinism in the strictest sense of the term. They themselves did not advocate the application of Darwin's theory of natural selection, "the law of the jungle," to human society'" Leonard, "Origins of the Myth," 41; see also Howard L. Kaye, *The Social Meaning of Modern Biology: From Social Darwinism to Sociobiology* (New Haven, Conn.: Yale University Press, 1986), 33–34.

5. Benjamin Kidd, "Sociology," in *Encyclopedia Britannica* (Cincinnati: Babson Press, 1911), 4:898.

6. W. E. B. Du Bois, *The Souls of Black Folk: Authoritative Text, Contexts, and Criticism*, ed. Henry Louis Gates and Terri Hume Oliver (New York: W. W. Norton, 1999), 10–11.

7. Frederick Douglass, *Address by Hon. Frederick Douglass, Delivered in the Metropolitan A.M.E. Church, Washington, D.C., Tuesday, January 9th, 1894, on the Lessons of the Hour* (Baltimore: Press of Thomas & Evans, 1894).

8. Ibid.

9. When discussing mob law in *Imperium in Imperio*, Griggs writes: "Our race has furnished some brutes lower than beasts of the field. . . . When, by violence a member of a despised race assails a defenseless woman; robs her of her virtue . . . hell is scoured by the Southern white man in search of plans to vent his rage." Sutton E. Griggs, *Imperium in Imperio* (Cincinnati: Editor Publishing, 1899), 101.

10. Henry Woodfin Grady, *The Race Problem: A Lecture* (Philadelphia: J. D. Morris, 1900).

11. Kelly Miller, "The Negro and Education," *Forum* 30 (1901): 693–705, here 696; Sutton E. Griggs, *Unfettered (Nashville: Orion Publishing Company)*, 4. Subsequent references to *Unfettered* are cited parenthetically in the text.

12. Miller, "Negro and Education," 696.

13. Many battles were fought, and the Scythians gained no advantage, until at last one of them thus addressed the remainder: "What are we doing, Scythians? We are fighting our slaves, diminishing our own number when we fall, and the number of those that belong to us when they fall by our hands. Take my advice—lay spear and bow aside, and let each man fetch his horsewhip, and go boldly up to them. So long as they see us with arms in our hands, they imagine themselves our equals in birth and bravery;

but let them behold us with no other weapon but the whip, and they will feel that they are our slaves, and flee before us." The Scythians followed this counsel, and the slaves were so astounded that they forgot to fight, and immediately ran away. Such was the mode in which the Scythians, after being for a time the lords of Asia and then forced to quit it by the Medes, returned and settled in their own country. Herodotus, *Herodotus in Four Volumes*, trans. A. D. Godley (New York: G. P. Putnam's Sons, 1928), bk. 4, chap. 3.

14. Though Griggs does not acknowledge Spencer by name in this passage, he is borrowing Spencer's ideas about the factors that lead one group to imagine that their crafted superiority is in fact natural. "Simultaneously there arise, between the ruling and subject classes, unlikenesses of bodily activity and skill. Occupied, as those of higher rank commonly are, in the chase when not occupied in war, they have a life-long discipline of a kind conducive to various physical superiorities; while, contrariwise, those occupied in agriculture, in carrying of burdens, and in other drudgeries, partially lose what agility and address they naturally had. Class-predominance is, therefore, thus further facilitated. 'And then there *are the* respective mental traits produced *by* daily exercise *of* power, *and by* daily submission *to* power. *The ideas, and sentiments, and modes of behavior, perpetually repeated, generate on one side an inherited fitness for command, and on the other side an inherited fitness for obedience; with the result that, in course of time, there arises on both sides the belief that the established relations of classes are the natural ones.'* By implying habitual war among settled societies, the foregoing interpretations have implied the formation of compound societies. The rise of such class-divisions as have been described is, therefore, complicated by the rise of further class-divisions determined by the relations from time to time established between those conquerors and conquered whose respective groups already contain class-divisions." Herbert Spencer, "Development of Political Institutions, IV — Political Differentiation," *Popular Science Monthly*, February 1881:441–42.

15. Griggs continues: "The traits of character acquired in one generation were transmitted to succeeding generations, so that notions of inherent superiority and the belief in the right of repression became ingrained in Southern character. In confirmation of this conclusion, we again quote from Mr. Herbert Spencer, who says: "The emotional nature prompting the general mode of conduct is derived from ancestors is a product of all ancestral activities. * * * The governing sentiment is, in short, mainly the accumulated and organized sentiment of the past." Taken from Herbert Spencer, *The Principles of Sociology* (New York: D. Appleton, 1891), 2:321.

16. James Robert Payne, "Afro-American Literature of the Spanish-American War," *MELUS* 10, no. 3, "Varieties of Ethnic Criticism" (Autumn 1983): 26.

17. William Thomas Stead, *The Americanisation of the World; or, The Trend of the Twentieth Century* (London: Review of Reviews Office, 1902).

18. Kelly Miller, "The Negro and Education," 694–95.

19. See Herbert Spencer, "Climate and Social Development," *Popular Science Monthly*, July 1874, 324–27.

20. Spencer, *Principles of Sociology*, 1:24.

21. Griggs pulls here from Kidd's original: "If we look to the native social systems of the tropical East, to the primitive savagery of Central Africa, to the West Indian Islands in the past in process of being assisted into the position of modern States by Great Britain, to the Black Republic of Hayti in the present, or to modern Liberia in the future, the lesson seems everywhere the same; it is that there will be no development of the resources of the tropics under native government." Benjamin Kidd, *The Control of the Tropics* (London: Macmillan, 1898), 53.

22. Miller, *A Review of Hoffman's Race Traits and Tendencies of the American Negro* (Washington D.C.: The Academy, 1897), 9–10.

23. This need for relocating the black populace extended to all ranks. The educated would need to be relocated not just from one region to the next but internationally as well. See Griggs, *Unfettered*, 256–57.

TESS CHAKKALAKAL

Reading in Sutton E. Griggs

Part autobiography, part sales pitch, Sutton E. Griggs's *The Story of My Struggles* (1914) recounts the challenges faced by an African American author during the Jim Crow era. These challenges were not only the result of discrimination in a publishing industry committed to promoting the work of popular white supremacist writers. In *The Story*, Griggs "shifts the blame" for his lack of success as an author to his fellow African Americans, who did not support him in his risky literary enterprise. Though his books were advertised in several newspapers, Griggs describes his disappointment at the poor sales of his first two novels, *Imperium in Imperio* (1899) and *Overshadowed* (1901). "There were practically no sales," he laments, "save such as were made in person."[1]

The disappointing reality of his ambitious literary labors that Griggs reveals in *The Story* goes against the long-held assumption, first asserted by Hugh M. Gloster, that "because Griggs was industrious enough to establish his own publishing companies and to promote the sale of his books among the black masses of the country, his novels, though virtually unknown to white American readers, were probably more widely circulated among Negroes than the fiction of [Charles Waddell] Chesnutt and [Paul Laurence] Dunbar."[2] Gloster's "probably" would become a certainty among later critics. The now widely held belief that "Griggs was exceedingly popular among his own people" rests almost entirely on the control— unprecedented for an African American author at the time—that Griggs exerted over the production and dissemination of his novels. While Chesnutt relied on the patronage and advice of white literary luminaries such as George Washington Cable and Walter Hines Page, and Dunbar found in W. D. Howells an important ally and critic, Griggs produced his novels practically alone, receiving little financial support or literary advice from external sources. Instead, Griggs acted as his own editor, his own publisher, and, ultimately, marketed his books himself. Though Griggs followed methods similar to those of the itinerant black ministers of the period, who, as John Giggie notes, sold goods to their congregations produced by northern white manufacturers, Griggs worked only for himself.[3]

What set Griggs apart from his better-known African American contemporaries was the fact that he relied almost exclusively on African American readers and presses to produce and disseminate his work.[4] Because Griggs did not modify his novels to suit the literary tastes of white editors and critics of his time, his novels may be viewed, in Wilson J. Moses's useful terminology, as exemplifying the principles of a "literary black nationalism."[5] As Moses outlines in his important study of Griggs's novels, Griggs's literary commitment to and investment in African American readers was routinely ignored or misunderstood. Excoriating African Americanist literary critics for their failure to appreciate Griggs's contribution, Moses declares: "There have been few readers to treat Griggs with any serious appreciation." Corroborating Moses's claim, Griggs notes in his own *Story* that all his attempts to reach African American readers through his novels ended in failure and bitter disappointment. The fact that the only way he could get African Americans to buy or even "appreciate" the value of his books was through "direct personal canvas" suggested to him that all his literary efforts were doomed to fail. "I decided to abandon the field of literature and devote my time fully to my other labors" (11).

These "other labors" involved the more practical tasks of pastoring the First Baptist Church in East Nashville and lecturing on the "Negro Problem" directly to black audiences throughout the South. Griggs's income was derived from his work as a minister and lecturer, but much to the chagrin of his congregation, Griggs viewed this work as secondary to his literary work.[6] In a 1907 lecture titled "How to Win the Battles of the Race," Griggs spoke of the writings of Owen Wister, Thomas Nelson Page, Thomas Dixon, and others. His novels, he explained to his audience at the Ebenezer A.M.E. Church in Baltimore, are intended to wage war against the sentiments expressed by those who are "creating sentiment against the Negro." The only way to win the war, presumably, was not to pray or to attend speeches and lectures but to read. Reading works that were opposed to those of Wister, Page, and Dixon would produce a demand for a new kind of literature, a form that did not subscribe to the racist principles of those writers. All that was needed was a new kind of reader, one who understood the experiences of former slaves and their descendants.

Though Griggs's emphasis on reading hardly seems radical to readers today, it did in fact mark a significant departure from the political and religious discourse of the early twentieth century. Long before early twenty-first-century critics pointed out that "celebrations of the black oral tradition and black vernacular" have undermined our understanding of African American literature, Griggs privileged the written word over the spoken. "To succeed as a race," he wrote in 1916, "we must move up out of the age of the voice."[7]

To achieve such success, Griggs committed himself to making and selling books, but doing so did not produce the results he envisioned. His attempt to establish a bureau in Philadelphia for the dissemination of literature favorable to the race never materialized; instead, he returned to the South and established the National Public Welfare League in Memphis, Tennessee, to focus on southern readers. The numerous books and pamphlets published under the National Public Welfare League did little to achieve his larger purpose. Though black literacy was on the rise and the number of black newspapers and journals was steadily growing, Griggs could not find enough readers for his works that would enable commercial success. Why? Part of the reason, as several of his readers have pointed out, lies in Griggs's own rhetorical failure. Another part lies in a lack of resources and support. But another, perhaps less obvious reason, was the simple fact that Griggs's books were difficult to read. They require a great deal of attention and time that most people, particularly poor people struggling to survive, could not afford. To enable his potential audience to move out of the age of the voice, Griggs would first have to teach "his race" how to read a novel.

Looking back on his short but highly productive career as a novelist in his *Story*, he recalls that in 1902 he "decided to write another book and put forth all that there was in [him], so that there could be no shadow of doubt as to where the fault [of reception] was. It was thus that [he] wrote 'Unfettered'" (10). In a glowing review of the novel that appeared in the *Colored American* under the headline "'Unfettered': A Story of Love and Politics involving a Sober Discussion of the Race Problem," the anonymous reviewer claims that the novel will "vastly increase one's stock of information, and [to] suggest a method which, if carried, would result in happier conditions for our people in this country."[8] This review, likely penned by Griggs himself, emphasizes the practical effects of reading the novel. Yet the immediate material benefits associated with reading his novels did little to attract readers.

Despite having decided to abandon literary fiction after the failure of his second novel, Griggs was persuaded by the National Baptist Convention (NBC) at its annual meeting on September 16, 1903, to write a third, *The Hindered Hand; or, The Reign of the Repressionist* (1905), as a response to Thomas Dixon's white supremacist *Reconstruction Trilogy*. However, the financial support promised by the NBC, as Griggs reveals in *The Story*, "never came" (13). Despite being in debt, Griggs published two more books, one a work of nonfiction, *The One Great Question* (1907), and the other, his last novel, *Pointing the Way* (1908), "with the same results" (14). After the publication of *Pointing the Way*, Griggs finally gave up on making books, moving instead to the less onerous task of publishing pamphlets: "Unable longer to issue books I began to publish small pamphlets which I took and peddled here and there" (14). For Griggs, peddling pamphlets rather than making books was a sign that "his people" were not yet ready to appreciate the value of literature.

Making books, especially the kinds of books that Griggs was making, was a costly enterprise. First editions of Griggs's novels are now rare and expensive. At the time, however, Griggs's novels were priced at only a dollar a copy, plus ten cents for postage. This was the standard price for most novels sold by subscription at the time. Griggs's first novel, *Imperium in Imperio*, was published by a vanity press in Ohio, which meant that he would have paid the Editor Publishing Company to publish his novel, rather than receiving an advance from his publisher (as did both Chesnutt and Dunbar). Similarly, his later novels were self-published, so he would have had to pay the costs of printing and reproducing his novels himself. Although Griggs would have had to borrow heavily to produce his books, these first editions were not made cheaply; they reveal an attention to certain production details of an author interested in the book as a physical object and the experience of reading. Even the first edition of *Imperium in Imperio* departs from most books produced by the Editor Publishing Company during the period. Its unique cover design suggests that Griggs was involved directly in its production (see fig. 1). Indeed the physical features of Griggs's books—beautifully bound in cloth, lettered in gold with particularly beautiful cover designs—were viewed by contemporary reviewers as a distinguishing feature (see fig. 2). *Imperium* was published the same year that Griggs became pastor of the First Baptist Church in East Nashville; based on the financial records of the church gathered by Randolph Meade Walker, it is likely that Griggs used money from the church to help finance the production and dissemination of his novels. Although Griggs did not give up on writing, he stopped making beautiful books for African Americans to read only because he could no longer afford to do so.

In many ways, Griggs's literary enterprise was doomed from the start. There was simply no way for his books, priced as they were, to make money unless he sold them in great quantities. Griggs ended his career as a novelist in 1908 be-

IMPERIUM IN IMPERIO.

BY

SUTTON E. GRIGGS.

CINCINNATI
THE EDITOR PUBLISHING CO.
1899.

Figure 1. Title page and cover illustration of first edition of
Imperium in Imperio (Cincinnati: Editor, 1899)

Figure 2. Detail of title page of *Imperium in Imperio*

cause he could not convince African Americans that reading novels was worth their time and money. Unlike those of Chesnutt and Dunbar, Griggs's novels reveal an author less interested in "becoming an author," that is, someone who lived "off" his writing, than an author who simply wanted to sell enough books to make more books. Griggs wrote, edited, published, and disseminated books so that African Americans living in the South might experience the pleasure of reading a book that made them feel as if they had the power to change their circumstances.

Like Olaudah Equiano and William Wells Brown, Griggs was deeply involved in the writing, production, and dissemination of his books. But unlike these early (and now canonical) African American writers, Griggs marketed his books almost exclusively to African Americans. His publishing activities shed considerable light on the development of African American literary culture at the turn of the century in the United States, but few book histories mention Griggs. Part of the reason for Griggs's absence from most literary histories and histories of book publishing is due to the lack of material evidence concerning the production and dissemination of his novels.[9] There are virtually no surviving manuscripts, business records, contracts, diaries, or personal correspondence related to Griggs's literary career. All that remains of Griggs's career as a novelist are the books he wrote, published, and sold.

Literary historians in the past two decades have worked hard to recover "real readers."[10] Their purpose has been to capture the nuances of the act of reading as a situated and embodied phenomenon. By looking at personal diaries and annotations and other marks left in books, they have been able to recover specific acts of reading with unprecedented detail and insight. Though considerable progress has been made in uncovering "African American reading acts," most of the scholarship on African American readers is, as Leon Jackson complains, "more akin to rhetorical analysis than reading history."[11] This is because, as Jackson and others argue, the story of the production, dissemination, and consumption of African American literature has not been adequately told.[12] But it is also the case, as Griggs notes in *The Story of My Struggles*, that "the masses" of African Americans were "unresponsive" to books. Although Griggs paints a rather bleak picture of African American readers as a group in his autobiography, his novels reveal a more hopeful image of the individual African American reader. Though this reader is entirely a figment of Griggs's imagination and is therefore considered unreliable evidence for most historians of reading, I suggest that Griggs's imagined African American reader reveals a marked shift away from collective or shared reading practices related to the conditions of slavery and the emancipation period toward the development of a solitary or private African American reading practice during Jim Crow.

During the last twenty years, with the burgeoning of reception studies, reading studies, and book history, scholars have begun to address the ways in which African American print culture developed in the postslavery era. Though several recent studies of nineteenth- and early twentieth-century African American readers have helped to expand our knowledge about this neglected interpretive community, "African American readers" remains a highly elusive category. "How can we know," Elizabeth McHenry asks in her seminal literary history of African American readers, "or historically document the act of reading, an activity that in our own day and age, at least, is mainly practiced in silent and individual ways that seem impossible to access?"[13] Given the "silent and individual ways" of most readers, historians of reading like McHenry have focused on African American readers as a collective category born out of slavery and the struggle for literacy.[14] This essay focuses on a different kind of African American reader, one who was not a member of the African American reading communities and literary societies or involved in other forms of communal reading projects that are the subject of most studies of African American print culture. Social segregation and voting restrictions associated with the Jim Crow era resulted in a retreat, particularly among African Americans, from the public sphere. Unable to hold political office, to vote, or even to enter various segregated spaces, such as libraries, schools, and government buildings, African Americans retreated to private spaces, such as the home and church, where they could be safe from acts of racial violence. And it was in these enclosed spaces that African Americans might experience the pleasure of reading. Foregrounding the silent and individual reading habits of readers in his fiction, Griggs believed, would enable African Americans to develop what he called "the habit of reading," a quality that would "secure the very highest and best form of co-operation" between the races.[15]

Griggs's novels primarily manifest the personal and social benefits of reading for politically disenfranchised and economically disadvantaged African Americans between 1899 and 1908. Historians generally regard this period as the Age of Restoration, when African American voters were legally eliminated from the electorate in the South.[16] Though this period of American history has figured prominently in the historical and literary imagination, the contemporary African American response to disenfranchisement has been largely ignored. Griggs's novels are about presenting "the race question in a new light."[17] Shedding new light on a rather old problem required shifting the mode in which it was presented. In a 1907 pamphlet, addressing the role black leaders played in the "Brownsville Affair," Griggs explains why he has chosen to address the political issues of his moment in print form: "A speech would have been heard and would have vanished, leaving only memories behind, whereas the reader, if he feels so inclined, may now read, re-read and ponder every word that is here said."[18]

Given the social and political reality of Jim Crow, Griggs turned to literature as an instrument with which African Americans might gain the political representation they were promised by the Fifteenth Amendment yet denied by state governments in the South. Due to the "very absence of social contact" between the races during his time, "it [is] necessary for the races to discover some other way of understanding each other better." Griggs asked, "Cannot literature become this bond of union?" "Cannot white men and women picture the inner life of the white South, and through these books give the Negroes a sympathy and knowledge of the whites?"[19]

Griggs answered his own call for such literature by publishing five novels, but his novels failed to achieve their purpose. For all his industry and eloquence, Griggs could not convince African Americans living in the segregated South that the highly individual and silent act of reading would produce a political coalition between blacks and whites in the South that would bring an end to Jim Crow. Of course, as Griggs himself would later admit, his dream of forming a coalition of like-minded whites and blacks in the South was a sign of his political naïveté. Though Griggs did give up on writing novels, he did not abandon the idea that without the right to vote, "making many books" was the only way to achieve political representation.[20]

The Price of Fiction

"Fiction," Booker T. Washington declares in his autobiography, *Up from Slavery* (1901), "I care little for. Frequently I have to almost force myself to read a novel that is on every one's lips."[21] Washington's disdain for fiction should come as no surprise for those familiar with his philosophy of education. Through his work as the founder and principal of the Tuskegee Normal and Industrial Institute for the Training of Colored Young Men and Women in rural Alabama— more commonly called "The Tuskegee Machine"—Washington espoused the value of teaching students practical labor skills over that of, what he called, "mere book education." The now-standard indictment of Washington's philosophy of education is that it made black schooling an instrument of active accommodation to a social system becoming more harshly discriminatory after the end of Reconstruction. While this critique of Washington's philosophy is well founded, it is also the case, as several of Washington's recent defenders argue, that his educational philosophy was itself generated by the particular historical and political circumstances of the late nineteenth century.

Washington didn't like reading fiction because he felt it was useless to newly emancipated African Americans, who had to learn how to feed and clothe themselves, how to run a household, and how to earn and spend money wisely. When Washington says that he does not care for fiction, he does not mean that he doesn't like to read. To the contrary, he does like reading. "The kind of reading that I have the greatest fondness for is biography. I like to be sure that I am reading about a real man or a real thing," he writes. It is not reading that is useless; it is reading fiction. For Washington, fiction had nothing to do with the business of real men doing real things. In fact, Washington went so far as to suggest that reading fiction served only to distract African Americans during the postemancipation era from moving up from slavery.[22]

Like Washington, who famously instructed southern blacks to "cast down your bucket where you are," rather than pursue greater opportunities in the North, Griggs was an ardent supporter of the South and its people. All his novels are set in the South, and he expresses some reservation for those, like Bernard Belgrave, the antihero of his first novel, *Imperium in Imperio*, and Astral Herndon, the ambivalent hero of *Overshadowed*, who leave the South to pursue an elite education in the North. It is, in fact, in *Overshadowed* that Griggs makes his sympathies for Washington's philosophy most explicit. Its heroine, Erma Wysong, is a student at Tuskegee but must quit her studies due to her mother's death. Though she does not complete her Tuskegee education, she does nonetheless pursue a path of self-improvement that mirrors Washington's philosophy. Later in the novel, Washington makes a cameo appearance to deliver a lecture on the "Race Problem." Washington's speech and ideas are essential to forming Erma's character; she is, to my mind, one of the most memorable and admirable heroines of Griggs's fiction.

While Washington plays an important role in Griggs's fiction and connections between the two authors can be easily drawn, the premium Griggs places on "book-education" and "the habit of reading" flies in the face of Washington's philosophy. Reading books forms a cornerstone of Griggs's political philosophy. In *Life's Demands*, Griggs deems the habit of reading "the climax of the qualities needed to secure the very highest and best form of co-operation." Reading, for Griggs, was not just a matter of practical literacy; instead, it involved the more abstract ability "to absorb what is written or printed" and "of being moved to action" by what is read.[23] The distinction Griggs draws between literacy and the habit of reading marks an important shift in the history of African American readers, from the reading habits formed by "slave culture" and emancipation to the development of a "New Negro" literary culture.

Imperium in Imperio opens with the words of Belton Piedmont's mother, Hannah, "a poor, ignorant negro [*sic*] woman," who is determined to give her four children "all de book larning dar is ter be had eben ef she has ter lib on bred an' herrin's, an die en de a'ms house."[24] Despite this very obvious contrast between Griggs's and Washington's philosophies of education, Griggs does not—like W. E. B. Du Bois—openly oppose Washington's model for black education.[25] Instead, he makes the habit of reading central to his program for "racial success." Rather than choose a side on the great debate over black education, Griggs decided to write novels that would appeal to the black masses, the kind of books that would be accessible and relevant to women like Hannah Piedmont, Erma Wysong, and their children. In other words, Griggs's target audience was poor African Americans living in the South. The question is why did Griggs insist on fiction as the form to disseminate his ideas among those who lacked the leisure and resources to read novels?

"The Habit of Reading"

The novel was increasingly prominent in mainstream literary culture toward the end of the nineteenth century; despite Washington's highly influential denunciation of fiction, it was the most popular genre in both the marketplace and the library. Echoing late nineteenth-century discourse that celebrated the "reading habit" in newspapers, magazines, and lectures, Griggs presented "the habit of reading" as one of the most important of "The Laws of Individual Success."[26] This "habit" could be acquired only by reading, by developing a desire to read. Unlike learning to read—becoming literate—developing a reading habit could not be taught by schoolteachers alone; a reading habit is formed primarily through individual practice. "Let this be done," Griggs instructs, "throughout all the years of one's life, and let it not be neglected, it matters not how busy, how very busy, that life may be."[27]

While Griggs solemnly asserted that "all that men have ever thought, felt or done that is recorded can become the help of him who has the habit of reading," he was also aware that developing this habit was not easy, especially for those who were being instructed about the negative effects of the reading habit. It is one thing to promise "individual success" by reading, but it is quite another to persuade those who "lack the leisure" and "general culture" of the benefits of reading.[28] It was through his fiction that Griggs hoped to instill the habit of reading in African Americans.

At the turn of the twentieth century, a growing mass of readers avidly consumed popular fiction, dime novels, detective fiction, and Westerns. The division between popular fiction and serious literature seemed to be widening at this time. Popular fiction was directed at the masses, while serious literature appeared disinterested in having a mass appeal. It was by reading popular fiction rather than serious literature that most people develop the reading habit, and it was by writing about the race problem in this form that Griggs believed it might be solved. Griggs's fiction depicts characters absorbed by reading. The act of reading, rather than their racial affiliation, shapes the lives of Griggs's characters. This neglected feature of Griggs's fiction is important not only to deciphering the meaning of his novels but also essential to broadening theoretical notions of the act of reading.[29]

Imperium in Imperio begins with an announcement to "The Public" by the author, declaring not just the truth of the narrative we are about to read but how the manuscript came into the author's hands. He claims that he is not, in fact, the author of the narrative but just its editor and goes on to declare that he has other documents in his possession to confirm the "truthfulness" of the "assertions made in the narrative" (3). The overall effect of Griggs's announcement was to respond to those like Washington who longed for true stories and practical advice in literature. By drawing the reader's attention to the storytelling process, Griggs gives the novel a greater immediacy, making the novelist less the story's creator than its mediator. Moreover, Griggs's insistence that he is not the writer of the story but an active reader places him on common ground with his readers. Part of the challenge of reading *Imperium in Imperio* is coming to terms with the status of the author, who remains elusive and, at the same time, maintains an intimate relationship with the reader throughout the novel.

Griggs's insistence that the narrative is not only true but "given" to him by a man named Berl Trout displaces his own role as author. Instead, Griggs acts only as its editor and one who intervenes only sparingly: "Having perfect faith in the truthfulness of his narrative I have not hesitated to fulfil his dying request by editing his Ms., and giving it to the public" (3). Echoing Nathaniel Hawthorne's well-known introduction to *The Scarlet Letter*, Griggs's explanation of how the manuscript came into his possession allows (in Hawthorne's memorable formulation) a personal relation with the public. By calling attention to the means by which the book was written, Griggs invites readers to approach the book as a collaborative enterprise: the book was written by Berl Trout, edited by Sutton E. Griggs, and tells the story of neither but rather introduces readers to two great black men, Belton Piedmont and Bernard Belgrave. Berl Trout only appears in the first person at the beginning and the end of the narrative to explain to readers why he has chosen to tell the story. In the final chapter, titled "Personal," we learn that Trout was a member of the Imperium, which ordered Belton to be slain. It is out of guilt for that terrible act that he feels compelled to reveal the secret of the Imperium in the form of a book. By reading the book we gain knowledge not only of this secret government but also of the *true* story of a great man, "a poor Negro," who is a figure for "the spirit of conservatism in the Negro race," and who is betrayed and executed by his political rival, Bernard Belgrave. Bernard's violent actions are directly related to a form of black radicalism that goes against the conservative political principles for which Belton died (175). The activity of the reader is not one of being a consumer of stories but rather one of learning and constructing a new ethical realm through a new set of political relations. Indeed, this is precisely the type of story that Washington would have appreciated because it is a story about "real life" with "real effects," even though it is "just" a novel.

Like Griggs's subsequent novels, *Imperium* employs the kind of narrating persona found in the novels of Owen Wister, Francis Marion Crawford, and Winston Churchill so popular at the time. Like Griggs, these writers used a rhetoric of direct address to reinforce an image of the reader as an active collaborator in a shared enterprise. Though these writers were more popular than their literary contemporaries—Edith Wharton, Charles Chesnutt, and Henry James—most of their novels, like Griggs's, are hardly known today. Part of the reason for this, as Barbara Hochman explains in her study of readers in the age of American realism, was purely formal: "The novelists who went on conceptualizing the reader as peer and confidant were forgotten or dismissed."[30] Another reason for the popularity of these writers in their time and their later disappearance is that they emphasized the political and social matters of their day, while ignoring the psychological complexities motivating their characters' actions.

Wister's novel *Lady Baltimore* (1906), which Griggs discusses in *The One Great Question*, presents "the current thought of the young North groping its way toward settled convictions [and] represents it as now feeling that the final status of the American Negro is to be and ought to be 'something between equality and slavery.'"[31] Griggs was understandably alarmed by such sentiments expressed in the popular literature of his day. In response to writers such as Wister and Thomas Dixon Jr., who expressed similar though more radical views on "the Negro" in his novels, Griggs wrote novels based on his personal experience of being African American in the Jim Crow South. "Being somewhat familiar with the actual workings of this system," he explains, "having seen it thoroughly tested on sundry occasions, we have thought to pilot our readers on a visit to the regions in question, that they may note the kind of fruit the tree of repression bears."[32] Judging by the metaphors Griggs typically employs when speaking either of or to his readers, he viewed his novels as offering an accurate description of the effects of racial segregation and disenfranchisement on African Americans in sharp contrast to the caricatures of African Americans found in the novels of Thomas E. Dixon and Thomas Nelson Page. As a novelist, Griggs acts as a guide who takes readers on a journey through the southern United States, where we are introduced to *real* (historically accurate representations of) African Americans and their experiences of family, education, love, politics, marriage, and death.

Imperium is typical of Griggs's rhetorical mode in this respect. Though Griggs presents the story in the voice of a native tour guide, he also presents himself as a self-conscious narrator: "Let us now acquaint ourselves with the circumstances under which the opening words of our story were spoken. To do this, we must need lead our readers into humble and commonplace surroundings" (7). Griggs's narrator often directly addresses his readers as a distinct group and always refers to himself in the third-person plural. Moreover, he never lets his readers forget that what we are reading is a story that only he can provide, given his knowledge and proximity to the people and events he describes: "Mrs. Hannah Piedmont, the colored woman whom we have presented to our readers as addressing her little boy, was the mother of five children,—three girls and two boys" (8). This narrative mode gives the impression that the novel's author is standing next to his readers while they read, pointing out significant details, though neither is participating directly in the action: "This morning we find Belton's mother preparing him for school, and we shall stand by and watch the preparations." Though the people of Griggs's story, upon first glance, appear to be entirely unremarkable, the narrator insists that these people are worthy of our attention: "A man of tact, intelligence, and superior education moving in the midst of a mass of ignorant people, ofttimes has a sway more absolute than that of monarchs" (10). Such lines as these are delivered for the benefit of those readers, like Griggs himself, who find themselves "in the midst of a mass of ignorant people" not knowing what to do with their knowledge and education. One objective of the novel is to provide practical advice to African Americans for what to do with their newly acquired ability to read.

Throughout *Imperium*, the narrator attempts to guide readers toward a more balanced perspective of the race problem in the South. To do this, he introduces readers to a character with whom they might easily identify. Belton Piedmont is black, poor, and the fourth of his mother's five children who have been abandoned by their father. Precisely because there is nothing remarkable about Belton, he "was singled out by the teacher as a special object on which he might expend his spleen" (23). Neither his teacher's racism nor the impoverished circumstances of his birth stand in the way of Belton's desire to learn. Rather than be led by his cruel teacher, Belton (like his more fortunate and light-skinned counterpart Bernard Belgrave) "ran to the sublime in literature" reading about "heroic deeds of man" (25). It is reading literature that ultimately saves Belton from falling into the trap of ignominy and humiliation that would otherwise be the inevitable result of his circumstances.

That reading figures prominently in *Imperium* should come as no surprise. Even in a novel so rhetorically and ideologically removed as Wister's *The Virginian*, reading appears as the linchpin of education. What is different about the way reading figures in Griggs's fiction is the various ways in which reading alters the course of the hero's life. It is, for instance, after Mr. King, the white editor of the *Richmond Daily Temps*, reads Belton's oration, "published and commented upon by the leading journals of England," that "he saw that the flame of liberty was in his heart, her sword in his hand, and the disdain of death stamped on his brow" (34). In writing *Imperium*, Griggs hopes that his readers will be so moved, that they will read his words, just as the newspaper editor reads Belton's speech, and be moved to reach out to thoughtful and educated black men like Belton who seek a political voice. Moreover, it is because Mr. King *reads* Belton's speech in the newspaper, rather than hears it at the graduation ceremony when it is first delivered, that he is moved to take action. Whereas the speech in oral form succumbs to the prejudices of the audience, when printed in the *Temps* it "created a great sensation in political and literary circles in every section of the country" (32). Like his hero, Griggs had great faith in the power of the printed word to transcend racial differences. Though the narrator celebrates his characters' "remarkable feats of oratory," *Imperium* concludes by endorsing the printed word over the spoken word. Speeches may move the masses to take action but often, as in the case of Erma Wysong of *Overshadowed*, listening to a passionate speech by Booker T. Washington, rather than reading a book about the lives of African Americans, leads to hasty judgments and political mistakes.

Though *Imperium* is decidedly a story about a great man, a fictional form of historical biography, it also depicts women reading and involved in politics. Both Belton and Bernard fall in love with "intellectual" women. Belton meets Antoinette Nermal when he is hired at a "local colored school," while Bernard meets Viola Martin at a "reading circle composed of the brightest most talented young men and women of the city" (69). Though both women are extolled for their beauty and virtue, Viola's association with the reading circle and with the "patriotic clubs among the women" in Norfolk distinguish her from the "musical circles in which [Antoinette] moved" (80). Antoinette, like Griggs's own wife, Emma J. Williams, is a schoolteacher who teaches African American children to read in the South. Although Antoinette and Belton marry without obstacles, a book thwarts the union of Viola and Bernard. Viola supports Bernard's efforts to enter politics, but she refuses to marry him because of his light skin. In her suicide note/love letter to Bernard she explains that her decision to kill herself is based on "a book entitled 'White Supremacy and Negro Subordination' [that] by merest accident came into [her] possession" (118).

Written by a northern medical doctor, J. H. Van Evrie, and published shortly after the Civil War, this book is no fiction. It is the result, as its author explains, "of many years of patient study and investigation of the normal order of American society."[33] Based primarily on census data and a broad cultural-historical study of American life from the colonial period to the mid-nineteenth century, the book "presents in language that can be easily understood by the commonest reader" that "the four millions of negroes in their so-called slavery in the South were happier and more improved, intellectually, than the same number of the same class in any other portion of the world." So moved is Viola by reading the book that she vows "to solemnly pledge God to never marry a mulatto man" because based on her reading of Van Evrie's book, such a union would be "sapping the vitality of the Negro race." In her letter to Bernard, she instructs him to "secure the book" and "to study the question of the intermingling of the races" (119). If, as she believes, miscegenation is what "is in reality destroying [African Americans]," then Bernard is to "dedicate [his] soul to the work of separating the white and colored races" (119). This is exactly what Bernard does. Viola's instructions (adapted from her reading of Van Evrie's white supremacist doctrines) form the cornerstone of the political philosophy that Berl Trout indicts in the novel's conclusion: "With Viola's tiny hand protruding from the grave pointing him to move forward, Bernard Belgrave, President of the Imperium in Imperio, was a man to be feared" (175). The book may be responsible for Bernard's radicalism and his rise to power, but it is Viola's singular act of reading that lies behind his political actions. Not unlike his later *Hindered Hand*, which responds to Dixon's popular white supremacist fiction, *Imperium in Imperio* offers a response to Van Evrie's earlier *White Supremacy and Negro Subordination* (1868). Though she is literate and cultured, Viola falls victim to a book that misrepresents African Americans. African Americans are simply reading the wrong books about the race problem because these are the only ones available to them. To correct their mistaken views, they must be more careful in choosing what books come into their possession. Possessing a book like *Imperium in Imperio* would yield drastically different results from those that result from Viola's accidental possession of *White Supremacy and Negro Subordination*.

Reading, thus, takes several distinct but related forms in *Imperium in Imperio*. First, reading takes the form of words "from the lips of a poor, ignorant, negro [sic] woman" whose insistence on "book larning" for her children is celebrated as having "vitally affected the destiny of the nation." Belton's and Bernard's "reading habit" models the kind of education that produces great men. When women read in Griggs's novels, however, the results are somewhat less predictable. Though Bernard's mother is "a woman with a very superior education" and exhibits a "remarkable" reading habit, it is a form of reading associated only with wealth and status. In sharp contrast to the poverty and ignorance of

Belton's mother, Bernard's mother "was a woman with a very superior education. The range of her reading was truly remarkable. She possessed the finest library ever seen in the northern section of Virginia, and all of the best of the latest books were constantly arriving at her home. Magazines and newspapers arrived by every mail" (61). However, Mrs. Belgrave's access to great literature and popular publications is the result of her illicit marriage to a white senator. Unlike Bernard's light-skinned and rich mother, Belton's "poor" mother exhibits a different kind of commitment to "book larning." Mrs. Piedmont's determination to acquire "book larning," according to the narrator, "saved the sun of the Nineteenth Century, proud and glorious, from passing through, near its setting, the blackest and thickest and ugliest clouds of all its journey" (7). Though both women dedicate themselves to their sons' educations, that dedication is manifested differently. Belton's mother makes a great economic sacrifice for his education, while Bernard's mother "superintended his literary training and cultivated in him a yearning for literature of the highest and purest type" (61). Through his representation of mothers, Griggs presents contrasting uses of reading. Reading is valued for distinct reasons and taught at distinct times in an individual's life, by distinctly gendered teachers, through distinct methods. Moreover, the kind of reading performed by Bernard's light-skinned, wealthy mother has strong racial implications that are reinforced by Viola Martin's suicide note. Reading only literature making claims to be of "the highest and purest type," it turns out, may not be as good for us as readers who belong to exclusive literary societies and book clubs seem to believe. Indeed, it may be precisely this type of race literature that enforces false ideas about blacks and whites and the relationship between them.

Griggs wanted to produce a different kind of literature, a form of literature that departed from aesthetic standards that were predicated on the dominant racial theories of his time. To read this new form of literature, however, required not just a new set of reading practices but also a new kind of reader, the kind of reader who, because she did not have access to an extensive library, must choose her books more carefully and read them intensively. In other words, for Griggs's readers, reading was not just a matter of good taste and social status; it was a matter of life and death.

A Reading Romance

It is difficult to overstate the importance of reading to almost every aspect of *Unfettered* (1902). From its plot, characters, and setting to its paratextual corollaries such as the dedication to Griggs's deceased sister (whom he calls his "one sympathetic reader") and preface (which declares the novel's aim "to lead the reader into the inner life of the Negro race"), *Unfettered* is a novel obsessed with the act of reading. This obsession takes shape in multiple forms but is fully realized in the novel's heroine, the beautiful Morlene Dalton. Morlene foregrounds the figure of the female reader that remains in the background of his first novel. Just as in *Imperium*, politics is central to the plot of *Unfettered*; here books and the act of reading are not merely a source for ideas and images. It is through writing and reading books that the legal and social strictures of Jim Crow are overcome.

Like Bernard's mother, Morlene has access to a library of many books, none of which belong to her. They, like the house she shares with Aunt Catherine, belong to a former slave owner, Maurice Dalton. Upon his death, she and Catherine are banished from the house by Dalton's misguided nephew, Lemuel. Though Morlene rejects Lemuel's offer to provide for her material comfort, she does take with her the habit of reading that she developed while living on the Dalton estate. Morlene does not own the books she reads. Instead, these books are available to her only while she is a resident on the Dalton estate. Once she is forced to leave the premises (significantly Lemuel informs her and Aunt Catherine that they must leave the estate in the library) she no longer has access to books. Because she does not own the books she reads, Morlene is unable to rely on them for sustenance. Reading, as her friend Beulah points out to her, only exacerbates the impoverished conditions in which they both live. Assuming an intimate connection with Morlene because they are both "poor country girls and can talk plainly to each other," Beulah goes on to point out that though she does not read like Morlene, there is no difference between them: "You have been reading books up at the Dalton house which set forth the deeds of mighty men. Out of all that you have gleaned from books you have constructed your ideal man whom you feel awaits you in the world. Morlene, we country girls have only a limited education and know but little of the requirements of the higher walks of life. The man whom your imagination has selected will be so much your superior in point of culture that he will not notice you" (42). Beulah is wrong on both counts: Morlene's reading habit distinguishes her from Beulah. The man she imagines to be ideal will notice her because of this difference. Beulah's misguided opinion of reading is informed entirely by her desire to have Morlene wed her ailing brother, whom she believes can be saved only by having Morlene as his wife. Even though she is sure she "could never love a man on

Harry's order" (42), Morlene agrees to marry Harry because Beulah convinces her that Morlene's "ideal [husband] is impossible of attainment" (43). Though her marriage does little to abate her love of books, it does result in a loveless marriage to a man who, "while not very proficient, had succeeded in mastering all that the teacher could impart." In Griggs's novels, "all that the teacher could impart" doesn't add up to much (25). Knowledge and success come not from teachers but from the books one chooses to read. We know that Morlene's marriage to Harry is doomed from the start not only because Morlene does not love him but also because Harry, like his sister, exhibits no interest in reading.

It is no wonder that Harry and Beulah are both killed and forgotten by the end of the novel. Because they, like Bernard's mother and his beloved Viola Martin, represent misguided or ill-informed views about reading and society, they are to be viewed as hapless victims of their own ignorance. That Morlene manages to overcome the ignorance they unwittingly thrust upon her would not be possible without the presence of the novel's unequivocal hero, Dorlan Warthell.

Morlene first encounters Dorlan after her marriage to Harry and the murder of Beulah has forced the couple (along with their neighbors) to leave their home in the country for the city. It is in her new home in the city that she meets Dorlan, whose physical description immediately reveals that he possesses the requisite qualities of Morlene's ideal husband: "His skin was smooth, his features regular, his eye intelligent and his head so formed as to indicate great brain power. As to color he was black, but even those prejudiced to color forgot that prejudice when they gazed upon this ebony-like Apollo. Wherever he appeared he was sure to attract attention as a rare specimen of physical manhood. His was evidently an open, frank nature, and his soul was in his face" (70–71). Dorlan's physical features distinguish him not only from the man Morlene "had married under a species of duress" but also manifest a particular history of reading that has brought him to Morlene's front door. Dorlan's early years were spent in school, where he received "great mental development." His learning continued when he found employment as a stable boy in the home of an eminent statesman. During his leisure hours, he perused his library and became thoroughly imbued with the spirit of the statesman. His residence in the South deemed it impossible for "men with black faces to aid in running the government" (80). Nonetheless, Dorlan is employed by a power-hungry Republican congressman to act as a political aid and speechwriter. It is important to note that Dorlan is a *writer*, not an orator. Dorlan's writing takes multiple forms in the novel. Besides writing political speeches, he also writes articles, dissertations, and love letters. Though we do see Dorlan repeatedly reading books, he is figured throughout the novel as producing literature that other characters, namely, Morlene, read and reread. The difference between them is precisely what makes them compatible. Although nonreaders like Beulah and Harry are responsible for keeping Morlene and Dorlan apart, there is a force even more powerful than they are. Morlene and Dorlan cannot marry and live happily ever after until the race problem is solved. This is exactly what *Unfettered* does: it solves the race problem by presenting its hero writing a book that the heroine reads.

To say that Griggs's love story is a trifle contrived is to state the obvious. But the romantic plot is only a literary device intended to interest readers in Griggs's political message. That the message is delivered through the fictional pen of the novel's hero makes it no less persuasive. In fact, it is by delivering the message that Dorlan *becomes* the novel's hero: "A Negro has been found to display political independence and moral courage of a high order. He has placed himself in a position where the unthinking will liken him unto the serpent that buried its fangs in the bosom that warmed it. None the less, his act is one of marked heroism" (97). For "Dorlan's Plan" to achieve its purpose, it must be read. This act takes "more courage," Griggs tells us in his "Foreword" to the plan, "than it does to fight a battle" (221).

In Griggs's fiction the act of reading is a critical step toward regaining political representation. Griggs's political objective can be achieved only after people read his books. Until African Americans invest in books that speak truthfully of their condition, they will be forced to represent the racial tenets of white supremacists writers. Buying a book, in other words, is tantamount to casting a vote, though the differences between the two acts are notable. *Unfettered* contains several dramatic scenes familiar to readers of African American literature: lynchings, mob violence, conspiracies, police chases, and the like. But the novel's primary action revolves around specific acts of reading. What is striking about the scenes of reading in this novel is that they occur in private. Unlike communal scenes of reading found in much African American literature, whether between slaves and their owners or among free African Americans who belong to literary societies, the scenes that Griggs presents depict his fictional readers as alone with the text. It is only by reading alone that "an era of independent thought among the Negroes" might begin and thus bring an end to the Jim Crow era (99).

While most viewed the struggle against Jim Crow as a battle between white and black or as an extension of the Civil War between the North and the South, Griggs saw the struggle as taking place wholly within the South between those few who read and consider issues "upon the highest plane" and the "many people in the South who never read, who never ponder grave questions, but assume the right to wreak vengeance on the heads of those who perchance wander from beaten paths in search of truth"(99). As we see in the case of Harry and Beulah Dalton, those who fall into the latter camp are not just white supremacists.

The book that Dorlan writes to solve the race problem, significantly, is not a novel. It is, as Griggs explains in the foreword to "Dorlan's Plan," a piece of particularly dry, dull, tedious writing that was a torture for its author to write and an even greater torture to read. No wonder it is subtitled "A Dissertation." Despite the challenges that the text poses to its reader, Griggs's novel presents the beautiful Morlene reading the dissertation "with much deliberation." Here is how Griggs describes Morlene's reading:

> After reading a while, Morlene laid the manuscript aside and spent the remainder of the day in meditating on what she had read. The second day she did likewise. Morlene began to be much elated, for, as the paper progressed, she saw that Dorlan was treating the subject in a most comprehensive way. Thus from day to day, she read and pondered, her hopes rising higher and higher. . . . By and by, after the lapse of many days Morlene drew near the close of the document. When, on the last day of her perusal, she read the last words of the last page, and her mind flashed back to the beginning and survey in general outline the whole, her enthusiasm knew no bounds. (202–3)

In some ways this mode of reading is not far removed from erotic reading, since both attempt to arouse the reader to express himself or herself freely, without inhibitions. This is, in other words, an intensely private form of reading that not only requires being left alone but also a lot of time, but it is something one can do anywhere. But unlike erotic reading performed solely for the purpose of pleasure, there is a significant pragmatic element in Morlene's reading. Though this kind of reading requires an investment, it is the kind of investment that those who lack leisure time can actually make, as long as they have the will. Griggs's fiction dramatizes the act of Morlene's reading "Dorlan's Plan" to "devise a solution to [the] Southern problem" as the means by which the mind of the Negro" will be "Unfettered" (175–76).

In the "dissertation" Griggs goes on to explain the more practical benefits of this mode of reading. Under the subtitle "Of Making Many Books There Is No End"—a line from Ecclesiastes that has since become the mantra of book historians—Griggs marks the historical shift in black reading practices at the turn of the twentieth century:

> The laboring Negroes have been accustomed to sing as they worked or have relieved the monotony of their labors by jovial bantering. The occupations of a race eventually make themselves felt in more or less marked racial characteristics. Thus, when a cotton factory was established recently to be operated by Negro labor, it failed, the manager assigning as a partial cause thereof the fact that the Negroes did not make the best operatives, in that sitting still and being quiet caused them to be rather listless and sleepily inclined. While, in other instances, tendencies in that direction have perhaps been overcome, this one case serves to suggest that inattention to reading on the part of so many may be traceable to the same inherited indisposition to sit still and be quiet, necessary concomitants of the reading habit. (250)

The stakes of reading and of reading intensively—of sitting still and being quiet—are high. Not being able to read in this way leads to the failure of the factory, the loss of "Negro jobs," poverty, violence, and crime. For Griggs, the only way to end this familiar story of "Negro life" is to tell a novel story showing African Americans how to develop the habit of reading, a habit that would eventually whittle away at the strictures imposed by Jim Crow.

Notes

1. Sutton E. Griggs, *The Story of My Struggles* (Memphis: National Public Welfare League, 1914), 10. Subsequent quotations from *The Story* are from this edition and are cited parenthetically in the text. It is worth noting at the outset that Griggs was not alone in his "door-to-door" publishing activities. At this time there were several "obscure" publishing houses that specialized in books by black authors sold door-to-door to black Americans too poor or too uncertain to enter standard bookstores. For instance, J. L. Nichols and Company of Naperville, Illinois, published in 1900 the first version of Booker T. Washington's autobiography, *The Story of My Life*. See Louis R. Harlan, "*Up from Slavery* as History and Biography," in *Booker T. Washington and Black Progress: Up from Slavery 100 Years Later*, ed. W. Fitzhugh Brundage (Gainesville: University Press of Florida, 2003), 21. Though not associated with a publishing company, Kathryn Johnson was a black bookseller who traveled through the northeastern and southeastern United States selling books specifically to African American readers out of the back seat of a Ford coupe in the early decades of the twentieth century. See Elizabeth McHenry, *Forgotten Readers: Recovering the Lost History of African-American Literary Societies* (Durham, N.C.: Duke University Press, 2002), 11.

2. Hugh M. Gloster, *Negro Voices in American Fiction* (Chapel Hill: University of North Carolina Press, 1948), 57. See also R. W. Logan, *The Betrayal of the Negro* (New

York: Macmillan, 1965), 357–58; William Loren Katz, untitled review in *Journal of Black Studies* 1, no. 4 (June 1971): 495.

3. John M. Giggie, "Preachers and Peddlers of God": Ex-Slaves and the Selling of African-American Religion in the American South," in *Commodifying Everything: Relationships of the Market*, ed. Susan Strasser (New York: Routledge, 2003), 170.

4. Although Chesnutt was well supported by his publisher, Houghton, Mifflin & Co., in selling and advertising his books, it should be noted that he, like Griggs, also met with African Americans one-on-one to promote his work to African American readers. Requesting from his publisher fifteen copies of his books *The Conjure Woman* and *The Wife of His Youth* "at the trade discount," he explains that these books will be sold by him personally "among a class of readers who are not ordinarily large buyers of fiction, but who can be very easily reached by a little personal attention." See Chesnutt to Houghton, Mifflin & Co., November 24, 1899, collected in *To Be an Author: Letter of Charles W. Chesnutt, 1889–1905*, ed. Joseph R. McElrath Jr. and Robert C. Leitz (Princeton, N.J.: Princeton University Press, 1997), 138.

5. Wilson J. Moses, "Literary Garveyism: The Novels of Reverend Sutton E. Griggs," *Phylon* 40 (1979): 204.

6. Bobby L. Lovett provides an intriguing discussion of Griggs's dealings with the National Baptist Conventions, highlighting his fraught relations with Richard Henry Boyd's National Baptist Publishing Board and Griggs's financial difficulties, which resulted in Griggs serving a short jail sentence "for illegally obtaining money for sale of stock in his Orion Publishing Company." See Bobby L. Lovett, *A Black Man's Dream: The First 100 Years, Richard Henry Boyd and the National Baptist Publishing Board* ([Jacksonville, Fla.?]: Mega Corporation, 1993), 100.

7. Sutton E. Griggs, *Life's Demands; or, According to Law* (Memphis: National Public Welfare League), 51

8. Anonymous review, "Unfettered," *Coloured American* 34, no. 3 (December 13, 1902): 3.

9. As Finnie Coleman explains, "there are no surviving letters, and his two-thousand-volume library seems to have simply vanished." Due in large part to a devastating fire in East Nashville in the second decade of the twentieth century, where Griggs's publishing company was located, the records of his press have similarly been lost. See Finnie D. Coleman, "*Sutton E. Griggs and the Struggle against White Supremacy* (Knoxville: University of Tennessee Press, 2007), xxi.

10. For two recent examples of such successful recovery efforts of African American readers, see Eric Gardner, "Remembered (Black) Readers: Subscribers to the *Christian Recorder*, 1864–1865," *American Literary History* 23, no. 2 (2011): 229–59; Barbara Hochman, *Uncle Tom's Cabin and the Reading Revolution: Race, Literacy, Childhood, and Fiction, 1851–1911* (Amherst: University of Massachusetts Press, 2011).

11. Leon Jackson, "The Talking Book and the Talking Book Historian: African American Cultures of Print—the State of the Discipline," *Book History* 13 (2010): 282.

12. See Gardner, "Remembered (Black) Readers."

13. McHenry, *Forgotten Readers*, 7.

14. See also Janet Duitsman Cornelius, "*When I Can Read My Title Clear*": Literacy,

Slavery, and Religion in the Antebellum South (Columbia: University of South Carolina Press, 1991), 3–10.

15. Griggs, *Life's Demands*, 25.

16. For an excellent overview of this period, see Michael Perman, *Struggle for Mastery in the South, 1888–1908* (Chapel Hill: University of North Carolina Press, 2001).

17. This phrase is the title of Griggs's 1909 political pamphlet, also published by Orion.

18. Sutton E. Griggs, *Pulled from Shelter* (Nashville: Orion, 1907), 3.

19. Sutton E. Griggs, *Wisdom's Call* (Nashville: Orion, 1911), 178.

20. Sutton E. Griggs, *Unfettered: A Novel* (Nashville: Orion, 1902), n.p. Subsequent quotations from *Unfettered* are from this edition and are cited parenthetically in the text.

21. Booker T. Washington, *Up from Slavery: An Autobiography* (New York: Doubleday, Page, 1907), 263.

22. McHenry's account of nineteenth-century African American literary societies confirms the repudiation of fiction in the black community, which viewed reading as limited to the practical purpose of social and economic progress (172–73).

23. Griggs, *Life's Demands*, 25.

24. Sutton E. Griggs, *Imperium in Imperio* (1899; New York: Modern Library, 2003), 7. Subsequent quotations from *Imperium* are from this edition and are cited parenthetically in the text.

25. See W. E. B. Du Bois, "Of Mr. Booker T. Washington and Others," in *The Souls of Black Folk* (1903; New York: Signet Classic, 1995), 79–95.

26. Griggs, *Life's Demands*, 25.

27. Ibid.

28. Sutton E. Griggs, *The Hindered Hand: or, The Reign of the Repressionist* (Nashville: Orion, 1905), 207.

29. I allude here to Wolfgang Iser's much-discussed theory of aesthetic response in his now classic book *The Act of Reading* (Baltimore: Johns Hopkins University Press, 1978). Following Iser's reading of Henry James, I am interested here in how Griggs sets up the terms by which a reader evaluates the meaning of the text by, in Iser's words, "becoming aware of his own prejudices" (8). Through his carefully constructed characters, Griggs's novels dramatize the ways in which the reader's prejudices might be overcome by the experience of reading itself.

30. Barbara Hochman, *Getting at the Author: Reimagining Books and Reading in the Age of American Realism* (Amherst: University of Massachusetts Press, 2001), 3.

31. Sutton E. Griggs, *The One Great Question* (Nashville: Orion, 1907), 5.

32. Ibid., 10.

33. J. H. Van Evrie, *White Supremacy and Negro Subordination; or, Negroes a Subordinate Race* (New York: Van Evrie, Horton, 1868), v. Van Evrie was a prolific publisher of racist works for the Democrats. Alongside his book-length study cited by Griggs, Van Evrie also published *The Abolition Conspiracy to Destroy the Union; or, A Ten Years' Record of the "Republican" Party.* (New York: Van Evrie, Horton, 1868) and *The Democratic Almanac and Political Compendium for 1868* (New York: Van Evrie, Horton, 1868).

HANNA WALLINGER

Sutton E. Griggs against Thomas Dixon's "Vile Misrepresentations"

The Hindered Hand *and* The Leopard's Spots

Published in 1905 as his fourth novel, Sutton E. Griggs's *The Hindered Hand* can be and has been read as an African American reply to *The Leopard's Spots* (1902) by Thomas Dixon, perhaps the major literary voice for white supremacy at the beginning of the twentieth century. In the office of the *Hindered Hand*'s protagonist, Ensal Ellwood, Mr. A. Hostility, a white fanatic, comes across the book "of a rather conspicuous Southern man" whose purpose it is to discredit the African American race.[1] The reference to Dixon's novel is so obvious that Griggs does not even bother to spell it out. Ensal, aware of Dixon's great popularity, fears his book will influence Americans decisively against the African American race because it manipulates the emotions and deep-seated fears of readers. He trembles at the havoc these "vile misrepresentations" (HH, 207) would play upon their minds. Griggs's intellectual hero recognizes that books such as *The Leopard's Spots* or *The Clansman*—Dixon's second Reconstruction novel—must be answered, especially considering recent incidents of terrible mob violence and brutality and an impending race riot, so that the public can be persuaded to see both sides of the color line.

By concentrating on *The Hindered Hand*; its supplement, "The Hindering Hand"; and *The Leopard's Spots*, this essay argues that despite their predictably discordant readings of slavery, Reconstruction, and the present state of race relations, the relationship of Sutton Griggs and Thomas Dixon was one of mutual dependency as both southerners and Baptist preachers in a Jim Crow United States. The pairing of Griggs and Dixon is no novel enterprise and has been noted by some Dixon and nearly all Griggs critics because it is well known that *The Hindered Hand* was commissioned as a reply to Dixon's *The Leop-*

ard's Spots.[2] Dixon's paranoid fear of race amalgamation and Griggs's obsessive treatment of race antagonisms stem from their biographical backgrounds, which need to be spelled out to a certain extent. Their lives collided at various points with mutual effects on their manners of writing and subject matters.

At the time of the publication of *The Hindered Hand* in 1905, Griggs was a thirty-three-year-old pastor and author of three previous novels (*Imperium in Imperio* [1899]; *Overshadowed* [1901]; *Unfettered* [1902]) and owner of the Orion Publishing Company in Nashville, Tennessee, which he had founded after the publication of *Imperium in Imperio*. Born in 1872 to a prominent and activist Baptist minister, Griggs became deacon and later pastor of the First Baptist Church of Berkley, Virginia (between 1893 and 1900), and pastor of the First Baptist Church in East Nashville, Tennessee (from 1900 to 1913). From all evidence, Griggs was very disappointed in the poor reception of his first three novels, which despite positive reviews did not yield any financial rewards. So when the delegates at the National Baptist Convention (NBC) in Philadelphia commissioned him in 1903 to produce a response to Thomas Dixon's *The Leopard's Spots* and promised considerable financial support, he gladly dedicated his time to writing a fourth novel, which he published under the title *The Hindered Hand.*[3]

By the time Griggs wrote his novelistic response to Dixon, the latter was forty-one years old and had been an actor, lawyer, and legislator. In 1905 he was a popular preacher, speaker, and published author. He had just published *The Clansman*, his second novel, and the autobiographical *The Life Worth Living* about his spacious home, "Elmington Manor," in Dixondale, Virginia, on the Chesapeake Bay, where he lived in comfortable circumstances with his wife and three children. Dixon was born in 1864 in King's Mountain, North Carolina, to a Baptist minister of English, German, and French ethnicity and the daughter of a wealthy plantation owner; he spent his youth in the turbulent Reconstruction years in the South. After various careers in politics, the law, and the Baptist church, Dixon founded his own nondenominational church, the People's Church, and enjoyed much attention and publicity.[4] At the same time, he made a name as the publisher of several volumes of nonfiction. In 1899 he resigned as pastor of the People's Church and traveled through the country on remunerative lecturing tours. Presumably he attended a stage adaptation of Harriet Beecher Stowe's *Uncle Tom's Cabin* and was offended by what he regarded as its inadequate representation of southerners. He was also increasingly concerned with the aftermath of the Spanish-American War and the civil rights promised to dark-skinned Cubans and Filipinos. *The Leopard's Spots*, published in 1902, established him as a spokesman for what he thought was the silent, misrepresented South and became the first of his *Reconstruction Trilogy*, comprising *The Clansman*, published in 1905, and *The Traitor*, published in 1907.[5]

The evident correspondence between the lives of these two writers, both southerners, both sons of Baptist ministers and Baptist ministers themselves, both involved in politics and fiction writing, stops short at the discrepancies between their careers and ideologies. It is hardly conceivable that any two persons could be as dissimilar on questions of race and racist characteristics, history and historiography as Dixon and Griggs. These differences are spelled out in their novels in fictional dialogues on history, politics, and religion and are acted out by the characters in separate or quasi-separate treatises.

Book 1 of *The Leopard's Spots* traces the fates of returned Confederate soldiers in Hambright, North Carolina, who battle the poverty and political insecurities of the early Reconstruction South, which is aggravated by the claim to power of several cruel and uncivilized white liberals and black men, among them Simon Legree and Tim Shelby (imported and adapted from *Uncle Tom's Cabin*), who plan to redistribute power and wealth in the South. When Shelby approaches a white woman, the white townspeople under the leadership of the Reverend Durham strike back and create the Ku Klux Klan as a defensive organization to protect white women. In book 2, twenty years later, the Republican Party is threatening to take control of the state and expand African American rights. The protagonist is Charlie Gaston, a struggling attorney and aspiring politician, who has been raised by the Durham family. He is deeply in love with Sallie, the beautiful daughter of General Worth, who has built a milling empire but who refuses his consent to the marriage because of the vile slanders against Gaston's character by Allan McLeod, one of the novel's villains. In book 3, on the eve of a race riot, Gaston drafts a "Second Declaration of Independence," in which he denounces corrupt and tyrannical (especially black and pro-black) leadership. To enforce their demand for the resignation of town officials and the closure of the black newspaper, Gaston and his political allies assemble a mob to keep African American and Republican voters away from the polls at the next election. Gaston's forceful personality and inspired speeches about white supremacy gain him popularity. He is elected governor and wins the hand of Sallie and the approval of her father.

The novel that Griggs wrote in response to Dixon revolves around the mysteries, mistaken identities, and misunderstandings between various couples.

Most of the novel's tragic events result from the reckless scheme of Mr. and Mrs. Seabright, who pass as white and pursue an ambitious project of undermining white society from within by "tainting" it with color. Their beautiful but dark-skinned daughter Tiara Merlow is in love with the novel's hero, dark-skinned preacher Ensal Ellwood, who ambitiously works for a moderate course of African American politics. His counterpart, the radical, rebellious, bitter, but almost white Earl Bluefield is linked with the equally light-skinned Eunice Seabright, who demonstrates the utmost self-hatred when it is made public that she possesses the fateful drop of black blood. And finally we have the innocent and well-meaning lovers Foresta Crump and Bud Harper, whose tragic deaths after terrible torture and burning forms the emotional climax of the novel. A fifth couple are white Alene Daleman and Ramon Mansford, who also become victims of the war between the races. At the end of the novel, most of the main characters are either dead or insane, and the two protagonists Ensal and Tiara, recently married, are on their way to Africa.

Griggs's and Dixon's novels clearly demonstrate their profound political differences. In *The Leopard's Spots*, for example, there are Charlie Gaston's "Second Declaration of Independence" and his nomination speech, and in *The Hindered Hand* Ensal Ellwood's race address (HH, 147–60).[6] There is also a supplement to *The Hindered Hand*, a separate thirty-page review of Dixon's *The Leopard's Spots*, included for the first time in the third printing of Griggs's novel.[7] Called "The Hindering Hand: Supplementary to the Hindered Hand. A Review of the Anti-Negro Crusade of Mr. Thomas Dixon, Jr.," this dense and polemical refutation of the race hatred behind such a novel as *The Leopard's Spots* serves as the starting point of the following intertextual reading. To support my premises about the emotional relationship between Griggs and Dixon, I discuss the contrasting historical-political interpretation of the Reconstruction period, the dominant race theories, the role of Christianity, and the function of literature in the discourse about race in general. As a point of clarification, it must be noted that Griggs knew about but did not want to respond to Dixon's more recent novel, *The Clansman*.[8]

An important part of Griggs's argument in "The Hindering Hand" rests on a history of slavery that highlights the legacy of bitter feelings and vengeance between the poor white class of the South and the "Negro." In the novel and its supplement, Griggs is especially eloquent in his condemnation of the poor segment of white southerners, whom he holds responsible for racism and discrimination. In Griggs's account, a feeling of hatred and hostility was handed down from generation to generation and forms the base of the race problem, and Griggs sees Dixon as one of many representatives of this group of ill-informed white southerners. Judith Stein correctly points out that it is inaccurate to see southern disenfranchisement and Jim Crow laws purely in terms of race and that all southern classes, including poor whites, were affected by these social forces.[9] Griggs, however, needed to polemicize on the grounds of clear-cut class lines because he believed his only hopes lay in the hands of the well-educated and more enlightened new young southerner. The personification of this type of enlightened southerner in *The Hindered Hand* is H. Clay Maul, who as the prosecuting attorney in the trial of the people responsible for the burning and lynching of Foresta and Bud speaks eloquently on behalf of justice. Maul does not criticize race hierarchy in itself but disputes the superiority of the Anglo-Saxon race because it is tainted by "the waves of the blood of the innocent and the helpless" (HH, 175).

Maul can be seen as the fictive heir to the former U.S. representative and senator from Maine James G. Blaine (1830–93), whose words Griggs quotes extensively in the supplement to the novel. He dedicates seven pages to an article in the *North American Review* about the passage from Reconstruction to the end of Reconstruction, which is an excerpt from a discourse titled "Ought the Negro to Be Disenfranchised? Ought He to Have Been Enfranchised?" solicited by the editors of the journal and answered in the March 1879 issue in fifty-eight pages written by Blaine and other famous politicians and leaders of public opinion. The excerpt that Griggs uses is taken from Blaine's answer to the other essays, which in turn replied to his original entry. Blaine writes about the danger of reenslavement of former slaves immediately after the war, the failure of the Fourteenth Amendment to bring about universal suffrage, and the necessity for the Reconstruction Acts and the Fifteenth Amendment. Griggs quotes Blaine as a white northern antislavery spokesman: "Nothing could have been more despicable than to use the Negro to secure the adoption of the Fourteenth Amendment and then to leave them exposed to the hazard of losing suffrage whenever those who had attempted to re-enslave them should regain political power in their States" (HH, 324).[10]

Dixon, the real-life opposite of the fictive Maul, sees himself as an advocate of the South against the dominant influence of northerners. His autobiographical *Southern Horizons* abounds in scenes that depict the general suffering of the postwar South and the specific ills affecting his own family. Dixon is particularly unstinting in his admiration for his uncle Colonel Leroy McAffee, one of the leading members of the local Ku Klux Klan. In an ironic response to Booker T. Washington's idea of slavery as a school in his *Up from Slavery*, Dixon interprets slavery as a "mild form of labor" (LS, 397), in which the slaves were better treated and taken care of than in a socialist system of the post-Reconstruction era.[11] While most African Americans in *The Leopard's Spots* are either happy and contented former slaves or brute savages, his white southerners are the culmination of Anglo-Saxon civilization; northern do-gooders and Republican statesmen are fictionalized as perverse henchmen working for the ruin of the South.

As Eric Foner has amply demonstrated, the scholarly study of Reconstruction has undergone tremendous changes since the treatments in the early twentieth century by William Dunning, John W. Burgess, and their students.[12] Their reading of Reconstruction—Dunning's *Essays on the Civil War and Reconstruction* appeared as early as 1897—as the darkest page in American history abounds in references to "negro rule" and large-scale descriptions of "negro incapacity" and uneducated and childlike African Americans.[13] Dixon calls the real-life northern politicians Thaddeus Stevens, Charles Sumner, and B. F. Butler "the triumvirate of physical and mental deformity" (LS, 95), whose sole purpose it is to "let the white man suffer" (LS, 91). Dixon's term for the period of Reconstruction is "reign of terror" (LS, 84) led by such men as ruffian Simon Legree, the mule-like Tim Shelby (a "full-blooded Negro"), and the revengeful former proslavery advocate Amos Hogg. The league of worthy southerners is led by the Reverend Durham, General Worth, and a number of former brave Confederate soldiers from the ranks of the "poor whites," who are supported by several well-meaning and loyal former slaves, such as Uncle Nelse or young Dick. Reconstruction is a war "the most ghastly and hellish every waged" (LS, 161) and at stake are the survival of the Anglo-Saxon race and the future of the South. Amalgamation leads to Africanization (see LS, 382) and must be hindered at all costs, even if it means that a father would rather kill his daughter than have her raped by a black man and survive.

Griggs repeatedly and obsessively turns against the ill-boding group of retrogressionists (Dixon prominent among them) who worked against the necessary political changes and racial attitudes that would revise the portrait of Republican rule in the South and revoke the myth of a "Negro rule" during Reconstruction. Griggs emphasizes the establishment of public school systems, equal citizenship, social and political progress, and the revolutionary potential of emancipation itself. He recognizes and fictionalizes the survival of the old planter class, the deep-seated racism, the social ferment of the time, and the changing role of women. In his overview of the black response to the historiography of slavery, historian John David Smith calls attention to the many inconsistencies and contradictions in such writers as Booker T. Washington, Kelly Miller, and Paul Laurence Dunbar, who, Smith argues, "offered seemingly contradictory statements regarding slavery, concurrently denouncing it soundly as an evil yet finding benefits in it for the bondsmen."[14] Griggs is one of these voices that condemn slavery in very obvious ways but also thematize the hope for racial harmony and tolerance. Against the background of Reconstruction historiography, Dixon and Griggs thus stand at opposite ends both as intellectuals and novelists about the alleged retrogression of African Americans toward savagery and bestiality, the threat of emancipation, and the inability of the two races to live together harmoniously.[15]

In "The Hindering Hand," Griggs distances himself from the purported inferiority of Africans and proposes what is basically known today as the environmental theory of races, which insists that the special condition of Africans arose from their geographical isolation, the hot climate, and the abundance of food, but not as coming from any innate racial inferiority.[16] Griggs thus joins a large group of black ethnologists whose ideas on the origin of the human races allowed them to counter white supremacist claims and accept the notion of a basic hierarchy of the human races with the important addition that the black race was not necessarily classified as inferior. Mia Bay conclusively argues that this school of thought ended with a paradigm shift, which was a break with racial determinism, effected through the research of Franz Boas.[17] Griggs and his fellow African American intellectuals fought for an egalitarian assessment of the races that recognized the values of the so-called black races.[18]

It was the prevalence of negative stereotypes about black Americans that led Griggs and many of his African American contemporaries (such as Charles Chesnutt and Pauline Hopkins) to return so often and obsessively to the notion of racial equality. *The Leopard's Spots* frequently describes the "thick-lipped, flat-nosed negro but yesterday taken from the jungle" (LS, 97), whose only intention is to "force social equality" (LS, 146), which would end "this nation's life" (LS, 242). "*Can you build, in a Democracy, a nation inside a nation of two hostile races?* We must do this or become mulatto, and that is death" (LS, 242) are the phrases that Dr. Durham uses over and over again. The paranoia in the logic of this character must be Dixon's own: "You cannot seek the Negro vote without asking him to your home sooner or later. If you ask him to your house, he will break bread with you at last. And if you seat him at your table, he has the right to ask your daughter's hand in marriage" (LS, 242). George Harris, Eliza Harris's son from *Uncle Tom's Cabin*, is accepted into the home of the Honorable Everett Lowell and eventually asks him for his daughter's hand, whereupon this liberal northerner dismisses him wrathfully: "One drop of your blood in my family could push it backward three thousand years in history. . . . I would . . . kill her with my own hand, rather than see her sink in your arms into the black waters of a Negroid life!" (LS, 394). Charlie Gaston later issues a race call: "Let the manhood of the Aryan race with its four thousand years of authentic history answer that question!" (LS, 436). With the inclusion of George Harris, who is well educated and patronized by Lowell before his proposal, Dixon highlights that every African American (regardless of education and position) lusts after white women and that miscegenation threatens the U.S. nation as a whole.

Griggs directly addresses this passage from *The Leopard's Spots* by pointing out the utter absurdity of comparing a white father judging a man's political aspirations and his approval of him as a future son-in-law: "The rejection of a man because he lacks generations of approved blood behind him is classed by Mr. Dixon as race discrimination, whereas such rejections are daily made for similar reasons within all civilized races" (HH, 314). Griggs's answer to Dixon's fear of the sexual power of black men is his portrayal of white men lusting after black women, a character constellation and motivation totally absent from Dixon's fictive world. White Arthur Daleman, for example, pursues beautiful Foresta Crump, who has no means to escape him without losing the protection of his father and provoking an insult by her black fiancé that might lead to another lynching.

The picture of the relationship between the races as seen from these two novels is more complex, however. There are scenes in *The Leopard's Spots* in which Dr. Durham and Charlie Gaston profess their love for the individual African American and even try to stop a lynching by the Klan and later the lynching of Charlie's childhood friend Dick, accused of rape. And in Griggs we find frequent patronizing attitudes toward other races and arguments of nativism.[19] Mr. A. Hostility in *The Hindered Hand* embodies the feared figure of the European immigrant who threatens to overthrow the system of Anglo-Saxon superiority. He represents the often-heard sentiment against the "Angry Saxons" as "a predatory race whose brutality spanned all of human history."[20] In this part of *The Hindered Hand*, the anarchic immigrant is positioned against the friendly and well-meaning African American. His scheme to overthrow the nation is interpreted as much more threatening than any real or futile attempt at race rioting. The future American in Dixon is the gentle, cavalier, manly son of the South who will protect the individual African American, and in Griggs it is the gentle and well-meaning former slave who will save the entire nation.

Although most readers agree that *Uncle Tom's Cabin* memorializes the suffering of African American characters and represents Uncle Tom as the prototypical Christian unwilling and unable to kill his oppressors, the religious background in Dixon and Griggs is equally obvious but less remarked upon. It must have irked Griggs endlessly that Dixon was a fellow Baptist minister with a similar background in religion, although he had turned his back on the Baptist Church when he founded his own nondenominational church. As the son of a prominent and activist Baptist minister; a graduate of Bishop College in Marshall, Texas, and Richmond Theological Institute; and an active participant in the National Baptist Convention, Griggs was certainly proud of the role that the Baptist Church played in fostering Christianity, a strict lifestyle, cultural richness, social activism, good education, and the uplifting of African Americans. Many of the most intelligent and prominent African Americans had a background in the clergy, had gained their success and respect from church work, and were expected to take a public stand in social and political matters.[21] Griggs, therefore, defends the African American against charges that black worship could be called "grotesque" and "heathenish" (HH, 309). As Paul Harvey points out, not all southern black Baptists were involved in politics, but Griggs was certainly the "best known voice of protest" responding with outrage to the emerging Jim Crow system in the 1890s.[22]

In *The Leopard's Spots*, the Reverend Durham, a Dixon-like Baptist preacher of "God, of Truth, of Righteousness, of Judgment, the same yesterday, to-day and forever" (LS, 40), speaks with heartfelt authority and gently guides his flock, while the black preacher, Uncle Josh Miller, hollers the word of God: "En such whoopin', en yellin', en bawlin'. Yer can hear 'em er mile" (LS, 40). Durham even accuses his fellow black preachers and their congregations of lying, stealing, and drinking (LS, 308). Griggs refutes Dixon's portrayal and defends African American ministers as a bulwark "against all who would assail these earlier gropings after the unknown God" (HH, 310). Because the African American was taught the "Gospel of peace" (HH, 310) in the United States, he should not be condemned by someone like Dixon. Griggs's Baptist minister Ensal Ellwood gently guides his people to what he considers the right course and prevents a planned race riot by wounding his more radical friend Earl Bluefield. Griggs interprets the emotionalism of the black preachers that Dixon derides so vehemently as a type of rhetorical power demonstrating the true religious fervor inherited from plantation melodies. He even goes so far as to claim that the black preacher "is beyond all doubt Mr. Dixon's spiritual parent so far as power is concerned" (HH, 330), a sentiment mirrored inadvertently by Dixon in his autobiography when he describes the powerful influence of old black Aunt Barbara's Bible readings.[23] In an essay about *The Birth of a Nation* as race melodrama, Jane M. Gaines analyzes the legacy of Dixon's rhetoric as a southern Baptist minister and notes the "tradition of exhortation from the pulpit, of the rendering of life's challenges in the most exaggerated and apocalyptic of terms." Just as in melodrama, "everything felt must be hyperbolized; everything described must be vivid; and everything spoken must be thunderous."[24] Griggs's voice, clearly heard in *The Hindered Hand*, is thundering. The oppositions are rendered in stark contrast; the victims are described in more than gory detail (see especially the terrible lynching scene of Foresta and Bud). The effect of the melodramatic in literature is to appeal straight to the hearts of the audience in a way very similar to the "feeling of the spirit" during Sunday worship. Justice, love, and forgiveness are the roots of both Dixon and Griggs's novels, although they differ diametrically on the matter of to whom that justice, love, and forgiveness should be given.

Attempting to explain Dixon's popularity in "The Hindering Hand," Griggs presents an analysis that has become a valuable pursuit in scholarship about intertextual connections between black and white writers. It is the idea of a closer connection between Dixon and African Americans, a kind of unwished-for Africanism—to use Toni Morrison's term—in his psyche. "Materially, psychologically, and culturally," Ralph Ellison writes in *Shadow and Act*, "part of the nation's heritage is Negro American, and whatever it becomes will be shaped in part by the Negro's presence."[25] Griggs precedes Ellison in this line of analysis by observing, "Mr. Thomas Dixon, Jr., beyond doubt owes his emotional power to the very race which he has elected to scourge" (HH, 330) because "the predominating element in his power is the gift of that race" (HH, 330). It is a "subconscious feeling" (HH, 330) that prompts Dixon to write what he writes. In his psychological analysis, Griggs anticipates both Ralph Ellison's and Toni Morrison's Africanism and sees the other side of hatred as deep-seated anxiety that the object of one's hatred might reflect back on oneself. There is the rumor even that Dixon's own father had a mixed son with his cook and that this had a devastating effect on the psychological health of the young boy.[26] In *Playing in the Dark*, Morrison writes about the "dark, abiding, signifying Africanist presence" in American literature and uses the term to designate the unspeakable in discourses about class, sexuality, and issues of power and domination, all of which are detectable in Dixon's fiction.[27] "The Real Problem," Griggs then says in "The Hindering Hand," is that "in myriad ways the Negro will write something upon the soul of the white man" (HH, 331). Ralph Ellison later pursues a similar argument when he says that the white man stepping behind the mask of the trickster fears "that he is not simply miming a personification of his disorder and chaos but that he will become in fact that which he intends only to symbolize."[28]

Earlier in "The Hindering Hand," Griggs claims that Dixon only uses "borrowed power" (HH, 328) because his "grasp upon the emotions of men, his ability to arouse and sway their feelings" (HH, 329) directly comes from his contact with African Americans. In contrast to the later enriching influence of African American stories and voices on American art, such as Shelley Fisher Fishkin sees in Mark Twain or Kenneth Warren in Henry James and William Dean Howells, Griggs judges Dixon's refusal to recognize the positive potential of "physical amalgamation" (HH, 331) as leading to a decline in white art.[29] This idea is reflected in Griggs's character Tiara, who warns her audience of the dehumanizing effect of race segregation because it will have a devastating effect on art. "It will cause your great race to be warped, to be narrow. Oratory will decay in your midst; poetry will disappear or dwell in mediocrity, taking on a mocking sound and a metallic ring; art will become formal, lacking in spirit; huge soulless machines will grow up that will crush the life out of humanity" (HH, 232–33). Dixon's other fervent critic, Kelly Miller, echoes this same idea when he directly addresses Dixon at the end of an open letter: "Race hatred is the most malignant poison that can afflict the mind. It freezes up the fount of inspiration and chills the higher faculties of the soul. You are a greater enemy to your own race than you are to mine."[30]

Despite the two men not having a personal relationship, their work clearly demonstrates a mutual influence as Griggs acknowledges: "There is nothing more patent to an observer of life in the South than the fact that the Anglo-Saxon and Negro races are producing in each other modifications of many of their racial characteristics" (HH, 328). Obviously Griggs spends a lot of energy on this review of Dixon, indicating that he read *The Leopard's Spots* very carefully, and I am not the first critic to recognize the deep-seated antagonism between Griggs and Dixon as a "unique" relationship.[31] *The Hindered Hand* was the first of Griggs's novels to include engravings, forcefully playing off Dixon's use of images in his novels. Griggs's attack on Dixon, as much as it rests on historical issues and race theory, takes on a very personal tone and becomes an assault on Dixon's integrity rather than on his art. Dixon invites attack from a position of popularity and strength. Griggs is like David throwing stones at Goliath. He is aggressive, self-assured, full of righteous wrath. He clearly strives for an art that will overcome and outdo his opponent's art. Griggs uses Dixon as the representative of an overpowering white dominance that is responsible for the great race antagonism of the first decade of the twentieth century. In this relationship, Dixon is the offender, and Griggs finds himself in the position of the weaker part who, to his great distress, elicits indifference rather than support. Dixon's increasing fame while he himself failed to attain large-scale popularity illustrates to Griggs his own defeat in the production of the kind of counter-discourse necessary to minimize the audience's favorable reception of Dixon. In *The Story of My Struggles* he records his repeated and insistent appeal to his fellow African Americans to buy his books. Most of all, he counted on the financial support of the National Baptist Publishing Board, which had initially commissioned his novel. This board was founded in 1896 and became a prosperous and influential organization of the National Baptist Convention.[32] By all evidence Griggs became a victim of the "wrangling for control of the publishing board" between its charismatic leader, Richard Henry Boyd, and the more moderate NBC president Elias Camp Morris.[33] Griggs was too radical and unconciliatory and did not have the support of the entire board.[34] Disappointed by his own people, seemingly let down by even sympathetic white readers, he made various calls for racial harmony, but his multiple plans to amend race relations ultimately fail. After 1905 Griggs increasingly turned to nonfiction writing (except for the publication of *Pointing the Way* in 1908) and his career as a preacher. Randolph M. Walker interprets his later, more conservative attitude as a turn from youthful idealism to more-adult pragmatism.[35] This conservatism demonstrates, I would add, his increasing frustration with the Jim Crow United States and his willingness to take a stand as a Baptist minister against injustice and discrimination.

Griggs even imagined an engraving on the future tombstone of Dixon that can and has been interpreted as a metaphorical killing of Dixon.[36] That epitaph reads: "This misguided soul ignored all of the good in the aspiring Negro; made every vicious offshoot that he pictured typical of the entire race; presented all mistakes independent of their environments and provocations; ignored or minimized all the evil in the more vicious element of whites; said and did all things which he deemed necessary to leave behind him the greatest heritage of hatred the world has ever known. Humanity claims him not as one of her children" (HH, 332–33).[37] Griggs knew well that humanity was often denied to the so-called children of Ham and that polygenist theories of races saw "Negroes" as subhuman or a separate species of humankind.[38] By denying Dixon any kind of humanity, Griggs paid him back for his retrogressionist and repressionist views. Griggs's aim, as I see it, was to leave behind a substantially revised version of Dixon's narrow-minded vision. Very early Griggs understood that the great popularity of Dixon did not make him a great writer.

In significant ways, Griggs and Dixon have to be seen as opposite voices in a discourse on races, the role of the South, and the role of religion, politics, and historiography. Griggs portrayed Dixon as going backward (see HH, 332) and fancied his inglorious end, while Griggs positioned himself as going forward, as being part of the main public sentiment rather than an isolated writer and activist. Though Griggs was decidedly unpopular in his own time, his own ideas make more sense to readers today than they did to early twentieth-century readers.

Both Griggs and Dixon clearly assumed that their audiences would agree with their basic ideas of southern race relations, their interpretation of the period of Reconstruction, and their vision for the future South. Both displaced their aggressiveness onto their characters and had them speak out on their behalf. Dixon caught the zeitgeist more fully than Griggs. D. W. Griffith's *Birth of a Nation*, based on *The Clansman*, brought him more enduring fame than even he had anticipated. Dixon may be said to have won the battle of the books in the movies with a film about the Civil War and Reconstruction considered one of the most influential early films, captivating an audience not despite but most often because of its racist imagery. At the same time, he has also been exposed and denigrated as a racist and retrogressionist, as appealing to the base instincts of the U.S. nation. His final novel, *The Flaming Sword*, has been called "the sick fantasies of a bitter, desperate, and isolated man."[39]

When it became clear to Griggs that the promised support of the National Baptist Convention would not materialize, he turned to peddling his works door-to-door: "I . . . visited, at dinner hours, places, where plain workmen toiled. I went to schools where poor Negro boys and girls were struggling for an education. These humble people of the race came to me with their dimes, and I was thus able to at least hold my head above the threatening financial flood."[40] Though his novel did not produce the response he had hoped for from those to whom it was addressed, he still managed to take a public stand against all "vile misrepresentations" of black people and culture during the Jim Crow era. Given the popularity of Dixon's fiction at the time, we should read *The Hindered Hand* as a great achievement of a complex and exciting writer.

Notes

I owe thanks to John Gruesser, Tess Chakkalakal, and Kenneth Warren for their helpful comments on the various drafts of this essay, to Linda Reschen for her careful reading, to John David Smith for helping me with some material, and to the panelists (Giulia Fabi, John Gruesser, Tess Chakkalakal) at the 2008 CAAR conference in Bremen.

1. Sutton E. Griggs, *The Hindered Hand; or, The Reign of the Repressionist*, 3rd ed. (1905; repr., New York: AMS, 1969), 206. Subsequent quotations from this work are from this edition and are cited parenthetically in the text as HH.

2. Most prominently, in *Blood Talk*, Susan Gillman has called them "procrustean bedfellows." Gillman traces a startling number of similarities between the two writers. Both Dixon and Griggs speak "not from the periphery but from different centers of late-nineteenth-century U.S. culture." Both were Baptist ministers, public speakers, and versatile writers. They share a historiographic mode that is melodramatic and informed by conspirational imagination, understand fiction as a "natural extension of their lifelong, proselytizing work in the pulpit and on the speaker's platform," and see politics as part of fictional art. Susan Gillman, *Blood Talk: American Race Melodrama and the Culture of the Occult* (Chicago: University of Chicago Press, 2003), 73–119, here 75. In an article included in Gillespie and Hall's *Thomas Dixon Jr. and the Birth of Modern America*, historian John David Smith sees Griggs as one of Dixon's African American challengers together with William Monroe Trotter, the editor of the *Boston Guardian*, and Howard University professor Kelly Miller. Black Americans, Smith argues, "challenged Dixon's Radical racist ideology, his retrogressionist view of blacks, his gross insults, and his lurid depictions of black men lurking after and raping white women." Smith, "'My Books Are Hard Reading for a Negro': Tom Dixon and His African American Critics, 1905–1930," in *Thomas Dixon Jr. and the Birth of Modern America*, ed. Michele L. Gillespie and Randal L. Hall (Baton Rouge: Louisiana State University Press, 2006), 50.

3. Biographical evidence is taken mainly from the following sources: Finnie D. Coleman, *Sutton E. Griggs and the Struggle against White Supremacy* (Knoxville: University of Tennessee Press, 2007); Randolph Meade Walker, "The Metamorphosis of Sutton E. Griggs: A Southern Black Baptist Minister's Transformation in Theological and Sociological Thought during the Twentieth Century" (PhD, Memphis State University, 1990).

Several dates are given for Griggs's move from Virginia to Tennessee. In his essay *The One Great Question*, which he published in 1907, he indicates that he had been in Nashville, Tennessee, for seven years. His move from Berkley, Virginia, to Nashville happened between his publication of *Imperium in Imperio* in 1899 and of *Overshadowed* in 1901. See *The One Great Question: A Study of Southern Conditions at Close Range* (Nashville: Orion, 1907). For a report about the National Baptist Convention, see Woolford Damon, "Twenty-Third Annual Session of the National Negro Baptist Convention," *Colored American Magazine* 6, no. 11 (November 1903): 778–93. For criticism about Griggs, see Arlene E. Elder, *The "Hindered Hand": Cultural Implications of Early African-American Fiction* (Westport, Conn.: Greenwood, 1978); Hugh M. Gloster, "Sutton E. Griggs: Novelist of the New Negro," *Phylon* 4 (1943): 335–45; John Cullen Gruesser, *Black on Black: Twentieth-Century African American Writing about Africa* (Lexington: University Press of Kentucky, 2000), 24–33; Maria Karafilis, "Oratory, Embodiment, and U.S. Citizenship in Sutton E. Griggs's *Imperium in Imperio*," *African American Review* 40, no. 1 (2006): 125–43; Stephen Knadler, "Sensationalizing Patriotism: Sutton Griggs and the Sentimental Nationalism of Citizen Tom," *American Literature* 79, no. 4 (2007): 673–99; Caroline Levander, "Sutton Griggs and the Borderlands of Empire," in this volume; Wilson J. Moses, "Literary Garveyism: The Novels of Reverend Sutton E. Griggs," *Phylon* 40, no. 3 (1979): 203–16; Sabine Sielke, *Reading Rape: The Rhetoric of Sexual Violence in American Literature and Culture, 1790–1990* (Princeton, N.J.: Princeton University Press, 2002), 54–59; Roger Whitlow, "The Revolutionary Black Novels of Martin R. Delany and Sutton Griggs," *MELUS* 5, no. 3 (1978): 26–36.

4. Raymond A. Cook, *Thomas Dixon* (New York: Twayne, 1974), 44; Anthony Slide, *American Racist: The Life and Films of Thomas Dixon* (Lexington: University Press of Kentucky, 2004), 21–22.

5. For biographical information about Dixon, see Cook, *Thomas Dixon*; Gillespie and Hall, *Thomas Dixon*; Slide, *American Racist*; Maxwell Bloomfield, "Dixon's *The Leopard's Spots*: A Study in Popular Racism," *American Quarterly* 16, no. 3 (1964): 387–401. The following websites are helpful: "Documenting the American South," University of North Carolina at Chapel Hill, http://docsouth.unc.edu/southlit/dixonleopard/summary.html; *Uncle Tom's Cabin and American Culture*, University of Virginia (2006), http://utc.iath.virginia.edu; "Thomas Dixon, Jr.," http://en.wikipedia.org/wiki/Thomas Dixon, Jr.

6. For Gaston's "Second Declaration" and his nomination speech, see Thomas Dixon Jr., *The Leopard's Spots: A Romance of the White Man's Burden 1865–1900* (1902; repr., Ridgewood, N.J.: Gregg Press, 1967), 409–16; 433–44. Subsequent quotations from this work are from this edition and are cited parenthetically in the text as LS.

7. The supplement replaces parts of the original chap. 31 in the first edition of the novel as Griggs explains to the reader: "The present edition of 'The Hindered Hand' differs from previous editions in that a review of Mr. Thomas Dixon's 'Leopard's Spots' appears in former editions in the form of a conversation between two of the characters of the book, whereas in the present edition the review is more fully given in an article appearing in the rear of this book after the closing of the story" (HH, 298). Griggs reprints

some of the material from both the novel and the supplement in his later essay *The One Great Question* (1907).

8. In the "Notes to the Third Edition," Griggs writes: "No attempt is here made to deal with Mr. Dixon's second book bearing on the race problem, it being the hope of the writer to give that matter serious and independent attention" (HH, 298).

9. Judith Stein, "'Of Mr. Booker T. Washington and Others': The Political Economy of Racism in the United States," in *Renewing Black Intellectual History: The Ideological and Material Foundations of African American Thought*, ed. Adolph Reed Jr. and Kenneth W. Warren (Boulder, Colo.: Paradigm, 2010), 41–43.

10. The other respondents/contributors are L. Q. C. Lamar, Wade Hampton, James A. Garfield, Alexander H. Stephens, Wendell Phillips, Montgomery Blair, and Thomas A. Hendrick. See James G. Blaine et al., "Ought the Negro to Be Disenfranchised? Ought He to Have Been Enfranchised?" *North American Review* 128, no. 268 (March 1879): 225–83. James Gillespie Blaine served in the Maine House of Representatives from 1859 to 1862 and was elected as a Republican to the Thirty-Eighth and the six succeeding Congresses between 1863 and 1876. He was the unsuccessful candidate for nomination for president on the Republican ticket in 1876, 1880, and 1884. He was appointed and subsequently elected as a Republican to the United States Senate and became secretary of state in 1881 in the cabinets of Presidents James Garfield and Chester Arthur, as well as in the cabinet of President Benjamin Harrison (1889–92). A powerful party leader, he was surrounded by suspicions of corruption. During Reconstruction he advocated black suffrage but opposed the coercive measures of the Radical Republicans during the Grant administration. His influence on American life rests on his foreign policy, focused on relations with Latin American countries and Britain (see *Biographical Directory of the United States Congress, 1774–Present*: http://bioguide.congress.gov/scripts/biodisplay .pl?index=b000519). His *Twenty Years in Congress* (1884–86) has served as a source about the period for later historians. John David Smith refers to him as one of several Northern neoabolitionists who spoke out against southern white racial thought. See *An Old Creed for the New South: Proslavery Ideology and Historiography, 1865–1918* (Athens: University of Georgia Press, 2010), 69–75. Although Eric Foner considers him one of the moderate Republicans who "viewed Reconstruction as a practical problem, not an opportunity to impose an open-ended social revolution upon the South," and who were not enthusiastic about black suffrage but endorsed civil rights for African Americans, in the essay from which Griggs quotes he appears as a rather outspoken advocate of black civil rights. Foner, *Reconstruction: America's Unfinished Revolution 1863–1877* (New York: Harper & Row, 1984), 241–42.

11. Dixon, *Southern Horizons: The Autobiography of Thomas Dixon; A Critical Edition*, ed. M. Karen Crowe (Alexandria, Va.: IWV, 1984); Booker T. Washington, *Up from Slavery: Three Negro Classics*, with an introduction by John Hope Franklin (New York: Avon, 1965), 37. In *Old Creed*, John David Smith classifies and analyzes the many works of white historians about slavery in the period before 1918 and describes the black response to these historians and the slavery-as-school analogy (see esp. 219–21).

12. See Foner, *Reconstruction*, xix. There are many other good historical sources on

the history of Reconstruction and post-Reconstruction. For an overview of historical research, see John Hope Franklin, "'Birth of a Nation'—Propaganda as History," *Massachusetts Review* 20, no. 3 (1979): 417–34; Francis B. Simkins, "New Viewpoints of Southern Reconstruction," *Journal of Southern History* 5, no. 1 (1939): 49–61.

13. Foner, *Reconstruction*, xx. Dunning was one of the teachers at Columbia University of Ulrich B. Phillips (1877–1932), whose *American Negro Slavery* (1918) became a landmark proslavery work on the history of slavery. His *Reconstruction, Political and Economic, 1865–1877* appeared in 1907. About the influence of Phillips, see Smith, *Old Creed*, 239–83.

14. Smith, *Old Creed*, 200.

15. See Smith, "My Books," 48.

16. Ibid., 56; Mia Bay, *The White Image in the Black Mind: African-American Ideas about White People, 1830–1925* (New York: Oxford University Press, 2000), 220–21.

17. See Bay, *White Image*, 187–217.

18. Ibid., 194. Bay notes the difficulties many black thinkers had with the evolutionary concepts of races and writes about the many facets of romantic, conservative, and essential racialism, black social Darwinism, and claims for black equality.

19. In *Black on Black*, Gruesser writes about the "warring ideals" of Africa and America in the novels of Griggs and points out the ambivalence of Griggs about Africa (see 24–33).

20. Qtd. in Bay, *White Image*, 221. Bay traces this idea back to a lecture by James W. C. Pennington in 1850 (see 264n5). See also F. Garvin Davenport Jr., "Thomas Dixon's Mythology of Southern History," *Journal of Southern History* 36, no. 3 (1970): 350–67, esp. 362; Samuel K. Roberts, "Kelly Miller and Thomas Dixon, Jr. on Blacks in American Civilization," *Phylon* 41, no. 2 (1980): 202–9. See also Gruesser's study *The Empire Abroad and the Empire at Home: African American Literature and the Era of Overseas Expansion* (Athens: University of Georgia Press, 2012).

21. For a good overview of the development of African American churches, see Anthony B. Pinn, *The African American Religious Experience in America* (Westport, Conn.: Greenwood, 2006), esp. 11–27 and 122–26. For a briefer overview, see Michael Corbett and Julia Mitchell Corbett, *Politics and Religion in the U.S.* (New York: Garland, 1999), 299–334. The most detailed study available on the religious cultures and racial identities among southern Baptists in the period between 1865 and 1925 is Paul Harvey, *Redeeming the South: Religious Cultures and Racial Identities among Southern Baptists, 1865–1925*. Harvey paints a very complex picture about so-called old time preaching and vernacular expressions of spirituality in both black and white churches as opposed to the "bourgeois codes of behaviour" (78) also in both black and white churches.

22. Harvey, *Redeeming the South*, 234.

23. Dixon, *Southern Horizons*, 60, 133. In general *Southern Horizons* can be read as a comment on both *The Leopard's Spots* and *The Clansman*. Many of the memorable scenes in the novels appear to have been taken directly from personal experience. Dixon obviously uses the autobiographical form to prove that his fiction is realistic.

24. Jane M. Gaines, "Thomas Dixon and Race Melodrama," in Gillespie and Hall, *Thomas Dixon*, 160.

25. Ellison, "Twentieth-Century Fiction and the Black Mask of Humanity," in *Shadow and Act* (New York: Random House, 1964), 24.

26. See Glenda Elizabeth Gilmore, "'One of the Meanest Books': Thomas Dixon, Jr. and *The Leopard's Spots*," *North Carolina Literary Review* 11, no. 1 (1994): 87–101, here 97. Gilmore draws her information from quotations by African American journalist and writer John Edward Bruce. There are several other interpretations of Dixon based on psychological childhood traumata, foremost among them that of Joel Williamson, which focuses on the young Dixon having to care for his invalid mother, who seemed to have suffered from a trauma due to her early pregnancy. Williamson writes about the motivation behind the writing of the book: "*The Leopard's Spots* functioned as a vehicle by which Dixon discharged a great store of aggressive potential, partially resolved his feelings of guilt, and repaid in some measure an imagined debt to his mother. As an attempt at psychic self-cure, it was a brilliant, disingenuous performance in which, in brief, Southern white maidenhood substituted for his mother, the black beast rapist was a surrogate for her never named violator, and the violator in the person of the black beast was horribly punished." Joel Williamson, *The Crucible of Race: Black-White Relations in the American South since Emancipation* (New York: Oxford University Press, 1984), 165–76, here 165.

27. Toni Morrison, *Playing in the Dark: Whiteness and the Literary Imagination* (Cambridge, Mass.: Harvard University Press, 1992), 5.

28. Ralph Ellison, "Change the Joke and Slip the Yoke," in *Shadow and Act*, 53.

29. Fishkin contextualizes her study about Mark Twain within the great number of books that demonstrate the hybridity of American culture. She comes to the provocative conclusion: "If we apply to our culture the 'one drop' rule that in the U.S. has long classified anyone with one drop of black blood as black, then all of American culture is black." In *Black and White Strangers* Kenneth Warren writes: "In a multiracial, multiethnic society, race, particularly black/white racial difference, emerges not merely as a problem but as part of the discursive building blocks that make expression—political and aesthetic—possible." See Fishkin, "Interrogating 'Whiteness,' Complicating 'Blackness': Remapping American Culture," in *Criticism and the Color Line: Desegregating American Literary Studies*, ed. Henry B. Wonham (New Brunswick, N.J.: Rutgers University Press, 1996), 275; Warren, *Black and White Strangers: Race and American Literary Realism* (Chicago: University of Chicago Press, 1993), 10.

30. Kelly Miller, *As to the Leopard's Spots: An Open Letter to Thomas Dixon, Jr.* (Washington, D.C.: by author, 1905), 20.

31. See Walker, "Metamorphosis of Sutton E. Griggs," 31.

32. See Harvey, *Redeeming the South*, 70.

33. Ibid., 246.

34. On the power play in the publishing board, see Harvey, *Redeeming the South*, 243–50.

35. Walker writes: "As a youthful idealist, Griggs wrote from the viewpoint of a crusader. He told all that was wrong with American society so far as the African American was concerned. He criticized lynching and disfranchisement. He called for fairness and

equality for the ebony-skinned Americans. However, age and experience taught Griggs that wrongs were not going to be righted simply because he brought them to the public's attention. Therefore, as an older crusader he replaced idealism with pragmatism." Based on a careful examination of his nonfiction works, Walker's study goes beyond the scope of this paper in his evaluation and appraisal of Griggs's sociological thoughts and later career. Walker, "Metamorphosis of Sutton E. Griggs," 158.

36. Smith, "My Books," 57.

37. Gilmore quotes a real obituary of Dixon in the *Chicago Defender* that is remarkably similar to this fictional engraving: It reads: "Another 'Methusaleh of race hatred' has gone to his reward. . . . He advocated the violation of the Golden Rule, although he was a minister. He loved to make men hate each other; he wrote some of the filthiest books on love and social problems. Wherever there was a foulness to be placed between bookcovers, he enjoyed the job. He sought to make every white man whiter, and likewise every black man blacker. . . ." Gilmore, "One of the Meanest Books," 100.

38. For a good overview of the development, nature, and effects of race theories, see Thomas F. Gossett, *Race: The History of an Idea in America* (1962; repr., New York: Oxford University Press, 1997).

39. John David Smith, "My Books," 71. In a recent publication William Link improbably calls Dixon a "Renaissance Man for his generation and beyond," a person of "considerable intellectual potential" with a "knack for attracting and keeping attention." William A. Link, "Epilogue: The Enduring Worlds of Thomas Dixon," in Gillespie and Hall, *Thomas Dixon*, 203.

40. Griggs, *The Story of My Struggles* (Memphis: National Public Welfare League, 1914), 14.

JOHN ERNEST

Harnessing the Niagara

Sutton E. Griggs's The Hindered Hand

As events heat to their expected boil in *The Hindered Hand; or, The Reign of the Repressionist*, Sutton Griggs has his moderate protagonist, Ensal, turn to writing in hopes of lowering the heat while still effecting cultural change. Ensal's militant friend, Earl, is planning armed conflict, a direct confrontation with white supremacist forces aimed at pressing the issues so long repressed by the racist protocols of the day. "Going to his desk," Griggs writes, Ensal procures "a rather bulky document" into which "he had cast all of his soul. Upon it he was relying for the amelioration of conditions to such an extent that his race might be saved from being goaded on to an unequal and disastrous conflict. He hoped that its efficacy would be so self-evident that Earl might stay the hand that threatened the South and the nation with another awful convulsion. No wonder that his voice was charged with deep emotion as he read as follows: 'To the People of the United States of America.'"[1] In the document is an impassioned and impressively reasoned plea, an attempt to change hearts and minds by referring "the People of the United States of America" to the nation's governing principles, to the dictates of Christianity, and to the forces of reason. Reasonable though it is, however, Ensal's document constitutes a great act of faith, for the racist social order that he is addressing was not developed according to reason, and it was not constricted by any national or religious principles, since the reinterpretation and corruption of such principles had been the primary effect of the system of racial domination.

Nevertheless, in publishing this document to the nation, Ensal takes part in a long and proud, if frustrating, African American tradition, one that extends back at least as far as the post–Revolutionary War petitions to legislative bodies for the recognition of African American rights, or even for basic liberty, based on the ideals articulated in the Declaration of Independence. This tradition also includes many pamphlets, orations, black national convention proceedings, and other documents published by African Americans from the late eighteenth century to Griggs's time, many of which included direct appeals to the public. Some of these documents were addressed specifically to those of African heritage—most famously, *David Walker's Appeal, in Four Articles; Together with a Preamble, to the Coloured Citizens of the World, but in Particular, and Very Expressly, to Those of The United States of America*. Others were directed primarily toward a white readership, though one contextualized in a document directed toward black communities, for example, the address "To the American People" included in the *Minutes of the Fifth Annual Convention for the Improvement of the Free People of Colour in the United States, Held By Adjournments, in the Wesley Church, Philadelphia, from the First to the Fifth of June, inclusive, 1835*. In the face of the absurd approaches to everything from theology to science required for the maintenance of the white supremacist regime, one might expect such public statements to have limited effect, but African Americans continued to turn to such measures, counting on the published word and the reasoned appeal to logic and principle to overturn the judgment of public opinion and, by that means, redirect the underlying logic that governed the cultural system.

These are the measures on which Ensal places his hopes—and, more significantly, the measures on which Griggs himself placed his hopes, for Ensal's document to the world is but a part of Griggs's own publication, the combination of fiction and appeals to reason that constitute *The Hindered Hand*. Griggs, however, handles his appeal more knowingly than does his character, for while Ensal publishes his document directly to the world, Griggs goes to some trouble to frame and contextualize his own appeals. Perhaps the central question behind Griggs's work concerns the means by which the published word might find its power, for both white readers and black. In a world governed by absurdities, by the corruption of all reason and principle, how might one secure a hearing for a document that *appeals to* and *depends on* reason and principle? What conditions are necessary for a successful statement to the world? It is a commonplace to note that Griggs's writing career turned eventually from fiction to nonfiction, but less often noted is that this turn to nonfiction was a change more of emphasis than of kind, for Griggs had always included and highlighted various documents in his fiction, sometimes as apparent supplements in appendices, and sometimes as appeals embedded in the fiction it-self. This highlighting of political statements has often led scholars to dismiss Griggs as a didactic or simply clumsy novelist, but such judgments are but re-minders that African American writers often are judged for failing at things that they were not trying to do, or for not fitting into traditions that they didn't try to fit into, traditions that often go unexamined in relation to race history.[2] For Griggs, I argue, fiction was a necessary means for publishing appeals to reason in an absurd and utterly unreasonable world. Through the use of fic-tion, Griggs could expose the various narrative lines of American political, eco-nomic, religious, and social history to locate the African American community historically. Ultimately, Griggs's novels are a knowing commentary on and in-tervention into official history, an attempt to reconstitute the many factions of American political and social life to provide African Americans with the means by which they might appeal to reason and principle in a nation that had largely abandoned both.

Beyond the Binaries

Perhaps the greatest challenge in understanding Griggs is that his work is so clearly concerned with the racial dynamics of U.S. history and culture at the turn of the century, a history usually approached with packaged simplifications. Certainly, the general outlines of the historical story are clear: a time of almost unimaginable racial oppression and violence, with African American strate-gies for responding to that violence defined by the two poles represented by Booker T. Washington and W. E. B. Du Bois. For many readers, this binary di-vision of black male leadership into the moderate and the militant—so persis-tent in U.S. culture—provides the most obvious framework for approaching Griggs's work, a body of literature that characteristically features a plot driven by radical and moderate black leaders.[3] Representative of such approaches is Robert A. Bone's rather predictable 1965 analysis of "Griggs's vacillation between one pole which is militant and fantastic and another pole which is re-alistic and accommodationist"—a vacillation that, Bone concluded, "reflects the political dilemma of the Negro intellectual prior to World War I. The ideo-logical contradictions which plagued Griggs were not personal but historical."[4] A similar line of analysis, though far more satisfying, is Eric Curry's view that Griggs "seems to occupy a middle ground—a political perspective mediating the binary often posited between Du Bois and Washington, and could be radical or conservative as the situation dictated."⁵ For Curry, Griggs's attempt to negotiate a middle ground led him to an ongoing "experiment with fiction," a search for "a vehicle for community and political action that strives to re-imagine the relationship between author and reader as a partnership—a joint exploration of matters of mutual concern, such as leadership, combinations, and education."⁶ Although I agree that Griggs recognized that the pursuit of African American possibilities operated necessarily within a leadership spectrum defined by the opposing poles of militancy and moderation, forceful resistance and measured accommodation, I think the middle ground he occupied remains to be adequately surveyed.⁷ Griggs occupied and emerged from that complex terrain, and while he might have sought a partnership with his readers, he understood that his first challenge was simply to secure a hearing.

Beyond the binary possibilities imagined for African American leadership is a world often reduced to a corresponding binary, white and black, which is no more useful a model of U.S. racial history than is the binary of black leadership for understanding the ideological diversity of African American communities. The U.S. racial landscape was in fact diverse, dynamic, and overwhelmingly complex. Of the many changes wrought by the Civil War—and by the economic, industrial, and political developments that followed in the war's wake—one of the most significant was that of race itself. As Matthew Frye Jacobson has demonstrated, from the 1840s to the 1920s U.S. culture was characterized by a "spectacular rate of industrialization" and a corresponding "appetite for cheap labor" that encouraged migration, a situation that fostered a "growing nativist perception of these laborers as a political threat to the smooth functioning of the republic."⁸ Responding to such changes and the shifting politics of American demographics, the nation moved "from the unquestioned hegemony of a unified race of 'white persons'" to "a contest over political 'fitness' among a now fragmented, hierarchically arranged series of distinct 'white races.'"⁹ These changes in conceptions of whiteness naturally presented challenges to black Americans in their efforts to define the terms of their collective identity. Although many of the most prominent African American writers and political leaders had argued against the relevance and even the existence of race, they had recognized as well that those of African heritage were subject to prejudices, laws, social practices, and scientific theories that insisted on its existence and relevance. African Americans were defined by simplified conceptions of their complex relations with Africans, other African Americans, white Americans, and various immigrant groups, conceptions that often were played out in political articles and books, scientific treatises, literature, drama, popular song, and the minstrel stage.[10]

Jacobson has managed the best study of "the fluidity of race" in the late decades of the nineteenth century yet available, though he does so by noting that the subject can be apprehended only in parts, by way of particular case studies.[11] "If race is so mutable," Jacobson asks, "then how is its instability registered at a single historical moment or in a single group's history? How is this instability manifest in social consciousness and in the political unconscious?"[12] Jacobson approaches his answer to these questions by considering constructions of Jewishness in 1877, but his explanation of his methods applies more broadly to the demands of locating any social group during this time. Jacobson presents his analysis as an attempt "to illustrate the changeable character of race" and also "to trace the circuitry of race from the various historic encounters that generate this mode of ascribing 'difference' to the uneven patterns of racial recognition which leave such encounters in their wake."[13] Offering a "quick catalogue" of the events of 1877, Jacobson observes that "this glacial process has left in play multiple, contradictory racial understandings of who is who: competing 'phenotypical significations' are etched upon the body (and the body politic) not only by the residual power of prior events and renewing acts of their cultural representation, but also by the untidiness of history itself."[14] In short, Jacobson emphasizes that the instabilities in the dynamics of race translate into instabilities in collective historical understanding—indeed, competing historical narratives that often combine in a single moment or even a single individual's experience and consciousness. "Race," he argues, "is a palimpsest, a tablet whose most recent inscriptions only imperfectly cover those that had come before, and whose inscriptions can never be regarded as final. Contradictory racial identities come to coexist at the same moment in the same body in unstable combinations, as the specific histories that generated them linger in various cultural forms or in the social and political relationships that are their legacies."[15] "Culture," he adds later, "as a creature of history, destabilizes race by layering different conceptual schemes atop one another in response to shifting social and political circumstances. The palimpsest of race maps the terrain of ascription, perception, and subjectivity for a number of immigrant groups whose 'American experience' has scarcely been recounted as a *racial* experience at all."[16]

The very instabilities of racial thought led to a new and increasingly insistent stability, for these instabilities led to an understanding of racial identity that, as

Mark Smith has argued, was "immune to logic, impervious to thought, and, as such, a perfect foundation for segregation."[17] Following the Civil War, the white rage to explain the perceived necessity of black subordination was the subject of numerous books, both fiction and nonfiction—including such overtly racist nineteenth-century books as J. H. Van Evrie's *White Supremacy and Negro Subordination; or, Negroes a Subordinate race, and (So-Called) Slavery Its Normal Condition* (1868) and Thomas Dixon Jr.'s celebration of the Ku Klux Klan in his enormously popular novels at the beginning of the twentieth century. "Segregationists," Smith observes,

> lived an illogical, emotionally powerful lie that relied on gut rather than brain to fix racial identity and order society. Their ability to make solid what was always slippery is annoyingly impressive. When it came to race, ordinarily thoughtful people contorted reason to fit a system of racial segregation riddled with so many exceptions and nuances that it should have imploded under its own nonsense. But that is not what happened. Sensory stereotypes—and the unthinking, visceral behavior they encouraged, even required—helped make the system seem entirely stable, reasonable, and appropriate to the people who sponsored it. This tension, along with the ability to reconcile the ostensibly contradictory, was present from the very beginning of formal segregation.[18]

In such a dynamic system, defining the course for African American uplift, individual and collective, involved much more than direct political action or intraracial organization. Before the Civil War, African American abolitionists understood well the ways in which slavery, racism, economics, and politics were intricately related, and the history of the black convention movements, fraternal societies, press, and educational initiatives demonstrates both their awareness of the comprehensive efforts required as well as the overwhelming complexity of the task. It is no wonder that so many black abolitionists viewed the Civil War as the second American Revolution. But the nation awaiting at the other side of that revolution was more complex still than the one that preceded it, and it was a nation in which race played a new, if familiar, and even more threatening role than it had before the war.

African Americans, confronted with a newly threatening and more emphatically national system of repression that included the competition with immigrant groups that so preoccupied leaders such as Booker T. Washington, found themselves facing the challenge of entering and countering many histories, many narratives, in a complex racial palimpsest that complicated even the terms by which their collective identity or political unity could be defined. As has often been noted, the tenuous alliance of the white North and South was a political union managed by way of racial unity. "American reunion," David Blight observes, was "achievable in the end only through new regimes of racial subjugation, a fated and tragic struggle still only in its formative years. The sections needed one another, almost as polar opposites that made the center hold and kept both an industrial economy humming and a New South on the course of revival. Some of the war's greatest results, the civil and political liberties of African Americans, were slowly becoming sacrificial offerings on the altar of reunion."[19] The terms of this reunion would become the guiding terms of U.S. politics from that time to the present day, with any alleviation to the ongoing sacrificial offerings, any partial granting of African American rights, marked as progress, regardless of whether the historical effects of the original sacrifice were in any way addressed or compensated. At various stages of U.S. history, African Americans would find themselves in a new configuration of the palimpsest of race, approaching with a Du Boisian double consciousness what Alice Fahs has termed white America's "doubled consciousness of blacks" after the Civil War that "enabled whites to maintain older stereotypes while looking ahead to the possibility of new social realities for African Americans."[20] Progress for African Americans was itself folded into a historical narrative that looked back as insistently as it looked forward.

The numerous commentaries on the Civil War and the years that followed the war only add to the confusion. In *Black Reconstruction* (1935), W. E. B. Du Bois famously presents excerpts demonstrating the centrality of the racist assumptions informing many white historians' accounts of the failures of Reconstruction, but more difficult to counter was the "emotional, visceral, and febrile understanding of racial identity" behind such narratives that had already qualified Du Bois's faith in the efficacy of historical evidence and scholarly reason in a white supremacist culture.[21] And behind such official narratives were various and influential unofficial histories (the "imagined Civil War," as Fahs has it) in the form of "war poetry, sentimental war stories, sensational war novels, war humor, war juveniles, war songs, collections of war-related anecdotes, and war histories—literature that has often been designated, then dismissed, as popular."[22] "In both the North and the South," Fahs observes, "popular war literature was vitally important in shaping a cultural politics of war. Not only did it mark the gender of men and women as well as boys and girls, but it also explored and articulated attitudes toward race and, ultimately, portrayed and helped to shape new modes of imagining individuals' relationships to the nation."[23] This was a literary history marked by various attempts to reestablish the bonds of white America—and like race itself, and like the complex category of whiteness that stands at the forefront of U.S. racial history, the Civil War offered not one but many narratives, together constituting various historical palimpsests to complement and reinforce the ever-shifting, dynamic palimpsest of race. "This variegated literature," as Fahs puts it, "created not just one but a multitude of different imagined wars, complicating notions of what kind of national community was created through the auspices of print culture."[24]

The effects of the racial landscape that supported these multiple wars, this national community organized by way of its own instabilities, were inscribed in turn in black literature. Observing that "terror, organized and random, was a persistent part of politics in the postwar South," Blight rightly notes that these conditions defined the needs of African American expressive culture, and that, accordingly, "black folklore, fiction, and reminiscence have reflected the legacy of violence that began during Reconstruction."[25] Bernard Bell similarly notes the challenges faced by black American writers of the time, observing that "as twenty-first-century readers, we are inclined to forget the tenacity of the tradition of white supremacy with which postbellum and post-Reconstruction black novelists had to contend and the gravity of their dilemma."[26] Indeed, this was both an intimate and a practical dilemma for those interested in publishing their work, for "the black novelists of the period were compelled to have their works printed privately, or to make compromises to appeal to predominantly white readers."[27] It is hardly surprising then—given the complex racial dynamics of the era, the competing historical and popular narratives for making sense of the era, and the racial politics involved in the production and distribution of literature—that, as Bruce observes, "much of what post-Reconstruction literature reveals about black American thought and action lies in its unresolved contradictions, not in the answers it gave to the pressing problems of racial injustice."[28] Unresolved contradictions, after all, had long been at the center of African American history, experience, and identity.

The American Eye

A writer who brought those contradictions to the center of his work, Griggs recognized that the struggle for African American rights and social recognition was being fought largely in the fields of literature. He recognized as well that the representation of African American history required something more than the correction of misrepresentations. Those who dismiss African American literature of this time either on the basis of sentimentalism or didacticism—or even on the grounds of formal incoherence—miss an essential point about the challenge African American writers faced, the challenge of intervening in a cultural history that itself deployed sentimentalism and didacticism in its oppression of African Americans, and that was itself incoherent. John M. Reilly years ago emphasized a basic point about the construction of history that we still cannot afford to forget. "The patterns devised to give the details of human experience coherence occur in discourse," Reilly observes, "and one is tempted to say that these patterns are the form given to history by human agency, rather than history itself, until one recalls that nearly all we know of the direction of events derives from discourse piled upon discourse, document upon document, interpretation upon interpretation. Together they comprise a collection of propositions, assertions, and counter-arguments that in its enormity makes summation difficult, certitude probably impossible. This shifting and never completed association of inscriptions, arguments, tales, reports, and hearsay is what we know of the past."[29] Griggs's novels are studied responses to this understanding of history, attempts to reach through "discourse piled upon discourse, document upon document," and "interpretation upon interpretation" so as to manage a clear statement that might have some chance of being effective.

Griggs wrote *The Hindered Hand* as a direct response to a literary misrepresentation, Thomas Dixon Jr.'s *The Leopard's Spots* (1902), and he made an extended critique of Dixon's work a supplement to the novel's third edition. Griggs makes a point of this added emphasis on the novel's original grounding, explaining in a note, "The present edition of 'The Hindered Hand' differs from previous editions in that a review of Mr. Thomas Dixon's 'Leopard Spots' appears in former editions in the form of a conversation between two of the characters of the book, whereas in the present edition the review is more fully given in an article appearing in the rear of this book after the closing of the story" (HH, 121). The point was not simply that Dixon had written a racist novel. Rather, the point was that what Griggs viewed as natural human prejudices were given shape and directed through fiction, and Dixon's novel stood as a significant shift in the literary currents. Griggs points to Stowe's *Uncle Tom's Cabin* as a significant force in directing those currents before the Civil War, observing that Stowe's novel "grappled in the mire of Southern slavery and lifted a despised and helpless race into living sympathy with the white race at the

North" (HH, 123). What was significant about Dixon was that his novel had the potential to equal Stowe's in influence, and thereby "to cut these chords of sympathy and re-establish the old order of repulsion, based upon the primitive feeling of race hatred" (HH, 123). Dixon attained that influence, Griggs suggests, not simply by writing a white supremacist novel but by strategically manipulating the post–Civil War dynamics of white culture, not simply representing a vision of history but representing contesting visions among white Americans, thereby placing African Americans as, in Blight's words, "sacrificial offerings on the altar of reunion."[30] "In his first Anti-Negro book," Griggs argues, "Mr. Dixon was shrewd enough not to make a Southerner who was persona non grata to the North the hero of the story. The poor old Ex-Confederate soldier, rank secessionist, the real hero and dominating figure of his times, in this book is tied out in the back yard, while the post of honor is given to a little boy whose father fought most unwillingly against the Union" (HH, 123). The challenge, accordingly, was not simply to meet a misrepresentation with a corrective but to intervene in the cultural process by which historical understanding is (re)formulated.

Griggs's response is to make cultural process and historiographical perspective driving themes in *The Hindered Hand*, a process that begins in the opening pages, where the entire novel is grounded, in effect, before the beginning of human history. "In the long ago when the earth was in process of formation," the novel begins, "it must have been that those forces of nature most expert in the fashioning of the beautiful were ordered to come together as collaborators and give to the world Almaville!" (HH, 4). These forces of nature, our narrator observes, "so charged the air and all the environments with the spirit of the beautiful, that the men who later wrought in building the city found themselves the surprised and happy creators of a lovely habitation" (HH, 5). By identifying the imposing landscape, Griggs highlights the human culture both shaped by and imposed upon that landscape; and by extending the time-frame relevant to this story beyond human history, Griggs prepares us to consider not only the ways in which human history has been defined but also the extent to which it has strayed from the natural order. From this perspective, readers watch as the story thunders into view. "To the pagan yet remaining in man," the narrator states, "it would seem that yon railroad train plunging toward the Southland is somehow conscious of the fact that it is playing a part in events of tremendous import, for observe how it pierces the darkness with its one wild eye, cleaves the air with its steely front and causes wars and thunders to creep into the dreams of the people by whose homes it makes its midnight rush" (HH, 5). This contrast between the "wild eye" of the train and "those forces of nature most expert in the fashioning of the beautiful" set the stage for *The Hindered Hand*, appealing not only to those familiar with the world of the train but also to "the pagan yet remaining in man," that part of human nature that can still trace its lineage to the forces of nature evident in the surrounding environment.

Significantly, Griggs was not alone in trying to draw readers' attention to culturally trained eyes and perspectives. Early in Charles W. Chesnutt's *The Marrow of Tradition*, two doctors—the northern white Dr. Burns and the southern black Dr. Miller—travel south together on the train. Looking at these two "very different and yet similar types of manhood," the narrator notes that "a celebrated traveler, after many years spent in barbarous or savage lands, has said that among all varieties of mankind the similarities are vastly more important and fundamental than the differences."[31] But as his narrative train speeds on its "journey southward," the narrator adds immediately that if we should find ourselves "looking at these two men with the American eye, the differences would perhaps be the more striking, or at least the more immediately apparent, for the first was white and the second black, or, more correctly speaking, brown . . . even a light brown" (*Marrow of Tradition*, 49). Having presented the view from the American eye, the narrator then offers the perspective of yet another eye, by which Dr. Burns represents "a fine type of Anglo-Saxon, as the term is used in speaking of our composite white population," while Dr. Miller's "erect form, broad shoulders, clear eyes, fine teeth, and pleasingly molded features showed nowhere any sign of that degeneration which the pessimist so sadly maintains is the inevitable heritage of mixed races"(*Marrow of Tradition*, 49).

These three perspectives on the two men indicate the terms and necessity of Chesnutt's attempt throughout the novel to deconstruct the discourse of race, exposing the binary oppositions of racialist thought that veil a world of unnamed variety. But a variety unnamed is a variety available to discursive appropriation—and it is worth noticing that here the perspective of the "American eye" is bracketed by, on the one hand, a perspective informed by trips to "barbarous and savage lands" and, on the other, a perspective that finds in one man Anglo-Saxon features and finds in the other a victory over the argument that miscegenation breeds degeneration. One wonders which of these three perspectives is the best representation of the American eye: the first, that finds its evidence of similarities within an evolutionary framework that itself promotes a hierarchy of differences; the second, that classifies by the labels "white" and "black" people whose skin color is neither white nor black; or the third, in which the individual subject becomes an embodiment of the mastering discourse of scientific racialism—and can hope to be, at best, a living argument against the informing authority of that discourse. Chesnutt here draws attention to the ways in which one's eye can be disciplined by culture—shaped by a history of social prejudices and racial domination—to see differences where others would see similarities. Culture thus becomes a closed perceptual field, training people to see a world that seems unchangeable when viewed from within that field.

Race, one might say, both enters and exits U.S. literature through what Chesnutt terms the American eye—transcribing perceptions shaped by social prejudices and assumptions and particularizing those prejudices and assumptions for the reader. This, of course, is hardly news, for if white readers and writers have been slow to acknowledge and confront the construction of race in literature, black readers and writers certainly have not. Such confrontations are at the center, for example, of Frances E. W. Harper's work. Harper's career as a writer was necessarily devoted not only to constructing a reconfigured black community but also to deconstructing white images (literary and otherwise) of black identity and potential. One character in Harper's intricate novel *Trial and Triumph* complains to a white merchant with whom he shares "kindred intellectual and literary tastes" that books by black authors go unread by white readers; and of the "unaspiring" inhabitants of one depressed neighborhood the narrator explains, "The literature they read was mostly from the hands of white men who would paint them in any colors which suited their prejudices or predilections."[32] Similarly, in her essay on "The Negro as Presented in American Literature," included in *A Voice from the South*, Anna Julia Cooper discusses the role literature plays in the promotion of distorted and essentialized images of races and cultures. Noting the tendency of white writers to base their black characters on the writers' perceptions of whatever black people they happened to encounter, Cooper complains that "a few with really kind intentions and a sincere desire for information have approached the subject as a clumsy microscopist, not quite at home with his instrument, might study a new order of beetle or bug. Not having focused closely enough to obtain a clear-cut view, they begin by telling you that all colored people look exactly alike and end by noting down every chance contortion or idiosyncrasy as a race characteristic."[33] Considered as a mode of envisioning, the American eye sees incorrectly but with increasing particularity, focusing on "chance contortions" as evidence of degeneration, and using idiosyncratic materials to construct what will count as representative images.

I want to offer here a rather extreme example of what Cooper calls a "clumsy microscopist," the author to whom (or against whom) Griggs's novel is addressed, Thomas Dixon Jr.—for in Dixon's *The Clansman* (1905), arguably the most influential racist work the United States has yet produced, Thomas Dixon Jr. brings his own microscope to bear on the American eye.[34] The novel builds to that all but inevitable moment in turn-of-the-century white supremacist literature when a black man rapes a white woman, presented as the flower of Southern culture and Aryan civilization. In this novel, two women are raped, a mother and a daughter, both of whom then immediately commit suicide. Looking to discover the identity of the rapist, Dr. Cameron acts on his belief that "a microscope of sufficient power will reveal on the retina of these dead eyes the image of this devil as if etched there by fire"—for, the doctor notes, just as "impressions remain in the brain like words written on paper in invisible ink," so, too, "images in the eye."[35] Nothing can be found in the daughter's eye, for she is too young, so the doctor turns to the mother who, at thirty-seven, "was the full-blown perfection of womanhood with every vital force at its highest tension" (*Clansman*, 313). When his young assistant can see nothing, the doctor explains, "Your powers of vision are not as trained as mine" (*Clansman*, 313). But when the doctor focuses his own trained vision on the dead mother's eye, unsurprisingly (in this novel) he finds "the bestial figure of a negro—his huge black hand plainly defined—the upper part of his face is dim, as if obscured by a gray mist of dawn—but the massive jaws and lips are clear—merciful God!— yes!—it's Gus" (*Clansman*, 314). Although his assistant suggests, "I'm afraid the image is in your own eye, sir, not the mother's," circumstantial evidence is taken as confirmation of the doctor's impressions—and they immediately take their findings to the head clansman of the township, the Grand Cyclops of the Den (*Clansman* 314, 318).

The eye projects the image; the microscope reflects the eye; and the Grand Cyclops envisions justice: this novel performs a trick done with pseudoscientific mirrors, projecting the violation of a racialized maternal eye to reconfirm the privileged vision of the paternal eye of justice.[36] Although Dixon himself asserts otherwise, clearly the image is, indeed, in the doctor's own eye, and Dixon supports that image in his handling of its fictive environment, the world of *The Clansman*. It is as Toni Morrison has said in her own exploration of such images on the American eye, "the subject of the dream is the dreamer.

The fabrication of an Africanist persona is reflexive; an extraordinary meditation on the self; a powerful exploration of the fears and desires that reside in
the writerly conscious. It is an astonishing revelation of longing, of terror, of
perplexity, of shame, of magnanimity."[37] *The Clansman* is only an obvious example of such fabrications, in which we can observe what Morrison has called
the transformation of the "old pseudo-scientific and class-informed racisms
whose dynamics we are more used to deciphering" to a metaphor used to refer
to and disguise "forces, events, classes, and expressions of social decay and economic division far more threatening to the body politic than biological 'race'
ever was."[38] And it is threatening precisely because, as Dixon realized, the image
of projected fears can be inscribed with invisible ink on the reader's eye.

Griggs works largely to make visible the social dynamics that Dixon worked
to manipulate, placing his characters in a world that cannot be easily divided
into black and white or northern and southern white. Whereas Dixon shaped his
characters, in Griggs's analysis, to appeal to a common bond between northern
and southern whites, Griggs shapes his narrative to indicate the world of tenuous and often disrupted affiliations that followed the Civil War. Noting, for example, the common view that the Civil War was "a rich man's war and a poor
man's fight," the narrator of *The Hindered Hand* asserts that "the highest interest
of the 'poor whites' who bore the brunt of the fighting was to be conserved by the
collapse rather than the triumph of the cause for which they fought with unsur-
passed gallantry. For, with the downfall of the system of enforced labor, the work
of the world became an open market, and the dignity of labor being restored, the
'poor whites' had both a better opportunity and a more congenial atmosphere
to begin their rise. Thus the stars in their courses fought for the 'poor whites' in
fighting bitterly against them" (HH, 8–9). Again we encounter a glimpse of an
overarching order, "the stars in their courses," again in tension with the cultural
trains that disrupt people's dreams (for the novel makes it clear that the surging
train at the novel's opening is a microcosm of the U.S. social order), but this time
those transcendent forces lay new tracks entirely, guiding the disenfranchised
(those manipulated by that social order) toward a new world of promise. And
the course of that alternate track cannot be ignored, the narrator emphasizes,
for "the human race has not thus far even approached the point of constructing such habitations as would render mankind indifferent to rumblings underground, nor has society such secure foundation that it can think lightly of its
lower elements" (HH, 10). "In the long run," we are told, the lower elements, like
"the pagan yet remaining in man," "will be heard from. It is inevitable" (HH, 10).

Griggs's handling of the world as envisioned by the "American eye," his attempt to represent the full range of a complexly contingent social and political world, leads him to cross and recross variously defined color lines. Although Dixon accounts for the mixing of the races, he does so to reinforce a firm division between black and white, whereas Griggs (following Chesnutt in *The Marrow of Tradition*) highlights the permeability of the color line in *The Hindered Hand* by raising the possibility of whites performing as black to avoid the discovery of their crimes. We discover this, though, not by such a performer but by a man who pretends to be black in order to solve a crime. In a letter to a friend in a "far away peaceful Northern home," Ramon Mansford, a white man whose fiancée was killed, reports:

> I am about at the end of one of the most shocking and most mystifying affairs known to the human race. In keeping with my resolve I disappeared into the Negro race for the purpose of fathoming the mystery of the murder of my beloved Alene. The fact that I could so disappear is one of far-reaching significance. It shows what an awful predicament the Negroes are in. Any white criminal has the race at his mercy. By dropping into the Negro race to commit a crime and immediately thereafter rejoining the white race, he has a most splendid opportunity to escape. And men who commit the darker crimes are not failing to take advantage of the open door. (HH, 46)

Mansford later finds that this is indeed the case in the murder of his fiancée, and thus does Griggs have white culture report on itself, dramatizing the discovery of the racial manipulations central to the maintenance of white supremacy. In this series of events we again encounter the "lower elements" of society, and again those elements expose the instabilities of the cultural order, the weaknesses in the foundations of a culture not in harmony with its harmonious natural environment. Here as throughout the novel, Griggs returns us to the novel's opening vision of two temporal realms contesting against one another, natural time and human history.

Human experience, Griggs suggests, functions within those tensions, sometimes drawn toward natural justice and sometimes toward unnatural manipulations of social divisions, and it is by such means that he identifies the two characters who represent the spectrum of possibilities for black activism, Ensal Ellwood and Earl Bluefield. "Ensal and Earl," we are told, "represented two types in the Negro race, the conservative and the radical. They both stood for the ultimate recognition of the rights of the Negro as an American citizen, but their methods were opposite" (HH, 20). Both men prove effective before the novel's end, though neither in the way they first conceived, and both men change their methods and find their successes compromised. I have more to say about that, but for the moment, I wish to note simply that Griggs distinguishes between the two men (and their favored methods) by placing them in different relations to history. While both men are devoted to "the procuring of the full recognition of the rights of the Negro," they differ in their readings of the foreground of that goal, with Ensal favoring historical negotiations and Earl historical interventions:

> Ensal felt that the acceptance of slavery on the part of the Negro in preference to extermination was evidence of adaptability to conditions that assured the presence of the Negro on the earth in the final wind up of things, in full possession of all the advantages that time and progress promise. Earl rather admired the Indian and felt that the dead Indian refusing to be enslaved was a richer heritage to the world than the yielding and thriving Negro.

> Ensal held that the course of the Negro during the Civil War in caring for the wives and children of the men fighting for their enslavement was a tribute to their humanity and would prove an invaluable asset in all future reckonings. While thoroughly approving of the Negro's protection of the women and children of the whites from violence, Earl was sorry that the thousand torches which Grady said would have disbanded the Southern armies were not lighted. Ensal deprecated all talk and thought of the sword as the final arbiter of the troubles between the races. Earl had his dreams—and his plans as well. (HH, 20)

In both cases, experience is the means by which collective character is forged, and history is the forum through which collective character is revealed. But how to interpret such historical revelations is itself a historical challenge. Ensal, one might say, believes that secular history is not so far removed from providential history as to be beyond hope, whereas Earl believes that human history is so corrupt as to require a violent interjection if it is to be realigned with any transcendent concept of justice.

And against this juxtapositioning of the conservative and the radical is a similar, though more complex, division among the whites. Arthur Daleman, a wealthy white southerner, lays out the basic divisions, beyond those of North and South: "My class was humane to the Negro in the days of slavery and under our kindly care developed him from a savage into a thoroughly civilized man. But I am glad slavery is gone. Under the system bad white men could own slaves and their doings were sometimes terrible. They were the ones who made

Uncle Tom's Cabin possible and brought down upon us all the maledictions of the world. Like 'poor dog Tray,' the humane class were caught in bad company and we have paid for it. But all of that is in the past" (HH, 40). Daleman's naïveté is matched only by his assumption of white supremacy, the assumption that slavery *could* have been and largely was a benevolent system, ruined only by "bad white men" who inspired the novel that finally defined the system in the cultural imagination. And his paternalism continues in his summary of the postwar situation, in which he distinguishes between white southern radicals and liberals: "The radical element at the South has always given us trouble. The radicals hate the Negro and nothing is too bad for them to do to him. We liberals like him and want to see him prosper. Such of us liberals as labor to keep the Negro out of politics do so, not out of hatred of him, but for his own good, as we see it. We hate to see him the victim of the spleen of the radicals and they do grow furious at the sight of the Negro in exalted station. In your Northern home bear in mind these two classes of Southerners and remember that some of us at least are anxious for the highest good to all" (HH, 40). Of course, there are more than two classes, and the tensions between and among them make possible the inevitable supremacy of, again, the lowest element, which offers the clearest response to the race question, one offered by one of a crowd of people who had come by special train to town to witness a lynching: "We lynch niggers down here for anything. We lynch them for being sassy and sometimes lynch them on general principles. The truth of the matter is the real 'one crime' that paves the way for a lynching whenever we have the notion, is the crime of being black" (HH, 54). One might say that such violence trumps all other positions, or that all inhabitants of the white political spectrum share complicity in a culture that leads inevitably to a murderous racism, but Griggs seems to insist otherwise, attending carefully to the tensions within and across the spectrum.

Constituting Social Change

Accounting for such tensions, of various social and political positions defined with and against each other in a world of contingencies beyond anyone's control, Griggs takes readers into the muck of the world while still drawing from his novel's opening vision of an encompassing historical realm from which human social orders and affairs should be viewed. The novel is filled with individuals and groups hell-bent on a mission, and it is hard to believe that the point of the novel should be to choose a single one, as if there were a solution for this mess of a world Griggs represents in this gorgeous mess of a novel. Indeed, the point seems to be that there is some degree of truth, or at least a hint of some ancient impulse, that drives all missions. Consider, for example, his elaborate introduction to a less-than-glorious example of a driven woman working to live beyond the color line, that of Mrs. Arabelle Seabright. "This world of ours," the narrator comments,

> thought of in comparison with man the individual, is so very, very large; its sons and daughters departed, now on hand and yet to come, form such an innumerable host; the ever-increasing needs of the living are so varied and urgent; the advance cry of the future bidding us to prepare for its coming is so insistent; the contest for supremacy, raging everywhere, must be fought out among so many souls of power—these accumulated considerations so operate that it is given unto but a few of those who come upon the earth to obtain a look of recognition from the universal eye; and fewer still are they who, by virtue of inherited capacity, proper bent, necessary environment and the happy conjunction of the deed and the hour, so labor as to move to admiration, sympathy or reverence the universal heart, an achievement, apart from which no man, however talented, may hope to sit among the earth's immortals. (HH, 13)

This breathless vision of determination (for it is presented in one extended sentence) could be applied to many people in this novel. From the "wild eye of the train" to the fragmented (even fractal) American eye, and beyond to the universal eye and heart, Griggs draws us into a world in which missions come easy but movements are rare. That the woman for whom this introduction is intended, Mrs. Seabright, largely succeeds in integrating her family into the highest classes of white society suggests that Griggs does not hope to whittle down his complicated plot to a choice between Ensal and Earl or any clear point between, for it seems that most anyone can enjoy some measure of success in this chaotic society, regardless of his or her position. While clearly this is a novel drawn to the hope of recognition and sympathy, it is not one that offers a clear path to those goals, and the path it offers is by no means populated solely by heroes.

I do not mean to suggest that Griggs is not interested in the possibilities of a clear mission, perhaps even one capable of leading to a movement. Indeed, he foregrounds certain messages that are clearly intended to resonate beyond the novel's end. Much is made, for example, of Ensal's address to the American people, including Tiara's decision to "choose as her mission the placing of a copy thereof in every American home" (HH, 87). This extensive address, so closely aligned with views Griggs expresses elsewhere, is clearly intended as a centerpiece of the novel. Tiara's mission extends still further, as she takes to the "lecture platform" and travels "from city to city, pleading her cause," including the cause of temperance (HH, 88). Similarly, the white minister Rev. Percy G. Marshall, is praised as "a pioneer spirit," and "by degrees," due to his efforts, "the white pulpit of the South was growing more and more aggressive and emphatic" (HH, 78). Similarly, too, when the white lawyer H. Clay Maul, serves as prosecuting attorney for the white lynchers of Bud and Foresta and actually tries to secure a guilty verdict, our solemn narrator reprints the whole of his long, eloquent, and hopeless speech. And one could go on—including some of the less admirable missions that I have already referenced.

All the missions have some force, but all are somehow compromised. Ensal leaves the United States for an impassioned mission in Africa and then finally returns for another equally impassioned mission: his love of Tiara. The novel's stance on these turns in his career is rather clear: "Now all of you who believe in altruism; who believe in the giving of one's self for others; who believe in fixedness of purpose; who have in any wise pinned your faith to that man Ensal—let all such prepare yourselves for evidence of the utter frailty of man" (HH, 110). Earl, in turn, is moved by Ensal's address but believes that Ensal's *Uncle Tom's Cabin* needs a John Brown and a Harpers Ferry if it is to have its full effect; when he strikes out on a military campaign, he is seriously wounded by Ensal himself, trying to stop him. As for Percy Marshall, the narrator notes that "it was the irony of fate that this young minister should be slain by a member of the race for which he had imperilled his own standing among the whites" (HH, 78). Young attorney Maul begins his statement to the jury with "a smile of triumph upon his face" and comes "into his spiritual inheritance" with the position he takes, but he sacrifices his bright future at the same time" (HH, 68). It was, after all, a closing argument that ended with Maul pronouncing his more fundamental stand: "I stand for white supremacy in intellect, in soul power, in grasp upon the esteem of others through sheer force of character" (HH, 71). Even the achievement of character, be it Maul's or anyone else's in this novel, is compromised before it can fully claim the attention of the universal eye and heart.

The one mission in *The Hindered Hand* that grows to a powerful movement is less a message than a method, a matter of working this cacophony of voices, this chaos of competing and always compromised missions—that of Earl Bluefield, who plays all sides against the others to gain political supremacy over the white southern repressionists. Earl himself states the essential nature of his mission when he first begins to conceive of it. "Groping for the light," as the narrator puts it, Earl states, "It is one thing to produce a Niagara and another thing to harness it. O for a means of harnessing all the righteous sentiment in America in favor of the ideals of the Constitution" (HH, 103). And, indeed, that's what Earl does. Under the alias of John Blue, Earl presents one message to the radical wing of white southern politicians, another to "Northern labor," another to "the business interests of the country," another to statesmen, and another to "the whole people" (HH, 107–9). Central to his efforts is the exposure of white supremacist thought—or, one might say, the elevation of white supremacist ideology as an unquestioned presence in white American life to a positive assertion—a call for the white people of America, in effect, to own up to the guiding principles of American social, political, and economic life. Earl begins this call with those prepared to answer it enthusiastically, radical white southerners, knowing that they would do his work from there, disrupting the dynamics of the U.S. racial order by making it explicit, conscious, deliberate, visible. He "invaded state after state in the South and conferred with the radical leaders wherever he went and found the sentiment everywhere prevailing that the time was ripe for the radical South to pull off its mask and let the world see its real heart" (HH, 107). He then turns his attention to the North: "With ceaseless, tireless energy Earl Bluefield went everywhere in the North during the campaign that followed, assailing the political power in control of the South. The heat of his heart warmed his words and his eloquence thrilled the nation" (HH, 107). By encouraging southerners to articulate the white supremacist position more boldly, more aggressively, more loudly, and by coaching all others on how to respond to protect their own interests (including the interest of veiling their racism), Earl becomes a representative not so much of a righteous message as of a devilishly righteous method, and a very successful one, leading to "a glorious triumph at the polls" (HH, 109).

The Hindered Hand, I suggest, is not a didactic novel, for its message cannot be reduced to any of even the most detailed and explicit position statements presented in its pages. This is a novel not of positions but of positioning, of process, an extension of Earl's attempt at "harnessing all the righteous sentiment in America in favor of the ideals of the Constitution" (HH, 103). As the Federalist Papers suggest, the Constitution is not based on a bright or optimistic vision of human nature. Rather, the Constitution is an attempt at formulating a method by which the whole might be greater than the sum of the parts, by which contending views and differing positions of self-interest might be managed. As the narrator of *The Hindered Hand* puts it when noting that both Tiara and A. Hostility wanted Ensal to remain in America, one for love and one for "evil genius," "How often do diverse spirits from widely differing motives work toward a common end!" (HH, 83). Differing spirits haunt the pages of *The Hindered Hand*, and their different motives work with and against one another throughout, keeping any single motive from finding unhindered advancement. Ultimately, *The Hindered Hand* is devoted to a historical intervention similar to that of the Constitution, an intervention of method over message, or of method *as* message, process over content, a guiding principle by which the chaos of social life—the righteous sentiment that Griggs identifies as the Niagara of this novel—can be anticipated and, indeed, harnessed. The "message" of this novel is that there is no singular message capable of accounting for, or succeeding in the face of, "all the righteous sentiment in America."

Like Earl, though, Griggs stacks the deck—or, perhaps, he works to balance a stacked deck by making clear the terms of the contending forces, to use Pauline Hopkins's term, in need of a governing method, and this is why he foregrounds Dixon's work in his own. As Earl's strategy involves awaking all sides to a heady contest by making white supremacist thought an unavoidable presence in U.S. politics, so Griggs's strategy involves turning to a white southern writer who made violent fountains of the underlying currents of U.S. social and political life. Sounding a warning as dire as anything Earl presents to his northern audiences, Griggs writes in his appendix to *The Hindered Hand*: "Let the use to which Mr. Dixon is putting his borrowed emotional power recall the nation to the slumbering Negro mind that must ere long awake to power. May the coming, then, of Mr. Dixon, the literary exotic, serve as a reminder to the American people that they give the Negro a healthy place, a helpful atmosphere in which to evolve all that is good within himself and eliminate all the bad. If this be done, even Mr. Dixon will not have lived and frothed in vain" (HH, 133). Dixon, in short, has work to do in Griggs's appendix, and it is easy to see why Griggs first approached that work in the body of the novel itself. Dixon is there not simply as a subject of Griggs's analysis, though teaching readers a certain degree of cultural literacy in reading racialized texts is an African American tradition that extends back at least as far as David Walker's *Appeal*. But Dixon has more important work to do in this novel—the work of simply being Dixon, author of novels unmistakably devoted to promoting a white supremacist ideology, with the Klan in full regalia and power.

Working to distance white readers from this frothing and exotic writer, Griggs reminds readers of the stakes involved, the extent to which we live in the worlds we create, or the worlds we allow to be created in our name. "Just now the American people seem much engrossed with the training of the hand of the Negro," Griggs writes, "confessedly a work of tremendous moment. But be it known unto you, oh Americans, that it is through his mind, his spirit, the exhalations of his soul, his dreams or lack of dreams, that the Negro is to leave his most marked influence on American life" (HH, 133). Significantly, Griggs presents the vision of this "marked influence" in literary terms. Noting that "Southern self-interest may be relied upon to keep the Negro here," Griggs lays out for the reader the inevitable cultural process that follows from that presence:

> Being here, no human power can prevent him from contributing his quota to the atmosphere of the group in which all the sons of the South must find their environing inheritance. In the contact of the street workman with his boss; in the cook kitchen; in the nursery room; in the concubine chamber; in the street song; in the brothel; in the philosophizings of the minstrel performer; in the literature which he will ere long create, by means of which there can be contact not personal; in myriad ways the Negro will write something upon the soul of the white man. It should be the care of American people that he write well. (HH, 133)

In short, Griggs goes a long way around, necessarily, to reach a fairly recognizable point: that republics depend on the education and character of their citizens. African Americans will be involved in the contending forces of the republic, as will every other problematic group in the novel, every manifestation of the "lowest element" of human society. The challenge is to prepare all sides for the ongoing debate—the interplay orchestrated by constitutional checks and balances—that is the American republican process of self-governance.

It is in this way that Ensal is as important to Griggs's purposes as is Earl, for while Earl articulates the method, Ensal identifies the field of battle, the constituencies in need of a governing method. When A. Hostility wants to "inflame" Ensal to join in his scheme of pitting Anglo-Saxons against the Slavs for world domination, he gives Ensal a "book written for the express purpose of thoroughly discrediting the Negro race in America," presumably a book by Dixon (HH, 84). Ensal is indeed inflamed, and his reflections on the book are revealing:

> The movement for which this book stood, constituted what Ensal regarded as one of the most menacing phases of the problem of the relation of the races. He knew

that in the very nature of things a policy of misrepresentation was the necessary concomitant of a policy of repression. Now that the repressionists were invading the realm of literature to ply their trade, he saw how that the Negro was to be attacked in the quiet of the American home, the final arbiter of so many of earth's most momentous questions, and he trembled at the havoc vile misrepresentations would play before the truth could get a hearing. (HH, 84)

In a novel that calls attention more than once to the enormous influence of Harriet Beecher Stowe's *Uncle Tom's Cabin*, this is a serious moment—serious enough, indeed, to constitute a major revision in the third edition of *The Hindered Hand*, wherein Griggs devotes his appendix to a cogent and blistering review of Dixon's novel. This invasion of "the American home," and of American minds and hearts, shifts the field of Earl's method of playing contending forces against one another from political arenas to home parlors. Griggs's work is driven by his conviction that African Americans would need to enter American homes as powerfully as did Dixon—all American homes if possible (as Ensal hopes to do in publishing his address to the American people), but at least African American homes, so that this most vulnerable constituency could be prepared for the contentious struggles needed for the nation to realize itself as a functioning republic. "Ensal thought of the odds against the Negro in this literary battle," we are told, and the odds against their equal participation in this most important of forums were considerable:

How that Southern white people, being more extensive purchasers of books than the Negroes, would have the natural bias of great publishing agencies on their side; how that Northern white people, resident in the South, for social and business reasons, might hesitate to father books not in keeping with the prevailing sentiment of Southern white people; how that residents of the North, who essayed to write in defense of the Negro, were laughed out of school as mere theorists ignorant of actual conditions; and, finally, how that a lack of leisure and the absence of general culture handicapped the Negro in fighting his own battle in this species of warfare. (HH, 84)

A specifically African American literature was needed, a literature capable of training African American minds not simply to receive literary correctives to violent misrepresentations but also to read aright the terms of their participation in the national battles.

Although Griggs was innovative in many ways, his strategically fractured and intertextual work is of a piece with many of the writings produced by African Americans throughout the nineteenth century. Attempts to create such a literature go back at least as far as David Walker's *Appeal*, in which Walker similarly embeds and comments on documents by white writers in a text that appeals to the governing authority of constitutional public realm. Griggs works in this same tradition, though by his time the plot lines required to represent the absurdities of U.S. racial culture and the many factions both divided and affiliated by the Civil War and Reconstruction were considerably more complex than they were for Walker. But the basic challenge of representation and interpretation remains. The conspicuous intertextuality of Walker's *Appeal* is central to its purposes, for the racial presence in the *Appeal* can be located not in its author or even in "the coloured citizens of the world" that Walker invokes in his title, but rather in the cultural politics of interpretation. So it is for Griggs as well, for while Griggs includes characters that represent various positions on the question of racial affiliation, ultimately the racial position he addresses comes down to matters of representation and interpretation. Indeed, it is on these grounds that he hopes to eventually win the battle against Dixon's misrepresentations. At the end of the appendix, constituting the final words of *The Hindered Hand*, Griggs closes with a vision of Dixon's epitaph, in which Dixon is remembered as a "misguided soul" who deliberately misinterpreted African American character and potential—presenting "mistakes independent of their environments and provocations," while ignoring or minimizing "all the evil in the more vicious element of whites" (HH, 134). In a conversation with the *somewhat* enlightened H. Clay Maul, Ensal gives voice to the one clear hope of this novel: "We Negroes are going to ask one favor of the nation, and that is that it enforce its constitution, which provides one test for all American citizens. If we win it will not only free us from the repressionists, but will free the better element of Southern whites as well" (HH, 115). The liberation of such elements and the contentious collective self-governance that would follow required the services of writers capable of placing a complex and contentious world in American homes. That is the service Griggs tries to perform in *The Hindered Hand*, a novel directed to the process and method of American history.

Notes

1. Sutton E. Griggs, *The Hindered Hand: or, The Reign of the Repressionist*, 3rd ed. (New York: AMS Press, 2010), 59. Subsequent references to the novel are cited parenthetically in the text as HH.

2. For thoughtful defenses of Griggs's achievements as a literary artist, see Wilson J.

Moses, "Literary Garveyism: The Novels of Reverend Sutton E. Griggs," in *Phylon* 40, no. 1 (1979): 203–16; Kali Tal, "'That Just Kills Me': Black Militant Near-Future Fiction," in *Social Text* 20, no. 2 (2002): 70–75.

3. As Dickson D. Bruce Jr. has observed, much of the criticism has attempted to locate Griggs as a political thinker—that is, to identify his position in the spectrum of possibilities at the time. Consider, for example, one of the most detailed studies of Griggs life and work to date, Finnie D. Coleman's consideration of Griggs as a case study in "conservative pragmatism as it shaped the psychodynamics of race relations and racial politics and colored intergenerational change in Black families and communities during this period," a position that echoes somewhat the earlier judgment of Yarborough that Griggs favored the racial conservatism associated with Booker T. Washington. See Bruce, *The Origins of African American Literature, 1680–1865* (Charlottesville: University Press of Virginia, 2001), 155–56; Coleman, *Sutton Griggs and the Struggle against White Supremacy* (Knoxville: University of Tennessee Press, 2007), xii. Ultimately, many readers conclude that Griggs was largely a product of the political confusions and tensions of his time, which he could replicate but not resolve. On this, see Arlene A. Elder, *The "Hindered Hand": Cultural Implications of Early African-American Fiction* (Westport, Conn.: Greenwood, 1978), 99–103; Robert E. Fleming, "Sutton E. Griggs: Militant Black Novelist," *Phylon* 34, no. 1 (1973): 73–77; Richard Allen Yarborough, "The Depiction of Blacks in the Early Afro-American Novel" (PhD diss., Stanford University, 1980), 501; Raymond Hedin, "Probable Readers, Possible Stories: The Limits of Nineteenth-Century Black Narrative," in *Readers in History: Nineteenth-Century American Literature and the Contexts of Response* (Baltimore: Johns Hopkins University Press, 1993), 42–43; Maria Karafilis, "Oratory, Embodiment, and U.S. Citizenship in Sutton E. Griggs's *Imperium in Imperio*," *African American Review* 40, no. 1 (2006): 140.

4. Robert A. Bone, *The Negro Novel in America* (New Haven, Conn.: Yale University Press, 1965), 34.

5. Eric Curry, "'The Power of Combinations': Sutton Griggs' *Imperium in Imperio* and the Science of Collective Efficiency," *American Literary Realism* 43, no. 1 (2010): 25.

6. Ibid., 24.

7. I do not mean to undervalue the work that has been done along these lines, among which Curry's is a particularly thoughtful example. Important, too, is Mary Crumpton Winter's exploration of Griggs's vision of "racial cohesion"; Stephen Knadler's consideration of Griggs's "shaping, in narrative, of a counter-representation of patriotic citizens of African descent at a historical moment of patriotic fervor and crisis"; Gabriel A. Briggs's examination of "the New Negro as an inherently *southern* figure," one "who finds his first ideological expressions and inspiration for long-term agitation of the race problem in Sutton Griggs's *Imperium In Imperio*"; Caroline Levander's demonstration of the value of locating that same novel "within the context of the specific region that the Imperium calls home, rather than within the context of a generic U.S. South or U.S. nation"; and John Cullen Gruesser's consideration of Griggs's ambivalent and uninformed portrayal of Africa in his fiction, leading to a perspective that ultimately played into white resistance to African American claims for full citizenship. See Winter, *American*

Narratives: Multiethnic Writing in the Age of Realism (Baton Rouge: Louisiana State University Press, 2007), 92; Knadler, "Sensationalizing Patriotism: Sutton Griggs and the Sentimental Nationalism of Citizen Tom," American Literature 79, no. 4 (2007): 675; Briggs, "Imperium In Imperio: Sutton E. Griggs and the New Negro of the South," Southern Quarterly 45, no. 3 (2008), 155; Levander "Sutton Griggs and the Borderlands of Empire," in this volume; Gruesser, Black on Black: Twentieth-Century African American Writing about Africa (Lexington: University of Kentucky Press, 2000), 24–33.

8. Matthew Frye Jacobson, Whiteness of a Different Color: European Immigrants and the Alchemy of Race (Cambridge, Mass.: Harvard University Press, 1998), 41.

9. Ibid., 42–43.

10. The scholarship on the construction of race in the nineteenth century covers a wide range of disciplines. For legal background, see John Hope Franklin and Genna Rae McNeil, eds., African Americans and the Living Constitution (Washington, D.C.: Smithsonian Institution Press, 1995); Ariela J. Gross, Double Character: Slavery and Mastery in the Antebellum Southern Courtroom (Athens: University of Georgia Press, 2000) and What Blood Won't Tell: A History of Race on Trial in America (Cambridge, Mass.: Harvard University Press, 2008); Leon A. Higginbotham Jr., In the Matter of Color: Race & The American Legal Process; The Colonial Period (Oxford: Oxford University Press, 1978) and Shades of Freedom: Racial Politics and Presumptions of the American Legal Process (New York: Oxford University Press, 1996); Rogers Smith, Civic Ideals: Conflicting Visions of Citizenship in U.S. History (New Haven, Conn.: Yale University Press, 1997). For scientific background, see William Ragan Stanton, The Leopard's Spots: Scientific Attitudes toward Race in America, 1815–59 (Chicago: University of Chicago Press, 1960). For general cultural background on the United States as a "racial state," see George M. Fredrickson, The Black Image in the White Mind: The Debate on Afro-American Character and Destiny, 1817–1914 (New York: Harper, 1971); Thomas F. Gossett, Race: The History of an Idea in America (1963; repr., New York: Schocken Books, 1965); Reginald Horsman, Race and Manifest Destiny: The Origins of American Racial Anglo-Saxonism (Cambridge, Mass.: Harvard University Press, 1981); David R. Roediger, The Wages of Whiteness: Race and the Making of the American Working Class (London: Verso, 1991); Alexander Saxton, The Rise and Fall of the White Republic: Class Politics and Mass Culture in Nineteenth-Century America (London: Verso, 1990). For general philosophical and theoretical frameworks that are especially relevant in this regard, see David Theo Goldberg, The Racial State (Malden, Mass.: Blackwell, 2002) and Racist Culture: Philosophy and the Politics of Meaning (Cambridge, Mass.: Blackwell, 1993); Charles W. Mills, The Racial Contract (Ithaca, N.Y.: Cornell University Press, 1997). I comment on this history more extensively in the first chapter of Chaotic Justice: Rethinking African American Literary History, a general consideration of the historical process of race from which I draw for this essay (Chapel Hill: University of North Carolina Press, 2009).

11. Jacobson, Whiteness of a Different Color, 137.

12. Ibid.

13. Ibid., 138.

14. Ibid., 141.

15. Ibid., 142.

16. Ibid., 170.

17. Mark M. Smith, *How Race Is Made: Slavery, Segregation, and the Senses* (Chapel Hill: University of North Carolina Press, 2006), 47.

18. Ibid., 66.

19. David Blight, *Race and Reunion: The Civil War in American Memory* (Cambridge, Mass.: Belknap, 2001), 139.

20. Ibid., 162.

21. Although Reconstruction has not fed nearly the publishing industry inspired by the Civil War, there have still been a number of good studies published, and recent studies indicate that the complexities of this period, especially including but beyond race, will receive increasing attention. For a good survey of scholarship on this subject, covering a broad span of years, see Gao Chunchang, *African Americans in the Reconstruction Era* (New York: Garland, 2000); Laura F. Edwards, *Gendered Strife and Confusion: The Political Culture of Reconstruction* (Urbana: University of Illinois Press, 1997); Eric Foner, *Reconstruction: America's Unfinished Revolution, 1863–1877* (New York: Harper & Row, 1988); John Hope Franklin, *Reconstruction after the Civil War*, 2nd ed. (Chicago: University of Chicago Press, 1994); Thomas Holt, *Black over White: Negro Political Leadership in South Carolina during Reconstruction* (Urbana: University of Illinois Press, 1977); Harold Hyman, ed., *New Frontiers of the American Reconstruction* (Urbana: University of Illinois Press, 1966); Leon F. Litwack, *Been in the Storm So Long: The Aftermath of Slavery* (New York: Knopf, 1979); Michele Mitchell, *Righteous Propagation: African Americans and the Politics of Racial Destiny after Reconstruction* (Chapel Hill: University of North Carolina Press, 2004); Susan Eva O'Donovan, *Becoming Free in the Cotton South* (Cambridge, Mass.: Harvard University Press, 2007); Howard N. Rabinowitz, *Race Relations in the Urban South, 1865–1890.* (New York: Oxford University Press, 1978); Heather Cox Richardson, *The Death of Reconstruction: Race, Labor, and Politics in the Post–Civil War North, 1865–1901* (Cambridge, Mass.: Harvard University Press, 2001); Amy Dru Stanley, *From Bondage to Contract: Wage Labor, Marriage, and the Market in the Age of Slave Emancipation* (Cambridge: Cambridge University Press, 1998); Thomas Adams Upchurch, *Legislating Racism: The Billion Dollar Congress and the Birth of Jim Crow* (Lexington: University Press of Kentucky, 2004); Richard M. Valelly, *The Two Reconstructions: The Struggle for Black Enfranchisement* (Chicago: University of Chicago Press, 2004); Forrest G. Wood, *Black Scare: The Racist Response to Emancipation and Reconstruction* (Berkeley: University of California Press, 1970).

22. Alice Fahs, *The Imagined Civil War: Popular Literature of the North & South, 1861–1865* (Chapel Hill: University of North Carolina Press, 2001), 1.

23. Ibid., 1–2.

24. Ibid., 10.

25. Blight, *Race and Reunion*, 108.

26. Bernard W. Bell, *The Afro-American Novel and Its Tradition* (Amherst: University of Massachusetts Press, 1987), 98.

27. Ibid., 97.

28. Ibid., xii.

29. John M. Reilly, "History-Making Literature," in *Studies in Black American Literature*, vol. 2: *Belief vs. Theory in Black American Literary Criticism* (Greenwood, Fla.: Penkevill, 1986), 87.

30. Blight, *Race and Reunion*, 139.

31. Charles W. Chesnutt, *The Marrow of Tradition* (Ann Arbor: University of Michigan Press, 1969), 49.

32. Frances E.W. Harper, *Trial and Triumph*, in *"Minnie's Sacrifice," "Sowing and Reaping," "Trial and Triumph": Three Rediscovered Novels by Frances E. W. Harper*, ed. Frances Smith Foster (Boston: Beacon, 1994.), 222, 240.

33. Anna Julia Cooper, "The Negro as Presented in American Literature," in *A Voice from the South by a Black Woman of the South* (New York: Oxford University Press, 1988), 186–87.

34. I say influential in part because from Dixon's work sprang *The Birth of a Nation*, in part because of the novel's ongoing importance to the members of the KKK, and in part because of Dixon's direct and indirect influence on subsequent writers—for example, Margaret Mitchell, who admired Dixon's fiction long before she wrote *Gone with the Wind*. As Thomas D. Clark notes in his 1970 introduction to the novel, "No scholarly historian of Reconstruction was ever able to reach so wide or impressionable an audience as did Thomas Dixon." See introduction to *The Clansman: An Historical Romance of the Ku Klux Klan*, by Thomas Dixon Jr. (Lexington: University Press of Kentucky, 1970), xvii.

35. Thomas Dixon Jr., *The Clansman: An Historical Romance of the Ku Klux Klan* (Lexington: University Press of Kentucky, 1970), 312–13.

36. On the intersections of "eugenics, motherhood, and racial patriarchy," see chapter 1 of Laura Doyle, *Bordering the Body: The Racial Matrix of Modern Fiction and Culture* (New York: Oxford University Press, 1994).

37. Toni Morrison, *Playing in the Dark: Whiteness and the Literary Imagination* (Cambridge, Mass.: Harvard University Press, 1992), 17.

38. Ibid., 47, 63.

M. GIULIA FABI

Jim Crow and the House of Fiction

Charles W. Chesnutt's and Sutton E. Griggs's Last Novels

In this essay I offer a comparative analysis of Charles W. Chesnutt's *The Colonel's Dream* (1905) and Sutton E. Griggs's *Pointing the Way* (1908), the least appreciated and least critically analyzed works of two of the most prolific black novelists at the beginning of the twentieth century. These novels have rarely been examined in relation to each other. Yet they do not simply share a close chronological proximity and related topical concerns (including disenfranchisement, the neoslavery of segregation, and the convict-lease system). Rather, *Pointing the Way* is a deliberate, systematic, illuminating revision of Chesnutt's earlier novel, and reading these works together opens up new vistas on the internal diversification of African American literature and on the specific aesthetic configurations that the faith in "the mightier weapon" of the pen to effect a "moral revolution" took in the early twentieth century.[1] The oft-voiced critical acknowledgment that Chesnutt and Griggs shared such faith in the power of the pen needs to be accompanied by an exploration of their specific literary goals and interventionist projects. Whether because of their conditional acceptance (in the case of Chesnutt) or utter marginalization (in the case of Griggs) by a white-dominated publishing industry, by the time they wrote *The Colonel's Dream* and *Pointing the Way*, both authors had become keenly aware that Jim Crow prevailed not only in society at large but also in the Jamesian "house of fiction," and they had devised significantly different literary ways of pursuing their projects of social and literary desegregation.[2] Exploring the intertextual connections between these two writers illuminates such differences most effectively, revealing how Griggs's revision of Chesnutt's novel is based on a brilliant critical reading of it that defied the obtuseness of contemporary reviews and that in many ways remains, to this day, still unparalleled in its subtlety.

In *The Colonel's Dream*, Chesnutt foregrounds how the very process of know-ing and interpreting reality is crucially related to the possibility of effective in-tervention in it. I argue that his devastating portrayal of the New South in *The Colonel's Dream* rests not only on the documentary realism with which he de-scribes the economy of exploitation and the neoslavery of segregation but also on the psychological realism with which he depicts how the good intentions of his protagonist are vitiated and ultimately thwarted by his self-satisfaction, his habit of thinking in stereotyped ways, and his overall limited capacities of in-terpretation. Anticipating the ironic economy of James Weldon Johnson's *The Autobiography of an Ex-Coloured Man* (1912), in *The Colonel's Dream* Chesnutt makes use of an unreliable limited point of view to offer a realistic portrayal of a character who, so to speak, cannot interpret reality realistically. Colonel French is neither an "ideal reformer" nor a villain who "succeed[s] in wors-ening race relations in his home town," and taking his liberalism at face-value misses the real focus of the novel.[3] By combining and contrasting documen-tary and psychological realism, Chesnutt aimed to explore "the quality of the mind" of the colonel and foreground ironically how, despite the protagonist's emphasized goodwill, the culture of racial prejudice and segregation make him an unreliable interpreter of his social context and fellow human beings.[4] As in the case of Johnson's novel, the sophisticated ironic economy of Chesnutt's novel has long been critically neglected in ways that reveal the inadequacy of approaching pre–Harlem Renaissance African American fiction as barely dis-guised propaganda rather than as aesthetically complex literary works. By con-trast, appreciating the dual (documentary and psychological) realism of *The Colonel's Dream* pushes in new directions our understanding of this novel and of Chesnutt's place in American literary history, foregrounding his modern(ist) experimentation with the kind of unreliable central consciousness that is cel-ebrated in the case of his contemporary Henry James.

Appreciating the ironic economy of *The Colonel's Dream* and the ways in which Chesnutt challenges his audience to perform the difficult task of reading and understanding, rather than simply feeling, right opens up new vistas also on the even more critically neglected significance and value of Griggs's *Pointing the Way*. In his revision of *The Colonel's Dream*, Griggs engages many of Chesnutt's central thematic concerns, changing their relative importance within the econ-omy of his own novel in order to shift the focus from the psychology of white supremacy to the psychological process of black empowerment and the explora-tion of contemporaneous strategies of black self-determination. Like Chesnutt, he challenges his readers to a new interpretation of reality, but he is not content with noting limitations, preferring instead to point the way toward alternative options. In his nuanced intertextual revision, for instance, Griggs carefully changes the relative prominence of various characters. Although he does present an unreliable white reformer, Seth Molair, he does not grant him narrative primacy as central consciousness. Rather, he foregrounds also the agency, projects, and internal dynamics of the black community, the representation of which, as Ryan Simmons has noticed, is "admittedly highly limited" in *The Colonel's Dream*. Instead of organizing his novel around an unreliable, limited point of view, Griggs opts for a structural unreliability that challenges the expectations of readers by subtly, "imperceptibly," as Chesnutt himself would have it, introducing into American fiction a new hero who exceeds literary and cultural stereotypes.[5] The very centrality of the elderly ex-slave Uncle Jack ironically subverts the narrative script that traditionally relegated him to the role of an irredeemably secondary character, while his *Bildung* epitomizes and at the same time heralds the ideological emancipation of a whole people into self-determination.

In order to do this Griggs, like Chesnutt, compounds the documentary realism of his critical portrayal of segregation and disenfranchisement with the psychological realism of his study of Uncle Jack's transformation into a civil rights activist. At the same time, Griggs also offers a detailed portrayal of the white supremacist assumptions, privileged reluctance, and limited interpretive powers of the main white reformer, limitations that qualify Seth Molair for repeated, explicit remedial lectures on nonracist thought by a variety of black characters who, in the process, acquire great narrative visibility and foreground a communal context of political self-awareness that eliminates any suspicion of singularity from Uncle Jack's conversion. In his revision of his more established contemporary, Griggs combines Chesnutt's interest in a "new body of thought" with a focus on a new body politic, a black political constituency that embodies a historical alternative to his contemporaneous Jim Crow nation.[6]

This change of focus is mediated literarily by a parallel change in representational choices. Griggs's intertextual rereading relies on nuanced differences in thematic and generic emphasis. In the very title of his novel, Chesnutt evokes the genre of utopian fiction that was widely popular in his time, but he frustrates his readers' expectations when the colonel's "faith in human nature and the triumph of right ideas" (CD, 188) clashes with the dystopian context of segregation, sanctioning the triumph of the latter. As a result, the eponymous "dream" acquires the negative connotations of an impossible project or an unrealistic perception of events. In *Pointing the Way*, instead, even as he explores the psychological costs and the present horrors of segregation, Griggs tilts the generic balance in favor of utopia as the presentation of a possible and better historical alternative. Griggs's choice of focusing on successful social change is neither escapist nor voluntaristic. As an active Baptist minister who was a member of the Niagara Movement and later of the NAACP, Griggs did not need to invent black political activism, but he did decide, unlike Chesnutt, to foreground and celebrate it in his fiction.

Reelaborating and expanding real-life trends of his time, Griggs retained Chesnutt's blend of documentary and psychological realism to offer a vision of "the way" to greater social justice. Griggs's narrative portrayal of a nationwide, nonviolent, social revolution is a "concrete" utopian vision based on a careful assessment of forces, possible alliances, tested strategies, and feasible short- and long-term goals that he draws from real-life practices of resistance to segregation and that he systematizes in his depiction of an interracial civil rights movement and a commitment to equality before the law.[7] In the following essay I explore the intertextual relationship between Chesnutt and Griggs by focusing first on *The Colonel's Dream* and then on *Pointing the Way*. Ultimately, this comparative analysis aims to move the discussion of the differences between Chesnutt and Griggs beyond summary sociological labels like "integrationist" and "separatist," enabling a greater appreciation of the sophisticated literariness that shaped the distinctive modes in which they "mined" segregation within and without the house of fiction.[8]

"Peace, Harmony, and Universal Good Will": The Colonel's Dream *(1905)*

Chesnutt's *The Colonel's Dream* opens on a metropolitan scene of modernity in the North characterized by manufacturing companies, financial speculation, trusts, "telephones and push buttons" (CD, 4).[9] Chesnutt returns to this New York setting in the last chapter of the novel, but within this urban frame and in contrast with it, the largest part of his novel focuses on the colonel's physical space travel and psychological time travel to what he perceives as a more backward and isolated civilization: the rural South of "the pine country" (CD, 9).[10] The "general decay" (CD, 16) of the "old Southern town" of Clarendon (CD, 14) is paradigmatic of a civilization "that lives mostly in the past" (CD, 102), a place where time and people move so slowly as to appear to stand still. Chesnutt, who is clearly playing with the lost-race and lost-empire novels that were popular in his time, portrays this time warp from the point of view of the ambivalent colonel, who sees his old hometown "through a mellowing glow of sentiment" (CD, 18), though he cannot avoid noticing how everything was "so like, and yet so different" (CD, 15) from what he remembers. Toward his memories of the Old South he left when he was nineteen (CD, 17), he feels both affection and a sense of distance. The balance between these feelings will change as he is drawn into the atmosphere of the past and starts thinking of Clarendon "as an established residence" (CD, 89). Yet throughout his stay, his "cheerful optimism" (CD, 166) will continue to remain at odds with and obfuscate his perception of a New South social context that is not only significantly poorer, less technologically advanced, and more isolated than the world he has left behind in New York but also governed by cultural mores whose deep-rootedness the colonel cannot gauge and consequently underestimates.[11] The increasingly more momentous and traumatic experiences that mark his descent into this world, which he perceives as more "primitive" (CD, 247), continually challenge the colonel's optimistic assessment of the great potential of the South for improvement, and he counters their dystopian thrust with plans to bridge the economic and cultural gap through his own actions and personal wealth.

Adopting quite uncritically contemporaneous popular portrayals of the South as a locus for tourism and entrepreneurial investment, the colonel reelaborates them into a vision of the South as a "backward" (CD, 48) land where modern spokespersons for "the forces of enlightenment" (CD, 118) like himself may reap easy and great returns for their generosity. Not unlike Hank Morgan in Mark Twain's *A Connecticut Yankee* (1889), a novel Chesnutt owned in his library, the colonel feels superior to the "lethargic" (CD, 106) civilization in which he finds himself.[12] Capitalizing on the benefits of hindsight, he thinks he knows "the car of progress" (CD, 105), but his "missionary enterprise" (CD, 106) amounts to little more than an attempt to reproduce northern practices in a southern context. Social change may require some work, maybe even more work than he expected initially, but he believes that its telos is clear to him. Money, technology, and the American dream of individual self-making will work the miracle of modernizing the backward South, changing its people and teaching them "habits of industry, efficiency and thrift" (CD, 106).

It is from the contrast between the colonel's self-satisfied sense of all-knowing omnipotence as a man from the future and his consistent inability to interpret the world that he initially "insensibly" (CD, 89) sets out to improve that the ironic economy of the novel and the unreliability of its central consciousness emerge. His sense of superiority toward the raw materials (human and otherwise) of the South is overwhelming, and he becomes only occasionally aware of it, as when he suspects that the townspeople "might not relish the thought that they were regarded as fit subjects for reform" (CD, 108). However, his intermittent, superficial awareness never reaches the point of making him analyze his own attitude and motivations or of making him question the less-than-utopian northern context he has adopted as a model to be imitated. After all, even in the North the colonel's optimism was mostly the result of cultivated ignorance, a privileged selective process of avoidance of uncomfortable truths, such as the unpleasant consequences that the successful sale of his firm will have on his employees. He will show this unchanged attitude on other occasions in the course of the novel, as when he "revels" in the diminished prominence of "labour unions, . . . women's clubs and women's claims" (CD, 66) in the South or when he appreciates how in the North one is not exposed to the (mal)treatment of convicts. He philosophizes: "There were certain functions of society, as of the body, which were more decently performed in retirement" (CD, 226–27).

The stunted self-awareness of the protagonist and his delusional sense of superiority based on a limited understanding of reality are a central concern in *The Colonel's Dream*. In his study of Chesnutt as a "substantial contributor to [realist] ideals and techniques," critic Ryan Simmons argues convincingly that the novelist aimed to change "not only what readers know, but also how they know it and how they are capable of responding to it."[13] What still needs to be emphasized, however, is that in *The Colonel's Dream* he explores such a consciousness-raising process indirectly and ironically by analyzing its absence in the case of the novel's central character. Through his sustained focus on the colonel's point of view, Chesnutt probes how his protagonist's self-satisfaction inhibits an in-depth understanding of reality; how his intentions to "help" coexist unwittingly with unexamined racial, gender, and sectional prejudices; how his self-proclaimed philanthropic efforts have personal, often self-aggrandizing and at times self-interested motivations; and how, in the absence of profound comprehension of the world he would like to improve, his "dream" of social enlightenment is simplistically and ineffectually superimposed on a dystopian reality of exploitation in ways that preempt the very possibility of successful systemic change.

Through his portrayal of an improvised and superficial, however well-intentioned, would-be reformer whose limited (in all senses) point of view dominates in the novel, Chesnutt challenges readers to find their way out of the maze of unexamined stereotypes, prejudices, assumptions, and self-interested rationalizations that guide even a "kind" (CD, 122) character like the colonel and undermine his effectiveness as a "man of action" (CD, 105). Focusing on prejudice as a hermeneutic system that distorts the perception of reality, in the case not only of those who mean evil but by default of anybody who does not consciously question the prevailing social system of exploitation, in *The Colonel's Dream* Chesnutt offers his last published novelistic analysis of the Jim Crow culture that dominates in the U.S. nation. Haunted and condescendingly reprimanded, after the publication of *The Marrow of Tradition* (1901), by accusations of bitterness for portraying the brutal realities of segregation that not only genteel William Dean Howells but also many contemporaneous naturalists and muckrakers preferred to overlook, Chesnutt responds ironically by organizing his new novel around the act of misreading.[14] He chooses as protagonist a "supremely confident" (CD, 195) character with a bona fide southern aristocratic pedigree and a prolonged northern experience as a successful businessman, and he dialogizes his character's far-from-bitter outlook by contrasting his "cheerful optimism" (CD, 166) with the violent social conditions and cultural mores he encounters. Taking on the "well-meaning advice of friends to treat less controversial themes," in *The Colonel's Dream* Chesnutt explores the practical (im)possibility, ethical (ir)responsibility, and negative consequences of such avoidance of reality.[15] In the process, he notes the impoverishment of self and other that is the price of a willful innocence rooted in the refusal to perceive or interpret.

In light of Chesnutt's central concern with "reality as a function of consciousness mediated through language," as William Andrews has insightfully noticed, it is quite ironic that he should continue to be critiqued for not being "realistic" enough.[16] The tendency to read Chesnutt only through the lenses of documentary realism goes against the evidence of his own emphasis on a more Jamesian and modernist notion that "impressions *are* experience."[17] Nevertheless, in many ways Chesnutt remains trapped between the rock of those who seem to blame him for alienating his audience by dealing with controversial topics that many other realists avoided and the hard place of those who take his unreliable protagonist at face value, missing the author's pervasive irony and attributing to him the contradictions of his character.[18] As a result, it is not surprising that the critical reception of *The Colonel's Dream* at the time of its publication and to some extent even today should continue to be less than enthusiastic and do little justice to the complexity of this novel.[19] To appreciate this complexity and the critical force of *The Colonel's Dream*, it is necessary to examine how they are rooted in Chesnutt's masterfully ironic narrative use of an unreliable central consciousness. Chesnutt's chosen narrative point of view foregrounds the contrast between the psychological realism of his description of the colonel's delusional optimism as the absence of any systematic problematization of the American dream, and the author's equally realistic description of the dystopian social conditions that prevailed in the segregated South. This interplay between psychological and documentary realism is crucial to the interpretation of the novel and to the comprehension of Chesnutt's aesthetic choices and related project of cultural intervention.

Chesnutt's deployment of an unreliable, limited point of view is also crucially connected with his systematic frustration of his readers' narrative expectations that critics have noticed.[20] As our narrative expectations are frustrated, so does the colonel's dream fail, and this double formal and thematic dissatisfaction is meant to make us question the cultural assumptions underlying both those narrative expectations and the colonel's failure. In his attempt to engage his audience in a consciousness-raising critical dissection of segregation not only as a social reality but as a hermeneutic system, Chesnutt indicts the prevailing culture of inequality as responsible for both horrifying social practices of exploitation such as the convict-lease system and also for its potential to perpetuate such practices by stunting our very humanity, our interpretive ability, our sense of moral responsibility, as well as our capacity to even conceive of a substantially different and better historical alternative and to devise means to realize it. As Andrews has noticed, in fact, the colonel's dream recapitulates many contemporaneous reform plans of which Chesnutt shows the underlying limitations and "piecemeal" approach.[21]

In my analysis of the interpretive significance of the interaction between psychological and documentary realism that governs *The Colonel's Dream*, I focus on three specific aspects: first, the colonel's relationship with the pre–Civil War past, which is mediated narratively by the central trope of the cemetery; second, the limitations of the colonel's dream as a project of social change; third, the colonel's perceptions of his ex-slave Uncle Peter and of the black community as paradigmatic of his interpretive unreliability.

The Cemetery

Michel Foucault has famously described the cemetery as a "highly heterotopic place since, for the individual, the cemetery begins with this strange heterocrony, the loss of life."[22] In *The Colonel's Dream*, the cemetery that frames the novel offers an early instance of the interpretive limitations that transform the colonel's "dream" into a self-fulfilling prophecy of failure. Oak Cemetery marks the temporary end of the colonel's earlier life in the North and the start of a new one. It functions as a portal, so to speak, that at the beginning the colonel crosses to enter into the "strange land" (CD, 184) of the South and that at the end he will cross again to return to the "outer" (CD, 22) world of the North. In *The Colonel's Dream* the cemetery also serves as a tool of characterization.[23] Many of the central characters reveal themselves in relation to this cultural institution, and this is particularly true in the case of the colonel. He offers a characteristic misinterpretation of his southern context during his visit to his family plot at the cemetery, the day after his arrival in Clarendon. Chesnutt orchestrates the colonel's experience of such a visit as a veritable journey back in time through careful references to changed practices of the cult of the dead. The colonel's perceptions of the "older part" (CD, 22) of the cemetery draw him back to the pre–Civil War past of the rural cemetery movement. The location outside town, the iron railings delimiting different plots, the natural setting, its use as a meeting place and leisure ground that the colonel and his son Phil visit on Sundays (CD, 143), and the republican simplicity of its monuments point to a pre–Civil War sensibility that the colonel is quick to embrace.[24] Looking at the dilapidated monuments through the rose-colored and distorting lenses of the "good times" of his youth (CD 26), the colonel superimposes his own nostalgia on the more complex reality of the cemetery, selecting out those elements that do not fit the old-time picture he would like to see. In the process, he reveals a tendency to separate his modern life in the North from the fascinatingly "remoter" one (CD, 119) he thinks he finds in Clarendon. Symptomatically, he judges upstart Bill Fetters's monument for his parents as "expensive but vulgar" (CD, 35), as "strangely out of keeping with the simple dignity and quiet restfulness of the surroundings" (CD, 34), refusing to see it as an expression of the New South and failing to connect its function as a status symbol to that of the "stately mausoleum, in keeping with similar memorials on every hand," that the colonel himself has erected in the "Northern cemetery where his young wife was buried" (CD, 144).

If Chesnutt's description of Oak Cemetery from the viewpoint of his protagonist effectively reveals the colonel's nostalgic approach to the land of his youth, it also lays the narrative groundwork for the author's ironic portrayal of his hero's complacent rediscovery of other traditional cultural institutions of the Old South. In this "quiet graveyard" (CD, 144), the colonel encounters Uncle Peter, who is tending the tombs of his former masters and seems to fit perfectly the role of the faithful "old retainer" (CD, 31). He also meets Laura Treadwell, whom he immediately perceives as a "lady" (CD, 31), even before recognizing her, and whose true womanhood is soon confirmed by her motherly attitude toward the colonel's son. By introducing the old-time setting of the cemetery, Chesnutt does not simply aim to foreground his protagonist's nostalgia for the "good times" (CD, 26) before the war but more subtly also reveals his unreliability as an interpreter. The colonel, in fact, does not regret the end of slavery, which he repeatedly indicts as an "incubus" (CD, 36, 264) from which he "had been emancipated by the same token that had made Peter free" (CD, 29). However, the ostensible progressiveness of such comments is ironically undercut by the simultaneous absence of any recognition of slavery as a racialized economy of exploitation, as becomes clear from the colonel's easy equation of the condition of masters and slaves, as well as from his slippage from actual to metaphorical bondage: "Had Peter remained a slave, then the colonel would have remained a master, which was only another form of slavery" (CD, 29). In similarly ironic fashion, while the colonel complacently rejoices at how "the shackles" had been struck from his own and "from a Nation's mind" (CD, 30), his uncritical, stereotyped reading of the cemetery and of the people he meets there reveals the deeper, if less conscious, fact that his very mode of perception of the South is still informed by the culture of slavery and that his attempt to enforce a clear-cut separation between the South as the land of the past and the North as the land of the future leaves open the problem of interpreting the Jim Crow present.

Foreshadowing many subsequent contrasts between the colonel's optimistic frame of mind and the more tragic plot of the novel, the happy reunion at the cemetery ends on an ominous note, as Uncle Peter is led away by "a white man, wearing a tinned badge upon his coat" (CD, 38). The reader will later learn that the white man is the constable who has arrested Uncle Peter for vagrancy. Post–Civil War modernity intrudes on the colonel's nostalgic time travel. As with Fetters's monument and, later, with his too-modern house (CD, 216) and too-business-like appearance (CD, 223), the colonel will continue to be surprised by such intrusions. This surprise, like his optimism, is dialogized in the novel, as Chesnutt points to the colonel's incapacity not only to read the present New South but also to problematize the past by noticing the ways in which "the same forces" (CD, 10) of capitalism (North and South) have reorganized old practices like slavery under a new, "modern" guise like the convict-lease system.

The ultimate, sophisticated irony of Chesnutt's narrative use of the cemetery is, in Foucauldian terms, its failure as a heterotopia. Rather than a counter-site where "all the other real sites that can be found within the culture . . . are simultaneously represented, contested, and inverted," the cemetery, from the colonel's limited point of view, simply mirrors prevailing racial and gender hierarchies.[25] Similarly, the past cannot seem to teach any useful lessons in this time warp and appears destined to be only "reproduced" (CD, 93). The colonel's "golden moment (CD, 103) in Clarendon, for instance, coincides with the successful organization of an "old-time party" (CD, 93), but he remains blind to the continuities between his resurrection of "old-time amusements" (CD, 96) that had been "prevalent fifty years before" (CD, 94) and other forms of staging the plantation nostalgia, such as the "sale" (CD, 67) of black convicts where the colonel himself buys Uncle Peter's labor "for life" (CD, 68).

Chesnutt hints at the contestatory heterotopic potential of the cemetery only in relation to the colonel's son.[26] "With his lively imagination," Phil finds pleasure "in looking into the future" (CD, 144) and asks his father to bury Uncle Peter near him, when the time comes. Phil's vision of a desegregated cemetery (though Uncle Peter's place would still be marginal, at the foot of the lot [CD, 145]) anticipates the final tragedy and raises expectations that will eventually be frustrated. Like his father's project of social reform, Phil will die in his early childhood. In Clarendon the integrated cemetery will remain an "unreal space" that signals the failure of the colonel's "dream."[27]

The Dream

At the height of his seemingly growing awareness of the unforeseen complexities of social reform, the colonel realizes that what is needed is "a new body of thought" (CD, 247). What he proposes, however, is hardly new. As Andrews has observed, the colonel's dream "is, after all, another application of the American Dream, in this case to the realm of socioeconomic reform."[28] Both share a faith in property, individualism, and freedom and, also, an implicitly racialized double standard of access to those rights.[29]

Having himself realized the American dream when he moved North after the Civil War, the colonel thinks he knows what he is talking about. A privileged immigrant who has enjoyed the advantage of being "offered employment in New York by a relative who had sympathized with the South in her struggle" (CD, 17), the colonel works his way up. He takes his relative's place at the head of the firm and eventually manages to sell it just before succumbing to the impersonal forces of big business that briefly but momentously enter the novel as "the board of directors of the bagging trust" (CD, 5) at the invisible other end of the colonel's phone receiver. Not unlike Edward Bellamy's Julian West, the colonel is among those who manage to ride on top of the "prodigious" coach of northern capitalism, showing no urge to fight for systematic reform, ignoring the inequalities he does not mean to confront, and preferring not to question the "singular hallucination" of feeling that his privilege is deserved.[30] Slipping into the colonel's limited point of view, the narrator notes that he "may have known . . . or guessed" that his own success was linked to the establishment of a monopoly that would make "labour . . . sweat and the public groan," but "he was between the devil and the deep sea—a victim rather than an accessory— he must take what he could get, or lose what he had" (CD, 5).

The northern context that has witnessed his success is the stuff the colonel's dream is made of. And to the extent that his dream aims to reproduce aspects of (what he sees as) the civilized, modern North in (what he sees as) the backward, preindustrial South (CD, 192), he emerges more as an unwitting colonizer than a conscious reformer.[31] His sense of superiority infuses with paternalism the hierarchical relationship he establishes with the natives as "subjects for reform" (CD, 108). Assuming that he knows them and that he knows better, he condescendingly (mis)interprets the natives' resistance as laziness or ignorance, and he is self-righteously shocked when he discovers that they do not *want* to accept his ideas. Chesnutt explores the limitations of his protagonist's self-reliance as an inability to learn. The colonel's self-satisfied individualism inhibits his naturalization in the different world he has entered, and even the two central insiders he trusts (Uncle Peter and Laura Treadwell) cannot function as guides because he thinks he has nothing to learn and only new things to offer. Similarly, the romantic subplot fails to resocialize him and frustrates the expectations of readers used to the mediating function of women à la Edith Bartlett Jr. in Bellamy's *Looking Backward*. He considers his fiancée Laura his muse, as a source "of spiritual strength and inspiration" (CD, 156), but he does not examine how implicated by segregation she really is, nor does he take seriously her comments when she tries to guide him toward a more accurate understanding of their townspeople and the social context of the New South.[32] From within the impermeable bubble of his self-satisfaction, the colonel can at best recycle stereotypes from the Old South or reproduce prevalent "modern" practices from the North.

The ironic economy of *The Colonel's Dream* is at work in the contrast between the fact that while the colonel's overwhelming paternalism is neither enlightened nor strategic, some of his ideas are indeed rather progressive, especially when compared with the virulent racism and violent exploitation that characterizes not only Fetters and his gang but also some of the "best people," like Dr. Mackenzie, "minister of the Presbyterian Church" (CD, 163). On the one hand, his plan to improve the educational opportunities, work conditions, and legislation in Clarendon mirrors on a local level the spirit of the Progressive Era, and in the colonel's mind it paves the way to his utopia of "a regenerated South, filled with thriving industries, and thronged with a prosperous and happy people, . . . where law and order should prevail unquestioned, and where every man could enter . . . the field of opportunity" (CD, 280). On the other hand, "even in his dreams the colonel's sober mind" cannot contemplate that "all men would ever be equal" (CD, 280). Seeing himself, once again like Twain's Connecticut Yankee, as a lone actor from the future, he never treats the natives as equals; he does not collaborate with them but rather hires them, using money to (re)produce hierarchies that he does not question. Those hierarchies effectively modernize older ones, as when in the attempt to buy Bud Johnson out of the convict-lease system he treats Fetters as if he were still a poor white (CD, 223–25) and is surprised when the latter "wouldn't be bullied" (CD, 269). Rather than "a new body of thought," the colonel's dream emerges as little more than a reactive project in which he gets "insensibly" (CD, 119) more and more involved because it initially seems to yield easy results.

The colonel's surprise at the increasingly more serious difficulties he encounters is systematically dialogized in the novel, as Chesnutt attempts to stimulate in the reader the kind of critical awareness that continually escapes his protagonist. The irony of this dialogization is compounded by the contrast between the colonel's self-righteous conviction of selfless generosity and his unwitting revelation of the personal motivations behind his most generous actions.[33] No longer driven by business, the now independently wealthy colonel can indulge in "a philanthropic zeal as pleasant as it was novel," as the narrator notes (CD, 155). Feeling as if he were in "a play" (CD, 50), he is ready for applause and for the gratification of community approval that initially comes easily and that, by contrast with a northern environment where he was a piece of a much larger machine, feeds his sense of exceptionality.[34] However, even his most ambitious reform projects reveal his self-centeredness. His plan for a modern cotton mill with more humane work conditions is an attempt to outdo adult Fetters; he organizes Bud's escape "to please Miss Laura" (CD, 231) and play the all-conquering prince with his fiancée; and he wants to build a library to revive his family name. Showing no change in this pattern, at the very end of the novel, when he is still planning a "crusade," he thinks of Clarendon as "a monument to mark his son's resting place" (CD, 276).

The ostensibly selfless motivations of the colonel's improvised career as a reformer have ironically tragic consequences for the "human means," so to speak, that he uses to his philanthropic ends. To protect his family name, the colonel "saves" Uncle Peter from the neoslavery of the convict-lease system only to buy his time for life (CD, 68), an ironic regression to old-time slavery that Chesnutt underscores through the satisfied comments of Clarendon's white citizens (CD, 78–79), as well as through the colonel's own ironically far-too-accurate description of his conspicuous consumption Jim Crow style: "My dear Laura, . . . I have been in Clarendon two days; and I have already bought a dog, a house and a man" (CD, 83). Similarly, the colonel's well-founded concern about Bud's tragic story of injustice and exploitation is superseded by the pleasant expectation of beating Fetters. When Fetters offers to release Bud Johnson if the colonel stops "his agitation on the labour laws," the latter does "not hesitate a moment" before turning down the offer: "He had risen now to higher game; nothing less than the system would satisfy him" (CD, 231).[35] Later, faced with the knowledge of Bud's revenge and without thinking of alternative options, he does not hesitate to rationalize the need to exchange Bud's capture for Ben Dudley's release from prison, thereby precipitating the series of events that will eventually lead to the former's lynching. In the unexamined greater value that the colonel attributes to white, as opposed to black, lives, Chesnutt sounds the depth of the colonel's unreliability and the racist underpinnings of his "universal good will" (CD, 247).

The Ex-Slave Retainer and the Black Community

The limitations of the colonel's reform plans become most glaring in his relationship with Uncle Peter and the black community. Although African Americans are not the primary object of his reform project, they are the ostensible primary cause of its failure, as opposition coalesces around the colonel's more liberal racial views. The irony, as emerges from Chesnutt's focus on his hero's unreliable point of view, is that the colonel's racial views are *not* very liberal. By contrast with his mildly more-enlightened racism, the strength of the opposition he encounters in Clarendon foregrounds in critical ways the extremism of prevailing race prejudice.

That the colonel thinks in stereotypes becomes evident quite early in the novel from the unwittingly parodic quality of his stereotyped comments about Uncle Peter, whom he sees, quite predictably, as an ever-contented and irresponsible "old retainer" (CD, 32), though he "was not really many years older than the colonel" (CD, 25), as the narrator notes pointedly. Moved by what he perceives as his ex-slave's almost "grotesque" (CD, 25) loyalty, the colonel decides to take care of him, since "nature first, and society next, in distributing their gifts, had been niggardly with old Peter" (CD, 29).[36] Typically stereotyped also is the colonel's reading of Bud Johnson, who first fits the role of the helpless but animalistic victim and, later, the complementary one of the beastly brute for whom freedom implies a reversion to supposedly senseless violence. The mildness of the colonel's liberal views on race is confirmed on several other occasions in the course of the novel. As critics have noticed, for instance, he does not object to Laura's suggestion that the new library be segregated, and while he hires black bricklayers to renovate the mill, his plan is to eventually give employment only to white workers (CD, 192).[37]

While Chesnutt's psychological realism explores the racial prejudices that underlie his hero's goodwill, undermining the attentive reader's faith in the reliability of the colonel's interpretive skills, the documentary realism with which the author describes the realities of Jim Crow enable alternative readings of those supposedly stereotyped characters, leading that same attentive reader to a more complex interpretation and a more systematic critique of segregation than the colonel himself is able to offer. Bud Johnson is a case in point. In the one episode where he is granted the power of direct speech, Bud, far from sounding like the one-dimensional victim or beast-like brute the colonel imagines, summarizes the injustice of the convict-lease system with a lucidity that the colonel never displays and that make the convict's anger at his unjustified incarceration easily understandable. Similarly, Bud's violence is hardly senseless or indiscriminate, since he aims to kill Constable Haines and Mr. Turner, the two persons who abused him most directly when he was a convict laborer.

Bud's desire for revenge, moreover, is hardly singular in the novel. Revenge, and of a much more irrational and unjust kind, motivates Constable Haines (CD, 61) to continue to torture Bud, the man he arrested unfairly in the first place. Fetters too, in organizing Bud's lynching, displays an analogously primordial instinct of revenge that does not acknowledge how his own violent greed is more directly responsible for his son's mutilation than Bud's faulty aim. The colonel's change of mind and reversion to reading Bud as an animalistic brute are also an instance of how "the very standards of right and wrong had been confused by the race issue" (CD, 247). Although the colonel recognizes it only in others, such confusion involves him too, insofar as he does not consider Bud entitled to self-defense or retributive justice even given the impossibility of legal recourse, an impossibility that the colonel is well aware of in light of his own unsuccessful attempt to fight peonage by appealing to the federal authorities (CD, 230). Expecting Bud to be contented to play the more passive role of grateful fugitive, the colonel is characteristically surprised to learn that Bud has a will of his own and is determined to avenge himself. At the very end of the novel, Chesnutt will return to and foreground the colonel's racialized double standard in suggesting patience to those, like Bud, who have been cruelly victimized. In fact, the colonel himself will taste the cup of anger and revenge for the desecration of his cemetery plot, and it is only after his return to the North that he "relent[s] sufficiently to contemplate making over to Miss Laura the old family residence in trust for use as a hospital" (CD, 291). The plan is aborted because the house burns down, and the colonel's reaction, as readers are told that "he was hardly sorry" (CD, 291), betrays his continuing anger and desire for revenge, a revenge that in a town without a hospital indiscriminately affects those who damaged him and those who did not, like Laura herself.

From the colonel's limited point of view, blacks remain part of the background throughout the novel. "Negro" (CD, 23), "black" (CD, 19), "mixed race" (CD, 171), and "mulatto" (CD, 17) secondary characters of different ages and occupations are mentioned repeatedly. They are part of the local southern landscape, not unlike the pine woods, but he hardly ever perceives them or relates to them as individuals. The only two who escape, in part, the colonel's stereotyping gaze are Henry Taylor, the schoolmaster, and William Nichols, the barber (the former because of his education and the latter because of his entrepreneurial spirit, which the colonel can relate to); in recognition of the carefully constructed ironic economy of the novel, it is worth noting that they are also the only two African Americans who are identified respectively as "Negro" and "mulatto" in the list of characters that opens the novel. Despite these partial exceptions, never does the colonel seem to entertain the suspicion that there may exist a black *community* and that it may have an autonomous life beyond his knowledge. Although he worries that whites may resent being considered subjects for reform, he never doubts that blacks would fit that role thankfully. During his meeting with "the leading coloured men" (CD, 161), he treats even them as objects of charity and delivers Washingtonian platitudes quite proudly.[38] Through the thick veil of the colonel's stereotyping gaze, Chesnutt offers to the attentive reader only brief, indirect glimpses into the life of the African American community: how they know Bud's whereabouts (CD, 245); how they may have actively protected the fugitive (CD, 278), thereby helping him to obtain the justice that they knew he could not get in court, as the colonel's own failed attempt to prosecute Bud's lynchers will confirm; how they overflow the church gallery to see Peter's desegregated funeral service (CD, 270); and how they ostracize Mr. Taylor for revealing Bud's hiding place (CD, 292).[39]

That the black community may have a life beyond the knowledge of outsiders like him is a possibility the colonel cannot even contemplate. Neither does he contemplate, when at the end of the novel the violence of prejudice turns against him and his family, the possibility of continuing "to help to preserve peace and good order" (CD, 244), as he had serenely recommended to Mr. Taylor when he was lamenting the systematic injustices of Jim Crow in Clarendon (CD, 244). On the contrary, the colonel's optimism and high-mindedness quickly turn into bitterness. His reaction to the profanation of his cemetery plot is final: emigration. Chesnutt's masterful portrayal of the colonel's quick and extreme reaction confirms that his hero's unwillingness to question his own privileged subject position is an indispensable precondition, as well as the most basic limitation, of his goodwill. In fact, even after Bud's lynching, the colonel is "beaten, but not dismayed" (CD, 279) by his failures. He can still dream of a better world and of his own role in hastening its creation (CD, 279). The structural irony that the act of desecrating his cemetery plot should occur while the colonel is sleeping and literally dreaming of "a regenerated South, filled with thriving industries, and thronged with a prosperous and happy people" (CD, 280) is followed by the subtler irony of Chesnutt's psychological exploration of his hero's reaction upon finding Peter's casket on the piazza. The colonel leaves "the coffin standing on the porch . . . all day" (CD, 282) but quickly drives over to the cemetery to see what has happened to his son's grave. What offends him even more than the deliberate exhumation of Uncle Peter is that the flowers on the grave of "little Phil had been trampled under foot—whether wantonly or not, inevitably, in the execution of the ghoulish task" (CD, 282). It is at this point that the colonel's "heart hardened," and he "turned away with an air of finality"

(CD, 282) from the tombs of his ancestors and from his own brief dream of so-cial usefulness in the South.

Why this particular episode "should destroy the Colonel's will to struggle" continues to be a "nagging question" for critics, as Andrews has noted.[40] Whereas the colonel explains his decision to Laura by denouncing the extremism of "mak[ing] war upon the dead" (CD, 283), Chesnutt's overall narrative construc-tion of his hero's unreliable point of view suggests alternative explanations. The trampling of Phil's grave is not only a crime against a basic tenet of the colonel, the sacredness of private property, but also a challenge to a more fundamen-tal property: his racial identity as a white man and its attending privileges. For instance, Fetters is sure that "no really white man would treat another white man" as the colonel has treated him (CD, 269); the discharged foreman, Jim Green, describes the colonel to the townspeople as "an enemy of his race" (CD, 271); and subsequently "a great deal of intemperate talk, concerning … Colo-nel French as the protector of Negroes and the enemy of white men" fills the local barroom (CD, 271). The profanation of his family lot is only a foretaste of the "social ostracism," "political death," or the "even more complete form of extinction" (CD, 195) that the colonel may yet encounter. The trampled grave of the colonel's "blue-eyed, golden-haired" (CD, 17) son opens the possibility of having to move from the freedom to champion the American dream in a backward land to the necessity of defending his own life and property, of hav-ing to step down from the superior position of generous benefactor to the os-tracized condition of fellow traveler of the oppressed. As the colonel glimpses, however briefly, into the momentousness of this fight, which he cannot control and may not win, he "turn[s] back" (CD, 293) and returns immediately to the "solid brilliancy" (CD, 128) of his privileged life in the North, a life that is safer not because it is, in itself, more utopian, but because he is less socially commit-ted there.

As the colonel realizes the real personal dangers of his "dream of useful-ness" (CD, 283) and quickly flees from a deeper involvement in it, so, too, does Chesnutt withdraw his focus from the colonel's point of view in the last chap-ter (39), mirroring his protagonist's return to the surface of things with a more superficial description of his actions rather than his thoughts. To the attentive reader aware of his unreliability, however, the colonel's actions speak as loud and ironically as his thoughts. The northern "land of plenty" (CD, 161) to which he returns at the end of the novel is not dramatically more enlightened than the South he has left behind.[41] The continuities emerge quite clearly, for instance, in the job discrimination faced by Mr. Taylor, the former schoolteacher now turned porter. The "extremely fortunate accident" (CD, 293) of their meeting on a train and of the colonel's subsequent intervention "to find him something better than menial employment" (CD, 293) only confirms the larger rule of discrimination also in the North. Even in the case of the blue-blood young lovers Ben Dudley and Graciela Treadwell, Chesnutt's devastating irony frustrates the expectation of a completely happy ending. Not unlike Herman Melville in *Benito Cereno* or Mark Twain in *Puddn'head Wilson*, the order that Chesnutt restores at the end of the novel is still pathologically rooted in the realities of racial domination. What saves Ben and Graciela from regressing to the status of "poor-white[s]" (CD, 288) is the former's invention of a model of a cotton gin and press that the colonel intends to patent and produce in the North. Their individual escape from poverty, then, is implicated in and may well reinforce the cotton economy in the South and such related practices of exploitation of black labor as peonage and the convict-lease system. To the end, Chesnutt foregrounds ironically and also challenges the reader to problematize the complicity of North and South in the culture and the economy of segregation, foreshadowing thematic concerns that a few years later will gain center stage in W. E. B. Du Bois's *The Quest of the Silver Fleece* (1911).

Ultimately, then, the failure of the colonel's dream coincides with the failure of his *Bildung*, for he never outgrows his initial limitations as an improvised reformer. He is, like the "best people" he blames for his decision to leave Clarendon, "an abstraction" (CD, 283). While he, characteristically, does not apply this critique to himself, in both cases it is indeed "not too much to say that what they permit they justify, and they cannot shirk the responsibility" (CD, 283). Because the colonel never questions his own racialized privilege or the ways in which he is implicated in the culture of Jim Crow, he possesses no firm alternative viewpoint to oppose to the prevailing segregationist credo of the likes of Bill Fetters. If the latter undoubtedly qualifies as a villain, the former never really acquires the stature of a hero, because he flees when he finally realizes the dangers of transforming his "pastime" of reform into a serious life commitment. Echoing his protagonist's earlier words, and eventual failure, at the end of the novel the narrator notes that a "new body of thought, favorable to just laws and their orderly administration" is visible only "to the eye of faith" (CD, 294). The ominous specter of the colonel's uninformed optimism and practical ineffectiveness hovers over the sobering tone of impotence that dominates the last paragraph of the novel, where Chesnutt focuses on "those who hope, and those who pray, that this condition will pass, that some day our whole land will be truly free ... and Justice, the seed, and Peace, the flower, of liberty, will prevail throughout all our borders" (CD, 294). Far from being a failed attempt to "attract readers with his optimism," these last lines of the novel echo almost verbatim the complacent musings in which the colonel indulged right before witnessing the auction of convicts (CD, 62), bringing full circle the ironic economy of *The Colonel's Dream*.[42]

It is precisely this paralyzing sense of impotence that in *Pointing the Way* Griggs tries to dissipate and convert into alternative social vision and action.[43] He starts precisely where the colonel failed, that is, from the *Bildung* of his protagonist. Uncle Jack's willingness to embrace "a new body of thought" and his courageous acceptance of the personal costs of questioning his own subject position sustain the concrete hope that informs Griggs's portrayal of the "way" to successful personal and communal change.

"I Done Voted": Sutton E. Griggs's Pointing the Way (1908)

Griggs's revision of *The Colonel's Dream* testifies to his most insightful critical reading of his primary intertext. Interested in compounding a hermeneutic critique, à la Chesnutt, of the contemporaneous Jim Crow culture with the presentation of a viable historical alternative that would expand the "horizon of expectations" of his readers, Griggs grants narrative centrality to African American resistance, presenting it as a driving force of social change informed by the concrete utopian planning of a better future.[44]

Griggs's own first authorial act of resistance is to free himself from the limited and limiting point of view of a privileged white liberal. Defying prevailing Jim Crow narrative hierarchies and representational practices, he privileges the limited point of view of an elderly, dialect-speaking ex-slave: Uncle Jack. Before presenting the interracial Belrose movement or "the plan" (PW, 141) to challenge political disenfranchisement, Griggs effects the hermeneutic revolution of establishing his aged "Negro servant" (PW, 15) as the central consciousness of *Pointing the Way*. He proceeds systematically by filtering from Uncle Jack's perspective most of the principal characters and events of the novel, and at the same time, he undermines from that same vantage point the assumed greater authoritativeness of more obvious, because more socially privileged and educated, candidates to narrative centrality. On the one hand, like Chesnutt, he foregrounds how Seth Molair, the aristocratic white reformer, a "strong, vigorous young scion of the white race" (PW, 42), cannot fully outgrow the culture of white supremacy, despite his active involvement in the Belrose movement. On the other, unlike Chesnutt, Griggs focuses only part of his last novel on the psychology of his well-meaning but unreliable reformer, privileging instead the exploration of Uncle Jack's psychology, the internal workings of the black community, and Uncle Jack's leading role in relation to younger, educated, free-born New Negroes like Clotille, Conroe, Eina, and Baug.

Unlike Chesnutt's Colonel French, Seth Molair is no estranged native son of the South. His unquestioned cultural belonging emerges from his first prolonged conversation with Eina, where he outlines the white supremacist ethos of the region. While he is less ambivalent than Colonel French on racial issues, he is not less self-deluded nor more self-aware, and his contradictions illuminate the larger ones of the culture to which he proudly belongs. After making clear with Eina that he has a "strong pride of race but [no] prejudice" (PW, 40), he closes their conversation in a way that ironically belies his previous statement and reduces the supposed complexity of his argument to commonplace segregationist social codes: "'Very well. If you claim your place in the white race, I hope to see you again. If you choose to cast your lot with the colored people farewell forever,' said Molair, his voice falling to a solemn whisper" (PW, 43).

Like Colonel French, Seth Molair never fully outgrows his racialist mode of thinking. Griggs foregrounds Molair's continued stunted awareness by detailing both his reluctance to get involved in an interracial political coalition and the multiple casualties that accompany his progress toward greater awareness of the injustices of racial oppression, as well as by examining the less-than-enlightened motivations that guide his actions even after he decides to participate in the Belrose movement. For instance, Molair is moved almost to "tears" (PW, 123) by his former mammy's death and grandly declares, "With the memory of her sublime self-renunciation, I am in a mood, as a sort of atonement, to forego vital interests of my own for the sake of the interests of others" (PW, 123). His goal, however, is not "equality before the law" (PW, 174) but rather the attempt to avoid "indirect amalgamation" (PW, 182) by improving the condition of black Americans in order to contain the tendency of those who are light skinned to avoid discrimination by passing into white society.

By contrast with the systematically sustained ironic economy of *The Colonel's Dream*, where the narrator does not overtly belie and at times even seems to validate his protagonist's misreading by echoing his words, in *Pointing the Way* Griggs offers metanarrative clues that point more directly to the dangers of misinterpretation and alert the reader to the need for attentive critical reading.[45] For instance, by inserting the text of Conroe's letter (chapter 14) and reading it from Molair's limited point of view, Griggs foregrounds his white reformer's racial bias and his resulting diminished interpretive skills. Echoing the proposal and the satiric tone of Chesnutt's 1900 "Future American" essays, Conroe's letter takes the violence of segregation to its extreme consequences in order to undermine its logic.[46] Molair realizes that there is a difference between the stated and the intended meaning of the letter, but his white supremacist beliefs inhibit a full decodification of Conroe's message. Molair does not take the suggestion of a "policy of cruelty" at face value (PW, 109), but he does take literally the complaint that "prejudice is actually operating to draw into the white race more Negro blood than would dream of getting there without its aid" (PW, 110) and decides to devote his life to prevent "amalgamation, direct or indirect, immediate or remote" (PW, 182). Molair's unreliability as an interpreter reveals the absence of a shared value system that would facilitate the comprehension of satire.[47] Although Conroe's letter has the desired effect of pushing Molair to get involved in politics, his reasons for doing so remain at odds with the egalitarian spirit of Conroe's letter.[48]

Such difference is no minor academic detail. Molair's *Bildung*, like Colonel French's, remains stunted by his unquestioned white supremacist alliances that limit the scope of his plans for social amelioration by keeping them mostly on the white side of the color line. If Molair's proud sense of racial superiority makes him willing "to deal honorably by a helpless people" (PW, 39), it also reveals the limits of his possible growth and capacity for alternative thinking.[49] Within the forward-looking economy of this novel and despite "the honors of a national character" (PW, 231) that a white-dominated nation is more ready to shower on him than on African American civil rights activists, those limits qualify Molair for the secondary role of follower, rather than initiator, of social change.[50] The ultimate test of his nonheroic status and interpretive unreliability is his relationship with Uncle Jack. Although Molair is ready to acknowledge with Eina that "a truer soul [than Uncle Jack] never lived," (PW, 28), Uncle Jack, who is the central driving force of utopian change, remains invisible to Molair if not in his role as Eina's servant.

Despite Molair's blindness, in *Pointing the Way* Uncle Jack is a more prominent figure than Molair himself both quantitatively, in terms of the space the author devotes to episodes and conversations in which he is an active participant, and qualitatively, as he is most often granted the power of direct speech.

It is through his point of view that the interpretive limitations of other characters are exposed. Griggs stages various scenes where his hero is misinterpreted. In these episodes Uncle Jack is not so much the object of the reader's knowing solidarity and more accurate interpretation, as was the case with Uncle Peter in *The Colonel's Dream*, but rather the central consciousness that notices the ironic contradictions on which such misinterpretations are based.[51] Through Uncle Jack, Griggs points the way to a subtler interpretation of those same scenes, establishing Uncle Jack's narrative reliability and earning him the reader's trust in ways that preempt the tendency to read this "servant" as a secondary character whose comic effect is unwittingly ironic.

The tendency to misinterpret Uncle Jack is shared by both white and black characters, though with differing degrees of complexity and nuance. Like Molair, the Republican politician and the election officials are blind to Uncle Jack's self-awareness and cannot even fathom, let alone decodify, his sarcasm. When he gets his way, as he does in both episodes, their first reaction of surprise quickly leads to physical violence. Within the "drama of . . . consciousness" staged through Griggs's consistent use of Uncle Jack's point of view, it is the very physicality of their reactions that sanctions these characters' secondary status within the novel.[52] Griggs foregrounds by contrast the subtlety and narrative prominence of Uncle Jack's self-awareness and the authoritativeness of his perspective.[53]

Uncle Jack, whose full name is Jackson Simpkins Hezekiah Morris (PW, 75), not only exceeds the stereotypically low expectations of uninformed, prejudiced whites but also acquires unequaled depth in relation to central, educated, sympathetic New Negro characters like Clotille, Conroe, Eina, and Baug. They love him, appreciate his goodness, and eventually learn "to esteem very highly [his] philosophizings" (PW, 88) but nevertheless regard him rather condescendingly as an "ever-faithful" (PW, 169), chattering Old Negro, in relation to whom they quite unthinkingly feel and act superior.[54] As Griggs focuses on Uncle Jack's point of view and opposes the ex-slave's angle of vision to that of his younger allies, their condescension proves to be based on misinterpretation. The irony of their unfounded sense of superiority reinforces the centrality and heroic stature of Uncle Jack. For instance, Eina thinks of him as an "untutored . . . child of nature" (PW, 57) and plans to "encourage Uncle Jack to talk, to enter with zest into his chatter and to have him thus in artless fashion lay bare his soul" (PW, 57), in order that he may unconsciously enable her "to get at the real essence . . . of the Negro soul" (PW, 57). However, Uncle Jack's conversation with Clotille and his reflections on Eina have already made readers privy to *his* own plan to use the conversations with all-but-white Eina to contrast the Molair family's biased presentation of blackness as "the most tragic situation in all this earth" (PW, 50) and to convince her to join the African American community. Similarly, Baug Peppers is condescendingly self-deluded when he thinks he can manipulate Uncle Jack. As we know from the latter's limited point of view, Baug's attempt to use him to have access to Eina is itself part of Uncle Jack's plan to promote their attachment. And later in the novel, while Baug will oppose his own "feelings of gloom" (PW, 170) to Uncle Jack's supposedly permanent lightheartedness and "rich store of humorous experiences" (PW, 170), the latter will explode such superficial characterization by outlining the plan to challenge disenfranchisement and also reunite the separated lovers.

The number of scenes that stage the misinterpretation of the ex-slave's intelligent self-awareness and dramatize his own ironic decoding of such misinterpretations lends insight into Griggs's awareness of the novelty of his portrayal of Uncle Jack. His aged "Negro servant," in fact, enters the house of fiction not through the back door of unwitting comedy but as the central consciousness and decoder of irony. In relation to *The Colonel's Dream*, Uncle Jack is a radical revision not only of Uncle Peter, as has already been noted, but also of Colonel French. If the ironic economy of *The Colonel's Dream* worked against the colonel, whose misinterpretations and contradictions are exposed through the author's focus on his limited point of view, in *Pointing the Way* Uncle Jack is the master of irony whose "thorough knowledge of conditions in the South" (PW, 73) and keen perceptions expose the misinterpretations and contradictions of others. From the very beginning, Griggs foregrounds this revised role through intertextual clues, such as the initial military characterization of Uncle Jack that evokes the colonel's. Despite their different official Civil War records (one becomes a colonel and the other cannot even join the army), Uncle Jack's "erect, soldierly carriage," though "somewhat modified by the humble carrying of his hat in his hand and the deferential inclining of his head slightly forward, a combination of dignity and humility" (PW, 15), is no caricature of the colonel's "erect" posture and "unconscious ease which one associates with military training" (CD, 3).[55] The qualities that inhibit any tendency to see Uncle Jack as a caricature in blackface of the colonel are the keenness of his consciousness and his reliability as an interpreter, the very attributes that also make him, rather than Colonel French or Seth Molair, a central spokesperson for and agent of radical social change.

What qualifies Uncle Jack for narrative centrality is the profound self-awareness with which he conceptualizes, articulates, and exercises his agency. From the very beginning, the elderly Uncle Jack functions as the ally of more-privileged, educated, younger African Americans characters. Yet with the help he provides, Uncle Jack exceeds the supportive role of an "ever-faithful" (PW, 169), however cunning, servant. He enters the realm of cultural critique, ideological opposi- tionality, and counterhegemonic discourse, as he tries to convince Eina to cast her lot with the black community and lays the ideological groundwork for the interracial Belrose movement (PW, 99). In the process, Uncle Jack's vernacular speech becomes an expression not only of his "everyday experience but also of those deeper labyrinths of dream and memory . . . to which nineteenth-century slave characters had little access," as Barbara Christian has noted in relation to later African American women's historical novels.[56]

Pointing the Way centers precisely on the ex-slave's consciousness and point of view. This narrative choice enables Griggs to foreground Uncle Jack's in- dependent decision-making processes, his active role in suggesting an inter- racial coalition, his keen ability to perceive and interpret the inner states of his younger, less experienced friends, and his courage to take action in ways that exceed the expectations of his allies (and of the reader) to the extent that he often has to explain himself and his motivations explicitly. In other words, Uncle Jack is the driving force of social change in the novel, the character whose *Bildung* runs parallel to and makes possible the process of social change. To counter the dystopian thrust of *The Colonel's Dream*, Griggs not only offers a feasible project of political alliances, protest activities, and litigation that leads to greater social equality, as I shall discuss in the next section, but also focuses on the process of forging a utopian humankind, of transforming individuals into worthy promoters and inhabitants of a better world. Unlike Molair, Uncle Jack is able to overcome his socialization and complete the process of growth from ex-slave to civil rights activist. Griggs's staging of his hero's successful *Bil- dung* is a key element of the process of perceptual reeducation of his readers, who follow from Uncle Jack's own perspective and point of view the "conver- sion" (PW, 69) of, so to speak, an Old Negro into a New Negro.

Revising his own generational model in *Imperium in Imperio*, where he had proposed a much-quoted definition of the New Negro in opposition to the Old Negro, Griggs offers a more stratified, inclusive vision of community that draws strength also from "go[ing] back into the past, that its mistakes might be

a guiding influence in any new movement projected" (PW, 88), and he reinter-
prets the historical experience of slavery not as an indelible taint but as a social condition(ing) that can be overcome. From Uncle Jack's narrative point of
view, we have access to his inner world as a slave, and it is the richness of this
inner world of conscious survival against the dehumanizing realities of slavery
that creates the possibility of his transformation into a political agent of social
change. Rather than a "left over from befo' the wah" (CD, 66), Uncle Jack's superior self-awareness becomes the narrative cornerstone of Griggs's vision of a
different future of which Uncle Jack himself is both an agent and a tenacious
spokesperson, as for the benefit of other characters (and of the reader) he reit-
erates the terms of his conversion. To the continued tendency, also on the part
of his younger allies, to impose on him a secondary, relational, supporting role
or to read his generosity as an involuntary automatism, as the unwitting result
of a life of servility and forced submission, Uncle Jack opposes a clear articulation of his goals and self-awareness as a political agent:

> "I ain't goin' into dis heah testin' businiss jes' ter bring yer an' Miss Eina nigh ter
> each udder, while dat is part uv whut I am atter. But I hez had time ter thort out dis
> thing, an' heah is my thorts.
>
> "Dey says dat Abe Linktum said dat Ameriky coulden' be kep' part one thing
> an' part er nudder, an' I sees dat dis whole country is one day goin' ter drink outen
> one spoon 'bout de cullud man. Ez er cullud man it is my lookout ter see ef dis one
> spoon is ter be er brass spoon er er silvah one.
>
> "Den ergin er ill littered white man is my arrival. I got ter work wid him, got ter
> go ter law wid him, an' sometimes got ter sass an' ter fight wid him, perhaps. Now
> ef yer let er ill littered white man vote, an' doan' let me vote yer give him dat much
> ekvantage uv me. Now I doan' want er ekvantage uv nobotty, but in jestice ter myself
> I doan' want nobotty ter git er ekvantage uv me." (PW, 207–8).

Uncle Jack's hard fought-for *Bildung* and emphasis on his autonomous decision-
making challenges Eina's and Baug's more simplistic notion of leadership that
sees "the masses of the colored people" biding their time while waiting for a
"group of cleanly, cultured, aspiring people in the colored race . . . to take charge
of and guide the racial thought and life" (PW, 101). The dynamics of the large,
diversified, active black community that revolves around Uncle Jack is more
complex than that, and while his self-awareness is emphasized as exceptionally
keen, it is not presented as unique or singular, as his interactions with other

former slaves like Aunt Melissa Crutcher or Aunt Lucy show. Centering the limited point of view of this respected insider, Griggs, unlike Chesnutt, moves the political activism of a resisting black community from the background to the foreground, exploring their internal workings not only in relation to whites but also among themselves, and opening an important narrative window on the vast panorama of black self-determination in the age of Jim Crow.

The "Plan"

Taking on and revising the negative connotations of Chesnutt's presentation of "the dream" as an impossible project or uninformed, delusional, wishful thinking, Griggs insists on the radical force of hope to inspire personal and social change.[57] He substitutes for "the dream" an inspirational focus on "the plan" (PW, 141) as an unfolding reality, a yet-to-be-realized but realizable project. To project historical alternatives, Griggs offers alternative narrative practices. He recovers the political function of utopian fiction as a genre that unites a critique of the "what is" with a strategic exploration of the "what if," defying the paralyzing oppressiveness of contemporary reality by expanding the horizon of expectations of his characters (and readers). The empowering political potential of utopian thinking is paralleled by the equally empowering literary effects of Griggs's decision to unsettle traditional narrative power relations by placing African American characters at the forefront of the process of social transformation.

As in his previous novels, Griggs presents the desire of social amelioration as a commitment that grows inside the black community, as its members face arbitrary but nevertheless societally enforced external obstacles to the realization of their existential dreams of love and freedom. In *Pointing the Way*, the desire to contrast Letitia Gilbreath's "diseased mind" and her hostility "to the marriage of dark couples" (PW, 34) like Clotille and Conroe is the impetus that initially leads Uncle Jack to suggest an interracial coalition to improve social conditions in Belrose. His plan will be adopted by Eina and Baug, who, being all but white, beautiful, and educated, will be accepted as mediators and "ambassador[s] of peace" (PW, 174) by reluctant Seth Molair.

Writing in the extremely malevolent climate of the Jim Crow "system of repression" he had described in *The One Great Question* (1907), a text that may be regarded as a nonfiction companion piece to *Pointing the Way*, Griggs relies on the utopian economy of his last novel to expand the "range of practicability" of his proposed interracial coalition and portray how Molair is able to support this black-initiated project while escaping the "terrible price socially, financially, and politically that an enemy of repression is so often called upon to pay," the very price that, once perceived, motivates Colonel French's speedy return to New York.[58] However, even within this utopian narrative economy, in order to preserve the potential feasibility of his project for those first readers who were living in a highly segregated social context, Griggs portrays the Belrose movement as a two-pronged attack against Jim Crow, where parallel black and white efforts converge at strategic moments (e.g., Molair's election or the desegregation of the fire brigades). On the one hand, the white side of the movement receives national recognition more easily, because of the greater social privilege and racial acceptability of its proponents but also, as Griggs underlines, because of the more limited scope of their project. On the other hand, Griggs not only insists on the black origins of the Belrose project but also emphasizes how it is the black community that continues to push ahead. While Seth Molair, his millionaire friend, and the president remain focused on the Belrose movement and on educating whites, the black activists are already working on defending the right to vote, a crucial step on the road to equality. They are the ones who lead and fund the legal challenge to disenfranchisement, enlarging their protest at a national level by taking the case to the Supreme Court and articulating the more radical goal of "equality before the law" (PW, 174). As Griggs focuses on African American resistance by referencing contemporaneous extraliterary real-life black efforts for self-determination and legal challenges to the grandfather clause, his continued narrative focus on the point of view of Uncle Jack links the process of communal liberation to that of personal transformation and outlines a vision of cooperation that cuts across class and generational differences, defying the more hierarchical model of the Talented Tenth.[59]

Uncle Jack, who has "thought long and deeply" (PW, 169) and has finally chosen to test the grandfather clause in Alabama, is no political pawn. He asserts his will to freedom and his role as voluntary ally who possesses a lucid awareness of the dangers of his mission and still accepts it, taking charge of devising the best means to carry it out.[60] Uncle Jack's repeated insistence on his free acceptance of this role ensures that his eventual death will not simply make him a casualty, but that it will actually confirm his status as the novel's hero. Unlike Uncle Peter, Uncle Jack does not unwittingly stumble to his death, nor is his self-sacrifice totally other-directed; rather, it is an expression of his existential commitment to freedom. By contrast with *The Colonel's Dream*, it is the meaningfulness of Uncle Jack's death that foreshadows, restores, and celebrates the radical heterotopic significance of Griggs's closing vision of a desegregated cemetery.

The Cemetery

In his systematic revision of *The Colonel's Dream*, Griggs registers and responds also to Chesnutt's cemeterial frame. He changes the relative significance of death and the cemetery by privileging an exploration of the former that leads to a redefinition of the latter. From the very first pages of *Pointing the Way*, Griggs links death with the possibility of rebirth. Eschewing explicit religious references, he focuses not on the promises of the afterlife but on the this-worldly possibility of a new and better life on earth. Eschewing also the conventional means (e.g., time or space travel, dreams, or suspended animation) by which utopian writers catapult the traveler into a different world that will change his or her consciousness, in *Pointing the Way* it is the change in consciousness that opens a portal onto a better future.

Griggs substitutes the cemeterial frame of *The Colonel's Dream* with a focus on useful death, on the heroism of voluntary self-sacrifice for a greater good. He rejects both the self-centeredness of suicide and the utter selflessness of other-directed self-immolation. He concentrates on the political significance and uses of self-aware martyrdom, foregrounding "representations of black agency," which in Chesnutt's novel were "admittedly highly limited."[61] In *The Colonel's Dream*, Uncle Peter's accidental death in the attempt to save young Phil's life was in keeping with and the culmination of his faithful career as a servant, for which the integrated funeral and the burial in the French family plot are, so to speak, a posthumous reward. Such reward does pose a challenge to the rule of segregation "from the cradle to the grave" (CD, 262), but in this challenge Uncle Peter plays a passive role. He provides the body that becomes a political object of contention among whites, and even the larger black community that overflows the church gallery (CD, 262) remains in the segregated background. In *Pointing the Way*, Griggs devises an original narrative means to enable the transition to a new life and details Uncle Jack's and the black community's agency in staging the "Funeral of a Live Man" (PW, 147), which marks Uncle Jack's transition to civil rights activism. The fake funeral is planned by Uncle Jack and organized by his Aunt Melissa (who is literally his aunt) and his cousin Horace, "who was now the owner of the old plantation on which Uncle Jack was a slave" (PW, 147–48). It is attended, as Uncle Jack puts it, by "all uv my frien's, white an' cullud, dat knowed me in de ole times" (PW, 148). As with the interracial Belrose movement and the Alabama project, Uncle Jack is the behind-the-scenes initiator of and an active participant in his own funeral. Once again, to those who may misunderstand his actions as a sign that he has "turnt ter er fool" (PW, 149), he offers a more complex interpretation: "Now I'se been picked out ez de cullud man ter tes' dat law. 'Fore I 'gin my life uv buckin' ergin er law uv de white folks I jes' wanted ter close up de life I had been livin', squar' an' even. . . . I hopes de white folks won't git mad at me fur tryin' ter git er ekal show in life fur a cullud an' er white boy. But ef dey doos git mad, dey done 'spressed deyself 'bout my charackter" (PW, 150). His funeral, unlike Uncle Peter's, is not the culmination of Uncle Jack's life but rather a communal event marking the transition to his new life of overt resistance that will culminate in his deliberate acceptance of the risk of dying for "a principull" (PW, 150) in the act of voting.

Uncle Jack's awareness that his individual commitment is part of a larger social movement grants political significance to his death at the polls and substantiates the radical import of Griggs's final focus on the cemetery. Within the prevailing utopian economy of *Pointing the Way*, Griggs's revision of Chesnutt's treatment of an integrated family plot does not only present an unchallenged heterotopic space in opposition to the prevailing reality of segregation. Griggs's final emphasis on a family plot, "Southern at that," where "there is no color line" (PW, 233) points to its exceptionality and also to its promise. The utopian valence of the cemetery as a metonym of a better historical alternative emerges from its contrast with the troubled fate of black bodies even "under the sod" (CD, 164) that characterizes the dystopian ending of Griggs's primary intertext.[62] At the same time, in *Pointing the Way* the utopian valence of the final integrated family plot is reinforced and broadened by the Molairs' visits to the grave of Aunt Lucy. These visits challenge segregation at a deep level, in that they signal an interracial acknowledgment of reciprocity and respect and, in their repetition, even a *commitment* to such reciprocity and respect.

As in his conceptualization of "the plan," in the closing cemetery scene Griggs foregrounds and celebrates the reality of African American resistance. The political significance of Aunt Lucy's death, which has contributed to Seth Molair's decision to join the Belrose movement in the first place, is emphasized by Griggs's final juxtaposition of the Molairs' visits to her grave with the visits of his New Negro protagonists to the graves of Conroe and Uncle Jack.[63] These visits intersect, temporally if not yet spatially, "on national decoration days"

(PW, 233), testifying to the "the spread of the Belrose movement throughout the South" (PW, 231) and foreshadowing a new shared culture in which the self-sacrifice of African American heroes and heroines will be revered by the entire American nation. Griggs compounds the revisionary evocation of Chesnutt's integrated family plot with the more overtly political inclusion of Uncle Jack, Conroe, and Aunt Lucy among "the dead who perished during the Civil War" (PW, 233). The Civil War references broaden the political significance of their death. In Uncle Jack's case, they reverberate with the initial description of his "soldierly carriage" (PW, 15), framing the novel with the image of Uncle Jack, who has successfully seized the opportunity to participate actively in a new civil war against Jim Crow practices that are "stretchin' color an' slavery down ter me terday" (PW, 216).

A "New Body of Thought"?

Unlike most of Chesnutt's contemporary reviewers and several later ones, Griggs registered and appreciated the irony and narrative subtlety of *The Colonel's Dream*.[64] His sensitive, precise, complex revision of the earlier intertext reveals as much. It also shows how Griggs reacted to what he perceived to be the limits of Chesnutt's dissection of white prejudice, foregrounding the former's narrative decision to propose alternatives by extrapolating from already-existing practices of black resistance and self-determination a broad vision of a more egalitarian social order. From this vantage point, Griggs's utopian vision points to new lines of intertextual exploration that link his lesser-known last novel to the more celebrated work of W. E. B. Du Bois, for instance. Familiar with Griggs's fiction and with the work of other mainstream and African American utopian novelists, including Edward A. Johnson, Du Bois will build on Griggs's legacy in his own first novel.[65] In *The Quest of the Silver Fleece* (1911), he will continue his antecedent's quest for "the Way" to personal growth, black self-determination, and effective social change in the South.[66]

In light of this rich and elaborate intertextual tapestry, the continued marginality of Chesnutt's and Griggs's last novels remains puzzling, especially given the established scholarly tradition of Chesnutt studies and the recent resurgence of critical interest in Griggs's work.[67] Chesnutt's and Griggs's sophisticated, ironic portrayals of, respectively, the unreliable colonel and Uncle Jack's misunderstood agency reverberate in ways that are themselves ironic on the residual tendency to see Chesnutt and Griggs as second-class dwellers in the house of fiction, as permanent literary apprentices whose last novels, in their supposed diminished effectiveness, are not even credited with the greater artistic self-awareness to be expected of such prolific and experienced writers. Rather, by comparison with earlier works like *The Conjure Woman* or *Imperium in Imperio*, *The Colonel's Dream* and *Pointing the Way* have been discussed as "reversions," so to speak, to literary incapacity. This critical propensity to underestimate the literary significance of pre–Harlem Renaissance novelists operates methodologically as a self-fulfilling prophecy of artistic inadequacy, since it emerges from long-standing, low critical expectations of literary artistry and leads to one-dimensional readings that end up confirming the initial assumption of poor artistry. In the case of Chesnutt and Griggs, this critical double standard becomes particularly obvious in the tendency to underestimate some of their most experimental works as unmediated expressions of the authors' political or social views, overlooking their ironic, multilayered, carefully crafted textual economy. The "new body of thought" (CD, 247) that continually eludes the colonel seems, to some extent, still beyond our critical reach.

Notes

1. Sutton E. Griggs, *Imperium in Imperio* (1899; New York: Arno Press, 1969), 246; Charles W. Chesnutt, May 29, 1880, in *The Journals of Charles W. Chesnutt*, ed. Richard Brodhead (Durham, N.C.: Duke University Press, 1993), 140. Although the scant biographical information currently available on Griggs provides no direct evidence that he read Chesnutt's novel, the internal evidence of references to *The Colonel's Dream* is so consistent and specific that it can hardly be supposed coincidental. Griggs and Chesnutt knew each other as members of the Niagara Movement (see Finnie D. Coleman, *Sutton E. Griggs and the Struggle against White Supremacy* [Knoxville: University of Tennessee Press, 2007], 140). Chesnutt's fame and the fact that his books had national distribution make it more than likely that Griggs would be familiar with his work, especially in light of his documented knowledge of other well-known writers on the race question such as Kelly Miller and, notoriously, Thomas Dixon Jr. It is also worth noting that Griggs advertised his Orion Publishing Company as a book distributor and that, as Tess Chakkalakal has recently discovered, he personally owned a large collection of books, seven hundred of which were posthumously acquired by LeMoyne College (Robert M. Ratcliffe, "Memphis Ministers Quiz Widow of Rev. Sutton Griggs," *Atlanta Daily World*, September 29, 1934, 1–2.). I thank Tess Chakkalakal for sharing her research findings.

2. Henry James, "Preface to *The Portrait of a Lady*" (1908), in *The Art of the Novel: Critical Prefaces by Henry James*, ed. Richard P. Blackmur (1934; Chicago: University of Chicago Press, 2011), 46.

3. Ernestine Williams Pickens, *Charles W. Chesnutt and the Progressive Movement*

(New York: Pace University Press, 1994), 102; Wiley Cash, "*The Colonel's Dream* Deferred: A Reconsideration of Chesnutt's Liberal Racist," *American Literary Realism* 37, no. 1 (2004): 35.

4. Henry James, "The Art of Fiction" (1884), in *Literary Criticism: Essays on Literature, American Writers, English Writers*, ed. Leon Edel and Mark Wilson (New York: Library of America, 1984), 64.

5. Ryan Simmons, *Chesnutt and Realism: A Study of the Novels* (Tuscaloosa: University of Alabama Press, 2006), 129; Chesnutt, May 29, 1880, in *Journals*, 140.

6. Charles W. Chesnutt, *The Colonel's Dream* (New York: Doubleday, Page, 1905), 247. Subsequent references to this novel are cited parenthetically in the text as CD.

7. Ernst Bloch describes the "apparently paradoxical term of concrete utopia" as indicating "the unfinished dream forward, the docta spes," the "known hope" (Ernst Bloch, *The Utopian Function in Art and Literature: Selected Essays*, trans. Jack Zipes and Frank Mecklenburg [Cambridge, Mass.: MIT Press, 1988], 107, 119, 120).

8. Chesnutt, May 29, 1880, in *Journals*, 140.

9. The quotation in the section title is from CD, 247.

10. The colonel has been away from Clarendon for about twenty-five years. The dilated sense of time travel to a different era stems from Chesnutt's focus on his protagonist's psychological perception of time and of his change during that time: "How far away it seemed . . . the time when he had thought of the Confederacy as his country!" (CD, 46).

11. Ryan Simmons offers an insightful reading of the colonel as a Bakhtinian fool: "French's basic stupidity about what he is undertaking . . . reveals the hidden workings of what are taken to be natural, inevitable elements of Southern life: it enables Chesnutt's analysis of racism and its relationship with capitalism" (*Chesnutt and Realism*, 127).

12. See Joseph R. McElrath Jr., "Charles W. Chesnutt's Library," *Analytical & Enumerative Bibliography* 8, no. 2 (1994): 115.

13. Simmons, *Chesnutt and Realism*, 2–3.

14. In a passage that deserves to be quoted in its entirety, William Dean Howells wrote: "'The Marrow of Tradition,' like everything else he [Chesnutt] has written, has to do with the relations of the blacks and whites, and in that republic of letters where all men are free and equal he stands up for his own people with a courage which has more justice than mercy in it. The book is, in fact, bitter, bitter. There is no reason in history why it should not be so, if wrong is to be repaid with hate, and yet it would be better if it was not so bitter. I am not saying that he is so inartistic as to play the advocate; whatever his minor foibles may be, he is an artist whom his stepbrother Americans may well be proud of; but while he recognizes pretty well all the facts in the case, he is too clearly of a judgment that is made up" (William Dean Howells, "A Psychological Counter-Current in Recent Fiction" [1901], in *Critical Essays on Charles W. Chesnutt*, ed. Joseph R. McElrath Jr. [New York: G. K. Hall, 1999], 82). On the limited or biased press coverage of segregation and racial violence, see Herbert Shapiro, "The Muckrakers and Negroes," *Phylon* 31, no. 1 (1970): 76–88; Jean M. Lutes, "Lynching Coverage and the American Reporter-Novelist," *American Literary History* 19, no. 2 (2007): 461. Interestingly, in 1968

Clarence Gohdes reprinted *The Colonel's Dream* presenting it as a "muckraking novel" (Clarence Gohdes, "Charles Waddell Chesnutt," in *The Colonel's Dream*, by Charles W. Chesnutt [Upper Saddle River, N.J.: Gregg Press: 1968], v–vi) and including it in a series, American Novels of Muckraking, Propaganda, and Social Protest.

15. Sylvia Lyons Render, "Tar Heelia in Chesnutt," *CLA Journal* 9 (1965): 50.

16. William L. Andrews, "The Representation of Slavery and the Rise of Afro-American Literary Realism, 1865–1920," in *Slavery and the Literary Imagination*, ed. Deborah E. McDowell and Arnold Rampersad (Baltimore: Johns Hopkins University Press, 1989), 76. For another recent, nuanced critical examination of scholarly assessments of Chesnutt's realism, see Simmons, *Chesnutt and Realism*.

17. James, "Art of Fiction," 53.

18. An undercurrent of impatience with Chesnutt's supposed obstinacy may be detected in the retributive tone of Joseph McElrath's discussion of Chesnutt's "disappointment" of Howells. He writes: "That Chesnutt could alienate a sympathizer who championed as well Paul Laurence Dunbar and Booker T. Washington should have alerted Chesnutt to the fact that he had strayed radically from ... the goal of seducing, rather than browbeating, the white American readership into a more benign attitude toward the African American. When he continued on the new heading in his next novel, *The Colonel's Dream* (1905), he did so in spite of the caution sounded by his onetime fan, and he reaped the harvest of *Dream*'s more bitter denunciation of the South as unredeemable: its publication ended his career as a professional novelist" (Joseph R. McElrath Jr., "W. D. Howells and Race: Charles W. Chesnutt's Disappointment of the Dean," in *Critical Essays on Charles W. Chesnutt*, ed. Joseph R. McElrath Jr. [New York: G. K. Hall, 1999], 243). Along similar lines, Matthew Wilson writes that in *The Colonel's Dream* "Chesnutt self-destructs as a writer, completely alienating his audience by bringing ... news that was not only unwelcome but was nearly unbelievable because it so contradicted conventional understandings of the time and he did so in a form that was purposely self-defeating" (Matthew Wilson, *Whiteness in the Novels of Charles W. Chesnutt* [Jackson: University Press of Mississippi, 2004], 149). The rhetoric of self-destruction seems to put the blame for such alienation on the writer, rather than on the prejudices of the audience. On the silencing effect of prevailing racial prejudice on black and white American authors, see Michael T. Gilmore, *The War on Words: Slavery, Race, and Free Speech in American Literature* (Chicago: University of Chicago Press, 2010).

19. See the numerous contemporary reviews available on "The Charles Chesnutt Digital Archive" (*http://faculty.berea.edu/browners/chesnutt/intro.html*). Even the renaissance of Chesnutt studies has not significantly altered the marginal status of *The Colonel's Dream* within the Chesnutt canon. See, for instance, the passing references to *The Colonel's Dream* in David Garrett Izzo and Maria Orban, *Charles Chesnutt Reappraised: Essays on the First Major African American Fiction Writer* (Jefferson, N.C.: McFarland, 2009).

20. See Gary Scharnhorst, "'Growth of a Dozen Tendrils': The Polyglot Satire of Chesnutt's *The Colonel's Dream*," in *Critical Essays on Charles W. Chesnutt*, ed. Joseph R.

McElrath Jr. (New York: G. K. Hall, 1999), 271–80, here 273; Simmons, *Chesnutt and Realism*, 117; Wilson, *Whiteness*, 149.

21. William L. Andrews, *The Literary Career of Charles W. Chesnutt* (Baton Rouge: Louisiana State University Press, 1980), 253.

22. Michel Foucault, "Of Other Spaces," *Diacritics* 16, no. 1 (1986): 26.

23. See, for instance, the "florid monument . . . of glaring design" that Fetters has erected for his parents "in an obtrusively conspicuous spot" in Oak Cemetery (CD, 34) and also the secret graveyard "in a secluded part of [his] plantation, where the graves of convicts who had died while in [his] service were very numerous" (CD, 219).

24. On changing pre–Civil War burial practices, see Stanley French, "The Cemetery as Cultural Institution: The Establishment of Mount Auburn and the 'Rural Cemetery' Movement," *American Quarterly* 26, no. 1 (1974): 37–59; Thomas Bender, "The 'Rural' Cemetery Movement: Urban Travail and the Appeal of Nature," *New England Quarterly* 47, no. 2 (1974): 196–211.

25. Foucault, "Of Other Spaces," 24.

26. From the beginning, Phil displays an innocence that differs from his father's willful ignorance. When he first meets Uncle Peter at the cemetery, he asks: "Oh, papa, . . . he must be some kin to us; he has the same name, and belongs to the same family, and you know you called him Uncle" (CD, 25). The naïveté of Phil's deduction is dialogized in the novel. Given the tangled genealogies of slavery that Chesnutt had explored in his previous novels and also in the story of Malcolm Dudley and Viney in *The Colonel's Dream*, Peter may very well be Phil's uncle.

27. Foucault, "Of Other Spaces," 24.

28. Andrews, *Literary Career*, 254.

29. Even as the colonel remains undoubtedly more open-minded than the locals, who see him as a radical, his racialized double standard becomes more explicit in the course of the novel. In his response to Dr. Mackenzie, a minister who in his readiness to exterminate blacks recalls Rev. Thomas Dixon, the colonel reveals his deep-seated racial ambivalence: "I am no lover of the Negro, *as* Negro—I do not know but I should rather see him elsewhere. . . . But they are men, and they should have their chance—at least *some* chance" (CD, 165). Similarly, to justify his employment of black bricklayers and a black foreman to build the new mill, he argues "in his usual good-humoured way" (CD, 191): "Even in the old slave times Negroes made the best of overseers; they knew their people better than white men and got more out of them. When the mill is completed it will give employment to five hundred white women and fifty white men. But every dog must have his day, so give the Negro his" (CD, 192).

30. Edward Bellamy, *Looking Backward, 2000–1887* (1888; repr., New York: Penguin, 1986), 7, 9.

31. Simmons notes: "Given his incapacity to alter his own outlook, French's attempts to reform Clarendon seem more like acts of aggression than of benevolence" (*Chesnutt and Realism*, 122). Along similar lines, Wilson compares the colonel to "nineteenth-century missionaries and imperialists" (*Whiteness*, 165).

32. See, for instance, the episodes on pp. 159 and 162–63.

33. Chesnutt's pervasive use of irony in *The Colonel's Dream* is often overlooked. A notable exception is Scharnhorst's "Growth of a Dozen Tendrils." In his overview of the critical reception of Chesnutt's work, McElrath's appreciation of Scharnhorst's approach emphasizes its novelty: "Scharnhorst's wholly unanticipated discovery is of a deftly ironic author who was capable of parody and satire. . . . On reading Scharnhorst's . . . interpretation of what once seemed the least significant, most 'obvious' novel, one may conclude that it is actually Chesnutt's tour de force" (Joseph R. McElrath Jr., introduction to *Critical Essays on Charles W. Chesnutt*, ed. Joseph R. McElrath Jr. [New York: G. K. Hall, 1999], 22). Yet the tendency to conflate Chesnutt with his protagonist has anything but disappeared in recent Chesnutt criticism. In 2005, Paul R. Petrie, for instance, reads *The Colonel's Dream* by approaching "Colonel French as a figure not of authorship per se but of the author, Chesnutt himself" (Paul R. Petrie, *Conscience and Purpose: Fiction and Social Consciousness in Howells, Jewett, Chesnutt, and Cather* [Tuscaloosa: University of Alabama Press, 2005], 136). Similarly, the significance of Chesnutt's narrative use of a limited point of view and of the ironic economy of the text continue to be neglected. This has led to the reiteration of critical assessments that, while noticing that the colonel is "racially ambivalent" (Sally Ann H. Ferguson, introduction to *The Colonel's Dream*, by Charles W. Chesnutt [New Milford, Conn.: Toby Press, 2004], xviii), still underestimate Chesnutt's authorial self-awareness and simply see the novel as "obscure or contradictory" (Dean McWilliams, *Charles W. Chesnutt and the Fictions of Race* [Athens: University of Georgia Press, 2002], 166). Wilson, for instance, writes: "The novel is at war with itself, designed (*almost* intentionally) to baffle and alienate the audience he once claimed he wanted to change" (*Whiteness*, 149, emphasis mine). This tendency to overlook Chesnutt's irony in his last novel is all the more surprising since it is a consistent vein in his fiction. In an interesting footnote, Wilson himself has noted that "as early as 1889, . . . Chesnutt had begun his career of subversion" with "A Roman Antique," "a sly satire of plantation school stories" that parodied Thomas Nelson Pages's 1887 "Marse Chan" (Matthew Wilson, "The Advent of 'The Nigger': The Careers of Paul Laurence Dunbar, Henry O. Tanner, and Charles W. Chesnutt," *American Studies* 43, no. 1 (2002): 49).

34. The "List of Characters" that opens the novel creates a similar impression for the reader (CD, ix).

35. This is a particularly clear instance of Chesnutt's construction of his unreliable protagonist and careful orchestration of the ironic economy of the novel. On the previous page, the colonel, acting as a spokesperson for "the victims of the system," argues that "it was hardly fair to sacrifice them to a mere punctilio" (CD, 230). That is, of course, precisely what he does just a few lines later in the case of Bud Johnson (CD, 231).

36. Contrary to the colonel's opinion, Peter may indeed act servile, but like Uncle Julius in *The Conjure Woman*, he is no fool. Chesnutt gives several textual clues to the attentive reader about the colonel's unreliable evaluation of Peter. See, for instance, the exchange between Peter and the colonel about the "value" that the colonel's slaveholding father placed on Peter:

"'It looked, Peter, as though he valued you more than me! more than his own son!'

"'Yas, suh, yas, suh! sho he did, sho he did! old Marse Philip wuz a monstus keerful man, an' I wuz wuth something suh, dem times; I wuz wuth five hundred dollahs any day in de yeah'" (CD, 28).

37. See Andrews, *Literary Career*, 244; Petrie, *Conscience and Purpose*, 142; Ferguson, introduction, xix.

38. On *The Colonel's Dream* as "a systematic and thorough refutation of Washington's program," see Susan L. Blake, "A Better Mousetrap: Washington's Program and *The Colonel's Dream*," *CLA Journal* 23 (September 1979): 49.

39. Relentless in his critical attention to the omnipresence of the culture of segregation, Chesnutt specifies that Uncle Peter's casket was "a little to one side" (CD, 270).

40. Andrews, *Literary Career*, 251.

41. Chesnutt hints at the continuities between North and South in the very first chapter of the novel, where he anticipates that the colonel would "fight another battle against the same forces [greed and craft and highly trained intelligence] and others quite as deeply rooted in human nature. But he was to fight upon a new field, and with different weapons, and with results which could not be foreseen" (CD, 10).

42. Gilmore, *War on Words*, 268. The critical reception of the ending of the novel confirms that neglecting the ironic economy of *The Colonel's Dream* and conflating the author with the unreliable central consciousness often lead to underestimating Chesnutt's craft and writerly self-awareness. Dean McWilliams, for instance, notices the "narrator's strained optimism" but concludes that it "achieves an effect opposite to the one intended" (*Charles W. Chesnutt*, 180). Similarly, Wilson describes the ending as invoking "a contradictory utopian hope for change" that "illustrate[s] his [Chesnutt's] own ambivalence" (*Whiteness*, 181). Chesnutt's final remarks do indeed "announce . . . the real bleakness of the moral landscape that has been portrayed" (McWilliams, *Charles W. Chesnutt*, 180). However, I would argue that they do so not because of "their inappropriateness to the narrative they conclude," as McWilliams remarks (*Charles W. Chesnutt*, 180), but precisely because of their consistency with Chesnutt's deliberate and sustained narrative use of irony.

43. Gilmore reminds us that the publication date of *The Colonel's Dream* (1905) "was also the year of Dixon's *The Clansman*" (*War on Words*, 268). As he had already done in the "A Hindering Hand: A Review of the Anti-Negro Crusade of Thomas Dixon, Jr.," a "Supplementary" essay that he added to the revised third edition of *The Hindered Hand* (Sutton E. Griggs, *The Hindered Hand; or, The Reign of the Repressionist*, [Nashville: Orion, 1905]), in *Pointing the Way* Griggs aims to counter what Gilmore has eloquently described as Dixon's abduction of "the prophetic voice to resurrect a dictatorship of racial caste as the only American dream worth fighting for" (Gilmore, *War on Words*, 268).

44. Hans Robert Jauss, *Toward an Aesthetic of Reception* (Minneapolis: University of Minnesota Press, 1982), 25. The subhead is drawn from Sutton E. Griggs, *Pointing the Way* (1908; repr., New York: AMS Press, 1974), 216. Subsequent references to this novel are cited parenthetically in the text as PW.

45. See, for instance, the different contexts in which the phrase "forces of enlighten-

ment" appears in *The Colonel's Dream*. If it speaks a note of hope when it first appears in the "Dedication" (CD, v), by the time it reappears in the colonel's reflections, it seeps with his self-deluded sense of omnipotence and serves to highlight his unreliability as an improvised reformer convinced that he "could, if need be, spare the year or two of continuous residence needed to rescue Clarendon from the grasp of Fetters" (CD, 118).

46. Charles W. Chesnutt, "The Future American Race," *Boston Evening Transcript* August 18, 1900, August 25, 1900, September 1, 1900, in *MELUS* 15, no. 3 (1988): 96–107.

47. Chesnutt faced a similar problem with his "Future American" essays, which anticipate the satiric tone and content of later works like George S. Schuyler's *Black No More* (1931). Griggs attempts to anticipate possible misreadings and clarifies his own stance by describing the "mulatto" woman (PW, 31) who takes the antimiscegenation plan seriously and is "hostile to the marriage of dark couples" as possessing a "diseased mind" (PW, 34).

48. Molair's motivation is to prevent "amalgamation": "But I want no amalgamation, direct or indirect, immediate or remote. I want no incorporation of the Negro blood into our race even after that blood has been so diluted as to lose its power of pigmentation. I don't want Negro blood in the blood of our race even though it be in the proportion to the waters of Lake Erie to those of the Atlantic and Pacific oceans combined" (PW, 182).

49. In a conversation with Baug Peppers, Molair agrees to support black enfranchisement, asserting his sense of racial and aristocratic superiority: "So far as I am concerned, if with a thousand years of civilization back of him a Molair cannot hold his own in an equal contest with the grandson of an uncivilized African, I say let him go to the wall. I scorn the idea of a weak test for a white man and a severe one for the Negro. It is a rank injustice to the white man. . . . The sooner the standard of voting for the white man is made as high as that for the colored man, the better for the white man. Indulgence leads to decay, not to advancement" (PW, 176). Gauging his audience and using their prejudices strategically in order to win his case against the grandfather clause, Baug will use a similar argument in his speech in front of the Supreme Court (PW, 228).

50. For a more extended discussion of Molair and his role as the spokesperson for even less enlightened whites, see M. Giulia Fabi, "Desegregating the Future: Sutton E. Griggs' *Pointing the Way* and American Utopian Fiction in the Age of Jim Crow," *American Literary Realism* 44, no. 2 (2012): 113–32.

51. See the previously cited episode at the cemetery where Chesnutt leaves up to the interpretive capacity of attentive readers the comprehension of Peter's more correct assessment of his master's interest in his "value" (CD, 28).

52. Henry James, "Preface to Roderick Hudson," in *The Art of the Novel: Critical Prefaces by Henry James*, ed. Richard P. Blackmur (1934; repr., Chicago: University of Chicago Press, 2011), 16.

53. The socially sanctioned force of the politician's kick or of the official's blows is also more practically offset by their inefficacy to prevent Uncle Jack from carrying out his plans.

54. See, for instance, the exchange between Baug and Uncle Jack in chapter 24 (PW, 170–72).

55. To this reverential description of Uncle Jack, Griggs adds: "His mustache, beard and hair were white, and his solemn face thus enveloped would have been a little awesome but for the kindly light that gleamed in his eyes" (PW, 15–16). Similarly, Chesnutt's description of the colonel reads: "His face indeed might have seemed austere, but for a sensitive mouth, which suggested a reserve of humour and a capacity for deep feeling" (CD, 3).

56. Barbara Christian, *New Black Feminist Criticism, 1985–2000* (Urbana: University of Illinois Press, 2007), 91.

57. In *The One Great Question* (1907), an essay published the year before *Pointing the Way*, Griggs critiques explicitly the definition of democratic ideals as idle dreams: "We have certain northern white men of wide repute suggesting that the nation abandon as idle its dream of establishing among its citizens an equality of citizenship without regard to 'race, color or previous condition of servitude'" (Sutton E. Griggs, *The One Great Question: A Study of Southern Conditions at Close Range* [Nashville: Orion, 1907], 10).

58. Ibid., 56, 57.

59. See Fabi, "Desegregating the Future."

60. See PW, chap. 24.

61. Simmons, *Chesnutt and Realism*, 129.

62. A much later work of fiction like Ann Petry's "The Bones of Louella Brown," which takes place in a northern cemetery like the one in which Uncle Peter was supposed to finally rest in peace, offers an ironic commentary on the troubled fate of black bodies "under the sod" (CD, 164). It also provides a significant historical perspective on the utopian valence of Griggs's closing image of a desegregated southern cemetery (Ann Petry, "The Bones of Louella Brown," in *Miss Muriel and Other Stories* [1971; repr., New York: Kensington, 2008], 163–80).

63. Through this juxtaposition, Griggs foreshadows the future of African Americans in another way as well. Reversing contemporary predictions of black extinction, Griggs refers to the "plot of ground that ... awaits the coming" of childless Molair and his mother (PW, 233), hinting implicitly at the extinction of the Molair family line, a theme that runs through *The Colonel's Dream* as well and that in the earlier novel is confirmed by Phil's death. By contrast, the black community lives on in new generations. The very names of Conroe Driscoll Jr. and "little Clotille Peppers" (PW, 233) point to an uninterrupted line of activism and resistance.

64. The subhead is drawn from Chesnutt, CD 247.

65. See Andrew Zimmerman, *Alabama in Africa: Booker T. Washington, the German Empire, and the Globalization of the New South* (Princeton, N.J.: Princeton University Press, 2010), 332. I thank Ira Dworkin for this reference.

66. W. E. B. Du Bois, *The Quest of the Silver Fleece* (1911; repr., Boston: Northeastern University Press, 1989), 296.

67. Recent critical essays (in alphabetical order) on Griggs's work include Dora Ahmad, *Landscapes of Hope: Anti-Colonial Utopianism in America* (New York: Oxford University Press, 2009); Adenike Marie Davidson, "Double Leadership, Double Trouble: Critiquing Double Consciousness and Racial Uplift in Sutton E. Griggs's *Imperium in*

Imperio," *CLA Journal* 48 (2004): 127–55; Fabi, "Desegregating the Future"; M. Giulia Fabi, *Passing and the Rise of the African American Novel* (Urbana: University of Illinois Press, 2001); Lynn R. Johnson, "A Return to the Black (W)hole: Mitigating the Trauma of Homelessness in Sutton E. Griggs's *Imperium in Imperio*," *Southern Literary Journal* 42 (2010): 12–33; Stephen Knadler, "Sensationalizing Patriotism: Sutton Griggs and the Sentimental Nationalism of Citizen Tom," *American Literature* 79 (2007): 673–99; Caroline Levander, "Sutton Griggs and the Borderlands of Empire," included in this volume; Kali Tal, "'That Just Kills Me': Black Militant Near-Future Fiction," *Social Text* 71 (2002): 65–91; Molly Crumpton Winter, *American Narratives: Multiethnic Writings in the Age of Realism* (Baton Rouge: Louisiana State University Press, 2007).

KENNETH W. WARREN

Perfecting the Political Romance

The Last Novel of Sutton Griggs

If we credit at all the account of Sutton E. Griggs's literary career provided in his brief autobiographical sketch *The Story of My Struggles*, it is difficult to see why Griggs's fifth and final novel, *Pointing the Way*, was written at all. His fourth novel, *The Hindered Hand; or, The Reign of the Repressionist* (1905), had been the crowning failure in a series of failed attempts to reach a popular black audience through his fiction writing. Griggs had undertaken *The Hindered Hand* with great expectations for its critical, financial, and political success because it seemed to be a work destined to reach a large audience. Seeking to counter the popularity of Thomas Dixon Jr.'s racist romance, *The Leopard's Spots* (1902)—a book that had persuaded many of its white readers of the need and justice of disenfranchising black Americans and driving them from the political life of the South—the National Baptist Convention had voted to ask Griggs to write a novelistic refutation. Despite his earlier disappointments, Griggs, a Baptist minister himself, was eager to respond. As he recalls in his autobiographical sketch,

> It seemed to me that that which I had needed all along, co-operation, had at last come. I felt here was a vast body of men who had voluntarily called upon me to be their spokesman and would therefore work vigorously for the general spread of the message as their message to the world. With that great host of people working with me I felt that the world would hear us. The volume of the power that we could send forth, I knew, could arrest the attention of the nation. Hitherto, it had been my lone voice. Now it looked as though it was to be the roar of the multitude.[1]

Griggs goes on to say that dazzled by a vision of "thousands of ministers going before millions of people Sunday after Sunday" with copies of his book in hand, he even persuaded some friends to form a joint stock company to promote the book. Yet despite all this support and optimism, popularity remained beyond the reach of Griggs's literary efforts. He concludes his recollection of the fate of his fourth novel by lamenting, "Yet my race failed to rally. The promised support of the National Baptist Convention never came. Thus 'The Hindered Hand' was a financial failure."[2] Perhaps even more galling was the fact that Dixon had followed up *The Leopard's Spots* with the even more successful *The Clansman* (1905), which in 1915 became D. W. Griffith's film, *The Birth of a Nation*. Notwithstanding the stunning rebuke to his ambitions represented by the failure of *The Hindered Hand*, Griggs, for reasons that may seem at first difficult to fathom, gave novel writing one more chance, in "the hope vain, vain hope that the result would be otherwise."[3]

It would be wrong, however, to identify Griggs's hope for success solely in terms of popularity as measured by sales. The goal of *Pointing the Way* was to keep within public view (and to persuade a key set of readers of) the urgency of redressing the disenfranchisement of black Americans throughout the South, at a moment when that cause was all but lost and would remain so for some sixty years. As indicated by a notice (possibly composed by Griggs himself) of the book in the *Washington Bee*, the "general aim of the book is to point the way for the solution of the race question at its most acute point, the question of suffrage at the South."[4] Or to put the matter slightly differently, *Pointing the Way* is a novel that believes it has a solution to the "race problem" and the question of suffrage.

As a consequence of this belief, the novel proceeds as if all that remains to be done is to persuade a significant number of Americans, or at the very least, a critical number of influential Americans, to adopt and support its solution. Indeed, a common aspect of Griggs's novels is the inclusion of scenes or moments in which characters declare they have a plan to solve the "race problem," one that needs only broader circulation to realize its efficacy. The voices of these characters, as I argue in regard to *Pointing the Way* and some of Griggs's other novels, are not dialogized, which is to say that they do not constitute "representations" of political or reformist discourse subordinated to the overall aesthetic goal of the novel.[5] Rather, these moments in Griggs's fiction are presented to the reader as arguments or propositions to be assessed in terms of their political accuracy and the likelihood that they might provide solutions to real political problems. That is, relative to the propositions offered within them, Griggs's novels appear to function primarily as delivery systems: the sugar coating around the medicine or, as the *Washington Bee*'s notice puts it, the "story of general human interest" that has been "wrapped about this question" of suffrage.

But what might not be quite right about this criticism as a general description of Griggs's fiction is that it creates an impression that the outer layers of his novels are not integral to what lies beneath them, such that the reader can attend to one narrative while more or less ignoring the other. Yet in a novel like *Unfettered* (1902), in which the romantic heroine predicates her acceptance of the hero's proposal of marriage on his ability to develop a plan to free the nation "from the narrow and narrowing problems of race," it would seem strange to assert that the novel's story of human interest is merely pleasant "wrapping" paper.[6] Rather, the story's romantic elements depend substantially, albeit not entirely, on the resolution of the political problems with which the novel engages. With respect to *Pointing the Way*, the description of the novel in the advertising notice as having an inner and an outer layer creates an impression that the relation of the "story of general human interest" to "the question of suffrage at the South" is a contingent rather than a necessary one, an impression that can deflect rather than assist clear apprehension of Griggs's intent in writing *Pointing the Way*.

With *Pointing the Way*, as with all of Griggs's novels, plot summary is never easy, but suffice it to say by way of beginning that the novel's comic romance (which nonetheless accommodates a myriad of tragic twists and turns) requires that the union of its romantic heroine, Eina Rapona, with its unfortunately named hero, Baug Peppers, be dependent on the romantic hero's efforts to redress the desperate political situation of southern blacks. The desperation of this situation is vividly described early in the novel by the white lawyer Seth Molair, who, although moved by the ulterior motive of persuading the racially ambiguous Eina to throw in her fortunes with whites, nonetheless paints a picture of southern society that we are urged to take as an accurate description of black subordination and degradation throughout the South. Molair observes:

> "Miss Rapona, was there ever in all the world a more pitiable spectacle than that which the presence of the colored man in America constitutes to-day? His return to Africa is precluded by the fact that Africa is projected on a lower economic and spiritual plane than that to which the Negro is willing to fall back, nor would the economic forces of the South quietly submit to a general exodus even if the Negro desired. So the Negro is riveted here by the economic conditions within and without.

"In the South there is a pronounced feeling against the absorption of the race into the political and social fabric, and he is a political and social Ishmaelite, with his hand against every one and every one's hand against him by the very logic of the situation. The door of hope is closed to him. There are no stars, no moons, no suns to light up his dark skies, so far as the body politic is concerned, and his spirit must struggle with all the darkness and briers and bogs of the spiritual jungle without the cheering light of hope, which, even when unrealized, serves to make men better. To work, to eat, to sleep, to die is the utmost programme that organized society in the South offers this race." (*Pointing the Way*, 40)

We quickly learn that lying behind this woeful state of affairs is the disfranchisement of blacks throughout the southern states.

Griggs was understandably preoccupied with suffrage during the period in which he wrote his five novels. In 1907, the year before *Pointing the Way* appeared, he put before the public a pamphlet titled *The One Great Question: A Study of Southern Conditions at Close Range*, in which he carefully and relentlessly drew a line from many of the ills afflicting blacks in the South to the fact of black disenfranchisement. Citing as an example the near lynching of a teacher at Tuskegee, Griggs observed: "Alabama is a repressionist State. Negroes have no voice in making and unmaking the administrators of the government. They may plead with the officials to perform their sworn duty, but there looms before these officials the day of reckoning at the ballot-box; and in their visions, seeing no Negroes present, they proceed to act or fail to act in a way to curry favor with the voters. How powerless is a voteless element even when buttressed by the walls of Tuskegee!"[7] Griggs structured *The One Great Question* as a rejoinder to a chorus of voices from both the North and the South asserting that it would be best for the nation to "abandon as idle its dream of establishing among its citizens an equality of citizenship without regard to 'race, color or previous condition of servitude,'" and to underwrite the "fixed policy of the white South to deny the Negro a share in government" (*One Great Question*, 9). Against those who touted the wisdom and benefits of a policy that would permanently lock blacks into a status "between equality and slavery," Griggs proposes that "a careful scrutiny of its fruitage would seem to be in order." Accordingly, he strives in the brief pages of his pamphlet to "pilot [his] readers on a visit to the regions in question, that they may note the kind of fruit the tree of repression bears" (*One Great Question*, 9).

Adverting to his status as a longtime resident of the South, Griggs proposes to speak from "at close range" about the social conditions there—a position from which he challenges the more sanguine views of other observers who were less familiar with the facts on the ground. More particularly, as a seven-year resident of Nashville, Tennessee, Griggs even tries to correct the "very favorable" impression that Booker T. Washington had given of that city in a recent talk. Asserting that the open-armed welcome Washington claimed to have received from aristocratic whites in the city was not indicative of the city's social relations, Griggs begins his rebuttal by noting that Nashville is "a repressionist city." He writes:

> The elimination of the Negro from the politics of the city of Nashville is not brought about directly by legislation, but by the predominance of the repressionist sentiment among the whites. Primaries are held from which Negroes are excluded because of their racial connection, and, when the primaries are regarded as having been fairly conducted, contumely is visited upon any white man who dares to attempt to thwart the expressed wish of the white primary by an alliance with Negro voters. (*One Great Question*, 13)

Griggs then proceeds to enumerate a host of injustices visited on blacks that derive from political disenfranchisement, including the lack of adequate space in the local schools set aside for blacks, inhumane treatment of black roustabouts, unjust arrests, as well as beatings and murders at the hands of police officers. In Griggs's view, Nashville officials "and all others under a repressionist regime, can afford to use the entire legal machinery for the protection of those who murder Negroes and yet fear nothing, as the white primary shields them from the Negro voter that would vote for court officials who would punish rather than shield crime" (*One Great Question*, 24). Injustice of all stripes, he asserts, can be tracked back to disenfranchisement. The next section of the pamphlet then canvasses the other states of the "repressionist" South, cataloging an array of unjust and barbarous practices, all of which go unchecked because blacks have been forcibly exiled from the political sphere.

Griggs, of course, was never content to be the kind of muckraker whose responsibility ended once he had drawn attention to injustice and corruption. Mirroring the heroes of his various fictions, he goes on to provide "A Plan of Action," which lays out several "suggestions" for remedying these problems. He first calls upon the "exponents of public sentiment in the country at large, the pulpit, the press, [and] the platforms of political parties" to declare in "forcible language" that the nation risked "moral death" by seeking to retain blacks in "some half-way house" between slavery and full citizenship. Second, he calls on prominent blacks and whites, including W. E. B. Du Bois, to establish agencies designed to educate "public opinion in the South" (*One Great Question*, 56–57). Third, he urges the nation to encourage white southern moderates, whether Democrats or Republicans, by inviting them "to high station" and eventually to elect a southerner president. Fourth, he urges "the intelligent Negroes of the South" to work with southern whites, "regardless of party." Finally, he insists that Congress act to ensure "that all men of equal merit are given like opportunities to express their choice as to who shall exercise rule over them" (*One Great Question*, 57).

Among the first things to understand about *Pointing the Way* as a novel, then, is that it not only seeks to depict some of the "suggestions" enumerated in *The One Great Question*, but it also exemplifies what had become for Griggs, at least since his writing of *Unfettered* and *The Hindered Hand*, his one great subject, namely, the restoration of the franchise to black men in the South on the same terms on which that right was extended to whites. In other words, from 1903 to 1908, Griggs was the novelist of the Fifteenth Amendment, which is, at once, to say everything but not quite enough, about him. On the one hand, it would be difficult to overstate the importance that Griggs attached to the franchise. For example, in *The Hindered Hand*, the ill-fated Eunice Seabrook is told by a ticket agent that she cannot book a first-class berth on a train because she belonged to "a voteless race." When she asks, "What has voting to do with my getting a suitable place to ride on a train?" she is told by the agent, who is not unsympathetic to her plight, "Everything."[8] Although the train companies had no commitment to Jim Crow, they would find themselves subject to reprisal if they took the economically preferred route of making first-class berths available to whoever could pay, regardless of race. But the lack of political power among blacks made this impossible. He concludes his explanation by saying, "If you people had voting power and could stand by us we could stand by you. It is a matter of business with us" (*Hindered Hand*, 245–46). Just as he will do later in *The One Great Question*, Griggs tracks the ills afflicting black Americans to their forcible expulsion from the political sphere of the nation.

Yet what makes it necessary to say more regarding the articulation of Griggs's novelistic writing with his commitment to ensuring the enforcement of the Fifteenth Amendment is that, in broad terms, at least qualified commitment to the Fifteenth Amendment formed the baseline of black political discourse during the early twentieth century. Although Isaiah Montgomery, the founder of the all-black town Mound Bayou and the only black delegate to the 1890

Mississippi Constitutional Convention, had voted to disenfranchise his fellow black Mississippians for the sake of good race relations, by the early twentieth century the writings and utterances of black politicians, writers, and spokespersons acknowledged the need to give minimal lip service to the idea that at least some number of southern blacks ought to remain enfranchised and able to participate in the political sphere. Accordingly, sorting out the politics of *Pointing the Way* demands attending to the particular case that Griggs makes for enfranchisement—a case that remains more or less consistent across his various fictions.

The claim that it is possible to derive a reasonably clear political policy from Griggs's fictional works runs against the grain of some recent criticism. Dickson Bruce, in one of the most comprehensive assessments of African American literature at the turn of the twentieth century, writes, "It is indeed difficult to draw any clear ideology—or even any clear pattern of ideology—out of Griggs's work," largely because "Griggs seems to have been especially aware of and unable to come to grips with the ambiguities that were so strong in black ideas and concerns during the late nineteenth and early twentieth centuries."[9] Likewise, Stephen Knadler has recently argued, "Rather than a coherent political statement, [Griggs's] novels offer the implosion and impossible realization of the sentimental black patriot," and Maria Karafilis remarks on the "multiple and often contradictory readings [that *Imperium in Imperio*] invites." Griggs, she says, in *Imperium* "lays out several strategies for political action without wholeheartedly endorsing any."[10]

Yet despite Griggs's penchant for staging debates among his characters—and despite the variegated surface of his fictions—he does lay out a rather consistent program for political action in the South that centers on responding to disenfranchisement. To be sure, his novels marshal a great many arguments about and examples of racial oppression in the South, but it is my contention that Karafilis gets it precisely backward when she asserts that in *Imperium* "liberty is neither a legal right nor an absence of formal impediments, but an economic and moral issue relating to access to capital and one's ability to exercise the rights inscribed within the law. It emphasizes that issues of economic inequality must be addressed in order to eradicate social and political inequalities."[11] Rather, for Griggs, liberty requires first and foremost access to the franchise for the elite of the black population. This point is not fully front and center in *Imperium*, but it is stated unequivocally. When the novel's more "conservative" protagonist, Belton Piedmont, addresses the Imperium in his most important speech to that body, he asserts, "The white man is still holding on to the stolen ballot box and he must surrender it. If we can secure possession of that right again, we shall use it to correct the many grievous wrongs under which we suffer. That is the one point on which all of our efforts are focused. Here is the storm center. Let us carry this point and our flag will soon have all of our rights inscribed thereon."[12] In Belton's view, the restoration of the franchise constitutes the "storm center" of black political efforts. What makes it difficult in *Imperium* to see this assertion as likewise central to Griggs's own beliefs at the time is that in the novel although Belton's oratory initially carries the day with the Imperium's congress, his more "radical" counterpart, Bernard Belgrave, responds with a different "Plan of Action." In a set of proposals that will conclude with Bernard telling Belton that the Anglo-Saxon "race" "will never admit you equality with him," Bernard urges the congress to "demand the surrender of Texas and Louisiana to the Imperium. Texas, we will retain. Louisiana, we will cede to our foreign allies in return for their aid. Thus will the Negro have an empire of his own, fertile in soil, capable of sustaining a population of fifty million people" (*Imperium in Imperio*, 253, 251–52). Reversing itself from the previous day, the congress, with the exception of Belton, votes for Bernard's plan. Belton explains his dissent by declaring such a plan treasonous. Accordingly, he announces his resignation from the Imperium, knowing that, according to the organization's laws, in doing so he will force the Imperium to execute him.

To readers who have come to the novel after its rediscovery in the 1960s, when despite civil rights gains, white racism persisted, and demands for black self-determination—understood in a variety of ways—became familiar features of black political discourse, it has been hard not to feel the affective pull of Bernard's plan. Indeed, as various scholars have pointed out, many blacks at the turn of the century signaled their endorsement of a more separatist course of action by establishing all-black towns or turning to emigrationist schemes. Yet the novel's decision to expose the existence of the Imperium through the actions of the self-described traitor, Berl Trout, who had served as the organization's secretary of state, and who, believing that with the death of Belton the organization has become a "serious menace to the peace of the world," decides to "reveal the existence of the Imperium that it might be broken up or watched," provides the key to unlocking its politics. Again, for contemporary readers, it is difficult to share Trout's mourning of the passing of the "last of that peculiar type of Negro heroes that could so fondly kiss the smiting hand,"

and it is hard not to hear an unspoken "good riddance" in the way that Griggs has Berl phrase his admiration of Belton (*Imperium in Imperio*, 263, 262). Yet for all of this, as Finnie Coleman has observed, Trout cannot betray the Imperium without the aid of Griggs. Because the Imperium has committed itself to remaining secret while it begins to carry out Bernard's plan, and has managed to do so until Trout brings his manuscript to Griggs, "Griggs then implicates himself in the betrayal by publishing the novel."[13] No one outside the Imperium knows of its existence until Griggs tells them of it. Although Coleman thinks that Griggs may have made a formal and aesthetic error by putting himself in the novel via its preface, the unavoidable fact is that, in the way that Griggs has constructed the story, to write the novel is to betray the Imperium—it is to suggest that telling the story of the Imperium will be more effective than allowing such an organization to do its proposed work.[14] In making this decision, then, Griggs aligns himself with Belton, whose original proposal to the congress includes a resolution that the members "no longer conceal from the Anglo-Saxon that the Imperium exists" (*Imperium in Imperio*, 244). Additionally, Griggs's publication of the novel enacts the conclusion that Belton reaches in placing his final resolution before the Imperium. After declaring that Bernard has erred in asserting that "the sword (and spear) and the ballot" are the strongest weapons available to blacks in their search for equality, Belton announces:

> There is a weapon mightier than either of these. I speak of the pen. If denied the use of the ballot let us devote our attention to that mightier weapon, the pen. . . . [It] would be a worthy theme for the songs of the Holy Angels, if every Negro, away from the land of his nativity, can by means of the pen, force an acknowledgment of equality from the proud lips of the fierce, all conquering Anglo-Saxon, thus eclipsing the record of all other races of men, who without exception have had to wade through blood to achieve their freedom. (*Imperium in Imperio*, 246–47)

In writing the novel, then, Griggs performs what Belton proposes, that is, he takes up the pen at the moment that southern states are moving en masse to complete the wave of disenfranchisement that will consolidate the region's embrace of Jim Crow.

It is not, however, until Griggs writes *The Hindered Hand* in response to Thomas Dixon's Jr.'s *The Leopard Spots* (1902) that he fully works out the dimensions of his fictions of antidisenfranchisement. Broadly speaking, at the point that Griggs turns to novel writing, the reestablishment of white rule in the South had zeroed in on disenfranchisement as its most important goal. As

Michael Perman has written, "In a society already divided and stratified along racial lines, it was odd to allow equality in one area of life." He continues:

> Even stranger, this lone outpost was the most significant and potentially the most dangerous in a society in which the right to vote was confined to adult males, the vote was the primary indicator of membership in a democratic system, and voting was the ultimate exercise of the power of citizenship, even of manhood. Until this right was taken away, it would be impossible for white men to be sure of their ability to dominate or for blacks to relinquish their aspirations. Disfranchisement would therefore remove the last remaining, and most important, obstacle to the installa-tion of a thoroughgoing and consistent system of racial separation and subordina-tion such as had existed in the years before emancipation and Reconstruction had turned race relations upside down.[15]

As Hugh Gloster has noted in regard to Griggs's novelistic project, the writ-ers whom Griggs sought to counter were those like Thomas Nelson Page and Thomas Dixon, Jr. whose works "helped to expedite disfranchisement."[16] In-deed, Dixon asserts forthrightly in his note to the reader in *The Clansman* that his previous novel, *The Leopard's Spots*, "was the statement in historical out-line of the conditions of the enfranchisement of the Negro to his disfranchise-ment."[17] In the climactic moment of *The Leopard Spots*, the Ku Klux Klan threat-ens "every negro in the county" with death if he shows up at the polls during the election. According to the Klan leaders, however, the threats are merely a test: "Those who come will be allowed to vote without molestation. . . . Any man, black or white, who can be scared out of his ballot is not fit to have one." The test "will be enough to show who is fit to rule the state."[18] Published a year after the Alabama Constitutional Convention had completed its work of disenfran-chisement and various challenges to disenfranchisement were making their way into courts across the South, Dixon's novel sought to underscore not only the necessity but the rightness and wisdom of disenfranchising black Americans.

In countering Dixon in *The Hindered Hand* and in the accompanying essay, "A Hindering Hand: A Supplement to *The Hindered Hand*," Griggs presents his formula, both literary and political, for reestablishing the franchise for black Americans. The components of this formula are more or less the same as those that would appear later in *The One Great Question* and include scenes dem-onstrating that the denial of the franchise to blacks allows white citizens and government officials to abuse and humiliate black citizens with impunity; as-sertions that, albeit for understandable reasons, blacks bear some of the responsibility for white southern opposition to black enfranchisement because blacks have voted implacably against the Democratic party; (as a corollary to the preceding) exhortations for blacks to resist or rise above party affiliation; and the representation of or calls for political cooperation among black and white moderate elites in the South. These elements are present in all of Griggs's fiction after *The Hindered Hand* and constitute the core of his political and aesthetic program.

Although Griggs shared with Booker T. Washington the belief that black misuse of the vote partly explains white southern commitment to disenfranchisement, Griggs's conviction that the problems in the South derived from disenfranchisement rather than from black incapacity or ignorance opened up some daylight between him and Washington. Griggs's criticism of Washington in *The One Great Question* provides only one example of this distance. Yet in distinguishing the two men from each other, one cannot overlook the general grounds on which they did agree. Like Washington, Griggs also insisted on the importance of good race relations as a means of reacquiring and securing the franchise. Race relations, a concept that, according to Michael West, Booker T. Washington invented, called upon African Americans "to modify their behavior, and in so doing, to disarm themselves as a combustible element in the lives of white Southerners, who would in turn disarm themselves under the good regime of good race relations."[19] According to this view, by making their actions and demeanors acceptable to whites, blacks could come to expect an extension of goodwill from their white fellow citizens. Baug Peppers in *Pointing the Way* exemplifies both the extent to which Griggs subscribed to the premises of good race relations and his unwillingness to make political equality conditional on anything else. In explaining Baug's initial reluctance to identify himself publicly with the effort to challenge disenfranchisement before the U.S. Supreme Court, the narrator reveals that Baug has

> realized fully that the good will of his southern white neighbors was a consideration second only in importance to achieving agreement that the race with which he was identified was to be dealt with according to the fundamental principle of the government, equality before the law. He had inaugurated in Belrose the harmonious working together of the white and "colored" people in local political matters, and he would have regretted much anything that rendered him personally unacceptable as an ambassador of peace. . . . He had all along been deeply concerned about the fundamental rights of his people [but had also hoped] to reserve himself for a task of equal importance, that of friendly adjustment. (*Pointing the Way*, 174)

Baug's fear that a premature disclosure of his intention to argue against disenfranchisement would derail his efforts to establish and maintain friendly relations with whites reveals the tension between these two commitments. Nonetheless, the formula that Griggs develops in his fiction requires that although his key characters should prefer political equality to everything else, they should value almost as highly the "friendly adjustment" of the black and white races. Griggs's method for resolving the tension that could arise from insisting simultaneously on full political equality and a friendly adjustment between the races is to support a policy favoring a political alliance of the "best" white and black southerners, which Griggs seeks to facilitate by urging black voters to rise above what he describes as their irrational and emotional commitment to the Republican Party, which will in turn loosen the white South's allegiance to the Democratic Party, making possible an interracial political alliance.

The establishment of such a political alliance is one of the major plot points of *Pointing the Way*. The white lawyer Seth Molair, who eventually becomes mayor of Belrose with the help of the enlightened black vote, defines this problem early in the novel in a conversation with Eina Rapona, when he observes, "The one thing needed in the South is political co-operation between the better elements of whites and the Negroes" (*Pointing the Way*, 41). This view, in varying permutations, was shared by any number of black writers and spokespersons during the period. Even W. E. B. Du Bois, in *The Souls of Black Folk*, laments that one result of the segregation of the races in the South is that "the best of the whites and the best of the Negroes almost never live in anything like close proximity," a situation that undermines the possibility of cooperation across racial lines.[20] In *Pointing the Way*, the lack of cooperation between the "best" whites and blacks becomes a refrain, mouthed by an array of characters who then set out to remedy the problem. The novel's primary vernacular character, Jackson Simpkins Hezekiah Morris, better known as Uncle Jack, puts the matter straightforwardly to Eina when he asks, "Do yer think de bes' white people will evah 'gree ter wuk 'long wid de cullud people in de same perlittercul yoke? Dat is de qusshun" (*Pointing the Way*, 99).

Eina readily agrees with Uncle Jack because sorting out the novel's romantic plot will turn on getting an affirmative answer to his question. Establishing the best of black society requires that the novel facilitate the marriages of two "black" couples, Eina Rapona and Baug Peppers, on the one hand, and Clotille Strange and Conroe Driscoll, on the other. Eina and Baug have light complexions—Eina, indeed, is racially ambiguous enough to pass as white if she so desires.

Clotille and Conroe, however, are quite dark. The complexions of these characters become an issue because Clotille's cousin and wealthy guardian, Letitia Gilbreath, who is "herself a mulatto," has her heart set on seeing her dark-skinned cousin, Clotille, marry Baug. Clotille, however, is secretly in love with Conroe, who returns her love. Standing in the way of their marriage, though, is their knowledge that Clotille will be disinherited if she defies Miss Letitia's matrimonial dreams.

With both satiric wit and sympathy, the novel gives us insight into Miss Letitia's objection to dark-skinned marriages among black Americans. We are told initially that she lacks sufficient race pride and is "a great believer in the white people" and in "the white man's temperament, traditions, character, and civilization," and that she laments profoundly the growing distance between blacks and whites. Believing that skin color constitutes the crux of the problem, Miss Letitia has come to believe that the solution to it lay in whitening the black race until there is no discernible difference between black and white. She does not, however, advocate accomplishing this through intermarriage ("She had no sympathy, however, for such Negroes of light complexion as illegally affiliated with the white race or surreptitiously entered that race"). Rather, she thinks blacks could take advantage of the race mixing that had already occurred under slavery and "thus bring good out of evil by making use of the light complexion contributed to the race to lighten its complexion from generation to generation until it finally lost its dark hue" (*Pointing the Way*, 31, 32).

Nevertheless, although the novel clearly condemns Miss Letitia's views, it does not paint her as pathologically self-hating. Her views, as we learn later when she confronts Seth Molair, make perfect sense as a reaction to black disenfranchisement. She remonstrates to Molair after he has objected to her scheme on the grounds that in the long run it will lead to racial amalgamation by saying, "You disfranchise, you ostracize, you jim crow, you lynch, you burn a man because he is colored, then hold up your hands in holy horror because he seeks, by honorable means, to get away from being colored. If you want a man to stay colored, why in the name of God don't you treat him right as colored?" (*Pointing the Way*, 181). Recognizing the logic within Letitia's rant, Molair commits himself to standing "for exact justice, impartial enforcement of the law, and the encouragement of all elements of our population to look upward and not downward" (*Pointing the Way*, 187–88).

Indeed, it is the political origins of Miss Letitia's objections to the marriage of Clotille and Conroe that mark them as being subject to a political resolution.

The novel is structured around producing a political solution that will enable the proper marriages to take place. Clotille realizes that her marriage to Conroe demands getting Baug Peppers "out of the way," and that this can be accomplished by getting Eina and Baug to fall in love and wed. But the second and, in some sense, the most necessary step is to dissolve Miss Letitia's objection to "colored" marriages, a step that will require converting "the white people of Belrose to a more kindly attitude toward the colored people." Knowing that Miss Letitia worshipped the "whites of Belrose" as "the most aristocratic people on earth," Clotille reasons that "if, therefore, Belrose could be brought to the point of according the colored people the full measure of citizenship rights and privileges, it would . . . operate to make Miss Letitia less pessimistic, more hopeful of the colored man's future as a colored man, and therefore less hostile to the marriage of dark couples" (*Pointing the Way*, 33–34). Although there is no doubt that as readers we agree with Clotille's assessment that her cousin possesses a "diseased mind," the political solution to Miss Letitia's ailment is one that is shared by all the sound minds in the novel.

As pointed out earlier, Griggs's belief that the South suffered because of the lack of cooperation among elite blacks and whites was shared across the black political spectrum at the turn of the century. Griggs's diagnosis differed from some, however, in laying the blame for current problems on what he regarded as the irrational (if understandable) party affiliations that developed during Reconstruction. Before Belton Piedmont in *Imperium in Imperio* declares the restoration of the franchise as the "storm center" of black politics, he first clarifies what the proper nature of the franchise is by avowing that the ballot

is a means employed to record men's ideas. It is not designed as a vehicle of prejudice or gratitude, but of thought, opinion. When the Negro was first given the ballot he used it to convey expression of love and gratitude to the North, while it bore to the South a message of hate and revenge. No Negro, on pain of being ostracised or probably murdered, was allowed to exercise the ballot in any other way than that just mentioned. They voted in a mass, according to the dictates of love and hate. (*Imperium in Imperio*, 240)

The "ballot," he concludes, "was never designed for such a purpose." Belton's account of the problematic emotional use of the vote is echoed in *Pointing the Way* by Molair, who laments how "the manner of the coming of emancipation, enfranchisement and the elevation to high public station seems to have riveted the Negro into one party, while the terror of being ruled by an alien and backward race have chained the real strength of the white race into an opposing party" (41). Consequently, in *Pointing the Way* and elsewhere in Griggs's anti-disenfranchisement fictions, exhortations for black voters to demonstrate their political independence by showing their willingness to vote against Republican candidates and for Democratic ones abound.

For example, the anti-imperialist sentiments in Griggs's 1902 novel *Unfettered* no doubt reflect Griggs's committed objections to a U.S. imperialism that sought to extend Jim Crow into the Philippines and everywhere U.S. military power had established sway over nonwhite peoples. Dorlan Warthell, the hero of that novel, declares that because the Republican Party will not guarantee that "in the final adjustment of things . . . the Filipino [will] be able to say that he stands upon the same plane, politically and otherwise, with all free and equal human beings," he has decided to disaffiliate from the party (*Unfettered*, 89). As John Gruesser has demonstrated in his essay in this volume, anti-imperialism became a noticeable current in early twentieth-century black politics, creating real perturbations among white Republicans that black voters would cross party lines in numbers significant enough to tip the balance of power nationally toward the Democrats. So powerful was this fear that W. E. B. Du Bois decided an important plot point in his 1911 novel *The Quest of the Silver Fleece* would be the Republican Party's manipulation of his hero, Bles Alwyn, to undercut those black spokespersons, "a small group of educated Negroes [who] are trying to induce the rest to punish the Republican Party for not protecting them."[21]

Yet as committed as Dorlan is to Filipino political equality as an end unto itself, he is also quite aware that anti-imperialism can serve to delaminate African American affections ("those tender memories which flourish in the sentimental bosom of the Negro," which constitute "one of the strongest attachments in all of human history") from the Republican Party (*Unfettered*, 90, 91). In fact, at the moment when Dorlan informs Morlene Dalton, the novel's heroine, of his plans to advocate for Filipino political equality by voting against any man, regardless of party affiliation, who "will not unequivocally and openly declare in favor of the ultimate political equality of the Filipinos," she is more moved by Dorlan's courage "in attempting to disillusion the Negroes with regard to the Republican party" than by his commitment to Filipino equal rights (*Unfettered*, 91).

As in the case of Earl Bluefield and Eunice Seabright in *The Hindered Hand* and the pair of lovers in *Pointing the Way*, the marriage of true minds in *Unfet-*

tered is made contingent on the race problem being solved. Dorlan must come up with a way of welding "two heterogeneous elements into a homogenous entity" (*Unfettered*, 176). Daunted only momentarily by so momentous a charge, both Dorlan and the novel move on to produce such a plan, which is printed in its entirety as a supplement to the novel. As an "initial step," the plan proposes creating a "device" or organization "whereby the several strengths of the millions of Negroes in the world may be harnessed to the huge stone of a world hate, to the end that said stone shall be swung aloft and hurled into the sea" (*Unfettered*, 234). But as with all of Griggs's fiction in this vein, the racial organization proposed by Dorlan will "arrange for a wiser participation" in politics, which will require that the "Negro . . . shake himself loose from all such feelings" of gratitude to the Republican Party (*Unfettered*, 261).

This pattern for restoring and protecting the franchise becomes indelible in Griggs's fiction. In *The Hindered Hand*, Ensal Ellwood describes a similar organization as he assures the southern liberal H. Clay Maul, the scion of a venerated family, whose name identifies him as a figure of compromise:

> The Negroes are going to organize in the South an Eclectic party that will serve as an antidote to the tendency toward party worship. We shall separate city from county politics, county from state, and state from national. We shall often, perhaps, be found supporting one party's candidate for governor and another party's candidate for president. The question of human rights and the civil and political equality of all men shall be a first consideration with us, and we shall go to the aid of the class of men of like faith on these points, it matters not in what political party they may be found. The best interests of the people, and not party loyalty, shall be our creed. (*Hindered Hand*, 292–93)

The prize for white, elite southerners in agreeing to join in a movement in which white and black elites exercised the franchise together is to be nothing less than a return to the highest office in the land. As Ensal states, "Nothing would give the Negroes greater joy than to see the right kind of white man from the South made President of the nation" (*Hindered Hand*, 279). Likewise, Baug Peppers in *Pointing the Way* seeks to woo Seth Molair into an interracial political movement by dangling before him and his fellow liberals the bait of the presidency, saying, "It is only a matter of a few years before the nation will again pick its Presidents from our section, and if such men as you are put forward as candidates you will find no happier, more enthusiastic supporters than will be the colored people" (122).

Ironically, Baug's prediction of the imminence of a southern presidency proved to be prescient. By 1912, four years after the publication of *Pointing the Way*, the nation would send a southerner, Woodrow Wilson, to the White House—the first southerner to be elected to the presidency since the Reconstruction era. Moreover, he would come to office with the support of many of the black leaders who would have received Griggs's seal of approval. As Mort Sosna notes, the cynicism of the Republican Party toward African Americans had

> resulted in a vocal minority of black leaders openly endorsing Woodrow Wilson during the campaign of 1912. These Negroes represented a resurgent black militance and were all diehard opponents of Booker T. Washington and his "Tuskegee Machine." Black Democrats included W. E. B. Du Bois, the Tuskegeean's most widely recognized critic and editor of *Crisis*, the monthly organ of the National Association for the Advancement of Colored People; William Monroe Trotter, head of the National Equal Rights League and the era's most tireless and outspoken advocate of rights for black people; Bishop Alexander Walters and J. Milton Waldron, prominent Negro clergymen and supporters of the NAACP.[22]

What made this support tragically ironic was that the turn to the South within the Wilson administration led to an extension of Jim Crow throughout the federal government. In Sosna's words, "not since the days of the Fugitive Slave Act and the Dred Scott decision had the federal government so thoroughly humiliated black men. Between April and September, 1913, gradually, discreetly, and without official public orders, the Wilson administration introduced wholesale segregation into federal departments. The Treasury, Post Office, and Navy departments assigned Negroes to separate working, eating, and toilet facilities; the government even installed screens around black men when the nature of their duties made moving impractical."[23] The numbers of blacks who had held appointive offices in the federal government dropped precipitously. Henry Blumenthal argues that Wilson's capitulation to white southern interests "practically amounted to the elimination of the small appointive official class of Negroes, frequently referred to as the 'Black Cabinet.' As members of the inner circle of governmental control, these officials used to render effective and prompt assistance to their race. At a time of a wide-spread feeling of insecurity the Negro minority now found itself without ready access to the sources of power."[24]

The various plans promulgated by Griggs and his many fictional characters took for granted Ensal Ellwood's assurance to Earl Bluefield that although "lesser governments within the government" were problematic in relation to the race question, "the spirit of the national government was very correct." Blacks could then rest assured that the national government would soon "mould the inner circles of government to its way of thinking" (*Hindered Hand*, 38). In essence Griggs's politics presumed a commitment to fair play at the national level that would radiate into the individual states—a commitment demonstrated in *Pointing the Way* when the president of the United States, though declaring himself "no special friend of the Negroes," still acknowledges a "direct relation" to blacks because "the great bulk of the colored people voted for [him]" (191). But the ascension of the Wilson administration and its extension of the "repressionist" tendencies of the lesser governments through federal agencies demonstrated how thoroughly and completely the political assumptions that undergirded Griggs's major fiction had collapsed less than a decade after Griggs had ended his career as a novelist. When William Monroe Trotter, on behalf of the Equal Rights League, secured a meeting with President Wilson in 1914 to protest Wilson's support of federal segregation, he found the president unreceptive. It was Wilson's view "that segregation benefitted Negroes and avoided friction between the races." When told by Trotter that because of the president's turnaround, "the black leaders who had supported Wilson were now regarded as traitors to their race," Wilson grew indignant and ended the meeting.[25] Racial adjustment under Wilson would mean more and not less segregation.

Of course Griggs could not have known when writing his last novel that the plan to throw black electoral support behind an apparently sympathetic southerner for president would backfire so thoroughly. Nonetheless *Pointing the Way* illustrates that Griggs did recognize that the politics he championed would likely come at price. Within the novel, Uncle Jack, whom Wilson J. Moses describes as Griggs's "best illustration of the homey virtues of the black underclass," is made to martyr himself for the sake of getting the question of the franchise before the U.S. Supreme Court.[26] Although Griggs drew on recent history for key elements to resolve the novel's plot, it was Griggs's political and aesthetic commitments and not current events that dictated Uncle Jack's martyrdom.

As noted earlier, the union of the two sets of lovers in *Pointing the Way* depends on instilling in Miss Letitia renewed faith in the political prospects of black Americans in the South. Even Molair, in order to deter efforts like Miss Letitia's to undermine racial purity, enlists in this project by establishing a black fire department unit and persuading Conroe to join it to demonstrate that a civic and political life might be possible in Belrose, even for a man as dark as Conroe. Encouraging as all of this is, however, Miss Letitia remains ill at ease because "she realized that it was the Negro's wise course in the matter of voting that had secured the company, and she, therefore, became deeply concerned about the right to vote." Accordingly, she tells Clotille, "Oh, I am so afraid that some of these old disfranchising laws will come here some day and upset all this nice work. I will never feel safe until the Supreme Court has spoken against the discriminating laws in other States. If that could be brought about, I believe I could sleep at night" (*Pointing the Way*, 140).

In response to Miss Letitia's fears, Clotille and Eina consult a knowledgeable Boston attorney, who outlines for them a "course of procedure" that would "beyond doubt force an unequivocal declaration from the Supreme Court" (*Pointing the Way*, 141). This plan, however, requires the "cooperation of an illiterate Negro" to provide a test case. Accordingly, Clotille and Eina decide to enlist Uncle Jack, who will have to establish residency in Alabama in order to launch the challenge. Uncle Jack agrees to participate, even though, as the narrative presents his situation, he realizes he may encounter some personal danger. But as he tells Aunt Melissa, a commitment to fairness and self-interest demand that he run the risk. He explains,

> "Yer see, Aunt Merllissa, my way and yer way uv managin' wid de white folks wuz to act kin' an' make out wid de bes' dat day seed fit ter do. I hez fell in wid som youngsters in Belrose dat wants things ter move 'cordin' ter some principull, an' not jes' ez er notion stracks de white people. Dey says dat de white people hez done gone an' disfrankshied ill-littered cullud folks 'thout disfrankshieng ill-littered white folks. Dese cullud young uns says dat ain't right. Dey says dat ill-littered white folks an' ill-littered cullud folks ought ter hab one law 'cordin ter de constertution." (*Pointing the Way*, 150)

Clearly some aspects of this part of Griggs's narrative were dictated by the historical record. Alabama had ratified its new constitution in 1901, putting in place a set of processes that the legislators believed would allow them to disenfranchise almost all black voters without running afoul of the Fifteenth Amendment. As R. Volney Riser has written in a recent study of black responses to disenfranchisement, the new Alabama constitution sought "the final political emasculation of black men." Even though "its plain text ... did not prescribe blacks' complete disfranchisement ... its purpose was no secret."[27] The key to the constitution's disenfranchising machinery was the power of discretion granted to the registrars under what was called the "Temporary Plan" to determine who could legally register to vote. Perversely, voters who were registered under the so-called Temporary Plan "would comprise a 'life electorate,'" and the discretionary powers of the registrars under this plan were intended to ensure that those whites who could not meet the property, literacy, ancestry, and poll tax requirements that would come into effect in 1903 under the "Permanent Plan" would not have their access to the franchise blocked. The registrars were also expected to keep virtually all blacks—even and especially those who met the explicit requirements for enfranchisement—from registering under the Temporary Plan.[28]

These measures would come under immediate legal attack by the state's black citizens. The "new constitution's defenders always claimed that educated, 'respectable,' propertied blacks were welcome as voters," but "they were not." It would be these same "educated, 'respectable,' and propertied blacks," however, who would "launch test cases," one of which, *Giles v. Harris*, would indeed reach the Supreme Court in 1903.[29] The man at the center of that case, Jackson W. Giles, cut quite a different figure from Griggs's Uncle Jack. As Riser describes him, "Jackson Giles was born a slave in 1859, had worked as a cotton sampler in his twenties, and, by his early forties, had won a coveted job as a U.S. Postal Service office clerk and mail carrier. . . . Giles had lived in Montgomery from his infancy, had kept his poll taxes current, and did not suffer from any of the character disqualifications prescribed by the 1901 constitution."[30] Upon being prevented from registering, Giles and several other "respectable" blacks formed the Colored Men's Suffrage Association of Alabama (CMSAA). With Giles as its president, the CMSAA issued an appeal to the black citizens of Alabama for support and attracted the attention of Wilford Smith, a Mississippi-born black lawyer who had been educated at Boston University and was at the time the first African American attorney to have "won an appeal to the U.S. Supreme Court."[31] Smith had the quiet backing of Booker T. Washington; he agreed to take the case and filed a suit on behalf of five thousand disenfranchised black citizens from the state of Alabama. Among the important things to remember about *Giles* in relation to *Pointing the Way* is that the line of attack pursued by Smith and the CMSAA "only asked that *qualified* men be admitted to the suffrage and that the registrars be forced to follow the letter of the law."[32] Someone like Uncle Jack would not have fit the bill.

Griggs, however, may not have been departing entirely from the historical record in placing someone like Uncle Jack at the center of his version of Alabama's challenge to disenfranchisement. Griggs was likely well aware that other efforts had been made to overturn disenfranchising constitutional provisions throughout the South. His representation of the Alabama case may have drawn on the ill-fated attempt by the Afro-American Council (AAC) in Louisiana to test the constitutionality of that state's "grandfather clause." The AAC had decided to center its case on David Jordan Ryanes, a sixty-year-old black Tennessee native who had been born a slave and had lived in New Orleans for more than forty years. Ryanes was a man more in the mold of Griggs's Uncle Jack. Though a "good and decent" man, Ryanes was both "illiterate and propertyless." More importantly, unlike the Alabama men in *Giles v. Harris*, but like Uncle Jack, Ryanes was not qualified to vote under stated criteria for franchise eligibility. Further, those who handled Ryanes's challenge had neglected to have him request or submit a registration form, with the result that Ryanes could not even demonstrate that he had been refused registration. As a result of this error and with the fact that Ryanes's illiteracy and lack of property were disqualifying factors, his case never had a chance of reaching the U.S. Supreme Court.[33]

What may have also determined Griggs's decision to conflate the two cases is that although Smith, unlike the lawyers for the AAC, was successful in bringing his client's suit before the U.S. Supreme Court, he was not able to win the day. When all was said and done, both efforts failed. In regard to *Giles*, Chief Justice Oliver Wendell Holmes, writing for the majority ruled, curiously, that relief could not be granted for two reasons. First, if the plaintiffs were right in declaring the 1901 Alabama constitution a fraud, then the court would be making itself party to this fraud if it ruled that Giles must be allowed to register to vote. Second, Holmes doubted the court's power to provide relief. His conclusion here is worth quoting at length. He writes that the disenfranchisement of Giles

> is alleged to be the conspiracy of a state, although the state is not and could not be made a party to the bill. *Hans v. Louisiana*, 134 *U. S. 1*. The circuit court has no constitutional power to control its action by any direct means. And if we leave the state out of consideration, the court has as little practical power to deal with the people of the state in a body. The bill imports that the great mass of the white population intends to keep the blacks from voting. To meet such an intent, something more than ordering the plaintiff's name to be inscribed upon the lists of 1902 will be needed. If the conspiracy and the intent exist, a name on a piece of paper will not defeat them. Unless we are prepared to supervise the voting in that state by officers of the court, it seems to us that all that the plaintiff could get from equity would be an empty form. Apart from damages to the individual, relief from a great political wrong, if done, as alleged, by the people of a state and the state itself, must be given by them or by the legislative and political department of the government of the United States.[34]

In Holmes's tortured reasoning, the question of the franchise remained a political matter, and its relief would have to come from the Alabama legislature itself or from the U.S. Congress.

As flawed as Holmes's decision was, the terms in which it was rendered are illustrative for the purposes of understanding Griggs's use of this case in *Pointing the Way*. There is no getting around the fact that from the standpoint of antidisenfranchisement efforts, Holmes's ruling was devastating. One U.S. senator described it as "worse than the Dred Scott decision."[35] Yet as demoralizing as the court's ruling was in real life, in Griggs's novel, the effort to bring the case before the court, though tempered by Uncle Jack's martyrdom for the cause, marks a triumph, both for the novel's politics and its romantic plot. In regard to the novel's comic romance, prior to the case reaching the Supreme Court, Baug and Eina have been separated by a misunderstanding. Through the machinations of Miss Letitia, Eina has come to believe, erroneously, that Baug loves Clotille and not her. But rather than confront either Baug or Clotille with what she believes is evidence of their perfidy, Eina sends Baug a note, calling off their engagement, after which she disappears.

When the distraught Baug seeks out Uncle Jack for consolation and aid in finding Eina, Jack reveals to him the plan to challenge disenfranchisement. At first Baug impatiently dismisses this information as irrelevant, but Jack tells him, "Jes' hole yer hosses," and then explains how the case and Baug's quest are related. He says, "Mis Eina kinder thort yer wuz er great man an' she wanted ter heah yer argify dat case in de S'preme Coat. She said dat ef dat case wuz evah called up dare she would be dare ef she lived. . . . I tell yer shuah ez yer bawn, ef yer git er case in de S'preme Coat to tes' dem disfrankshieing laws, Miss Eina will be on han' ter hear yer argify. Baug I tell yer I knows" (*Pointing the Way*, 172). It turns out, then, that unknown to Baug, Eina had been planning all along for him to litigate the case. Accordingly, getting the case before the court becomes a means of reuniting the lovers. As such, the importance of winning the case wanes in comparison with its utility in bringing Eina back to Baug, which it does when Eina, who has attended the court case disguised as a Chinese woman, lifts her veil and reveals herself to Baug. Her presence inspires Baug to speak eloquently, and even though the narrative does not have the temerity to rewrite history and give Baug the victory, we are told "it was common thought that regardless of what the decision of the Supreme Court might be, no human code could be made effective against the Baug Peppers type of men" (*Pointing the Way*, 229). Indeed, the chapter following Baug's appearance before the court is titled "Disfranchisement Forgotten." Lest we think this is a lament, the narrator quickly assures us that if the narrative's concern about disenfranchisement has fallen by the wayside, it is only because something more important has come to occupy Baug's attention. He has found Eina. As a result, "Disfranchisement, Constitutions, Supreme Courts, the Belrose movement now all faded from Baug's mind as he once more stood in the presence of the queen of his heart" (*Pointing the Way*, 230).

Nonetheless, as readers, we still might want to ask how can a novel that has placed so much emphasis on protecting the franchise now suddenly allow that issue to recede, at least for a time, into the background, and, more specifically, how can it transform what was a judicial defeat into something that feels like a victory?

By way of answering these questions, we need first to note that Baug's dismissal of his political cause in favor of his romantic one is another example of what has become by the writing of *Pointing the Way* a device that Griggs uses to acknowledge the demands of his romantic plotting. On a couple of other occasions in his novels, after having allowed political motivations to dominate his characters' actions, Griggs then seems to recall, or wishes to remind his readers, that his story is, nonetheless, a love story and that his characters will act from time to time as if love were the most important thing in the world. So, for example, in *Unfettered*, after having risked his life and reputation by insisting that a concern for Filipino civil rights ought to trump all other emotional ties that blacks have in the political realm, Dorlan discovers that Morlene, the woman he has loved all along, is now available and consequently decides that U.S. imperial expansion is now of secondary importance because, he explains, "I have a little problem of desired expansion on my own hands, and I fear the government will have to wag along without me the best way it can for awhile." The narrator then comments archly on Dorlan's momentary apostasy by observing, "The ultimate status of Morlene Dalton was now of more importance to him than the ultimate status of the Filipinos" (*Unfettered*, 159). Likewise, in *The Hindered Hand* the narrator of that novel has some tongue-in-cheek fun with Ensal Ellwood when he warns his reader that those of you who have "pinned your faith to that man Ensal—let all such prepare yourselves for evidence of the utter frailty of man" (272). We then learn that Ensal, after having declared himself unalterably committed to serving the race in Africa above all else, turns on a dime upon discovering that his beloved Tiara Merlew has not betrayed him. When his astonished landlady asks what has become of his intention to devote his life to "the uplift of Africa, the redemption of your race," Ensal tells her, "My *race*, dear madam, is to catch the first steamer returning to America" (*Hindered Hand*, 273).

The narrative tone in which these incidents are recited indicates that such momentary reversals are not meant to lower our estimation of these characters. Rather, Griggs's intent is to raise our appraisal of these individuals by demonstrating their constancy as devoted lovers. Griggs also uses these instances to make another point crucial to his politics. As we have seen, part of his diagnosis of the problem with the franchise in the South is that it has been wielded emotionally rather than with reason. As a result, political cooperation between white and black southerners has been, for the most part, impossible. These heightened moments of romance in his novels, however, serve to illustrate that the proper channels for intense irrational feelings are those that run into the personal sphere. With intense emotions siphoned off into the private realm of lovers, his political actors are then prepared to act reasonably and effectively in the political realm.

Of course, Griggs is writing at a moment when access to politics for blacks in the South has been severely constricted, if not all together interdicted, which means that he must also create a realm for political cooperation of a sort that Jim Crow was intended to prevent. This realm of political cooperation is to be the domain of the best of both races acting together on behalf of the good of the South. If by the end of *Pointing the Way* the Supreme Court's negative ruling has disappeared, it is because, as Griggs's readers, we are supposed to be encouraged by news of "the spread of the Belrose movement throughout the South, of the happy results that came from the harmonious co-operation of the better element of the two races, of Seth Molair's great popularity throughout the nation and the honors of a national character that evidently awaited him for having pointed the way for the peaceful adjustment of the race question in Belrose, which adjustment stood as a model of procedure for other communities" (231). In essence, the novel believes it has created the blueprint for biracial, elite rule throughout the South. In order for this rule to be established, the novel also must signal the willingness of the black lower classes to acquiesce in being ruled by the "better element," and for this to happen, Uncle Jack's sacrifice is necessary.

It would be wrong to characterize Uncle Jack as embodying the insurgent emotions of the black working and agricultural classes. He may represent what Eina describes as "the ground work of the Negro soul, its basal philosophy of life" (*Pointing the Way*, 57), but we are told from the outset of the novel that class deference is essential to his makeup. Uncle Jack is "very sensitive on the point as to the class of people he was to serve, and was a keen judge of what he called 'quality folks'" (*Pointing the Way*, 16). Yet at the moment of his martyrdom, when in defiance of the Alabama constitution's grandfather clause, he slips his ballot into the ballot box, Uncle Jack declares himself to be asserting *his* right to the franchise under the U.S. Constitution. Just before being dealt a mortal blow by an outraged election judge, he tells the onlookers, "I is er ill-litterd man an' my granddaddy wuz er slave. Dey wouldn't put my name on der reg'stration books 'cause my granddaddy couldn't vote. Ez my granddaddy wuz kept frum votin' cause uv his color an' cause he wuz er slave, it is stretchin' color an' 'slavery down ter me terday fur me ter be shet out on 'count uv my grandaddy's shortcomin's. Ter stretch color an' slav'ry lak dat is pointedly 'gainst de consterution uv de United States" (*Pointing the Way*, 216). What is striking about Uncle Jack's vernacular eloquence here is that at this moment, for the first time in the novel, the motivation for protecting the right to vote is expressed in fundamental constitutional terms. Uncle Jack declares that the Constitution has now ended slavery and prohibited all badges of servitude, and that the Fifteenth Amendment has extended the franchise to him. His grounds of defiance are that in light of the rights that have been extended to him by the post–Civil War constitutional amendments, the state of Alabama has illegally barred him from legally registering to vote.

Up to this point, Uncle Jack's justification for participating in the case has rested not on the fundamental claim of his right to vote but rather on a claim of class fairness. The problem is not so much that black men like him have been denied the franchise but rather that white men like him—that is, whites who are illiterate and have no property—are not likewise denied the franchise. A few pages before he casts his vote in Alabama, he tells Baug, "[The] ill littered white man is my orrival [i.e., rival]." Uncle Jack continues: "I got ter work wid him, got ter go ter law wid him, an' sometimes got ter sass an' ter fight wid him, perhaps. Now ef yer let er ill littered white man vote, an' doan' let me vote yer give him dat muc ekvantage uv me. Now I doan' want er ekvantage uv nobotty, but in jestice ter myself I doan' want nobotty ter git er ekvantage uv me" (*Pointing the Way*, 208). On this account, the franchise is not imagined at all as a matter of putting all men, regardless of class, on par politically. Rather, it is a matter of making sure that lower-class whites don't have an advantage over lower-class blacks. Politics is not depicted here as a realm where the rule of the better classes might be subject to challenges from below. Indeed, to the extent that such challenges have come from below in the South, the novel describes them as having been facilitated by the South's unfair approach to the franchise. The long and the short of it is that prior to Uncle Jack's speech at the polls, fairness in relation to the franchise, as described in *Pointing the Way*, could be more easily achieved by disfranchising poor, illiterate whites than by extending the franchise to blacks who were similarly situated. When Baug waits with Uncle Jack at the train station before the latter's fateful trip to Alabama, the narrator writes that Uncle Jack is there for "the purpose of inaugurating a test of the clause of the recently adopted state constitution that provided for the elimination of the illiterate Negro voter without affecting to the same degree the illiterate white voter" (*Pointing the Way*, 207). Expressed in these terms, Uncle Jack's goal may be less an attempt to secure the vote for himself than an effort to deny it to his poor white counterparts.[36]

Despite the plea for universal manhood suffrage that appears embedded in Uncle Jack's polling-place speech, it is the view of suffrage as a matter of group fairness and sectional pride, more than as an individual right, that prevails in the novel. What persuades Seth Molair to support the fight against disenfranchisement is "race" pride. When Baug Peters lays before him the patently invidious way that voting eligibility is being determined, Molair responds with disgust, saying,

> I scorn the idea of a weak test for a white man and a severe one for the Negro. It is a rank injustice to the white man. When you remember that mother nature coddled, made life easy for Africa, but was stern and penurious with England, you can see the danger that will come to the Southern white man if we indulge him while making exactions of the Negro.
>
> The sooner the standard of voting for the white man is made as high as that for the colored man, the better for the white man. (*Pointing the Way*, 176–77)

Giving voice to a Darwinian account of the current differences between the races, a view that Griggs endorses in "A Hindering Hand," Molair takes the position that human advancement demands imposing the same strictures on whites and blacks alike. In fact, when Baug concludes his plea before the U.S. Supreme Court, the moment that "seemed to catch the fancy of the justices and audience as well" is when Baug quotes Molair's objection to unequal franchise restrictions: "I want no laws of indulgence for me and mine. I spurn the thought of a lower test for Anglo-Saxon blood" (*Pointing the Way*, 228).[37]

The possibility that Uncle Jack dies for his own disenfranchisement (provided poor whites are likewise disenfranchised), rather than in an heroic attempt to ensure the vote for himself and other poor, illiterate black southerners, may make his sacrifice all the more poignant. Indeed, we are told that on national decoration days the families of Baug, Eina, and Clotille make sure that Uncle Jack's final resting place is not neglected—an acknowledgment that the politics of *Pointing the Way* has secured its vision of political rule by an interracial alliance of the better classes by making dead certain there will be no challenges from below.

Notes

1. Sutton E. Griggs, *The Story of My Struggles* (Memphis: National Public Welfare League, 1914), 10
2. Ibid. 13.
3. Sutton E. Griggs, *Pointing the Way* (Nashville: Orion, 1908) n.p. Subsequent references to the novel are given parenthetically in the text.
4. "Literary Notes," *Washington Bee*, July 11, 1908, 4.
5. Claudia Tate in *Domestic Allegories of Political Desire: The Black Heroine's Text at the Turn of the Century* (New York: Oxford University Press, 1996), 5–9, likewise notes that many turn-of-the-century African American novels provide reliable guides to the politics of their authors and readers.
6. Sutton E. Griggs, *Unfettered: A Novel* (Nashville: Orion, 1902), 215. Subsequent references to this work are cited parenthetically in the text.
7. Sutton E. Griggs, *The One Great Question: A Study of Southern Conditions at Close Range* (Nashville: Orion, 1902), 34. Subsequent references to this work are cited parenthetically in the text.
8. Sutton E. Griggs, *The Hindered Hand; or, The Reign of The Repressionist* (Nashville: Orion, 1905), 245. Subsequent references to this work are cited parenthetically in the text.
9. Dickson D. Bruce Jr., *Black American Writing from the Nadir: The Evolution of a Literary Tradition 1877–1915* (Baton Rouge: Louisiana State University Press, 1989), 156.
10. Stephen Knadler, "Sensationalizing Patriotism: Sutton Griggs and the Sentimental Nationalism of Uncle Tom," *American Literature* 79, no. 4 (December 2007): 126; Maria Karafilis, "Oratory, Embodiment, and U.S. Citizenship in Sutton E. Griggs's "Imperium in Imperio," *African American Review* 40, no. 1 (Spring 2006), 140. Debates about whether Griggs's novels constitute a coherent body of political work have attended the scholarly reception of his novels for some time now. In a 1973 *Phylon* article, Robert E. Fleming dissented from Robert Bone's assertion that Griggs was "ideologically confused" and from Hugh M. Gloster's attempt to distinguish *Imperium in Imperio* from Griggs's later work, by labeling it "militant," by noting that an "aversion to violence" and the construction of stories designed to "appeal to the white reader's sense of fair play

as well as to win sympathy for black people" (74–75) can be found throughout all of Griggs's novels. Robert E. Fleming, "Sutton E. Griggs: Militant Black Novelist," *Phylon* 34, no. 1 (1st qtr., 1973), 73–77.

11. Karafilis, "Oratory, Embodiment," 136.

12. Sutton E. Griggs, *Imperium in Imperio* (1899; repr., Miami: Mnemosyne, 1969), 241. Subsequent references to this work are cited parenthetically in the text.

13. Finnie D. Coleman, *Sutton E. Griggs and the Struggle against White Supremacy* (Knoxville: University of Tennessee Press, 2007), 45.

14. Ibid.

15. Michael Perman, *Struggle for Mastery: Disfranchisement in the South, 1888–1908* (Chapel Hill: University of North Carolina Press, 2001), 36.

16. Hugh Gloster, "Sutton E. Griggs: Novelist of the New Negro," *Phylon (1940–1956)* 4, no. 4 (4th qtr., 1943): 335.

17. Thomas Dixon Jr., *The Clansman: An Historical Romance of the Ku Klux Klan* (Lexington: University of Kentucky Press, 1970), n.p.

18. Dixon, *The Leopard's Spots: A Romance of the White Man's Burden* (New York: Doubleday, Page, 1903), 160.

19. Michael Rudolph West, *The Education of Booker T. Washington: American Democracy and the Idea of Race Relations* (New York: Columbia University Press, 2008), 197.

20. W. E. B. Du Bois, *The Souls of Black Folk*, in *Du Bois: Writings* (New York: Library of America, 1986), 477.

21. W. E. B. Du Bois, *The Quest of the Silver Fleece* (New York: Oxford University Press, 2007), 146.

22. Mort Sosna, "The South in the Saddle: Racial Politics during the Wilson Years," *Wisconsin Magazine of History* 54, no. 1 (Autumn 1970): 32.

23. Ibid., 33.

24. Henry Blumenthal, "Woodrow Wilson and the Race Question," *Journal of Negro History* 48, no. 1 (January 1963), 7.

25. Sosna, "South in the Saddle," 34, 35. It is worth noting that one of the historical ironies of a southerner's ascension to the White House is that D. W. Griffith's film *The Birth of a Nation*, adapted from Thomas Dixon's *The Clansman* was screened in the White House in 1915. Although the degree of Wilson's enthusiasm for the film has been the source of some dispute (a recent biography suggests that Dixon or Griffith mousetrapped Wilson into showing the film), it would be Dixon's work and not Griggs's that would reflect the tenor of the federal government. See John Milton Cooper Jr., *Woodrow Wilson: A Biography* (New York: Vintage, 2011), 272.

26. Wilson Jeremiah Moses, *The Golden Age of Black Nationalism, 1850–1925* (New York: Oxford University Press, 1978), 179.

27. R. Volney Riser, *Defying Disfranchisement: Black Voting Rights Activism in the Jim Crow South, 1890–1908* (Baton Rouge: Louisiana State University Press, 2010), 130.

28. See Riser, *Defying Disfranchisement*, 143–53; Perman, *Struggle for Mastery*, 183–94.

29. Riser, *Defying Disfranchisement*, 145.

30. Ibid., 150.

31. Ibid., 103.

32. Ibid.

33. Ibid., 127–28.

34. Giles v. Harris, 189 U.S. 475 (1903).

35. Quoted in Riser, *Defying Disfranchisement*, 123.

36. There is some possibility that Griggs also may have had in mind here the fact that forces of disenfranchisement in the South knew that they could only triumph by alleviating, to the greatest extent possible, fears among poor whites that they, too, would be pushed out of politics by the new state constitutions. Had those favoring disenfranchisement openly declared themselves in favor of disenfranchising white and black voters alike, the disenfranchisement campaign would have collapsed immediately. As it was, the Alabama state constitution was voted heavily against by a significant number of lower-class white voters, many of whom would, indeed, lose the franchise in the wake of its adoption.

37. In "A Hindering Hand," Griggs writes: "The soil of Africa fed the Negroes so bountifully that they did not acquire the habit of industry, and with a plenty of time on their hands they warred incessantly. The hot, humid atmosphere made them black and sapped their energies. To save them from yellow fever, nature gave them pigment and lost them friends. Other peoples have hesitated to intermarry with them because of their rather unfavorable showing in personal appearance" (*Hindered Hand*, 315).

Chronology

The Life and Times of Sutton E. Griggs

1872
June 19: Sutton Elbert Griggs born in Chatfield, Texas.

1883
October 15: The U.S. Supreme Court declares the Civil Rights Act of 1875 unconstitutional. The court declares that the Fourteenth Amendment forbids states, but not citizens, from discriminating.

1890
Griggs graduates from Bishop College, Marshall, Texas.
January 25: National Afro-American League established under leadership of Timothy Thomas Fortune.
November 1: Mississippi Constitutional Convention votes to disenfranchise black Mississippians.
Frances Ellen Watkins publishes her novel *Iola Leroy, or Shadows Uplifted* with James H. Earle, publisher.

1894
Griggs receives bachelor of divinity from Richmond Theological Seminary, Richmond, Virginia (renamed Virginia University in 1899).
Begins term as editor of the *Virginia Baptist*.

1895
September 18: Booker T. Washington speaks at the Atlanta Cotton States and International Exposition, where he gives his famous and controversial "Atlanta Compromise" speech urging racial accommodation.
Founding of the National Baptist Convention of the U.S.A.; the Baptist church is the largest black religious denomination in the United States.

1896

May 18: U.S. Supreme Court upholds constitutionality of state laws requiring racial segregation in public facilities under the doctrine of "separate but equal" in the *Plessy v. Ferguson* case.

October 11: Griggs installed as pastor of the First Baptist Church in Berkley, Virginia.

November 3: William McKinley (Republican) elected president.

1897

May 10: Sutton E. Griggs and Emma J. Williams marry in Berkley, Virginia. They adopt one daughter, Eunice.

1898

February 15: Explosion of the USS *Maine* in Havana Harbor.

February 22: Lynching of U.S. postmaster Frazier Baker in Lake City, South Carolina.

April 21: U.S. declares war against Spain. Sixteen regiments of black volunteers recruited; four saw combat.

November 10: Race riot in Wilmington, North Carolina, leads to the destruction of the *Daily Record*, the only African American newspaper in the state.

1899

February: U.S. annexation of the Philippines

March: Charles Chesnutt publishes first collection of short stories, *The Conjure Woman*, with the Boston publishing house Houghton, Mifflin & Company. Later the same year, Chesnutt's second collection of short stories, *The Wife of His Youth and Other Stories of the Color Line*, is brought out by the same publishing house.

Griggs publishes *Imperium in Imperio* with the Editor Publishing Company based in Cincinnati, Ohio.

1900

Houghton, Mifflin & Company publishes Chesnutt's first novel, *The House behind the Cedars*.

November 3: Griggs publishes an "Appeal to Negroes!" in the editorial pages of the *Indianapolis World* in an attempt to persuade southern blacks to reject the Republican Party and "glance at the program of the Democratic Party."

1901

November: Alabama passes educational requirement to its voting law, which included the "grandfather clause," in order to enfranchise whites over blacks.

March 4: George H. White, last African American congressman for twenty-eight years, gives up his seat.

Griggs establishes his own publishing firm, the Orion Publishing Company, in Nashville, Tennessee. Its first publication is his second novel, *Overshadowed*.

Charles Chesnutt's *The Marrow of Tradition* is published by Houghton, Mifflin, and Company.

Booker T. Washington publishes his autobiography, *Up from Slavery*, with Doubleday & Company.

1902

Griggs publishes his third novel, *Unfettered*, under the auspices of his own publishing company, Orion. It is dedicated to the memory of his recently deceased sister, Mary.

Griggs becomes pastor of the First Baptist Church of East Nashville, Tennessee. He remains in this position until 1913.

Thomas Dixon's *The Leopard's Spots: A Romance of the White Man's Burden—1865–1900*, published by Doubleday, Page & Company, becomes an immediate bestseller. It is the first in Dixon's Klan trilogy, which includes *The Clansman* (1905) and *The Traitor*. The novels are adapted for the screen by D. W. Griffith under the title *The Birth of a Nation* (1915).

1903

April 27: W. E. B. Du Bois publishes *The Souls of Black Folks* with A. C. McClurg & Company. Its third chapter critiques Washington's ideas and leadership, holding Washington partially responsible for "the disfranchisement of the Negro."

1905

Griggs publishes his fourth novel, *The Hindered Hand: or, The Reign of the Repressionist*, as a response to Dixon's Klan novels. It is initially commissioned by the National Baptist Convention. Griggs dedicates this novel to his parents, Allen R. Griggs and Emma Hodge.

Charles Chesnutt publishes *The Colonel's Dream* with Doubleday, Page & Company.

1906

Griggs becomes corresponding secretary of the National Baptist Convention's Educational Department.

August 13: Brownsville affair, in which a white police officer is wounded and a white bartender killed in Brownsville, Texas. Black members of the Twenty-Fifth Infantry Regiment are falsely accused, and President Theodore Roosevelt orders the dishonorable discharge of 167 black soldiers.

August 15–18: Griggs appointed state secretary for Tennessee at the second annual meeting of the Niagara Movement at Harpers Ferry, West Virginia.

1907

In response to President Roosevelt's actions against black troops and the National Baptist Convention's stand on the Brownsville affair under the leadership of the Reverend E. C. Morris, Griggs publishes his most overt critique of his fellow Baptists, *Pulled from Shelter*.

1908

Griggs publishes his fifth and final novel, *Pointing the Way*, under the auspices of the Orion Publishing Company.

November 3: William Howard Taft (Republican) elected president.

1909

February 12: The National Association for the Advancement of Colored People (NAACP) is formed to promote use of the courts to restore the legal rights of African Americans.

1911

Griggs publishes *Wisdom's Call*, his last book to appear under the auspices of his flailing publishing company.

Niagara Movement disbands and remaining members, of whom Griggs is not one, join with the NAACP.

October: National Urban League established, with Kelly Miller as a founding member.

1913

May 15: As educational secretary of the National Baptist Convention, Griggs delivers address to the Southern Baptist Convention in St. Louis, Missouri, expressing a desire for conference with and advice and cooperation of white Baptists of the South.

Griggs moves to Memphis, Tennessee, where he becomes pastor of the Tabernacle Baptist Church.

1912

November 5: Woodrow Wilson (Democrat) elected president.

James Weldon Johnson publishes *The Autobiography of an Ex-Coloured Man* anonymously with small Boston-based publishing house Sherman, French, & Company. Republished in 1927 by Alfred A. Knopf under Johnson's name and with preface by Carl Van Vechten.

1913

April 11: Wilson administration implements government-wide segregation of workplaces, restrooms, and lunchrooms.

1914

September 11: Griggs arrested and charged with fraud by Richard H. Boyd and the National Baptist Publishing Board for selling stock illegally in his Orion Publishing Company.

Griggs establishes the National Public Welfare League in Memphis, Tennessee, and continues to publish pamphlets and nonfiction tracts, including his autobiography, *The Story of My Struggles*, under its auspices.

1915

Booker T. Washington dies.

1920

November 3: Warren G. Harding (Republican) elected president, dies unexpectedly three years later; Vice President Calvin Coolidge succeeds him as president.

1922

May 7: Allen R. Griggs dies in Denison, Texas.

1925

May 8: Griggs unanimously elected president of the American Baptist Theological Seminary, a branch of Roger Williams University.

1928

September 18: Griggs records four of his sermons in Memphis, Tennessee, on the Victor label: "Saving the Day," "A Hero Closes a War," "Self-Examination," and "A Surprise Answer to Prayer."

1929

October: Stock market crash—Tabernacle Baptist Church declares bankruptcy and is forced to relocate. Griggs loses his position as pastor.

1931

Griggs returns to Texas and assumes role as pastor of Hopewell Baptist Church previously held by his late father.

1933

January 2: Griggs dies in Houston, Texas, from complications with pneumonia. Funeral held three days later at the New Hope Baptist Church in Dallas.

1948

January 27: Emma J. Griggs dies in Memphis, Tennessee, due to undisclosed illness at Collins Chapel Hospital. She had been the founder and president of the Griggs Business and Practical Arts College, whose mission was to put into practice the ideas of her late husband.

1954

May 17: In the *Brown v. Board of Education* decision the U.S. Supreme Court unanimously votes to overturn the *Plessy* verdict, declaring that "separate educational facilities are inherently unequal."

1965

August 6: U.S. Senate and House of Representatives pass the Voting Rights Act of 1965, whose purpose is to enforce the Fifteenth Amendment to the Constitution of the United States. Annulling southern state constitutional amendments to disfranchise blacks, it states: "No voting qualification or prerequisite to voting, or standard, practice, or procedure shall be imposed or applied by any State or political subdivision to deny or abridge the right of any citizen of the United States to vote on account or race or color."

1969
Imperium in Imperio reissued for the first time by Arno Press–The New York Times, with a preface by Hugh M. Gloster.

Selected Bibliography

WORKS BY SUTTON E. GRIGGS

Imperium in Imperio. Cincinnati: Editor, 1899.

Overshadowed. Nashville: Orion, 1901.

Whose Principles Shall Die—Vass or Boyd's. Nashville: Orion, 1902.

Unfettered; or, Dorlan's Plan. Nashville: Orion, 1902.

The Hindered Hand; or, The Reign of the Repressionist. Nashville: Orion, 1905.

The One Great Question: A Study of Southern Conditions at Close Range. Nashville: Orion, 1907.

Pulled from Shelter. Nashville: Orion, 1907.

Pointing the Way. Nashville: Orion, 1908.

Needs of the South. Nashville: Orion, 1909.

The Race Question in a New Light. Nashville: Orion, 1909. Enlarged as *Wisdom's Call.* Nashville: Orion, 1911.

The Story of My Struggles. Memphis: National Public Welfare League, 1914.

How to Rise. Memphis: National Public Welfare League, 1915.

Life's Demands; or, According to the Law. Memphis: National Public Welfare League, 1916.

The Reconstruction of a Race. Memphis: National Public Welfare League, 1917.

The Science of Collective Efficiency. Memphis: National Public Welfare League, 1921.

Light on Racial Issues. Memphis: National Public Welfare League, 1921.

Meeting the Great Test: Constructive Criticism of the Negro Race. Memphis: National Public Welfare League, 1922.

Guide to Racial Greatness; or, The Science of Collective Efficiency. Memphis: National Public Welfare League, 1923.

Missing Links; or, Unfolding the World's Greatest Mystery. Memphis: National Public Welfare League, 1923.

The Negro's Next Step. Memphis: National Public Welfare League, 1923.

Stepping Stones to Higher Things. Memphis: The National Public Welfare League, 1923.

Kingdom Builders' Manual: Companion Book to Guide to Racial Greatness. Memphis: National Public Welfare League, 1924.

Negroes Steadily Recording Progress. Memphis: National Public Welfare League, 1924.

Paths of Progress; or, Co-operation between the Races. Memphis: National Public Welfare League, 1925.

Triumph of the Simple Virtues; or, The Life Story of John L. Webb. Hot Springs, Ark.: Messenger, 1926(?).

The Winning Policy. Memphis: National Public Welfare League, 1927.

Unfolding the World's Greatest Mystery. Memphis: National Public Welfare League, ca. 1927.

Co-operative Natures and Social Education: A Philosophy of Civic Life. Memphis: National Public Welfare League, 1929.

Proper Approach to the Race Question in the South. Memphis: National Public Welfare League, 1929.

Friction between the Races: Causes and Cure. Memphis: National Public Welfare League, 1930.

SELECTED CRITICISM

Ahmad, Dora. *Landscapes of Hope: Anti-Colonial Utopianism in America*. New York: Oxford University Press, 2009.

Bell, Bernard W. *The Afro-American Novel and Its Tradition*. Amherst: University of Massachusetts Press, 1987.

Bone, Robert. *The Negro Novel in America*. New Haven, Conn.: Yale University Press, 1965.

Brown, Sterling Allen. *The Negro Caravan*. New York: Dryden Press, 1941.

Bruce, Dickson D. *Black American Writing from the Nadir: The Evolution of a Literary Tradition, 1877–1915*. Baton Rouge: Louisiana State University Press, 1989.

Coleman, Finnie D. *Sutton E. Griggs and the Struggle against White Supremacy*. Knoxville: University of Tennessee Press, 2007.

Curry, Eric. "The Power of Combinations: Sutton Griggs' *Imperium in Imperio* and the Science of Collective Efficiency." *American Literary Realism* 43, no. 1 (2010): 23–40.

Davidson, Adenike Marie. "Double Leadership, Double Trouble: Critiquing Double Consciousness and Racial Uplift in Sutton E. Griggs's *Imperium in Imperio*," *CLA Journal* 48 (2004): 127–55.

Davis, Arthur P., and J. Saunders Redding. *Cavalcade: Negro American Writing from 1760 to the Present*. Boston: Houghton Mifflin, 1971.

Elder, Arlene A. *The "Hindered Hand": Cultural Implications of Early African-American Fiction*. New York: Greenwood Press, 1979.

Fabi, Giulia M. "Desegregating the Future: Sutton E. Griggs' Pointing the Way and American Utopian Fiction in the Age of Jim Crow." *American Literary Realism* 44, no. 2 (Winter 2012): 113–32.

———. *Passing and the Rise of the African American Novel*. Urbana: University of Illinois Press, 2001.

Fleming, Robert E. "Sutton E. Griggs: Militant Black Novelist," *Phylon* 34 (March 1973): 73–77.

Gillman, Susan. *Blood Talk: American Race Melodrama and the Culture of the Occult*. Chicago: University of Chicago Press, 2003.

Gloster, Hugh M. *Negro Voices in American Fiction*. Chapel Hill: University of North Carolina Press, 1948.

———. "Sutton E. Griggs, Novelist of the New Negro," *Phylon* 4 (1943): 335–45.

Higginbotham, Evelyn Brooks. *Righteous Discontent: The Women's Movement in the Black Baptist Church, 1880–1920*. Cambridge, Mass: Harvard University Press, 1993.

Karafilis, Maria. "Oratory, Embodiment, and U.S. Citizenship in Sutton E. Griggs's *Imperium in Imperio*." *African American Review* 40 (Spring 2006): 125–43.

Knadler, Stephen. "Sensationalizing Patriotism: Sutton Griggs and the Sentimental Nationalism of Citizen Tom." *American Literature* 79, no. 4 (December 2007): 673–701.

Moses, Wilson Jeremiah. *The Golden Age of Black Nationalism, 1850–1925*. New York: Oxford University Press, 1988.

———. "Literary Garveyism: The Novels of Reverend Sutton E. Griggs." *Phylon* 40 (1979): 203–16.

Schmidt, Peter. *Sitting in Darkness: New South Fiction, Education, and the Rise of Jim Crow Colonialism, 1865–1920*. Jackson: University of Mississippi Press, 2008.

Tal, Kali. "That Just Kills Me: Black Militant Near-Future Fiction." *Social Text* 20, no. 2 (2002): 70–75.

Tracy, Steven C. "Saving the Day: The Recorded Sermons of Sutton E. Griggs." *Phylon* 47, no. 2 (1986): 159–66.

Walker, Randolph Meade. *The Metamorphosis of Sutton E. Griggs: The Transition from Black Radical to Conservative, 1913–1933*. Memphis: Walker, 1990.

Winter, Molly Crumpton. *American Narratives: Multiethnic Writing in the Age of Realism*. Baton Rouge: Louisiana State University Press, 2007.

Contributors

TESS CHAKKALAKAL is an associate Professor of Africana studies and English at Bowdoin College and is the author of *Novel Bondage: Slavery, Marriage, and Freedom in Nineteenth-Century America* (Urbana: University of Illinois Press, 2011).

FINNIE COLEMAN is an associate professor of English at the University of New Mexico. He is the author of *Sutton E. Griggs and the Struggle against White Supremacy* (Knoxville: University of Tennessee Press, 2007).

JOHN ERNEST is a professor of English at the University of Delaware. He is the author of *Chaotic Justice: Rethinking African American Literary History* (Chapel Hill: University of North Carolina Press, 2011); *Liberation Historiography: African American Writers and the Challenge of History, 1794–1861* (Chapel Hill: University of North Carolina Press, 2004); and *Resistance and Reformation in Nineteenth-Century African-American Literature: Brown, Wilson, Jacobs, Delany, Douglass, and Harper* (Jackson: University Press of Mississippi, 1995).

M. GIULIA FABI is an associate professor of American literature at the University of Ferrara, Italy, and the author of *Passing and the Rise of the African American Novel* (Urbana: University of Illinois Press, 2001). She has translated numerous works of African American literature from English to Italian, including *Imperium in Imperio* (Ravenna: Longo Editore, 2004). She is the editor of the Penguin Classics edition of William Wells Brown's *Clotel; or, The President's Daughter* (New York: Penguin, 2004) and of a series of Italian translations of African American novels, including *Imperium in Imperio* (Ravenna: Longo Editore, 2004). She is coeditor of Barbara Christian's *New Black Feminist Criticism, 1985–2000* (Urbana: University of Illinois Press).

JOHN GRUESSER is a professor of English and the coordinator of Master of Arts in Liberal Studies at Kean University. He has written five books: *The Empire Abroad and the Empire at Home: African American Literature and the Era of Overseas Expansion* (Athens: University of Georgia Press, 2013); *Race, Gender, and Empire in American Detective Fiction* (Jefferson, N.C.: McFarland, 2013); *Confluences: Postcolonialism, African American Literary Studies, and the Black Atlantic* (Athens: University of Georgia Press, 2005); *Black on Black: Twentieth-Century African American Writing about Africa* (Lexington: University of Kentucky Press, 2000); and *White on Black: Contemporary Literature about Africa* (Urbana: University of Illinois Press, 1992).

CAROLINE LEVANDER is the vice provost for interdisciplinary initiatives, Carlson Professor in the Humanities, and a professor of English at Rice University. She is the author of *Cradle of Liberty: Race, the Child and National Belonging from Thomas Jefferson to W. E. B. Du Bois* (Durham, N.C.: Duke University Press, 2006) and *Voices of the Nation: Women and Public Speech in Nineteenth-Century American Culture and Literature* (Cambridge: Cambridge University Press, 1998).

ROBERT S. LEVINE is a professor and Distinguished Scholar-Teacher at the University of Maryland. He is the author of *Dislocating Race and Nation: Episodes in Nineteenth-Century American Literary Nationalism* (Chapel Hill: University of North Carolina Press, 2008); *Martin Delany, Frederick Douglass, and the Politics of Representative Identity* (Chapel Hill: University of North Carolina Press, 1997); *Conspiracy and Romance: Studies in Brockden Brown, Cooper, Hawthorne, and Melville* (Cambridge: Cambridge University Press, 1989).

HANNA WALLINGER is an associate professor of American studies at the University of Salzburg, Austria. She is the author of *Pauline E. Hopkins: A Literary Biography* (Athens: University of Georgia Press, 2005).

KENNETH W. WARREN is the Fairfax M. Cone Distinguished Service Professor at the University of Chicago and teaches in the Department of English. He is the author of *What Was African American Literature?* (Cambridge, Mass.: Harvard University Press, 2011), *So Black and Blue: Ralph Ellison and the Occasion of Criticism* (Chicago: University of Chicago Press, 2003), and *Black and White Strangers: Race and American Literary Realism* (Chicago: University of Chicago Press, 1993).

ANDREÁ N. WILLIAMS is an associate professor of English at Ohio State University. She is the author of *Dividing Lines: Class Anxiety and Postbellum Black Fiction* (Ann Arbor: University of Michigan Press, 2012) and coeditor of the collection *North Carolina Slave Narratives* (Chapel Hill: University of North Carolina Press, 2003).

Index

Andrews, William, 220, 224
Arthur, Chester A., 182n10
Aryanism, 133
Ashworth brothers, 40
Asia, 120
Atlanta, Ga., 107n23
Atlantic (magazine), 69, 73
Austin, Stephen, 54
Austin, Tex., 41, 79
Autobiography of an Ex-colored Man
  (J. W. Johnson), 9, 12, 215

back-to-Africa movements, 104; and
  mass migration of U.S. blacks, 67n32.
  See also black colonization schemes
Baker, Frazier, murder-lynching of, 5, 24,
  51, 57, 67n29
Baptist Church, 3–5, 7; and fostering of
  Christianity, 175
Barr, Alwyn, 55
Battle of San Juan Hill, 52
Bay, Mia, 173
Baylor University, 32
Baym, Nina, 97
Bellamy, Edward, 225
Benito Cereno (Melville), 232
Bethune, Mary McLeod, 123
Bird, Henry, 36
Bird, John, 36
Birmingham, Ala., 107n23
Birth of a Nation, The (film), 176, 179,
  213n34, 255, 281n25
"Black Cabinet," 270
black colonization schemes, 53, 55–56,
  66n25, 121–22, 261; back-to-Africa
  movements, 67n32, 104
black cowboys, 41
Black No More (Schuyler), 251n47
Black Reconstruction (Du Bois), 192
black Seminoles, 41
Blaine, James G., 171, 182n10
Blair, Montgomery, 182n10
Blake (Delany), 30

Blight, David, 192–93, 195
Bloch, Ernst, 246n7
Blood Talk (Gillman), 23, 180n2
Blumenthal, Henry, 270
Boas, Franz, 173
Bone, Robert A., 51, 188, 280–81n10
"Bones of Louella Brown, The" (Petry),
  252n62
Boston, Mass., 107n23
Boyd, Richard Henry, 165n6, 178
Braithwaite, William Stanley, 123
Brann, William, 31, 33, 36, 43;
  assassination of, 32
Briggs, Gabriel A., 210–11n7
Brown, William Wells, 148; *Clotel*,
  108n40
Brownsville, Tex., 47n44
Brownsville affair, 6–7, 150
Bruce, Dickson D., Jr., 1, 193, 210n3, 260
Bruce, John Edward, 184n26
Bryan, William Jennings, 82
buffalo soldiers, 39
Burgess, John W., 172
Burr, Aaron, 70–72, 76, 79
Butler, B. F., 172

Cable, George Washington, 143
Caesar, Julius, 57
Calhoun, John, 34
Castronovo, Russ, 102
Central Africa, 57, 142n21
Central America, 25
Chakkalakal, Tess, 101, 245n1
Charlotte, N.C., 107n23
Chatfield, Tex., 38
Chesnutt, Charles W., 19n20, 146, 165n4,
  173, 245, 245n1, 247nn18–19, 249n33,
  249nn35–36, 250n41; and American
  eye, 196–97; and binary oppositions
  of racialist thought, 196; "Future
  American" essays of, 235, 251n47
—works of: *The Conjure Woman*, 165n4,
  245, 249n36; *The House behind the*

Griggs, Sutton Elbert (*continued*)
106; print culture invested in by, 8, 33, 35; on printed word's power and racial differences, 157; as prolific, 50; publishing ventures of, 7; reading as important to, 144–45, 150, 152–53, 159, 162–64; religious background of, 175; and self-sacrifice, 117–18; on slavery, 173; and social Darwinism, 15, 128, 132, 279; southern residence of, 1; and Spanish-American War, 130–31; as speaker, 3; and Spencer, 127–28, 135–36, 141nn14–15; and Talented Tenth, 7, 113, 123; Texas as important to, 14, 30, 54–56, 62; and *Uncle Tom's Cabin*, 194–95; as underappreciated, 12; unpopularity of, and critique of black community, 15; U.S. imperialism objected to by, 82, 268; and utopian fiction's political function, 61, 240; voice of, 3; Booker T. Washington's disagreements with, 264; and white supremacy, 81, 118; written word preferred by, 145
—fiction of: African American social hierarchy in, 94; armed violence as option in, 51; black messianism in, 105; political discourse in, 95, 276–77; race problem as central to, 11, 255–56; reading as important in, 153, 255–56; romantic plotting demanded in, 276–77; social agenda of, 96
—and race: cooperation, 6–7; differences, 157; equality and geospatial assumptions, 29; justice solutions, 38; problem sources, 170–71; uplift doctrine contributions, 104, 112, 132, 137
—works of: *Co-operative Natures and Social Education*, 111; *Friction between the Races*, 119; *Guide to Racial Greatness*, 84, 111–12, 123; "A Hindering Hand," 173, 176–77, 263, 279, 282n37; *Kingdom Builders' Manual*, 111; *Life's Demands*, 152; *Missing Links*, 111; *Negroes Steadily Recording Progress*, 111; *The Science of Collective Efficiency*, 7, 111–12, 114, 117, 119, 139n1; *The Story of My Struggles*, 7, 30, 57, 143, 145–46, 149, 178, 254; *Triumph of the Simple Virtues*, 111; *Wisdom's Call*, 30, 54, 123. See also *Hindered Hand, The*; *Imperium in Imperio*; *One Great Question, The*; *Overshadowed*; *Pointing the Way*; *Unfettered*
—writing of: as borderland region, 25; literary value of, as compromised, 30–31
Gruesser, John Cullen, 210–11n7, 268
Guam, 56
Guide to Racial Greatness, The (S. E. Griggs), 84, 111–12, 123

Hagar's Daughter (Hopkins), 9
Haiti, 142n21
Hale, Edward Everett, 15, 69–74, 77–82, 85; *How to Conquer Texas, before Texas Conquers Us*, 34, 79. *See also* "Man without a Country, The"
Hampton, Wade, 182n10
Hans v. Louisiana, 274
Harlem Renaissance, 9
Harper, Frances E. W.: *Iola Leroy*, 9; *Trial and Triumph*, 197
Harper's Weekly (magazine), 56, 66n25
Harrison, Benjamin, 182n10
Harvey, Paul, 175, 183n21
Hawaii, 53, 56
Hawthorne, Nathaniel, 154
Hayes, John B., 39
Haymarket Riot, 46n22
Hazeley Family, The (A. E. Johnson), 9
Hearts of Gold (J. M. Jones), 11
Hendrick, Thomas A., 182n10
Henry, Patrick, 71, 82
Heraldo, El (newspaper), 36
heterocrony, 221–22

heterotopia, 224
Higginbotham, Evelyn Brooks, 7
Hindered Hand, The (S. E. Griggs), 6,
52, 60, 62, 63n5, 180, 269, 276, 282n37;
appendix to, 206, 208; colored line
permeability in, 200; Cuban revolution
in, 51; Dixon psychologically analyzed
in, 176–78; enlightened southerner
type in, 171; Ensal and Earl in, as two
types of Negro race, 200–205, 207–8;
Ensal document in, 186–87; Ensal's
address in, as centerpiece, 203–4;
failure of, 254–55; fear of European
immigrant in, and Anglo-Saxon
superiority, 174–75; as *Leopard's Spots*
response, 12, 16, 52, 146, 167–70,
194, 262; lynching foreshadowed
in, 107n17; ministers in, 175–76; as
novel of positioning, 205; opening
pages of, 195–96, 199–200, 202; as
Reconstruction Trilogy response, 146;
supplement to, 170, 194, 263; white
supremacist thought in, 205. *See also*
"Hindering Hand, A"
"Hindering Hand, A" (S. E. Griggs),
173, 176–77, 263, 279, 282n37. *See also*
Hindered Hand, The
History of Black Baptists, The (Fitts),
66n27
Hochman, Barbara, 155
Hoffman, Frederick L., 137–38; "Race
Traits and Tendencies of the American
Negro," 137
Hofstadter, Richard, 139–40n3
Holland, Sharon Patricia, 103; *Raising the
Dead*, 91
Holloway, Karla, 107n17; *Passed On*, 91
Holmes, Oliver Wendell, 274–75
Holsey, Lucius H., 56
Hopewell Baptist Church, 2
Hopkins, Pauline, 1, 19n20, 173, 206; *Con-
tending Forces*, 9, 59; *Hagar's Daughter*,
9; *Of One Blood*, 9; *Winona*, 9

Horne, Gerald, 25, 39
Houghton, Mifflin & Co., 165n4
House behind the Cedars, The (Chesnutt), 9
Houston, Sam, 54
Houston, Tex., 39
Houston Riot, 40
Howells, William Dean, 143, 177, 220,
246–47n14, 247n18
"How the Worm Turned" (Remington),
39–40
*How to Conquer Texas, before Texas
Conquers Us* (Hale), 34, 79
Huxley, Thomas Henry, 118, 133–34
Hyde, Carrie, 71–72

Iconoclast (newspaper), 31, 33
imperialism, 50, 57, 131; and colonialism
and mercantilism, 116; U.S.
expansionist, and black relocation
schemes, 66n25; and white supremacy,
118
Imperium in Imperio (S. E. Griggs), 2,
6, 50, 89, 122, 143, 146, 280–81n10;
author status in, 154; Baker lynching
in, 5, 57; Belton in, 74–76, 262; and
black enfranchisement, 267; and black
nationalism, 95; as "borderland" novel,
14, 23, 25–26, 36–37, 44; conclusion
of, as bleak, 61; Cuban revolution
in, 51; direct address in, 154–56;
disappointing sales of, reasons for,
95; emigration and assimilation
debate in, 25–26, 35, 53; fictional
black revolutionary independence
movement in, 21–22; imperialism in,
57; liberty in, and black elite access,
260–61; lynching in, 75–76; "Man
without a Country" resemblance of,
69–70, 72, 74, 76–81; mob law in,
140n9; narrative logic of, and print
culture, 31; as object of study, 24;
patriotism and treason in, 37–38,
40–42; periphery in, and independent

Imperium in Imperio (*continued*)
black society, 28–30; print in, and
race debates, 33; race and religion
dialogue in, 33; reading in, 156–59;
reason for writing of, 37; as revenge
fantasy for black readers, 62; ruling
body in, modeled after U.S., 59; Texas
occupation plans in, 26–27, 30, 53, 58;
third-person narrative of, 74; Trout's
betrayal in, 60–62, 80–81, 261; U.S.
blacks as colonized peoples in, 62;
U.S. declaration of war in, 58; Booker
T. Washington's accommodationist
policies satirized in, 59; white
supremacy in, 157–58; women in,
157–59
Indianapolis World (newspaper), 82
Industrial Revolution, 116
Inter-Racial League, 2
Iola Leroy (Harper), 9
Iser, Wolfgang, 166n29

Jackson, Leon, 149
Jacobson, Matthew Frye, 189–90
James, Henry, 155, 166n29, 177, 215
Japan, 21
Jefferson, Thomas, 34, 77, 134–35; *Notes on the State of Virginia*, 135–36
Jewishness, 190
Jim Crow laws: and African American
literature, 11–12; as barrier to African
American success, 122–23; and black
segregation, 10; death compared with,
90–91; and exclusion, 10; and literary
culture, 214; as "Negro Problem"
solution, 10; and Philippines, 268; and
Pointing the Way, 241, 244; and poor
whites, 171; and private black reading
practice, 16, 162–64; during Wilson
administration, 270
J. L. Nichols and Company, 164n1
Johnson, Amelia E., 9
Johnson, Britton, 41

Johnson, Edward A., 244
Johnson, Harvey, 56; "Texas Movement"
plan of, 66n27
Johnson, Jack, 36
Johnson, James Weldon, 2, 123;
Autobiography of an Ex-colored Man,
9, 12, 215
Johnson, Kathryn, 164n1
Jones, Everett, 25
Jones, J. McHenry, 11
Juneteenth, 55

Kansas, 55
Kaplan, Amy, 23–24; *The Anarchy of Empire in the Making of U.S. Culture*, 23
Karafilis, Maria, 89, 260
Katz, William Loren, 24–25
Kaye, Howard, 140n4
Kazanjian, David, 93
Kellman, Stephen G., 51
Kermode, Frank, 89
Kidd, Benjamin, 15, 114, 116–18, 133,
142n21; *Control of the Tropics*, 136
Kingdom Builders' Manual (S. E. Griggs),
111
King Ranch, 41
Kipling, Rudyard, 131–33; "The White
Man's Burden," 131
Knadler, Stephen, 51, 59–60, 65n15, 95,
210–11n7, 260; *Remapping Citizenship and the Nation in African-American Literature*, 59
Knights and Daughters of Tabor, 42
Koger, A. Briscoe, 66n27
Ku Klux Klan, 31, 42, 169, 172, 174, 191,
206, 213n34, 263

Lady Baltimore (Wister), 155
Lamar, L. Q. C., 182n10
Lamon, Lester C., 51
Latin America, 32, 54
Lecky, William E., 118
Leiker, James, 25

LeMoyne College, 245n1

Leonard, T. C., 139–40nn3–4

Leopard's Spots, The (Dixon), 12, 16, 52, 167–68, 170, 173, 178, 183n23, 184n26, 194, 254–55, 263; disenfranchisement in, 263; ministers in, 175–76; miscegenation as threat in, 174; plot of, 169; slavery in, 172

Leopold, King, 67n32

Levander, Caroline, 53–54, 60–61, 65n15, 210–11n7

Liberia, 55

Life's Demands (S. E. Griggs), 152

Life Worth Living, The (Dixon), 168

Limón, José, 24

Lincoln, Abraham, 52

Link, William, 185n39

Livingstone, Stanley, 133–34; *Missionary Travels*, 134

Lodge, Henry Cabot, 132

Logan, Greenbury, 36

Logan, Rayford W., 9, 30

Looking Backward (Bellamy), 225

Loughran, Trish, 25

Louisiana, 28, 122, 261, 274

Louisiana Purchase, 66n25, 76, 79

Love of Landry, The (Dunbar), 9

lynching, 5, 75–76, 107n17, 128–29, 174, 184–85n35, 202

Maine (ship), 57, 67n29

Manifest Destiny, 119

"Man without a Country, The" (Hale), 15, 80, 85; aim of, 79; dispossession in, 69, 71, 78; outcast patriotism in, 72; patriot-traitor paradox in, 71, 73; plot of, 70; preface to, 71, 73–74, 79, 82; Texas plotline in, 71–72, 81

Marrow of Tradition, The (Chesnutt), 9, 196, 200, 220, 246–47n14

Martin, Elias Camp, 6

Martina Meriden (A. E. Johnson), 9

Marx, Karl, 117

Mason-Dixon Line, 23

Masons, 42

Massachusetts, 32

Massey, Sara, 25

McAffee, Leroy, 172

McCaskill, Barbara, 13

McElrath, Joseph, 247n18, 249n33

McHenry, Elizabeth, 149, 166n22

McKinley, William, 5, 82, 129, 131

McWilliams, Dean, 250n42

Melville, Herman, 49; *Benito Cereno*, 232

Memphis, Tenn., 94

Messenger (magazine), 41

Methodist Church, 3

Mexican-American War, 22, 51

Mexican Revolution, 40

Mexico, 14, 21–23, 34, 39, 53–54, 76–77; and black relocation plan, 66n25; Plan de Iguala of, 36

Miller, Kelly, 123–24, 137–38, 173, 177, 245n1; on "Negro Problem," 132

—works of: "The Negro and Education," 123, 133; *A Review of Hoffman's Race Traits and Tendencies of the American Negro*, 137

minstrel shows, 128

Minutes of the Fifth Annual Convention for the Improvement of the Free People of Colour in the United States, 187

Missing Links (S. E. Griggs), 111

Missionary Travels (Livingstone), 134

Mississippi Constitutional Convention, 260

Mitchell, John, Jr., 7–8; Griggs's war with, 4–6

Mitchell, Margaret, 213n34

Mizruchi, Susan, 30

Monroe Doctrine, 130

Morgan, John T., 56

Morris, Elias Camp, 4, 6–7, 178

Morrison, Toni, 176–77, 198–99; *Playing in the Dark*, 177

in, 23, 53; secession of, 55; separate
black state proposed within, 56; as
separate nation, 33; slavery in, 54–55;
as slave state, 76–77; and squatting
laws, 40; white privilege in, 35; as
world apart, 24–25, 58
Texas Declaration of Independence, 34
Texas in 1840 (Allen), 34
Texas Register (newspaper), 34
Texas Revolution, 34
Thompson, Betty Taylor, 8
Tiempo, El (newspaper), 36
Tracy, Steven C., 3
Traitor, The (Dixon), 169
Treaty of Paris, 130
Trial and Triumph (Harper), 197
Triumph of the Simple Virtues
(S. E. Griggs), 111
Trotter, William Monroe, 123, 270–71
Tucker, David M., 51
Turner, Henry McNeal, 52, 56
Tuskegee Normal and Industrial Institute,
151
Twain, Mark, 177, 184n29, 226; *A
Connecticut Yankee in King Arthur's
Court*, 218; *Puddn'head Wilson*, 232
Twenty-Fourth Infantry, 39; court martial
of, 40
Tyler, John, 54

Uncalled, The (Dunbar), 9
Uncle Tom's Cabin (Stowe), 59, 137, 168–
69, 174–75, 194–95, 202, 204; influence
of, 208
Unfettered (S. E. Griggs), 18n4, 62, 63n5,
276; Anglo-Saxons in, 125–26; blacks
compared with Filipinos in, 52; Cuban
revolution in, 51; "Dorlan's Plan" in,
117–18, 120, 123–24, 127, 133–34, 137–
39, 162–63; Dorlan Warthell as "New
Negro" in, 129; political message in,
160, 162; preface in, 124; race problem
solution in, 162, 268–69; reading

in, 159–62; Republican Party in, 119,
129–30; self-sacrifice in, 117–18; social
Darwinism in, 112; and Spanish-
American War, 82; storyline of, 95–96;
treatise of, 96, 118, 124; writing of, 145
United Brothers of Friendship, 42
United States, 14–15, 17, 23, 24, 27, 28,
37, 43, 47n44, 49, 114; Americanizing
world as destiny of, 132; as Anglo-
Saxon nation, 132; black presence
in, 67n30; blacks as nation within,
25; black soldiers of, on Mexican
border, 38–39; constitution of,
205–6, 278; foreign policy of, and
expansionism, 131; imperialism of, 53,
118; industrialization in, and cheap
labor need, 189; land of, reclaimed for
independent Negro republic, 21–22;
Monroe Doctrine of, and Spanish-
American War, 130–31; and "one drop"
rule, 184n29; racial fluidity in, 190;
racial landscape of, as complicated,
189; segregation in, 119; Texas as threat
to, 34–35; whiteness as concept in,
189; white privilege in, and African
American contestation, 35. *See also*
U.S. North; U.S. South
Up from Slavery (B. T. Washington), 151,
172
U.S. Constitution, 205–6, 278
U.S. North, 44, 114, 119, 192
U.S. South, 28, 43, 44, 114, 119, 192; black
disenfranchisement in, 128–29, 262–
63, 273–74, 279; and black emigration
schemes, 53, 56; and Jim Crow laws, 91,
277; as "repressionist," 64n9

Vallandigham, Clement, 73
Van Evrie, J. H., 157–58; *White Supremacy
and Negro Subordination*, 158, 191
Vassilowitch, John, Jr., 109n47
Villa, Pancho, 39
Virginia, 67n30

The New Southern Studies

Sacral Grooves/Limbo Gateways: Travels in Deep Southern Time,
Circum-Caribbean Space, Afro-creole Authority
by Keith Cartwright

Jim Crow, Literature, and the Legacy of Sutton E. Griggs
edited by Tess Chakkalakal and Kenneth W. Warren